Faulkner

AND HIS CRITICS

A *Modern Fiction Studies* Book
John N. Duvall, Series Editor

Faulkner

AND HIS CRITICS

Edited by John N. Duvall

The Johns Hopkins University Press
Baltimore

© 2010 The Johns Hopkins University Press
All rights reserved. Published 2010
Printed in the United States of America on acid-free paper
9 8 7 6 5 4 3 2 1

The Johns Hopkins University Press
2715 North Charles Street
Baltimore, Maryland 21218-4363
www.press.jhu.edu

ISBN 13: 978-0-8018-9698-9 (hardcover)
ISBN 10: 0-8018-9698-3 (hardcover)
ISBN 13: 978-0-8018-9699-6 (paperback)
ISBN 10: 0-8018-9699-1 (paperback)

Library of Congress Control Number: 2010922705

A catalog record for this book is available from the British Library.

Previously published essays © Purdue Research Foundation, 1956–1958, 1962–1963, 1967, 1970, 1975, 1982–1983, 1988, 1996, 1998, 2001, 2004

Special discounts are available for bulk purchases of this book. For more information, please contact Special Sales at 410-516-6936 or specialsales@press.jhu.edu.

The Johns Hopkins University Press uses environmentally friendly book materials, including recycled text paper that is composed of at least 30 percent post-consumer waste, whenever possible. All of our book papers are acid-free, and our jackets and covers are printed on paper with recycled content.

Contents

Gender and Race: Affect, the Body, and Identity

Modernity and Modernist Technique

Preface

Since its founding in 1955, *Modern Fiction Studies* (*MFS*) has published seventy-three articles on William Faulkner's novels and short stories. *Faulkner and His Critics* brings together nineteen of the most significant of these essays as a resource for scholars and students. This volume contains essays on all of Faulkner's major fiction from 1929 to 1942—*The Sound and the Fury*, *As I Lay Dying*, *Sanctuary*, *Light in August*, *Absalom, Absalom!*, and *Go Down, Moses*. In addition to articles on individual novels, several of the essays speak more broadly to issues and themes in Faulkner's work.

Early in its history, *MFS* took a leading role in shaping the emerging field of Faulkner studies. The journal's founding editor, Maurice Beebe, published the first special issue of an academic quarterly devoted to Faulkner in the fall of 1956.[1] Beebe again made Faulkner the subject of a special issue in spring 1967. When *MFS* published its 1956 special issue on Faulkner, the Nobel Prize–winning novelist was certainly a major figure in contemporary American literature. By 1967 and the second *MFS* Faulkner issue, however, the novelist's canonical status was undeniable. Beebe, who provided a checklist of Faulkner criticism in both these special issues, notes in the latter that "one only has to compare the length of the following checklist with that which appeared in the first Faulkner special number . . . to realize that Faulkner has probably received more critical attention than any other American novelist" (115).[2] The numbers bear this out: Beebe's first checklist was fourteen pages long; his second ran forty-five pages.

With the inception of *Mississippi Quarterly*'s annual summer issue on Faulkner (1964–99), along with the creation of the *Faulkner Journal* in 1985, it no longer was necessary for *MFS* to devote entire issues to Faulkner; nevertheless, the journal has continued publishing important scholarship on Faulkner. Reading through the history of the Faulkner criticism that *MFS* has published gives a pretty clear picture of the paradigm shifts in the profession since the mid-1950s. The earliest essays on Faulkner follow the dictates of New Critical practice. In reading the literary work, these critics seek the organic unity of Faulkner's narratives, showing how apparent tensions resolve into thematic coherence. If the essays from the 1950s and 1960s seek thematic unity, those from the 1970s and the twilight of the New Criticism often take coherence to another degree, identifying "theme clusters," the notion not only that a particular theme creates a unified work of art but also that various themes are themselves mutually reinforcing.

By the 1980s, however, the dissemination of structuralist and poststructuralist notions of textuality had displaced the search for the thematic unity of the organic work of art. What has emerged since then is a Faulkner whose texts are more fragmented, multivalent, and intertextual. Feminist critique also openly challenges the conservative world picture that was part and parcel of the New Critical enterprise, even as that enterprise presented itself as aesthetic rather than political. Since the 1990s the Faulkner essays published in *MFS* often embody the principles of New Historicism, seeing his fiction as deeply embodied in a variety of cultural and historical contexts.

Because the Faulkner essays that appear in this volume, viewed chronologically, tell a familiar story of the changing critical reading practices over the last six decades, I have chosen instead to present the material thematically. Not surprisingly, some of my categories privilege contemporary concerns. A critic in the 1960s, for example, would not have thought of his or her work as having anything to do with gender, but from our contemporary vantage point, we at times can see that this earlier work, although written using a different critical idiom, nevertheless speaks to issues that still shape the contemporary conversation about Faulkner. One modest hope I have for this volume is that it helps those just beginning to write about Faulkner become aware that some of their interests have a longer history than they may have imagined.

The opening section, "Myth and Religion," explores an earlier generation's attempt to understand the nature of moral and ethical values in Faulkner's fiction. Beekman W. Cottrell's "Christian Symbols in *Light in August*" from 1956 identifies a number of parallels not only between Joe Christmas and Jesus but also between other characters and their counterparts in the gospels. Beyond laying out the importance of Faulkner's deployment of Christian symbolism, Cottrell anticipates the work of subsequent scholars, such as Virginia Hlavsa, who sees *Light in August* as explicitly structured on the Gospel of John.[3] In 1962, Alwyn Berland in "*Light in August*: The Calvinism of William Faulkner" looked at the ways in which *Light in August* imagines predetermination and a belief in the natural depravity of man. For Berland, Joe Christmas's race, his blackness, is uncertain, but the racial meaning of blackness and whiteness is overwhelmed by connotations of evil and goodness.

Ultimately, whatever is racial in blackness is always intertwined in depraved, blackly figured sexuality. In tracing Joe's relationships with women, Berland is perhaps the first to see Joe's childhood encounter with sexuality while hiding in the dietitian's closet as an instance of Freud's primal scene. Berland argues that Faulkner rejects Calvinism intellectually and emotionally, yet it persists as a residue shaping Faulkner's representation of a static time of discrete presents that is congenial to predetermination. Strikingly, Berland briefly links the flow of black blood when Joe is castrated to Bobbie Allen's menstrual blood—something Joseph Urgo would develop much more fully in a 1988 article.[4] For Berland, it is the Keatsian allusion in both scenes that returns us to Joe's primal scene.

The first section is rounded out by Donald M. Kartiganer's 1963 essay, "The Role of Myth in *Absalom, Absalom!*" Kartiganer turns our attention away from the nature of Faulkner's belief in order to let us see the novelist more as a modernist than as a Southerner. Kartiganer does so by emphasizing the mythological elements of *Absalom, Absalom!* Using Sir James Frasier's *The Golden Bough*, Kartiganer explores the ways in which the novel dramatizes the problems that result when the old god, Thomas Sutpen, fails to give way to the new god, Charles Bon. If the replacement of the old god by the new was meant to ensure the fertility of the land, Sutpen has destroyed his domain (a symbol for the Old South) by denying his heir. Kartiganer further suggests that Sutpen figures an Old Testament jealous and protean Jehovah, while the Bon imagined by Quentin and Shreve evolves into a figuration of Christ, one who can appreciate the sufferings of others. If Sutpen's desire for absolute power is born in a moment of failed acknowledgment (a servant sends him to the back door), Bon becomes the sacrifice who refuses to repeat the father's will to power when Sutpen fails to acknowledge his son.

The second section, "Temporality, History, and Trauma," contains five essays and opens with Robert Hemenway's essay from 1970, "Enigmas of Being in *As I Lay Dying*." Based on close readings of some of Darl's more abstract meditations on the nature of being, Hemenway seeks to articulate the nature of Faulknerian temporality. For Hemenway, Faulkner's present is inescapable because Darl's main distinction is between "is" and "is not" rather than "is" and "was." The is/is not distinction governs many of the episodes in *As I Lay Dying*, and for Hemenway, Faulkner's purpose is to know what "is" is. Hemenway uses this perpetual present as a way to reconcile the competing views of the novel as, on the one hand, a triumph of the human spirit and, on the other hand, an absurd comedy. Five years later, James G. Watson published "'If *Was*

Existed': Faulkner's Prophets and the Patterns of History." Watson examines Darl Bundren from *As I Lay Dying* and Quentin Compson (in both *The Sound and the Fury* and *Absalom, Absalom!*) and their relation to history. For Watson, these prophetic figures are not so much historians as historicists who sense the laws of historical evolution in which the past anticipates the future. In their relation to the past, Watson argues, Darl and Quentin recall T. S. Eliot's "Gerontion" inasmuch as both characters find in their own versions of history the portents of their own immanent destruction, a destruction that has already begun even as the pattern is being discovered.

Rebecca Saunders's "On Lamentation and the Redistribution of Possessions: Faulkner's *Absalom, Absalom!* and the New South" from 1996 considers the role of lamentation as a response to historical trauma both in Faulkner's novel and in post-Reconstruction Southern rhetoric. The essay attempts to reconcile deconstruction's emphasis on rhetoricity and cultural studies' sense of historical materiality. What Saunders notices in both Faulkner's discourse and New South rhetoric is that lamentation marks the redistribution of both material goods and ideological values. Saunders's rhetorical analysis focuses on privatives—instances in which prefixes of negation blend with adjectival privatives that signal loss or privation. For Saunders, this means not only that Faulkner's language constantly stages the loss of Southern identity parallel to the material losses of the Civil War, but also that the very possibility of identity exists primarily as sustained catastrophe.

Donald Kartiganer published a second essay in *MFS* in 1998. The latter one bridges the autobiographical and the historical. In "'So I, who had never had a war . . .': William Faulkner, War, and the Modern Imagination," Kartiganer begins with the influence of the French symbolists (particularly Mallarmé) on Faulkner, an influence that led to a language of gesture rather than representation. Kartiganer points out similarities between Mallarmé's gestural aesthetics and Julia Kristeva's theory of language as a signifying process. Kartiganer then follows out this aesthetic of gesture from Faulkner's fictionalization of his autobiography (one in which Faulkner fabricates a war-hero persona for himself) to the author's fictions of war—from *Flags in the Dust*, *Light in August*, *The Unvanquished*, *A Fable*, and *Absalom, Absalom!*

The second section concludes with Erik Dussere's essay from 2001, "Accounting for Slavery: Economic Narratives in Morrison and Faulkner." Dussere's essay contributes to the ongoing discussion regarding Morrison's reading of Faulkner by providing a fascinating cultural context for understanding the two novelists' representations of slavery. Dussere examines the role that critical accounting (theoretical reflections on the history and purposes of accountancy) can play in understanding a text's treatment of economics. The economic tool that matters crucially is the ledger, which becomes a mode of historical narration with its own generic characteristics. Paying particular attention to the emergence of the ledger as a tool of modern accounting, Dussere carefully examines Isaac McCaslin's encounter with the plantation ledgers in *Go Down, Moses*. The essay concludes by looking at ways in which Morrison refigures this Faulknerian matter of economics and slavery in *Beloved* and *Sula*.

The third section, "Gender and Race: Affect, the Body, and Identity," opens with an essay from 1956, Karl E. Zink's wide-ranging essay, "Faulkner's Garden: Woman and the Immemorial Earth." Faulkner's representation of nature, according to Zink, shows that the novelist is less concerned with ultimate causes than with the processes of life in the here and now. For Zink, Faulkner's nature is life-giving and eternal, characteristics Zink also sees in many of the novelist's women. Although recognizing certain male figurations of nature in Faulkner's work, Zink sees the fluidity and flux of nature most often embodied in Faulkner's women characters. He focuses particularly on Faulkner's pregnant and pubescent female characters. For Zink, women's reproductive capacity gives them a more immediate knowledge of nature that always escapes men's comprehension.

Zink's identification of Faulkner's women as closer to nature than his men is one that had a long life in Faulkner studies. Zink's claim, for example, anticipates Cleanth Brooks's similar sense of the natural order of gender difference that he articulates in *William Faulkner: The Yoknapatawpha Country* (1963). Zink's understanding of Faulkner's women, one should note, is one of the more positive articulations of this position. Zink, for example, insists on the integrity of Faulkner's unwed mothers. In the hands of subsequent New Critics, the woman-as-nature claim often becomes more judgmental, if not openly misogynistic. This consensus view was only overturned when feminist critics began to scrutinize its implications in the 1980s.

However, an interesting prefeminist essay from 1967, Catherine B. Baum's "'The Beautiful One': Caddy Compson as Heroine of *The Sound and the Fury*," argues that other critics have not listened to Faulkner's comments about Caddy Compson and that this failure has resulted in an overly harsh view of this character. Baum inverts the focus—rather than looking at what other characters' responses to Caddy reveal about them, Baum looks for what these instances tell us about Caddy. Baum's New Critical attempt to re-value Caddy might profitably be read against Minrose Guin's later French feminist reading of Caddy in *The Feminine and Faulkner*.[5] What Baum highlights is Caddy's ability to love unselfishly, something that is otherwise in short supply in the Compson family. The issue of love recurs in a poststructuralist light in Linda Kauffman's essay from 1983, "Devious Channels of Decorous Ordering: A Lover's Discourse in *Absalom, Absalom!*" Against those who would see Rosa Coldfield as pathetic or grotesque, Kauffman sees her as passionate. The essay draws on Roland Barthes's *A Lover's Discourse* to examine the ways in which the rhetoric of love helps readers see elements of Rosa Coldfield as the Lover-as-Artist. Focusing particularly on Rosa's love for Charles Bon, Kauffman sees Rosa's discourse based on abandonment and the absence of the beloved. It is this abandonment that enables her to articulate the fictions of loss that structure the lives of the novel's other major characters.

If Baum is a feminist before the letter, Keith Louise Fulton writes expressly from the position of American feminism in her "Linda Snopes Kohl: Faulkner's Radical Woman," which appeared in 1988. Fulton explores the Snopes trilogy, emphasizing the ways in which Eula Varner Snopes and her daughter, Linda Snopes Kohl, move Faulkner away from the patriarchal design he originally conceived in imagining a project called "Father Abraham." For Fulton, Faulkner's depiction of these two women characters raises questions about a tradition dating back to Zink (see chap. 9) that sees Faulkner's men as bearers of culture and his women as close to nature. Fulton details a progressive subversion of such simplistic gender roles from *The Hamlet* through *The Town* to *The Mansion*. Fulton speculates that Linda particularly allowed Faulkner, who was in the 1950s engaging issues of civil rights and the cold war, to articulate a more radical position than he himself could take publicly.

Doreen Fowler's psychoanalytic essay "Faulkner's Return to the Freudian Father: *Sanctuary* Reconsidered," published in 2004, turns our attention from femininity to masculinity. For Fowler, Faulkner's *Sanctuary* compulsively revisits and refashions Freud's conception of the primal scene, an image out of the unconscious mind that explains the origin of masculine identity-formation and a cultural order founded on castration anxiety. Faulkner's inscriptions of the primal scene, however, dismantle Freud's image of the invincible father and reveal that a model of identity-formation based in repression is its own undoing. In part, Faulkner does so, accord-

ing to Fowler, by anticipating Lacan's revision of Freud that substitutes a figurative, linguistic father for the actual father.

Ellen Crowell's "The Picture of Charles Bon: Oscar Wilde's Trip
through Faulkner's Yoknapatawpha," which also appeared in 2004,
brings queer theory to bear on *Absalom, Absalom!* and underscores
the imbricated relation of race and queer sexuality in Faulkner's fiction. Crowell juxtaposes Wilde's trip to the South in 1882 with
Faulkner's infatuation with the Irish writer's fin de siècle decadence.
For Crowell, the Gothicism of Wilde's *The Picture of Dorian Gray*
(1890) in part is born of the same aesthetics of ruin as William
Faulkner's *Absalom, Absalom!* (1936). In Wildean dandyism (expressed through both Wilde's self-aestheticization and his writing),
Faulkner recognized a model through which to critique the multiple
and contradictory performances of Southern aristocracy. By allusions to Wilde and an intertextual recasting of the temptation
scene in Wilde's *The Picture of Dorian Gray*, Faulkner reinterprets
dandyism for the South in the character of Charles Bon and his
blackness. Crowell shows how both Wilde's and Bon's bodies are
read for signs of moral perversion and its threat to the postbellum
South.

The third section concludes with Erin E. Edwards's essay from
2009, "Extremities of the Body: The Anoptic Corporeality of *As I
Lay Dying*." Edwards provides an account of *As I Lay Dying*'s "necropoetics," Faulkner's radically experimental tropology that simultaneously composes and decomposes the body. Edwards considers
both Foucault's "inscribed" body (one produced by social power)
and Judith Butler's theory of embodiment (in which the body is
ontologically prior) and sees the unstable figurative bodies in
Faulkner's novel as a tropological space that negotiates these two
competing models. Turning to Deleuze and Guattari's notion of
becoming-animal, Edwards produces a reading that challenges the
mimetic interpretations that have almost always been central to discussions of Addie's corpse. For Edwards, Addie's body is not know-
able through visual power structures or medical discourse; rather,
her bodily materiality, disease, and eventual decomposition are
displaced onto other characters' metaphorical reconfigurations of
bodily form. Through what Edwards terms the "anoptic" reconfigurations of bodily form, Faulkner's novel allows for new definitions of
corporeality and subjectivity.

The final cluster of essays focuses on Faulkner's relation to
modernity and modernist technique. This section opens with
Donald T. Torchiana's essay from 1957, "Faulkner's *Pylon* and the
Structure of Modernity," still one of the best essays on *Pylon*, the

novel Faulkner wrote when he became stuck drafting *Absalom, Absalom!* For Torchiana, Faulkner's representation of modernization—an increasingly mechanized world of alienated human relations, fashioned on Eliot's wasteland—stages a critique of finance capital. Focusing on the novel's depiction of economic transactions, Torchiana illustrates capital's fundamental disregard for the workers, who in the novel are figured by the pilots and mechanics who compete at the air races that are part of the dedication of a new airport. The central symbol of the novel, the pylon, symbolizes both capitalism's requirements of labor (the pylons mark the arbitrary course the racers repetitively follow) and the phallic possibilities of human sexuality and human relationships that suggest Faulkner's basis for resistance to capitalism.

In "Gothicism in *Sanctuary*: The Black Pall and the Crap Table," published in 1956, David L. Frazier catalogs the ways in which Faulkner uses and modifies gothic conventions in *Sanctuary* in order to express the theme of the "breakdown of traditionalism" in the modern world. In his treatment of Judge Drake, Frazier notes the father's failure to protect the daughter and is the first critic to note parallels between Judge Drake and the blind man named Pap who "witnesses" Temple's rape at the Old Frenchman place.

If the first two essays in this section emphasize Faulkner's views of modernity, the latter two turn to Faulkner's modernist narrative technique. Ronald Schleifer's "Faulkner's Storied Novel: *Go Down, Moses* and the Translation of Time," which appeared in 1982, uses psychoanalytic and deconstructive perspectives to discuss the modernist structure of *Go Down, Moses*, which uses shorter narratives to construct what Schleifer calls a "storied novel." Focusing on the role of initiation as a form of possession, the essay explores the novel's twin concerns for ritual violence (hunting) and ritual love (courtship). Both are forms of initiation that deconstruct conventional temporality by refashioning origin: initiations, which are repetitions, make the repeated act seem to be prior to the past. Looking particularly at Ike McCaslin and Lucas Beauchamp, Schleifer teases out the ways in which temporality is challenged by the relation of the son to the father. Because "son" and "father" are not absolute but merely like linguistic positions ("I" and "you"), they undo and constantly reverse the possibilities of past/present. For Schleifer, the structure of *Go Down, Moses* is generated by the novel's concerns for violence and love, which are repeated in the novel's ostensibly discrete stories that are constantly translated into one another in a fashion that ultimately creates novelistic form.

The volume concludes with Cheryl Lester's 1988 essay, "From Place to Place in *The Sound and the Fury*: The Syntax of

Interrogation." Lester takes issue with a common practice in criticism on *The Sound and the Fury*, namely, identifying the first three parts of the novel as, respectively, the Benjy section, the Quentin section, and the Jason section. To do so, Lester argues, is to miss what exceeds soliloquy and to reduce the novel's complexity and uncertainty to various forms of unity and identity. This tendency, she believes, applies especially to readings that privilege the fourth section's seemingly omniscient narrator and leads to totalizing interpretations based on a sense of a linear movement from obscurity to clarity. Lester pays particular attention to Faulkner's use of pronouns without antecedents to illustrate the problem of trying to clarify reference by appealing to other passages. Such attempts to stabilize meaning often obscure other ambiguities. For Lester, Faulkner's constantly differed referentiality is key to understanding what turns language into the literary.

The essays appear in this volume as they were originally published. Citation and documentation conventions have changed more than once since 1955, and no effort has been made to regularize these. Additionally, essays published prior to the 1990s could not have used Noel Polk's corrected editions of Faulkner's texts; however, the documentation in each essay makes clear which edition was cited. In most cases, the pagination of the paperback editions used in earlier essays corresponds to the pagination of the first editions. For those seeking an alternative arrangement of these essays, Appendix A provides groupings by major novel and general studies. Appendix B lists all essays on Faulkner that *MFS* published from 1955 through 2009.

Notes

1. A short-lived annual, *Faulkner Studies*, published from 1952 to 1954, of course was devoted to criticism of Faulkner before it was reborn as *Critique: Studies in Modern Fiction* in 1956. The New Critical little magazines edited by former Southern Agrarians— *Southern Review* (Cleanth Brooks and Robert Penn Warren), *Kenyon Review* (John Crowe Ransom), and *Sewanee Review* (Allen Tate)—also published groundbreaking essays on Faulkner in the 1940s and 1950s.

2. "Criticism of William Faulkner: A Selected Checklist," *MFS* 8 (1967): 115–61.

3. See Hlavsa's *Faulkner and the Thoroughly Modern Novel* (Charlottesville: UP of Virginia, 1991).

4. See Urgo's "Menstrual Blood and 'Nigger' Blood: Joe Christmas and the Ideology of Sex and Race," *Mississippi Quarterly* 41 (1988): 391–401.

5. See chapter 2, "Hearing Caddy's Voice," of Guin's *The Feminine and Faulkner: Reading (Beyond) Sexual Difference* (Knoxville: U of Tennessee P, 1990).

MYTH AND RELIGION

CHAPTER I

CHRISTIAN SYMBOLS
IN *LIGHT IN AUGUST*

Beekman W. Cottrell

The novel-allegory *A Fable* provides clear evidence of the importance of Christian symbol in William Faulkner's work. Despite the many expressions of surprise at his direct use of such symbol, the Christian story in all its aspects has been of major concern to Faulkner at least as far back as *Light in August,* published in 1932 at the end of his "major period." Where *Light in August* used the elements of the Christian myth in a variety of ways and on various levels of importance and significance, at least the central story of *A Fable* màkes use of a more direct symbolism. In it, the corporal is a discernible representation of Jesus, the old general, of God, and the actions of the corporal are roughly comparable in effect to those of Jesus during His ministry on earth. Crucifixion, mourning, burial, and resurrection are quite literally represented in the story of the corporal, whose quiet example brought about a temporary halt in war.

The story of Christ is no less meaningful as a framework for interpreting *Light in August*. Faulkner uses symbolism on three levels throughout the novel, and the result is a comprehension of love and joy and death in the human condition which unifies the all-but-separate stories of Lena Grove and Byron Bunch, Joe Christmas, and Gail Hightower.

As if for proof that such a symbolic interpretation is valid, Faulkner gives us, on the outer or upper level of symbolism, certain

Originally published in *Modern Fiction Studies,* Winter 1956.

facts which many readers have noted and which are, indeed, inescapable. There is the name of Joe Christmas, with its initials of J. C.
There is the fact of his uncertain paternity and his appearance at the
orphanage on Christmas day. Joe is approximately thirty-three years
of age at his lynching, and this event is prepared for throughout the
novel by Faulkner's constant use of the word *crucifixion.* These are
firm guideposts, and there are perhaps others as convincing.

A second level of symbolic meaning follows close on the first.
In this use of symbol Faulkner follows the manner of such poets as
Eliot and Pound. Using stories or facts or symbols familiar to all,
whole or in part, in or out of logical time, he creates a new and richer
pattern of meaning, and, in Matthew Arnold's phrase, "a current of
true and fresh ideas."

On this level, too, Faulkner leaves sufficient clues to indicate
his purpose, but he does not restrict himself to an overly literal following of the well-known pattern. Nevertheless, the central story
of Joe Christmas does follow the life of Jesus, and interwoven with
this story (and in the case of Lena Grove, framing it) are many familiar people from the life of Christ.

Christmas himself, we are told, was fifteen years in formation,
then fifteen years in the world—"the street which was to run for
fifteen years" (Modern Library, p. 195)—before he committed murder, was hunted, imprisoned, and lynched. He bears the name of
Mary's husband. As an adopted child in the home of the fiercely
religious McEachern, Joe sees "no incongruity at all in the fact that
he was about to be punished, who had refrained from what McEachern would consider the cardinal sin which he could commit, exactly
the same as if he had committed it" (p. 139). The one who admin-
isters this punishment is named Simon, a veritable Simon Peter,
and for a time at least he and Christmas walk side by side in unspoken understanding. Simon McEachern is the type, the rock upon
which the puritan evangelical church of Yoknapatawpha County is
based.

As for Christmas awaiting punishment, "The boy's body might
have been wood or stone; a post or a tower upon which the sen-
tient part of him mused like a hermit, contemplative and remote
with ecstasy and self-crucifixion" (pp. 139–40).

Joe's foster mother symbolically washes his feet after his arrival from the orphanage and for fifteen years realizes that she
cannot come between him and the hardships (at this stage of his
life, whipping by Simon) he must bear.

When Joe Christmas leaves the McEachern home, he wanders
about the entire country, seeking love and self-fulfillment. He finds

them, or a travesty of them, and at the same time meets the crisis of his life, back in Jefferson with Joanna Burden. During his first nocturnal visit to her house he finds food set out in the dark. "It's peas," he said aloud. "For sweet Jesus. Field peas cooked with molasses" (p. 201). And before Joe enters her home the last evening,

> The dark was filled with the voices, myriad, out of all time that he had known, as though all the past was a flat pattern. And going on: tomorrow night, all the tomorrows, to be a part of the flat pattern, going on. He thought of that with quiet astonishment: going on, myriad, familiar, since all that had ever been was the same as all that was to be, since tomorrow to-be and had-been would be the same. Then it was time (p. 246).

It is the hour for Joe's baptism in blood.

Joanna stands, with her name of John, her half-ascetic, half-passionate nature, her body, over and over again described as thin and more like a man's than a woman's, as the John the Baptist (again the initials) of the story. It is she who says to Joe, just before the cataclysmic murder, "Light the lamp," and asks him to pray. "'Joe,' she said, 'for the last time. I don't ask it. Remember that. Kneel with me'" (p. 247).

The words of John the Baptist, preaching in the wilderness of Judea (as Joanna is preaching tolerance, "something between a hermit and a missionary to Negroes," in the wildnerness of the post–Civil War South), were "Repent ye: for the kingdom of heaven is at hand." Joanna's head is severed from her body by the knife which Christmas uses to kill her. Often afterward he thinks that all might have been different if she, like Simon McEachern before her, had not asked him to kneel and pray.

It is in his flight from the law that Joe enters the Negro church and goes wildly to the pulpit, laying about him with weapon in hand, as did Jesus in driving the money-changers from the temple.

And it is on Friday that Joe Christmas gives himself up quietly, with the same certainty and serenity which Christ felt that night in the Garden of Gethsemane. Joe makes one break for freedom ("My God, My God, why hast thou forsaken me?") before the death-by-lynching party at Hightower's home. In this scene Hightower tries, too late, to save the boy, crying,

> "Listen to me. He was here that night. He was with me the night of the murder. I swear to God—"
> "Jesus Christ!" Grimm cried . . . (p. 406)

and fired five shots into Christmas' body. Grimm, here the Roman soldier who pierced Jesus' side, performs his horrible ritual act of mutilation on Joe. Immediately Faulkner continues, as the words "He gave up the ghost" echo from all four Gospels,

> But the man on the floor had not moved. He just lay there, with his eyes open and empty of everything save conscious-ness, and with something, a shadow, about his mouth. For a long moment he looked up at them with peaceful and unfath-omable and unbearable eyes. Then his face, body, all, seemed to collapse, to fall in upon itself, and from out the slashed gar-ments about his hips and loins the pent black blood seemed to rush like a released breath. It seemed to rush out of his pale body like the rush of sparks from a rising rocket; upon that black blast the man seemed to rise soaring into their memories forever and ever. They are not to lose it, in what-ever peaceful valleys, beside whatever placid and reassuring streams of old age, in the mirroring faces of whatever chil-dren they will contemplate old disasters and newer hopes. It will be there, musing, quiet, steadfast, not fading and not particularly threatful, but of itself alone serene, of itself alone triumphant. (p. 407)

The story which surrounds the central events of Christmas' life is concerned with the arrival in Jefferson of Lena Grove, great with imminent child, her meeting with Byron Bunch and his ar-rangements for her refuge in the cabin near Joanna Burden's home. Lena sees the light in the August sky which the burning Burden home makes and this is her first connection with Joe Christmas, who has set the fire after murdering Joanna. Lena later learns that her new home has been the home of Christmas and Lucas Burch, the man she is seeking, the father of her child.

Lena symbolizes Mary, as she gives birth in a manger, is cared for by Joseph (Byron and his ever-present mule), and departs with him and the baby in the closing scene of the novel. Byron Bunch loves Lena as soon as he sees her, and is more than willing to marry and care for her, no matter what the paternity of her child. He and Joseph are humble, faithful, unquestioning in devotion. He works in a planing mill, a worker in wood as was the other Joseph, and Christmas is employed in the same mill for as long as he is in Jefferson. The birth of Lena's child means more in the texture of the story than a simple event. It is responsible for a kind of regen-eration, a rejoining of the human race, by the complex figure of Hightower. Old Mrs. Hines, having come to Jefferson in search of the grandson she believes is Joe Christmas, is present at the birth and relives the earlier birth of Joe in all its vividness. Through the violence of murder, chase, and lynching, Lena remains calm, "her face fixed in an expression serene and warm, as though she were about to smile" (p. 357). ("But Mary kept all these things and pondered them in her heart.") She is the Mona Lisa, the mother, all mothers at moments when Mrs. Hines has pressed her with the idea that this baby just born is really little Joey Christmas. Lena says to Byron,

> "She keeps on talking about him like his pa was that . . . the one in jail, that Mr. Christmas. She keeps on, and then I get mixed up and it's like sometimes I cant—like I am mixed up too and I think that his pa is that Mr.—Mr. Christmas too—" (p. 359).

At least two other figures from Christ's ministry are present in *Light in August*. One is Lucas Burch, alias Brown, the father of Lena's child, the man who shares the cabin with Joe Christmas before Joanna's murder. It is Burch who plays Judas (and thinks of Joe in the term "master"), turning state's evidence when he thinks there is the hope of the thousand dollars' reward, the thirty pieces of silver. But for all his pains, Burch does not get his reward. His shifty ways bring suspicion instead, and his cowardice in the face of Lena and the baby sends him fleeing from the cabin, from the novel, leaving behind only a pitiful note to the sheriff, "rapp it up in Paper 4 given it toe barer yrs truly" (p. 382).

The second figure is more complicated. It is Gail Hightower, and he is Pontius Pilate. The name Hightower has close associations with a whole group of Latin words centering on *pila,* a pillar, *pons,* a bridge or the floor of a tower, and *pilatus,* bald or close-shaved. The Roman first name of Gaius, for Gail, is associated in Tacitus with the Pontius family. Like Hightower in the novel, Pontius Pilate was a figure of mystery around whom subsequent legends have grown up. One of these is that Pilate, having failed his job in Judea, was recalled, exiled to Gaul, and driven to suicide by jumping from the peak of a mountain now called Pilatus, to perish in the lake at its foot. And like Hightower, too, Pilate was known for his loud voice.

Hightower presides as midwife at the birth of Lena's baby, as he has done earlier for another, a Negro child. After this act of commitment to humanity—Hightower's first in many years—"'And so I have surrendered, too,' he thinks, quiet still. He begins to rub his hands, gently at first, a little guiltily" (p. 356). But later, when Doc and Mrs. Hines and Byron have asked him to provide an alibi to save Christmas, Hightower refuses, shouting, "I won't do it! I won't!" with his hands raised and clenched, his face sweating, his lip lifted upon his clenched and rotting teeth from about which the long sagging of flabby and puttycolored flesh falls away. "Get out of my house! Get out of my house!" Then he falls forward, onto the desk his face between his extended arms and his clenched fists. As, the two old people moving ahead of him, Byron looks back from the door, he sees that Hightower has not moved, his bald head and his extended and clench-fisted arms lying full in the pool of light from the shaded lamp. (p. 342)

Where Pilate ruled in Judea as a representative of Rome, Hightower's realm is the Church, and in his youth he tried to serve it well. But events have made him an outcast in an unimportant corner of the kingdom and he has been reduced to putting out a small sign advertising Christmas cards for sale. "I have bought immunity . . . I paid for it. I didn't quibble about the price. No man can say that. I just wanted peace" (p. 271). It is nevertheless in his very corner of the world—his kitchen—that Christmas is lynched, and Hightower is denied in the last-minute urge to save him.

Hightower also has been peculiarly able to observe all of the people in the story, as was Pontius Pilate, and in a final apotheosis before death or madness overtakes him, he imagines a halo of faces. Most of the faces are alike,

composite of all the faces which he has ever seen. But he can distinguish them one from another: his wife's; townspeople, members of that congregation which denied him, which had met him at the station that day with eagerness and hunger; Byron Bunch's; the woman with the child; and that of the man called Christmas. This face alone is not clear. It is confused more than any other, as though in the now peaceful throes of a more recent, a more inextricable compositeness. (p. 430)

The last vision of Gail Hightower is focused upon "the twin blobs of his hands upon the ledge" (p. 432).

But before this final scene Hightower has asked himself the question which Pilate must have asked after the Crucifixion. "Perhaps I accepted more than I could perform. But is that criminal? Shall I be punished for that? Shall I be held responsible for that which was beyond my power?" (p. 428).

Pilate and Hightower each preside over the birth of something not fully understood. For Pilate the result is a jeopardy to his peace of mind; Hightower's assistance to Lena allows him to return to the condition of caring deeply about the welfare of some. Yet he cannot understand what it is that has returned his ties with humanity or that he has, by the very act, brought back dignity and stature to his life. Pilate tries to save Jesus by offering to crucify another condemned criminal; Hightower cries out in his kitchen to save Joe, but the offer comes too late.

On the third or overall level of symbolism it cannot be said that Joe Christmas represents Jesus Christ in the literal sense that the corporal of *A Fable* does. But Joe is the humanity for which Christ died. He asks Joanna Burden, "Just when do men that have different blood in them stop hating one another?" (p. 218). Convinced that he is part Negro, he puts on, after the murder, a pair of black work shoes from a Negro cabin and feels at last a member of the black abyss of humanity, thinking, "That was all I wanted . . . That was all, for thirty years. That didn't seem to be a whole lot to ask in thirty years" (p. 289). And he attains, like Jesus, the inner peace, the cessation of struggle, the inevitable feeling of necessary sacrifice.

Christmas personifies the belief of Jesus, expressed in *Light in August* by Hightower, that "him whose spirit alone required healing was not worth the having, the saving" (p. 416). He is betrayed by Burch, ironically enough, the father of Lena's baby. Thus in the large sense both the Nativity and the Crucifixion are being played simultaneously in the novel, and Lucas Burch as Judas is responsible for both. Hightower's help at the birth expresses his unconscious recognition of the Resurrection, the hope which this birth (and by extension through Mrs. Hines and the memories of Joe Christmas' birth, all births) brings for the world.

Joe's death somehow frees Lena and Byron and the child, somehow relieves tensions even in those who had no direct contact with him. In Christmas' character and the cumulative, callous, brutal events of his life are the full heights of horror and pity and beauty which the crucifixion of Jesus represents to the world. Nor is it inconsistent with the view of Jesus in His day to picture Him as a common criminal.

Thus the theme of both *Light in August* and the Christian story is that the mingling of evil and good can bring hope.

While Joe Christmas presents no positive beliefs to the world, as did Jesus Christ, his story offers great lessons in passion and compassion and argues strongly for the acceptance of an inevitably tragic view of life. This tragedy is only slightly relieved—as Faulkner may feel the Christian story can only relieve, not modify, the human condition—by the contentment or balance of mind with which Lena and Byron close the novel.

The title *Light in August* touches symbolic meaning on all three levels. The light is certainly two things in connection with

Joanna Burden—the light in her bedroom which brings about her ruin, and the subsequent blaze of her home. The same light is seen by Lena as ominous but she does not understand its full implications. Several lights concern Hightower—the light from the street which filters in through the trees to his house, the lamplight which bathes his symbolic, guilty hands, and the halo of light which Faulkner describes as surrounding his head. Lena's baby is born in the light of dawn, and the birth makes her, in the country phrase, "light" again in the month of August. Joe Christmas' skin is light—neither black nor white—and this very fact spurs on the lynching.

The light which Joanna Burden demanded is surely Christianity, and she asked it of the appropriate person. But Joe reacted violently, and the people of Jefferson and the world "looked at the fire, with that same dull and static amaze which they had brought down from the old fetid caves where knowing began, as though, like death, they had never seen fire before" (p. 252). So did the Romans, the Jews, and the subsequent centuries gaze upon Christianity. And so, perhaps, do they still misunderstand the Light of the World which blazed during the reign of Caesar Augustus.

To suggest such specific symbols for *Light in August* is not to proclaim that the novel offers no more than this. In the areas of complex story and suspense, folklore, and character portrayal it is one of Faulkner's major works. But it is a testament to his equally major place in fiction that he can use symbols so subtly, both overtly and covertly, to enrich his story, to give it added significance, and finally by them to suggest at least one framework which makes of the divergent stories in *Light in August* a comprehensible whole.

CHAPTER 2

LIGHT IN AUGUST
THE CALVINISM OF
WILLIAM FAULKNER

Alwyn Berland

In discussing so inventive and complex an author as William Faulkner against so codified and consistent a doctrine as Calvinism, one is at once confronted with several inconsistencies and paradoxes. Not the least of these is that in *Light in August* Faulkner creates a Calvinist world in order to reject its doctrine at the same time that the novel exhibits Faulkner's unconscious but continuing adherence to Calvinism as an attitude, a limiting frame to vision, an emotional set.

The doctrine of the absolute sovereignty of God, with its hieratical consequences in both church and state, nowhere concerns Faulkner even though, strictly speaking, this is the cornerstone of historical Calvinism. Faulkner's concern with doctrine—let it be said at once—is neither historical nor complete. The Calvinism of Faulkner is a religious and cultural residue filtering down through the Presbyterianism of the 19th and 20th centuries of the American secular South, in which form it is the doctrine, or set of doctrines, which he attacks in *Light in August*. Removed one step further from its institutionalized base, and seen as a dominant element in the very atmosphere which conditions a man's responses without benefit of credo—like a citizen yelling "I've got my rights!" to an over-stepping policeman at a moment when he neither knows, nor cares, that

Originally published in *Modern Fiction Studies*, Summer 1962.

ultimately his doctrine is that of John Locke—it is at this level that Faulkner's abiding Calvinism survives his conscious rejection of its hold on the human imagination.

The Calvinism which conditions and shapes the world of Joe Christmas, protagonist of *Light in August*, is the institutional belief that elevates righteousness above love, that accepts depravity as the natural condition of man, that suggests a strong measure of predestination. Joe Christmas' story is set within a contrasting framework of pastoral simplicity—the story of Lena Grove, who has traveled penniless and on foot from Alabama to Mississippi in search of the father of the child she bears during her long and beautifully evoked pilgrimage. Placid, trusting, innocent, her transparent goodness protects her as invincibly as her very trust removes her from the need for protection. Good begets good; evil generates evil: her world and Christmas' represent two extremes.

Joe Christmas had lived for his first five years as a white child in a white orphanage, where he had been abandoned one Christmas Eve. Two circumstances here shape his future even more than the orphanage itself (although it is worth remembering that Faulkner's most famous villain, Popeye, is reared in an orphanage, as is a later figure, far less sinister but also unsympathetic, General Gragnon of *A Fable*). One of these circumstances, which Joe does not understand, is the pathological hatred which the school dietician comes to feel for him. Joe has been going to her room every day to steal a taste of pink toothpaste, taking each time so little that the loss is never noticed. But one day he must hide at the approach of footsteps; he sits on the closet floor, piled with the dietician's "soft womansmelling garments," eating toothpaste, hardly aware of the assignation with a young intern on the other side of the closet curtain. Only this time, trapped as he is, he eats too much toothpaste and is sick. The dietician, convinced that he intends to report her transgression, cannot conceive that Joe has nothing to tell, except his own crime; that his silence under her questioning is not cunning, but fear; that he expects not the dollar bribe she gives him, but a whipping. He is profoundly shocked by the failure of punishment: this is the first dislocation in what is to be a long series for Joe:

> He was still with astonishment, shock, outrage. Looking at the dollar, he seemed to see ranked tubes of toothpaste like corded wood, endless and terrifying; his whole being coiled in a rich and passionate revulsion. "I don't want no more," he said. 'I don't never want no more,' he thought.[1]

In *The Sound and the Fury*, Quentin Compson's father tells him, "A man is the sum of his misfortunes"—a phrase which will haunt Quentin all through the day of his suicide. This is Joe's first misfortune: the child's miniature Calvinist world of rewards and punishments has been tampered with. Moreover, the dietician has been led to believe that Joe is a Negro, and now she taunts him with this. She goes further: she tries to get him evicted by telling the school matron that he is a Negro.

Here the second circumstance enters. The janitor of the orphanage, a dirty, half-crazed old man, has all along had some special secret interest in Joe; whenever the children are playing outdoors, the old man appears, quietly but unfailingly, to watch Joe. The dietician has observed this, and she comes to the old man now. She evokes not his aid but his curse: "Womansinning and bitchery!" He is not surprised that Joe has found her out (though the dietician has not told the janitor anything about the intern): "I knowed he would be there to catch you when God's time came. I knowed. I know who set him there, a sign and a damnation for bitchery" (p. 111).

The old man kidnaps Joe to prevent his being placed in a Negro orphanage. Before long he is found, however, and Joe is returned: a flight into Egypt after the discovery of the child on Christmas.

This whole episode in the orphanage establishes a cluster of associated ideas or motives that is of paramount importance all through the novel. Faulkner has juxtaposed Sex (as "primal scene," which the old man, who only much later will we learn is Joe's grandfather, sees as emblematic of natural depravity) and Joe's Negro blood—or not the fact of it, but only the taunt, the gibe. Heretofore, in the economy of his five years' life, this has had no importance for him, though some of the children sometimes confront him with the word. How they know is never explained; the grandfather claims they simply "*know*." But at this crisis, at the moment of his ambiguous discovery of sex, the Negro claim looms large. "'You little rat!' the thin, furious voice [of the dietician] hissed: 'You little rat! Spying on me! You little nigger bastard!'" (p. 107). And her "wild and dishevelled hair" will be worth remembering when we come to Joe's relationship with Joanna Burden.

Together with the motif of Sex and Negro blood, one more element enters here: the evasion, by women, of Law. Instead of beating Joe, the nurse tries to bribe him. Later, after he has been adopted by the McEacherns, a Scottish farm couple childless and isolated—he a strict and literal Calvinist; she a wan, ineffectual shadow in her husband's life—Joe will come to despise his foster mother for her vague conspiratorial attempts at tenderness, at love, at some consolation for both of them for what McEachern has made of her. Each time Joe tries to come to terms with some clear-cut system by which he can safely measure his relations with the world, accepting even

McEachern's system of unrelenting punishment as something he can understand and conform to, a woman like Mrs. McEachern will try to cut under the system, to establish a more personal and tender relationship—to replace, that is to say, Law with Love. It is this evasion of Law which Joe distrusts and which, ultimately, leads him to murder.

This significant pattern makes for several implications in the novel which have for the most part evaded criticism. That *Light in August* is "about" Calvinism is no new insight; the novel is discussed in these terms by William Van O'Connor.[2] One is grateful to him for pointing out the importance of this theme and its unifying power in a work that has been called "brilliantly written" but "disjointed," or "structurally unsound." But Mr. O'Connor does not see how very deeply committed to its subject the novel really is.

He does not see, for instance, that the only times that Joe's "black" blood becomes important in the novel are when sex is important too: first in the episode with the dietician; later in his first love affair with the waitress, who is also a prostitute (although Joe, seventeen and countrybred, does not know this at the time); and later still, with Joanna Burden, spinster, virgin, Puritan, who will at first yield to Joe only after fighting, but then will pursue, almost "corrupt" him: "wild then, in the close, breathing halfdark without walls, with her wild hair, each strand of which would seem to come alive like octopus tentacles, and her wild hands and her breathing: 'Negro! Negro! Negro!'" (p. 237). But during the long harrowing years of McEachern's domination, the issue of Joe's blood does not once enter; his foster parents do not know that he may be a Negro. Neither do the people of Jefferson, until after Joe has killed his white mistress.

As in any Calvinistic universe, the world of *Light in August* is a world of black and white, a world in which natural depravity, original sin, tends inevitably, even exclusively, to mean Sex. This leads one, I think, to a crucial thesis about the novel: the terms *black* and *white* here refer not so much to race as to something within the individual, to the antinomies of the Calvinist world—to such a double use of the same terms as may be found in Melville's *Benito Cereno*. As in that work, the conception of original sin, so important in the anti-Emersonian tradition of Hawthorne, Melville, James, and Faulkner, goes far beyond the ordinary connotations of human fallibility and *sinfulness*, to an insistence on absolute *depravity*. Like Melville's Babo, Joe Christmas comes to represent the Calvinist extreme. It is an extreme that will be found nowhere else in Melville (unless it is suggested in the figure of Claggart in *Billy Budd*); nowhere in Hawthorne; nowhere in James (unless in the rather exceptional *The Turn of the Screw*). The recent tendency in fashionable circles to erect the conception of original sin as a kind of touchstone for great American literature almost invariably overlooks what seems to me a crucial distinction.

Joe Christmas' father *may* have been part Negro—we never know for sure. Joe himself is not sure. "I don't know," he says. "I may be." That is relatively early in his life; later he will insist on his blackness savagely, vindictively. His blackness is significant precisely because he believes in it. The black *is* original sin; his bastard birth, his propensity to evil. More than that: the black here is not so much a symbol for *part* of each individual, as in the central Christian tradition that deals with original sin, so much as it is symbol for one total view of the individual. For in Calvinism, as distinct from the central Christian tradition, the human beast *is* black. Joe Christmas' identity—the sum of his misfortunes—stems not simply from his displacement in two sociologically ordered worlds; it stems also from the old Manichean conflict between potential good and evil. Joe's vision of himself is finally of evil only, and it hurls him to a damnation which he believes is inevitable. The possible good in Joe is frustrated time and time again, ironically enough by women. If Joe figures as a kind of perverted Christ symbol, he is surely also an upside-down Adam. But that irony is Joe's; the reader sees that his frustration comes not from any absolute truth in his vision of himself, but from his rejection of women, of the feminine principle that transcends Law—as Lena Grove transcends it. Lena's presence in the novel establishes the black-white conflict not as an inner struggle of man's dual nature, but as a war between two conceptions of the human possibility: the Calvinistic, which Joe's history imposes upon him, and another, the term for which is perhaps a little more evasive—Romantic, Rousseauistic, beatific—the belief in natural man and in his goodness, the conception exemplified in the novel by Lena Grove and Byron Bunch. If Joe's vision of evil hurls him to a damnation which he believes inevitable, it is balanced in the novel as a *necessary* view of human nature by the vision of Lena Grove, whose innocent assumption of universal goodness carries her in an opposite direction.

Joe has been pushed all of his life toward the black—toward that world view which the Reverend Hightower sees the Church as too often embodying, its steeples "empty, symbolical, bleak, sky-pointed not with ecstasy or passion, but in adjuration, threat, and doom." Joe has committed himself to evil and to damnation; still, when Joanna Burden, at that juncture in their relationship when the first outrageous passion has passed, proposes that they marry,

Joe will think: "Why not? It would mean ease, security, for the rest of your life. You would never have to move again. And you might as well be married to her as this—" (p. 232).

But the wary reader will at once feel the separateness of this possibility from Joe's whole life. Its alien quality is emphasized by the fact that this is the only time in Joe's career that he thinks of himself as another person, as *you* rather than as *I*. Such a marriage can mean something more than ease and security: an end to flight, to his rejection of the world. But in another moment he thinks: "No. If I give in now, I will deny all the thirty years that I have lived to make me what I chose to be."

What he has chosen to be is what is in fact predetermined: to be black and to fly from it; to see the possibility of white and to reject it. The paradox (familiar to Calvinism) of *choosing* the predestined is echoed not long after, when Joe is sitting outside waiting for that hour when he knows he will go up to Joanna's room and murder her. Faulkner describes his state in a rather tricky way: "he was the volitionless servant of the fatality in which he believed that he did not believe" (pp. 244–45).

It is a fatality because Joanna Burden has started to pray for him.

She is the granddaughter of a New England abolitionist named, with a kind of double underlining, Calvin Burden; a man who delivers to his son what he remembers of his own father's sermons, "half of . . . bleak and bloodless logic . . . and half of immediate hellfire and tangible brimstone," a man who tells his children: "I'll learn you to hate two things . . . or I'll frail the tar out of you. And those things are hell and slaveholders" (p. 212). The irony is more sublime still when he comments on the waywardness of the world: "Let them all go to their own benighted hell. . . . But I'll beat the loving God into the four of you as long as I can raise my arm" (pp. 212–13).

Joanna's father had taken her to see the graves of her grandfather and half-brother, who had been shot down by the zealous Colonel Sartoris, and the graves hidden for fear that townspeople still inflamed by the passions of Reconstruction might "find them. Dig them up. Maybe butcher them." Her father tells her at the grave:

> "Remember this. Your grandfather and brother are lying there, murdered not by one white man but by the curse which God put on a whole race before your grandfather or your brother or me or you were even thought of. A race doomed and cursed to be forever and ever a part of the white man's doom and curse for its sins. Remember that. His doom and his curse. Forever and ever" (p. 221).

The conception of the black man as the white man's curse, the white man's cross, appears elsewhere in Faulkner; its racial, sociological implications take one far afield. But in the context here—especially when we remember Joanna Burden's taking with so furious a passion Joe Christmas as her lover—it is clearly synonymous with the idea of original sin—"the curse which God put on a whole race"—the blackness which is not racial, not a partial element of humanity, but the Calvinistic conception of man's total depravity.

Ultimately Joanna Burden comes to exemplify still another aspect of Calvinism: the way in which sin can come to be welcomed, even celebrated, as the only medium through which some ultimate victory is possible—the extreme form of the doctrine of the fortunate fall. Or perhaps as the only medium through which man can at last recognize his essential humanity and so fulfill his destiny. We remember Quentin Compson's insistence that his sister Caddy has committed incest with him because he wants to deny her stupid, meaningless promiscuity which her world can no longer recognize as evil, which her father shrugs off as "a piece of natural human folly." Quentin prefers the "clean flame" of damnation to "the loud world." When Joanna Burden at last succumbs to Joe Christmas—to sex, to natural depravity—it is as with the sense of an inevitable if long-delayed collision with the very meaning of her life.

> At first it shocked him: the abject fury of the New England glacier exposed suddenly to the fire of the New England biblical hell. . . . she appeared to attempt to compensate each night as if she believed that it would be the last night on earth by damning herself forever to the hell of her forefathers, by living not alone in sin but in filth (pp. 225–26).

We can no longer believe that either is the victim of the other; they are both victims together. Except that for Joanna, the inevitable New England passionate remorse follows the passionate sin; she turns from Joe as lover in order to reform him, to establish him in the world. And when this effort fails, she begins to pray for him. Once more we have that pattern of black blood, and sex, and a woman's tampering with inevitable law. Unlike Joe, she cannot accept her total, final damnation. Trapped, as he feels, by a woman who will neither let him go nor accept him for what he is, for what he "chose to be," Joe murders her and flees, the sinister figure with a baleful glare in his face, the sum of his misfortunes embodied in his very clothes, the constant uniform of white shirt and black pants which tell his story.

There is still another story in the novel—that of the Reverend Gail Hightower, who had come to Jefferson because his grandfather had fought and died there in the Civil War. The circumstances of his death are not revealed until the latter part of the novel: he was shot in a raid on Grant's stores in the town—shot not during the raid, which was successful, but later, on a looting expedition, shot by a householder while stealing a chicken from a hen-house. Bizarre as this is, it is the central fact of Hightower's life, the vision recreated for him in childhood by his Negro servant and foster mother: the moment of apocalyptic glory when the horses' hooves come thundering down the street and the troops descend on the town. If the exact circumstances of the grandfather's death are kept from the reader until almost the end, it is because Hightower himself manages, until then, to block them from his romantic vision. And so central is this vision for Hightower that it becomes inextricably part of his religion. His early sermons, before he is forced to resign his pulpit, are compounded of a violent mixture of Christian dogma and martial glory: "like phantoms God and salvation and the galloping horses and his dead grandfather thundered."

It is late in the novel, only after Joe has been caught and murdered, and after Lena has had her baby, that Hightower comes to realize that he has forfeited his life, and—quite literally—his wife's, by his allegiance not only to a dream-vision of the past (a theme common to a whole gallery of Faulkner's characters), but to a conception of religion which is violent, apocalyptic, and dead: "skypointed not with ecstasy or passion, but in adjuration, threat, and doom" (p. 426). His great sin has been the rejection of his wife, who had offered him love, a love which Hightower dismisses in favor of his dead vision of violent glory, of Old Testamentary wars in heaven and on earth. So too will Joe consistently reject love from all the women in his life, taking only sex, recognizing only this as his human need and human damnation. Hightower's wife commits suicide, and this murder, as at the end of the book he comes to see it, is in miniature Hightower's murder of the church. For what he has brought to the church has been "instead of the crucified shape of pity and love, a swaggering and unchastened bravo killed with a shotgun in a peaceful henhouse, in a temporary hiatus of his own avocation of killing" (pp. 427–28).

One other figure is important in the novel: Percy Grimm, the man who shoots and emasculates Joe Christmas. Faulkner was later to describe him in a letter as a kind of proto-Fascist conceived two years before Hitler's Annunciation.[3] He *is* a proto-Fascist, but even in this characterization we are taken back to the Calvinist's Old Testament note of righteousness, of violence, of judgment and doom. The seed of Calvinism has flowered into the public life; Percy Grimm is not a departure from but an extension of the Calvinistic pattern of *Light in August*. His pursuit of Joe Christmas, who has escaped his guard in the Jefferson square, takes on the echoing tone of some infallible, inflexible Jehovah, relentlessly pursuing the enemy of Law. So that in the midst of the pursuit we are given this startling image: "Above the blunt, cold rake of the automatic his face had that serene, unearthly luminousness of angels in church windows" (pp. 404–5). And a little later we get this curious passage, not about Grimm himself, but about the mob that has followed him into Hightower's house, where Christmas has fled:

> Their faces seemed to glare with bodiless suspension as though from haloes as they stooped and raised Hightower, his face bleeding, from the floor where Christmas, running up the hall, his raised and armed and manacled hands full of glare and glitter like lightning bolts, so that he resembled a vengeful and furious god pronouncing a doom, had struck him down (pp. 405–6).

It is a full gallery: Christmas himself, shaped by a Calvinist *milieu* and pursuing a Calvinist fate; McEachern, his Presbyterian foster father who will spend all one Sunday torturing Joe, in righteousness, because he has not learned his catechism—will beat and starve him almost to insensibility and then, late that night, bid Joe get out of bed and onto his knees to pray with him, that God forgive his (*Joe's*) evil, ending his prayer with the request that "Almighty be as magnanimous as himself." Percy Grimm, Hightower, Joanna Burden, and Eupheus Hines, the crazed white grandfather who returns to the novel near its end, a fanatic who preaches a kind of pentecostal white supremacy in Negro churches, who calls himself an agent of God but who (like McEachern) sometimes forgets that he is agent only—who, at the end, will stand in the Jefferson streets screaming for the lynching of his grandson. The indictment of Calvinism, its implications, its myriad forms and consequences, seems devastating.

Yet somehow a residue is left. One senses an underlying Calvinism that belongs to Faulkner himself, rather than to the rejected world of his characters. Against those characters, the story of Lena and her pilgrimage, and her baby, and the attending Byron Bunch, should read like a final displacement of violence, of the resistance of evil with evil—like the coming of Mary and Joseph and, perhaps now, a real Christ to take the place of the crucified Joe Christmas. But the balancing of vision is not altogether convincing. It is as though Faulkner has come to reject Calvinism intellectually, even in some measure emotionally; but he has not been able, in Keats's fine phrase, to convince his nerves. For what I have spoken of as the last residue of Calvinism, as a conditioning to vision and to emotional set—this endures in Faulkner.

It endures in Faulkner's typical style, for instance: violent, tortured, doom-ridden, apocalyptic. It endures, more curiously, in Faulkner's treatment of time. I am convinced that it is just the note of fatality, of predetermination, which is responsible for the phenomenon that Jean-Paul Sartre,[4] among others, has noted in Faulkner: the impression he gives of static time, of a *present* constantly exploding its connection with the past and disgorging not into the future, but into the moment which succeeds and is another *present*. Faulkner's time, to apply in a different way one of his own favorite images, is like a string of beads, each of which is the present moment as it meets the eye, and each alone. For in the Calvinistic conception of predestination, all time past and future lies in the present moment, caught suspended in the eternity of God's mind; foreknowledge and predestination are equally divine attributes, and so all human experience becomes static in the fixed focus of the divine vision. Thus, at the very moment that Joe Christmas waits for the hour when he knows he will kill Joanna Burden, driven as he believes by some force outside himself, he will think of himself as "volitionless servant of the fatality in which he believed that he did not believe." Faulkner stresses not only the note of fatalism, but the separation of this act from the normal (that is to say, the causal) flow of time: "He was saying to himself *I had to do it* already in the past tense: *I had to do it*" (p. 245).

The Calvinism of Faulkner is revealed in two other important ways in *Light in August*: first, in the recurring theme of vengeful and fatalistic pursuit; second, in the almost universal coupling of sex and love with sin and destruction. It is a remarkable, if unnoted, fact that there are three pursuits in the novel, all accomplished under astonishingly similar circumstances. The first (in order of the sequence of telling, rather than of the events themselves) is McEachern's pursuit of Joe Christmas, when McEachern discovers Joe sliding down a rope from his room for what the foster father *knows* is the pursuit of lechery. We are told, in fact, that though he "had never committed lechery himself and . . . had not once failed to refuse to listen to anyone who talked about it," and though Joe has never once intimated that he even knows a girl, he nevertheless *knows*. He pursues Joe, who has long ago disappeared in Bobbie Allen's automobile:

> He turned into the road at the slow and ponderous gallop, the
> two of them, man and beast, leaning a little stiffly forward . . .
> as if in that cold and implacable and undeviating conviction of
> both omnipotence and clairvoyance of which they both par-

took known destination and speed were not necessary. He rode at that same speed straight to the place which he sought and which he had found out of a whole night and almost half a county . . . (pp. 176–77).

Hearing music at a schoolhouse, he goes directly to it, not knowing, in our ordinary sense, even yet that Joe is there. And inside, his movement never once stopped, abated, he moves directly to Joe and accosts him, as the "actual representative of wrathful and retributive Throne." Joe strikes him and runs away; we never learn for sure whether the man is dead.

The second pursuit is that by Eupheus Hines, after his daughter and the circus man with whom he *knows* she is running away. Like McEachern, he does not know which way to follow; but he too sets off on horse without question or hesitation:

And yet it wasn't any possible way that he could have known which road they had taken. But he did. He found them like he had known all the time just where they would be. . . . It was like he knew. It was pitch dark, and even when he caught up with a buggy, there wasn't any way he could have told it was the one he wanted. But he rode right up behind the buggy, the first buggy he had seen that night. He rode up on the right side of it and he leaned down, still in the pitch dark and without saying a word and without stopping his horse, and grabbed the man that might have been a stranger or a neighbor for all he could have known by sight or hearing . . . and shot him dead and brought the gal back home behind him on the horse. He left the buggy and the man both there in the road (p. 329).

The last pursuit is that by Percy Grimm, hunting down the escaped murderer, Christmas. Here too, if not at such length, we have the same sense of fatality, of foreknowledge: "he seemed to be served by certitude, the blind and untroubled faith in the rightness and infallibility of his actions." Faulkner develops in at least three varying references the image of Grimm as functioning in "swift, blind obedience to whatever Player moved him on the Board."

Once might seem coincidence; twice, a cleverly calculated strategy of a very careful craftsman. But *three* so closely paralleled episodes, each involving an infallible pursuit by a vengeful judgment—this surely suggests something more basic. For all three of these men to believe of themselves that they are infallibly guided is of course part of the very doctrine that Faulkner wants to reject. That all three should prove, in fact, actually to *be* infallibly guided—that is a fatalism that belongs no longer to the characters, but to the author himself.

Finally, there is the matter of love—sex—sin. It is curious that the criminality of Joe Christmas (as of all of Faulkner's most villainous characters) should be sexual, and that the motif of blackness, of depravity, should be worked out so exclusively in this novel in terms of sex. That sex becomes equated with natural depravity becomes even more clear near the end, when Grimm shoots Christmas and then emasculates him. We are told that Joe, for the first time in his adult life not "baleful," not "sinister," looks through eyes that are *peaceful*. A moment later we are told that "from out the slashed garments about his hips and loins the pent black blood seemed to rush like a released breath." On this "black blast" the man soars into the memories of the Jefferson mob forever: "It will be there, musing, quiet, steadfast, not fading, and not particularly threatful, but of itself serene, of itself alone triumphant" (p. 407).

If, de-sexed and dying, Joe should invoke so startlingly the imagery of Keats's Grecian urn, it is all the more startling when we remember that Joe's first sexual experience with Bobbie is delayed by her being "sick," by her being subject to that same periodic process which earlier in his life had caused Joe, learning of its existence, to shoot a sheep, and to kneel, "his hands in the yet warm blood of the dying beast, trembling, dry-mouthed, backglaring." When Bobbie tells him that she is sick, Joe strikes her and runs, entering the woods where

> as though in a cave he seemed to see a diminishing row of suavely shaped urns in moonlight, blanched. And not one was perfect. Each one was cracked and from each crack there issued something liquid, deathcolored, and foul. He touched a tree, leaning his propped arms against it, seeing the ranked and moonlit urns. He vomited (p. 165).

One is taken back, of course, to the primal experience at the orphanage, when "ranked tubes of toothpaste" become all confused, in physical revulsion, with sex.

But we are also taken forward by the Keatsian urn allusion, to Faulkner's use of it elsewhere, as in *The Bear*, as a symbol of "honor and pride and pity and justice and courage and love" untainted by human appetites and greeds. And we are taken to the figure of Joe Christmas dying, an image "of itself serene, of itself alone triumphant." It is difficult to imagine a stronger rejection of the entire human sexual process. The curse of Original Sin has been lifted; in mutilation lies our peace. What remains as serene and triumphant is purified, made white. The dying god, the maimed fisher-king, is translated to the heavens where no spring may touch him with renewal.

If we look elsewhere in Faulkner—as W. R. Moses has done[5]—we will find it hard, almost impossible, to find the theme of love or of sex anywhere treated as something positive in value, or as involving anything like the integrity of human choice. It will be seen either as an expression of a compulsive, involuntary curse or "possession." or, as in *Light in August*, as an expression of depravity and evil. Besides the fuller, more highly charged documentation of love and sex seen in this way, the pastoral legend of Lena Grove and Byron Bunch, beautifully as it is handled for the most part, seems at the end something projected rather than achieved, something wished for rather than seen. Their story has just begun at the end of *Light in August;* even there it must be reported, rather archly, at second hand by the furniture dealer. And Faulkner has nowhere taken this story, or its equivalent, up again.

Notes

1. *Light in August* (New York: Modern Library, 1950), p. 109. All subsequent references are to this edition.

2. *The Tangled Fire of William Faulkner* (Minneapolis: University of Minnesota Press, 1954).

3. Cited by Malcolm Cowley in *The Portable Faulkner* (New York: Viking Press, 1946), p. 652.

4. "Time in Faulkner: *The Sound and the Fury,*" in Frederick J. Hoffman and Olga Vickery, eds., *William Faulkner: Two Decades of Criticism* (East Lansing: Michigan State University Press, 1951), pp. 180–88.

5. "The Unity of *The Wild Palms,*" *Modern Fiction Studies*, II (Autumn 1956), 125–31.

CHAPTER 3

THE ROLE OF MYTH IN
ABSALOM, ABSALOM!

Donald M. Kartiganer

Recent criticism of Faulkner has shown increasing tendency to draw him away from the confines of Yoknapatawpha County and his Southern heritage and to link him with larger and more universal areas of thought and culture. Not that Faulkner's Southern roots are in any sense shallow or unimportant; but the depth and intensity of his writing is such that it transcends sectional bounds and becomes involved in racial experience itself. In addition to this extension of Faulkner's thought, the method of his work has been connected with the greatest of traditional art forms, completing the transition "from Jefferson to the World."[1]

Such an approach to *Absalom, Absalom!* may be particularly fruitful because of the almost unbearable intensity of the work, as if plunging to the very roots of human existence, and because of the obvious scope of its implication, describing the rise and fall of a man, a way of life. Beneath the surface of the novel, beneath the bitterness of Negro-white relations in the South, the lost innocence of the wilderness, is a darker soul of universal myth: of fathers and sons, of kings and heirs, of gods and the successors of gods. Recreated out of the combined narrative efforts of the four speakers (Miss Rosa, Compson, Quentin, and Shreve) is the legend of Thomas Sutpen—the man who would become god and erect an immortal dynasty, who rises to power and opulence, yet fails to understand that the god must die and be succeeded by the elder son, or at

Originally published in *Modern Fiction Studies*, Winter 1963.

least must meet the face of that son, touch his flesh, and grapple with him for the right to rule. To refuse the right of the son to confront his god is to destroy the health and potency of the dynasty, for without the proper heir the god eventually becomes weak, the crops grow brown, and the dwellings become skeletons of their former grandeur. While the god lives and thrives the land remains prosperous; but when he fails to honor the code of succession, when he cannot say "son" to the product of his body, then the godhead and the land are corrupted, and the tribe, or the section, or the nation trembles at its base, crumbles in fire and violence.

I

Sutpen is the grand center of this myth of ascendancy and doom, the brave, "fine figure of a man," the man who "if God Himself was to come down and ride the natural earth, that's what He would aim to look like,"[2] the man who creates house and gardens, wife and children "out of the soundless Nothing" (p. 8). Yet, for all his power and courage, he cannot comprehend the truth that his refusal to acknowledge the part-Negro Charles Bon as the son of his own body must be the irrevocable violation of his gigantic design, and of his attempt to fulfill the words of God to David of Israel, that "your house and your kingdom shall be made sure for ever before me; your throne shall be established for ever."[3] For David twice reaffirmed the relationship with his son Absalom, once when the latter had killed his half-brother Amnon: "So he came to the king; and bowed himself on his face to the ground before the king; and the king kissed Absalom" (2 Samuel 14, xxxiii); and again when his son had rebelled unsuccessfully against him: "Would I had died instead of you, O Absalom, my son, my son!" (2 Samuel 18, xxxiii).[4] But Sutpen can never affirm his fatherhood of Bon, who seeks his recognition in vain: "And he sent me no word? He did not ask you to send me to him? No word to me, no word at all?" (p. 356).

From the very beginning of his astounding rise to power there is a quality of myth surrounding the actions of Thomas Sutpen, and not even the cynical rationality of Compson or the humorous aloofness of Shreve can deprive him of this palpable sense of might and presence. The original journey of the Sutpen family, from an unidentified place ("there wasn't any West Virginia in 1808") (p. 220), at an uncertain time, is specified no further than as a pilgrimage from the mountains to the valleys. It is a movement rightly characterized by Miss Lind as a fall from grace to corruption,[5] but may be recognized also as the epic journey from one world to another, from Canaan down to the land of Egypt, from Troy to Latium, from Milton's Paradise to the land of men: it is a movement to a new way of existence.

No reason is given for the move, just "the whole passel of them . . . slid back down out of the mountains. . . . He didn't know just where his father had come from, whether from the country to which they returned or not, or even if his father knew, remembered, wanted to remember and find it again" (p. 223).[6] The vagueness of this entire story, Sutpen's concern only with the results rather than the explicit details of actions taken, provides the incidents with a legendary quality of mythical heroism, of the potential tribal god entering, a stranger, into the land, viewing its mores, and dedicating himself to the task of eventually ruling it. The key to his ambition, according to Sutpen, is the episode of rejection "when his father sent him to the big house with the message" (p. 229), "how it was the nigger told him, even before he had had time to say what he came for, never to come to that front door again but to go around to the back" (p. 232), again reiterated with a loyalty to fact and outcome, rather than to incidental ornament and description. The incident has a parabolic quality not unlike Kafka's fable of the young man before the door of the law in *The Trial*. And like an ancient legendary hero Sutpen re-flects on the problem, the injustice, constructs the ultimate aims to be achieved, and then begins his quest: "You got to have land and niggers and a fine house to combat them with. You see? and he said yes again. He left that night. He waked before day and departed just like he went to bed: by rising from the pallet and tiptoeing out of the house. He never saw any of his family again" (p. 238). No thought, no indecision, no heartache for faces never to be seen again: Sut-pen's departure is clearly biblical in its tone, with its heroic tran-quility, its bloodlessness, its inhumanity because it is larger than human.

"The little lost island" (p. 253) of Haiti is Sutpen's "solitary furnace experience" (p. 32), an elemental, brutal proving ground, "halfway between the dark inscrutable continent . . . and the cold known land" (p. 250), an island on which he is to meet his tests and bare himself before the furies. The native siege against the badly outnumbered planters is the initiatory rite of Sutpen: "on the eighth night the water gave out and something had to be done so he put the musket down and went out and subdued them. That was how he told it: he went out and subdued them, and when he re-turned he and the girl became engaged to marry" (p. 254). The gigantic bareness of the episode, the heroic inability to see any importance in speaking or explaining further, is the measure of Sutpen. One recalls such a typical biblical incident as Samson seiz-ing the "fresh jawbone of an ass . . . and with it he slew a thousand men" (Judges 15, xv). We are not told *how* such a feat could have been accomplished, how it was possible for a jawbone to fend off the swords of a thousand; as in the case of Sutpen, we are told merely that "he subdued them." Sutpen's putting aside of the fire-arm parallels Ike McCaslin's similar act in "The Bear," yet the obvious difference in tone is a clue to Sutpen's larger-than-life-size implications. He conquers via "an indomitable spirit which should have come from the same primary fire which theirs came from but which could not have, could not possibly have" (p. 254). This incident of the confronting of the Negroes single-handedly is, like the boy at the door of "the big house," a symbol repeated elsewhere in the novel: by the French architect when he vainly tries to escape, by Charles Etienne Bon struggling for an identity; but none can go forth like Sutpen and "subdue" them.

The marrying of the planter's daughter, whose first name Sutpen did not even know at the time, echoes the mythical awarding of the king's daughter to the knight that slays the marauding dragon, but in this case it is a prize that contains the germ of Sutpen's eventual fall. His discovery that his wife and son are part Negro causes the rejection of the two, and it is this repudiation, particularly of Charles, that is clearly the key to Sutpen's later decline and destruction.

In mythic terms (by no means far distant from the more obvious sociological ones) Sutpen's rejection of his elder son is a refusal to abide by the law of succession which demands that the tribal god eventually relinquish his rule to that son, who, in turn, may seize the throne only by demonstrating that the present god is no longer fit to guide his subjects. As Frazer has pointed out in his study of myths, the health of the god is irrevocably bound up with the health and fruitfulness of the land; by dethroning their leader at the first sign of decay, and by installing a new, young, and virile god in his place, the people may ensure continued prosperity.[7] Sutpen's error is his refusal to recognize Bon as his son, thus forbidding Bon even the right to challenge him for supremacy. Recognition, it is important to notice, does not imply abdication or voluntary relinquishment, but merely invests the son with the right to engage his father in combat. It is the right that Apollo grants to Phaeton by the opportunity to drive his chariot across the heavens; it is the right granted by David to Absalom when he kisses his son after the latter has murdered his half-brother. Both Phaeton and Absalom fail in their attempts to supplant the present god, yet their sacred privilege as the royal heir to accost him is never questioned. By violating the birthright of Bon, and subsequently of Bon's children, Sutpen is allowed indeed to decline, to sink from the baronial splendor of Sutpen's Hundred to the proprietorship of a small crossroads store. His lands, and the lands of the South, grow sterile and barren, his mansion becomes an iron shadow of itself. The tribal god has destroyed his domain by denying his natural heir, even as the Old South, symbolized in Sutpen, has denied its own "heir," the product of its plantation system. By having Sutpen marry Eulalia without knowing of her Negro blood, Faulkner seems to be implying that the South itself may have been "deceived" in its very installation of the slave system. But it is the very point of the novel that such possible deception cannot excuse the moral debt of that system.

There is an additional complexity, of course, in the fact that Sutpen's direct descendants are increasingly inept, particularly when compared to Sutpen himself, but this is due largely to the very denial of them. The final impression of Charles Bon is not clear, because of the colorations of the various speakers, but from the weight of Rosa's idolatry and Shreve's insistence on making a martyr out of him, Charles emerges as a fairly dominant figure, not without his share of worshippers and disciples, as well as bravery in combat. Because of Sutpen's original denial of him, however, he has been raised in the voluptuous surroundings of nineteenth-century New Orleans, a place of lush sensuality, of delicacy, ornament, and effeminacy, as opposed to the Spartan rearing of Henry, with his "granite heritage where even the houses, let alone clothing and conduct, are built in the image of a jealous and sadistic Jehovah" (p. 109). Bon's son Etienne is led still further away from the ideal "god-grooming" by the torture of his divided identity. He turns in anguish to a coal-black bride "resembling something in a zoo" (p. 209) and sires the idiot Jim Bond, who at last succeeds to his birthright by being the last Sutpen, bellowing before the fiery blaze that climaxes the ruination of Sutpen's Hundred. On the other hand, one might say that although Faulkner is aware of the necessity for the South to recognize its "natural heir," which is the freed Negro slave, he is unwilling to admit that the products of such miscegenation can approach the magnificence of the pure-blooded if unforeseeing giants who engendered the system. Thus, while he is advocating justice as the only possible preventative against continued decline and the only method of restoring to some degree the health of the land, Faulkner's loyalty to his own heritage forbids him from saying that such recognition, such justifiable acknowledgment, can ever produce men of the stature of the young Thomas Sutpen. The latter, as the founder of a dynasty, is not defeated by the Negro servant at the door, while those who come after him are indeed defeated by similar symbols of rejection. In terms of the myth, however, it is sufficient to say that recognition of the son is the irrevocable requirement of the tribal god; Sutpen's failure to do so causes his decline to go unchecked, finally resulting in the deterioration of the land he rules, which, symbolically speaking, is the South itself.

Following his repudiation of Eulalia and Bon, which is ultimately the destruction of the design he has yet to fashion, Sutpen comes to Jefferson, Mississippi, and it is there that he creates his world. Like the Creation itself, Sutpen's Hundred is formed "violently out of the soundless Nothing" (p. 8), as if with no greater effort than the Lord saying Let there be light: "the *Be Sutpen's Hundred* like the olden-time *Be Light*" (p. 9).[8] This apparently conscious allusion to the Creation is continued in the amount of time necessary to complete the foundation of his design: six years (1833–89) to build a house and plantation, to marry, and in the sixth year to create man, to beget a son. Jehovah-like, Sutpen "was not liked (which he evidently did not want, anyway) but feared, which seemed to amuse, if not actually please, him" (p. 72); and, creator-like, "he named them all, the one before Clytie and Henry and Judith even, with that same robust and sardonic temerity, naming with his own mouth his own ironic fecundity of dragon's teeth" (p. 62).

In spite of his subsequent decline he never loses his powerful presence and the awe in which others hold him, from his sister-in-law Rosa to the diseased, adoring Wash, until the very final moment when Wash wilfully violates the traditional taboo against touching the tribal god,[9] "I'm going to tech you, Kernel" (p. 286), and mutilates him for his crassness to his—Wash's—granddaughter. Rosa views him alternately as demon and god, never denying his power even when damning him. Her conviction that it was only for this ogre's crimes that "God let us lose the War" (p. 11) is in perfect harmony with the tribal god myth, which also blames Sutpen for the ruin of the South. Nor is this conviction inconsistent with Rosa's deep respect (if hatred) for the power of the man, Rosa, "who doubtless used to watch . . . from the window or door as he passed unaware of her as she would have looked at God probably, since everything else within her view belonged to him too" (p. 363).[10] As far as Sutpen is concerned, he is fulfilling the obligations of the godhead by his periodic and brutal bouts with his Negro slaves, constantly reasserting the supremacy which is his.

Yet all Sutpen's diligence and resourcefulness, his heroism in going forth to fight for his land, cannot overcome the corruption of his sin against the son. By the end of the War, when he should have been able to cease his struggle and give over to the younger Bon, Sutpen is still battling to prolong his lineage, sinking lower and lower in each attempt at fathering an heir. "The fat, the stomach, came later. It came upon him suddenly, all at once, in the year after whatever it was happened to his engagement to Miss Rosa" (p. 81).

It is significant that his final idolator (and murderer) is the diseased, malaria-ridden Wash, who achieves a kind of grandeur in his adulation of this "fine proud man" (p. 282), who believes hopefully that "me and him can still do hit and will ever so, if so he will show me what he aims for me to do" (p. 288). Yet he represents in his own corrupt form the deterioration of Sutpen's magnificence.

II

The supreme task of the tribal god, beyond the obligation to ensure the health of the land and subjects, is to prolong his own race, extend the line of kings. Charles Bon, with his princely title, is the elder son of Thomas Sutpen, and as such is the only one who can fulfill the hope of immortality. But it is Sutpen's error and his "one mistake" that he cannot comprehend this fact. In ritualistic fashion Bon is groomed for his natural role as heir by his embittered mother, although he himself is unaware until he meets Henry Sutpen what his task is to be: "Maybe she was grooming him for that hour and moment which she couldn't foresee . . . the moment when he (Bon) would stand side by side (not face to face) with his father . . . grooming him herself, bringing him on by hand herself, washing and feeding and putting him to bed and giving him the candy and the toys and the other child's fun and diversion and needs in measured doses like medicine with her own hand" (pp. 296–97).[11] Bon is not the figure that Sutpen was, lacks surely the gigantic mythic quality of that originator; yet, like Sutpen, he too appears to the inhabitants of Jefferson as a mysterious being "phoenix-like, full-sprung from no bones nor dust anywhere" (p. 74), "Yes, shadowy: a myth, a phantom" (p. 104). Bon also has his followers: young men like Henry "who aped his clothing and manner and . . . his very manner of living, looked upon Bon as though he were a hero out of some adolescent Arabian Nights" (p. 96). But it is particularly to Henry and Judith that Bon appeals the most: "it would be hard to say to which of them he appeared the more splendid" (p. 95). Evidence of Henry's complete admiration is his statement, "I am trying to make myself into what I think he wants me to be; he can do anything he wants to with me; he has only to tell me what to do and I will do it" (p. 330), a conscious echo of Wash's self-commitment to Sutpen, quoted above.

As in the case of Sutpen himself, the treatment of Bon by the various narrators depends greatly on the particular character of the speaker. To Compson, cynical and disillusioned, longing for a time that has passed, Bon is an epicene child of New Orleans, shrewd and sophisticated, yet lacking that dynamic boundlessness of Sutpen, that raw strength and virility of the Southern puritan's "granite heritage." To Shreve, however, the Canadian, as different from the Southern plantation owner as Bon must have been, Shreve, with his "pink-gleaming and baby-smooth, cherubic, almost hairless" (p. 181) body, Bon becomes a hero in battle and a martyr in death. He reverses Compson's version, which says that Henry saved Bon's life, and explains the picture of the octoroon mistress in the metal frame Judith gave Bon—which she finds after he is killed by Henry—as an example of his humane consideration: "It was because he said to himself, 'If Henry dont mean what he said, it will be all right; I can take it out and destroy it. But if he does mean what he said, it will be the only way I will have to say to her, *I was no good; do not grieve for me*. Ain't that right? Aint it? By God, aint it?' 'Yes,' Quentin said" (p. 359).

In short, Bon slowly evolves through the interpretations of Compson and Shreve into a kind of Christ Himself, a son to the stern Jehovah but a son of a different quality, possessed of a certain softness, a sense of human consideration, of appreciation for another's love and another's suffering. Easily comparable are Sutpen's callous behavior toward Rosa, toward Wash's granddaughter Milly, and Bon's attitude toward the New Orleans octoroon mistresses that so disgust the puritanical Henry: "But we do save that one, who but for us would have been sold to any brute who had the price, not sold to him for the night like a white prostitute, but body and soul for life. . . . Sometimes I believe that they are the only true chaste women, not to say virgins, in America, and they remain true and faithful to that man not merely until he dies or frees them, but until they die" (pp. 116–17); or consider Bon's gentleness in his treatment of Henry, his covering of his younger half-brother with a cloak to protect him against the cold (p. 356)—a complete contrast to the brutal and egoistic behavior of the dynamic Sutpen. At the end of his life Bon is doing little less than giving himself up to Henry's hands, refusing to assault the "system" that is forbidding him his birthright. His essentially passive, outwardly calm response to Sutpen's refusal to acknowledge him is diametrically opposite Sutpen's own response when, as a boy, he is barred from entrance to the white mansion. Unlike Bon, Sutpen reacts with a burning conviction to destroy those barriers which block him from success, to become, at all human costs, the master and ruler of his own mansion, his slaves, his women, and his heirs.

One of the keys to the relationship of Sutpen and Bon is their respective attitudes toward fate. Sutpen, like the Old Testament God on whom he is modeled, is a creating being, ambitious and aspiring, a basically fate-defying character, who will not give in to circumstance, even in his final attempt to father an heir on the young and ignorant Milly Jones. Bon, on the other hand, seems terribly aware of his fate, in fact seems continually racing toward it, anxious to embrace it. Never does he seek to overcome violently the "system" that denies him, never does he endeavor to seize the empire that is rightfully his. He seeks only the recognition of hearing "my son" spoken to his face: "He will not even have to ask me, I will just touch flesh with him and I will say it myself: You will not need to worry; she shall never see me again" (p. 348). And with this desire seems to come the deeper realization that the little he asks is far too much for the father. Rather, Bon is moving purposely toward an inevitable rendezvous with Henry at the gates of Sutpen's Hundred, where the devoted disciple must become the betrayer and shoot him down. Bon's final journey to Sutpen's house, with his knowledge of Henry's attitude to miscegenation, is clearly suicidal, becomes the completely passive act that hangs upon another's choice: *"You will have to stop me, Henry.* 'And he never slipped away' Shreve said. 'He could have, but he never even tried'" (p. 358).

The dichotomy of Bon and Sutpen is apparent in nearly every fact regarding the two: the lushness and extravagance of New Orleans vs. the granite, puritanical severity of Sutpen's Hundred; the mulatto vs. the white man; Catholic vs. Protestant; a softness and generosity vs. ruthlessness; passiveness and acceptance vs. the active and aspiring; the human and humane vs. the Titan. Sutpen is the antebellum warrior resisting the ascendancy of a new era: "His old man's solitary fury fighting now not with the stubborn yet slowly tractable earth as it had done before, but now against the ponderable weight of the changed new time itself as though he were trying to dam a river with his bare hands and a shingle" (p. 162). Faulkner's theme is no less than the epic one of changing orders, of Rome rising out of the shambles of Illium.

The dichotomy of Bon-Sutpen is ultimately extended into the world of 1910, into the lives of Quentin and Shreve, who find themselves swept up in the swift current of the Sutpen narrative. On the one hand the two Harvard undergraduates are assimilated with each other and with the Southern past: "Both born within the same year: the one in Alberta, the other in Mississippi; born half a continent apart yet joined, connected after a fashion . . . by that Continental Trough . . . the geologic umbilical" (p. 258). Yet the differences between them still outrank the similarities: the Deep South vs. Canada; warmth vs. frigidity; Shreve's basic indifference and ironic aloofness to the Sutpen story vs. Quentin's passionate involvement, which is ultimately his destruction. The division of Bon-Sutpen is represented in the single figure of Henry: son, yet not the legitimate heir; lover, yet pander to his sister Judith; disciple to

Bon, yet his father's agent in the murder of Bon; ultimately divided between Bon *and* Sutpen, and utterly incapable of choosing once and for all between them. This irreconcilable split in Henry's mind is carried on in Quentin, with his problems of incest desire and, more importantly in this novel, of torn loyalties between his "father" (Compson, Sutpen, the Old South) and his "elder brother" (Bon, the Negro, the Canadian, the New, postwar South). His similarity to Henry is subtly pointed out by Faulkner in the single, nearly hysterical affirmation each one makes regarding his divided soul. Henry is intent on believing in the integrity of his brother Bon, in freeing himself from the corrupt tribal god: "I will believe! I will! I will! Whether it is true or not, I will believe!" (p. 111). Quentin is torn between his love of and yet deep moral dismay for the South, crying out through "the cold air, the iron New England dark; *I don't. I don't! I don't hate it! I don't hate it!*" (p. 378). Both Henry and Quentin are incapable of facing boldly up to the corruptions of the South, and perhaps trying to cleanse them; nor are they capable of divorcing themselves completely from this land that has so enveloped and taken possession of their beings. This division of Bon-Sutpen, of Henry, of Quentin-Shreve, can perhaps be traced to the division in Faulkner himself of passionate admiration yet moral disgust for the deeds of Thomas Sutpen. And it is this division out of which the novel is finally created.

III

With the death of Bon and the fleeing of Henry, the damage of Sutpen's "error" is done and awaits only the increased perversion of Bon's children for the final destruction of his design. Interestingly enough, both the son, Charles Etienne Bon, and the grandson, Jim Bond, receive a kind of preparation and grooming parallel to Bon's own, as if they too were heirs-apparent. After Etienne's mother's death (Bon's octoroon wife whom, unlike Sutpen's first wife, he never renounces) the boy is brought by Clytie back to Sutpen's Hundred after Sutpen is dead and the plantation is completely rundown. Within this poverty and dilapidation Clytie, in almost a mockery of the succession, attempts to "groom" the young boy, as if he should take up one day the reins of power left by Sutpen himself. She "fed him, thrust food which he himself could discern to be the choicest of what they had, food which he realized had been prepared for him by deliberate sacrifice . . . (she) dressed him and washed him, thrust him into tubs of water too hot or too cold yet against which he dared make no outcry, and scrubbed him with harsh rags and soap, sometimes scrubbing at him with repressed fury as if she were trying to wash the smooth faint tinge from his skin" (p. 198). And even in this mock grooming are the echoes of the identical sin which Sutpen committed against Bon, reenacted by Judith on the son of her half-brother. Etienne is compelled to sleep on a trundle bed, halfway between Judith's regular bed and Clytie's floor pallet, illustrating his condition of denial by both. Even when she is trying to dissuade him from his marriage to the ape-like Negress, Judith is incapable of reaching out to him as her father could not reach out to Bon: "she not daring to put out the hand with which she could have actually touched it but instead just speaking to it, her voice soft and swooning" (p. 208). Denied once more is "the living touch of that flesh" (p. 319), the "hot communicated flesh" (p. 320) that, beyond all language, all speech, is the source of contact between two human beings.

In a manner that reaches the ironic, the idiot Jim Bond, the last of his race, "the scion, the heir, the apparent" (p. 370), is dressed in "clean faded overalls and shirt" (p. 370), a fact which is stated earlier in the novel: "in patched and faded yet quite clean shirt and overalls too small for him" (p. 214). One imagines the old Negro Clytie, too impoverished to buy new garments, or to restore the old mansion, yet insistent upon the cleanliness of the prince of Sutpen's Hundred.[12]

The death of Sutpen himself by the hand of the insulted grandfather points up the callousness of his treatment of Milly Jones but by no means destroys the gigantic figure he has hitherto presented. Granted that he has grown old and flabby, to Wash he is still "the fine proud image of the man on the fine proud image of the stallion . . . the apotheosis lonely, explicable beyond all human fouling: *He is bigger than all them Yankees that killed us and ourn*" (p. 287). For this diseased old man Sutpen is still the true godhead, the emblem of everything that a mere mortal could not hope to be, yet could somehow approach merely by believing in the god: "Maybe I am not as big as he is and maybe I did not do any of the galloping. But at least I was drug along where he went" (pp. 287–88); and the wonderful pathos of the old man's cry, embodying both the grandeur and the tragedy of the post–Civil War South: "Well, Kernel, they kilt us but they aint whupped us yit, air they?" (p. 184). Yet, as Sutpen's cruelty to Milly is the nadir of his ruthlessness, it is fitting that he should not be permitted to live beyond it, and that the agent of his destruction should be Wash, the high priest of his later years. In brandishing the old, long-unused scythe, Wash becomes fate itself, the mindless Demogorgon of the outraged land that can endure no longer the corruption that Sutpen has inflicted upon it. When the sons are defiled, when the subjects are crushed beyond retaliation, then it is the natural force itself which must cast out the offender. As in classic tragedy one marvels not only at the brutality of the punishment, but at the colossal presence of the protagonist himself, at the tremendous waste of such might, such potential, that through pride and blindness has risen up vainly against the laws of succession and blood and has contaminated the land it could have made fruitful.[13]

It is the figure of Sutpen, the demon, the god, the creator of a strategic design, the symbol of all that was grand and noble, all that was depraved and perverted, in the dynasty of the Old South that is being purged in the final flames, sweeping irrevocably away the time that has passed with only the howling idiot to signify that it ever existed, and that it was, however gallant, however magnificent, ultimately diseased, ultimately poisoned. *Absalom, Absalom!* is unquestionably tragedy of the highest order, with its colossal heroic figure doomed by a tragic blindness, the god himself destroyed by his unwillingness to kneel before necessity. As in high tragedy there is the element of catharsis in the final purgation through fire and, in Compson's final letter to his son Quentin, with its mention of hope, the element of long-sought order and definition, of pieces falling into place:

> —or perhaps there is. Surely it can harm no one to believe that perhaps she has escaped not at all the privilege of being outraged and amazed and of not forgiving but on the contrary has herself gained that place or bourne where the objects of the outrage and of the commiseration also are no longer ghosts but are actual people to be actual recipients of the hatred and the pity. It will do no harm to hope—You see I have written hope, not think. So let it be hope. —that the one cannot escape the censure which no doubt he deserves, that the other no longer lack the commiseration which let us hope, (while we are hoping) that they have longed for, if only for the reason that they are about to receive it whether they will or no. The weather was beautiful though cold and they had to use picks to break the earth for the grave yet in one of the deeper clods I saw a redworm doubtless alive when the clod was thrown up though by afternoon it was frozen again. (p. 377)

For a moment the supplanting of chaos with balance, and even the final wry suggestion of new life in the dormant earth (though quickly rejected by the cynical, disillusioned Compson); perhaps even the unspoken hope for future giants, though for Faulkner (as for Compson), one would think, the Sutpens of this earth, like its Lears, were of a special, grander substance, of a breadth and strength, a catastrophic power, that is buried eternally in the fleeting dust of a distant time.

Notes

1. A very select list of such criticisms: R. D. Jacobs, "Faulkner's Tragedy of Isolation," in L. D. Rubin, Jr., and R. D. Jacobs, eds. *Southern Renascence* (Baltimore: Johns Hopkins Press, 1953), dealing in part with Faulkner's relation to traditional Greek tragedy; R. M. Slabey, "Faulkner's 'Wasteland' Vision in *Absalom, Absalom!*" *Mississippi Quarterly,* XIV (Summer, 1961), 153–61, connecting Faulkner to Eliot, and "Myth and Ritual in *Light in August,*" *Texas Studies in Language and Literature,* II (1960), 328–49, utilizing the work of Frazer; H. H. Waggoner, *William Faulkner: From Jefferson to the World* (University of Kentucky Press, 1959), seeing Faulkner, in part, in the context of Christian myth; and, more recently, J. H. Justus, "Epic Design of *Absalom, Absalom!*" *Texas Studies in Language and Literature*, IV (Summer, 1962), 157–76, relating Faulkner to the classical epic tradition.

2. William Faulkner, *Absalom, Absalom!* (New York: Modern Library, 1951), p. 282. All further references to this work are given in the text.

3. *The Old Testament*, Revised Standard Version (New York: Thomas Nelson & Sons, 1952), 2 Samuel 7, xvi, p. 617. See Ilse Dusoir Lind, "The Design and Meaning of *Absalom, Absalom!*" *PMLA*, LXX (December, 1955), 887–912.

4. Faulkner's own comment on his use of the David-Absalom story: "As soon as I thought of the idea of the man who wanted sons and sons destroyed him, then I thought of the title." F. L. Gwynn and J. L. Blotner, *Faulkner in the University* (University of Virginia Press, 1959), p. 76.

5. Lind, p. 890.

6. This quotation, as well as the ones which follow in this section, is from part vii of the novel, in which Quentin and Shreve take up the narrative, but it is supposedly from the lips of Sutpen himself, as he related the history of his youth to Quentin's grandfather (p. 218).

7. Sir James George Frazer, *The New Golden Bough*, ed. Theodor H. Gaster (New York: Criterion Books, 1959), pp. 224–25. R. M. Slabey, in "Myth and Ritual in *Light in August,*" p. 330, indicates that there is good reason to believe that Faulkner was acquainted with Frazer's work.

8. Justus, p. 162, points out this role of Sutpen as God himself.

9. Frazer, p. 165.

10. Rosa's hatred of yet fascination for Sutpen seems related to her early repudiation of her father and the male principle itself (p. 60). Sutpen, with all his virility and power, comes to symbolize the essence of that principle for Rosa, and her proposed marriage to him is her lone attempt to adjust herself to it.

11. Eulalia can be compared to Gaea, the Earth Mother, grooming her son Cronus to dethrone her husband Uranus, who had imprisoned all her children.

12. The deterioration of the Sutpens is pointed out by Leslie Fiedler in the decline from "Bon," which means "good," to "Bond," which means "chain"—*Love and Death in the American Novel* (New York: Criterion Books, 1960), p. 398.

13. Faulkner's comment on Sutpen's fall: "the Greeks destroyed him, the old Greek concept of tragedy." *Faulkner in the University,* p. 35.

TEMPORALITY, HISTORY, AND TRAUMA

CHAPTER 4

ENIGMAS OF BEING
IN *AS I LAY DYING*

Robert Hemenway

In a strange room you must empty yourself for sleep. And before you are emptied for sleep, what are you. And when you are emptied for sleep, you are not. And when you are filled with sleep, you never were. I don't know what I am. I don't know if I am or not. Jewel knows he is, because he does not know that he does not know whether he is or not. He cannot empty himself for sleep because he is not what he is and he is what he is not. Beyond the unlamped wall I can hear the rain shaping the wagon that is ours, the load that is no longer theirs that felled and sawed it nor yet theirs that bought it and which is not ours either, lie on our wagon though it does, since only the wind and the rain shape it only to Jewel and me, that are not asleep. And since sleep is is-not and rain and wind are *was,* it is not. Yet the wagon *is,* because when the wagon is *was,* Addie Bundren will not be. And Jewel *is,* so Addie Bundren must be. And then I must be, or I could not empty myself for sleep in a strange room. And so if I am not emptied yet, I am *is.*[1]

Darl Bundren's reverie is one of the most difficult passages in all the Faulkner canon and is probably the most difficult single paragraph in *As I Lay Dying*. Detailed interpretation of it is frequently avoided and its significance for Faulkner's achievement has gone largely unexamined.[2] The reverie is important, however, because it defines an existential dilemma basic to Faulkner's fictional

Originally published in *Modern Fiction Studies*, Summer 1970.

world. Darl's tortured logic represents an uncertainty about personal reality; confronted by a dilemma of being, the enigmatical nature of existence, he finds himself asking, "Do I exist?" Although Darl never realizes an answer to this question, ending the novel on the train to Jackson and an asylum, his struggle with the enigma of being informs the theme and structure of *As I Lay Dying* and grants important insights into Faulkner's other fiction as well. For not only did he create Darl's dilemma, Faulkner also responded to it; he assigned "being" coextension with the present tense and asserted the necessity of living a highly personalized *present* existence, untrammeled by the past, untroubled by the future. This response explains much about Faulkner's art and life; it even helps to explain his attitude toward the reality which generated his fiction: the reality of a profound American artist living in a twentieth-century Mississippi obsessed with its ancestral past. Darl's passage can well bear close study.

When interpretation of Darl's meditation is attempted, the one easily understood sentence, "I don't know what I am," is usually cited as proof of an identity crisis, and there is no question that Darl struggles with the burden of his identity;[3] his attempt to explain himself as a Bundren, to reconcile himself to all the peculiar relationships of that condition, is a major narrative thread in the novel. But limiting Darl's emotional struggle to an identity crisis ignores the existential implications of Faulkner's language.[4] The passage is structured around the verb *to be,* and this verb's grammatical function is to describe a "condition or state of being," said condition or state dependent upon the predicate nominative completing the intransitive construction. Questioning identity, Darl should ask "Am I ——?" or "I am ——?"—his identity described by the verb's completing element. It becomes clear, however, that Darl's primary concern is the subsuming question of being: "I am?" or "Am I?" He wants to know nothing less than, What is existence? What is the nature of *being?* What is *is?* His words are not "I don't know who I am," but "I don't know what I am. I don't know if I am or not."

Such uncertainties of being are not unusual in *As I Lay Dying;* they in fact serve as a unifying motif for the entire novel. As Maurice Le Breton has stated, there is "beaucoup de peine à concevoir la notion d'Etre."[5] The Bundrens are Mississippi hill farmers struggling to comprehend, and act appropriately towards, the idea of death. To understand death, however, they must establish a definition of life, and this painful effort becomes a kind of ontological quest. Using the most common verb of their speech, "to be," the Bundrens seek to define life while confronted with its opposite, the corpse of Addie Bundren. What is the difference between her "state of being" and theirs? Should they say Addie "is," Addie "was," or Addie "is not"?

This may appear tautologous, but to the Bundrens it is a very real conundrum, demanding solution at both physical and metaphysical levels. Dewey Dell carries with her the fear of a night in which *"I couldn't think what I was I couldn't think of my name I couldn't even think I am a girl I couldn't even think I"* (423). Vardaman lives with a perpetually confused identification between his mother and a fish: "It was not her because it was laying right yonder in the dirt. And now it's all chopped up . . . Then it wasn't and she was, and now it is and she wasn't" (386). The Bundrens seek comprehension of a world where a human being can *die,* where a person can cease "to be," and *As I Lay Dying* questions not only the "state of being" called identity but, more importantly, the boundaries of existence: the temporal limits of "being"; it asks if "is not" equals "was." Ultimately such questions of identity and time are incorporated into an examination of the concept of being itself, the subject of Darl's passage and the source of the novel's toughest questions: "Is" is? What is the difference between "is" and "is not"? The responses to such enigmas illuminate a way of seeing which enables a writer to create successful fiction from the absurdities and tragedies observed in human experience. They define William Faulkner's "angle of vision."

I

Darl's soliloquy occurs after he has divined Addie's death, but before he and Jewel have returned home to begin the burial journey. It is a remarkable linguistic *tour de force* and must be examined with extreme care. (My explication of the passage follows and is designed to be read contiguously with the passage itself—indeed, it will only be meaningful if read in this manner.) Confronted with an alien situation, Darl starts with a metaphorical truth which is scientifically false: "In a strange room you must empty yourself for sleep." One's mind cannot be "emptied" for sleep; sleep is but the alteration of consciousness, the movement from awakened consciousness to sleep consciousness. Darl senses that something, perhaps indefinable, is taken away, that the consequent void is filled with a "never were" of simulated oblivion, and he is uncertain about that essential "state of being" which apparently vacates the premises: "Before you are emptied for sleep, what are you." The entire passage is designed to answer this question, and when Darl concludes[6] in the last sentence, "I am is," he has unknowingly defined existence as consciousness itself, a definition that limits man's essence to the "is" of present tense reality.[7]

When Darl admits "I don't know what I am," he is only second-arily concerned with his subjective identity (as Bundren, Mississip-pian, brother, son); he is primarily struggling with the abstraction of existence and the epistemological dilemma inherent in the idea. How does one *know* this human "state of being"? How does one know whether he "is" or not? A compulsion to ask such questions is critical, for it exhibits an awareness that living is not necessarily knowing. Darl is conscious of the uncertainty of existence ("I don't know if I am or not") but Jewel is unaware. Then can Jewel be said to "exist"? He does, of course, but his existence is significantly lim-ited in nature: Jewel "knows" that "he is" in only a narrow, physical sense, because he is unaware ("he does not know") of his ignorance of the enigma of being ("that he does not know whether he is or not"). To Darl's mind, Jewel "cannot empty himself for sleep" be-cause he "exists" at only one level; almost his entire life is defined in physical terms, and no emptying process need take place because no change in Jewel's "state of being" occurs. "He is not what he is"—he does not fulfill the potential of human consciousness. In a way, he is not quite human—for "he is what he is not": his lack of consciousness confirms his virtual dehumanization, a condition sug-gested by his substitution of a horse for his mother. Darl's evaluation of Jewel is reiterated throughout the novel: he is instinctive action, without intellectual perspective. He lacks the consciousness for paradox.

Having struggled with the abstract idea of human existence, Darl's tormented inquiry expands to include other "states of being" which surround humanity: existence as nature (rain and wind) and man-shaped natural existence (the lumber). His first discovery is obvious; man cannot presumptuously label existences outside him-self in relation to his own material being. How could any one think he "owned" the lumber on the wagon? It is really no one's, not the loggers', nor the buyers', nor the teamsters'. Thus, Darl is uncer-tain about how "things" outside the self exist, and he comes to a position which is roughly that of philosophical idealism, although he arrives there via a curious route. The lumber does not belong to man physically; it belongs, as all objects do, to nature, to the wind and rain which "shape it" through growth. But man is a part of na-ture too, endowed with imagination and memory, and Darl (even though he lies in a darkened, strange room) can imagine the wagon and its load because he has an idea of it. Hearing the rain hit the wagon, he can create its existence outside the house with his imagination. The wind and rain can even "shape it" (at least bring it to mind) for Jewel, although he will not be aware, as Darl is, of the complex processes of consciousness which make this possible; in any event, this perceiving capability is limited to the awakened mind.

How does this knowledge compare with Darl's conception of sleep? "Sleep is is-not" but "rain and wind are was." The rain and wind are only experienced by Darl with the auditory senses, and thus the total reality of rain and wind must be created by correlating the experienced sounds with the memory's significations of those sounds, with the "idea" of rain and wind. The "shaping" of the lumber that the wind and rain do, therefore, is a creation of the "was" of Darl's memory operating in the "is" of his consciousness, and in a purely literal sense, the lumber "is not." Yet it does exist because Darl has conceived of it, and he is left to ponder which is real: the idea of lumber or the lumber-filled wagon. This is a paradox, perhaps the major paradox of being. How does one reconcile subjective and objective reality? Mind and body? Existence and Essence?

Troubled by this paradox, Darl is returned to the starting point of the reverie. Still sure that sleep is an emptiness ("sleep is is-not"), he now hesitantly reasons that existence is primarily a function of the mind: rain and wind exist as they are experienced in the senses, organized in the imagination, and identified by the "was" of memory; the primary existence of the lumber, then, is mental, and in a primary physical sense, "it is not." Yet the paradox is not solved; Darl, like Dr. Johnson kicking the stone to refute Bishop Berkeley, is not ready to abdicate "literal" reality, an absolute existence outside the self. The stone he kicks is the wagon, for the wagon "is ours" and it defines Darl's existence in a way that the impersonal rain, wind, and lumber do not. Darl unconsciously withdraws from his semi-idealist position because its temporal significance has frightening implications for his relationship with Addie. For when the wagon, as it exists now with its lumber, becomes "was" (the lumber a memory, and the wagon in this strange place a memory), Addie Bundren's death will have to be faced (she will "not be"). Darl cannot master this fact, even though he knows she has died. He retreats into a completely literal perception of reality based on the family relationship that enables him to think of Addie as still existent. Jewel "is" (he exists) so "Addie Bundren must be" (alive in Jewel). Thus, Darl "must be" too, since he also is a son of Addie; such "being" implies an awakened consciousness, or there would not be anything to be emptied for sleep. And if you are not yet asleep, not yet emptied, you must be "is," the answer to the original question.

But is this an answer? Not really, since Darl is still the victim of the existential paradox within the passage; he is still uncertain about his very existence, and his acceptance of Jewel's level of being exposes a retreat from the possibilities of his ontological quest. He senses ambiguities in "states of being" and insoluble epistemological questions, but he remains essentially confused about any determination of existence, and it is a confusion which prefigures his ultimate madness. This does not necessarily mean, however, that his answer is without value; "I am is" actually does define the limits of human existence—although Darl does not realize it—a paradox which will be discussed presently.

Darl's clairvoyance is also a major factor in this "to be" reverie, for if he did not know of Addie's death, the dilemma of "being" would perhaps not be posed. Darl experiences events mentally even when he is absent physically, as when he describes Addie's death while miles away from the scene. Thus, in what manner can the death scene be said to exist? Only in the mind? In "objective" reality? Faulkner satisfied the reader by designing Peabody's account of the death scene to confirm Darl's subjective vision, but Darl himself is given only the warrant of the body; he cannot be sure that the death occurred as he imagined it.

In *As I Lay Dying* even those unhindered by the gift of clairvoyance cannot define existence. Life and death seem to overlap. Peabody suggests that death is "merely a function of the mind—and that of the minds of the ones who suffer the bereavement" (368), but when he enters Addie's room to try to save her he reports semi-clinically, "She has been dead these ten days" (368). Death to Vardaman is the substitution of a living fish for a dead mother and a refusal to accept the fact of the corpse: "My mother does not smell like that" (483). Yet Vardaman only half fools himself, for one part of his mind knows that his mother has died and is not a fish: he drills holes in the coffin's lid to give her air, but they are not holes that a fish could escape through. Vardaman knows Addie is in the coffin but dedicates his child's mind to refusing the knowledge. Dewey Dell is similarly hindered. Problems of her own prohibit her from acknowledging Addie's passing: "I heard that my mother is dead. I wish I had time to let her die. I wish I had time to wish I had" (422).

Almost every experience of *As I Lay Dying* calls into doubt the certainty of existence. The Bundrens discover that the difference between "is" and "is not" is indefinable. Addie "is" because they do not really consider her dead until she is placed in the Jefferson grave, but she "is not" too, a fact made painfully evident by the putrifying corpse. Yet the smell itself proves a kind of existence, so in some sense she "is." Jewel loves his mother—his love "is"—but it also "is not," since he can only express that love to a horse. Anse's reason for going to Jefferson "is" to bury the body, but this also "is not" the reason—he wants his teeth. Dewey Dell illustrates the same paradox with her desire for "medicine," and her problem is confounded by an existential dilemma going on in her own body. Should one say her foetus "is," "is not," or "about to be"? In fact, the entire narrative technique of the novel emphasizes the uncertainty of "states of being." Individual sections appear to be in direct address to the reader reporting fictional events, but often an interior monologue is solipsistic within the fictional experience. For example, Whitfield's "confession" both "is" and "is not." The technique of multiple narration calls into doubt even observed events: did Darl malevolently abandon Cash at the river (as Tull thinks) or did he jump because Cash told him to (as Darl reports)?

Faulkner ponders, at every level and with almost every scene, the frustrating enigma of being. What is *is*? Can one prove *is*? Although the answers seem to be uncertain, Faulkner does suggest that a boundary for *isness* can be identified. He shows that the boundary of existence is time, that tense serves as the only certain functionary of being. Indeed, Darl's "I am is" comes to be Faulkner's answer to the enigma of being, for it posits reality exclusively in the present tense. Ultimately *As I Lay Dying* teaches the same lesson that Chick Mallison learns from his uncle, Gavin Stevens, in *Intruder in the Dust:* "all man had was time, all that stood between him and the death he feared and abhorred was time."[8]

II

As I Lay Dying is a novel obsessed with time.[9] Dewey Dell knows her time is running out; Anse has waited twenty years for teeth; Vardaman is told to wait for Christmas; Darl and Jewel do not return in time to witness Addie's death; Cash's leg must be fixed soon; time measures the progressive decay and putrescence of the body. An important "to be" passage illuminating the theme is the following exchange between Vardaman and Darl, and again my explication is designed to be read contiguously with the passage:

> "Jewel's mother is a horse," Darl said.
> "Then mine can be a fish, can't it, Darl?" I said.
> Jewel is my brother.
> "Then mine will have to be a horse, too," I said.
> "Why?" Darl said. "If pa is your pa, why does your ma have to be a horse just because Jewel's is?"
> "Why does it?" I said. "Why does it, Darl?"
> Darl is my brother.
> "Then what is your ma, Darl?" I said.

"I haven't got ere one," Darl said. "Because if I had one, it is *was,* and if it is was, it can't be *is.* Can it?"

"No," I said.

"Then I am not," Darl said. "Am I?"

"No," I said.

I am. Darl is my brother.

"But you *are,* Darl," I said.

"I know it," Darl said. "That's why I am not *is. Are* is too many for one woman to foal." (409)

Jewel's identification between Mother and horse is a source of much anguish to Darl for various reasons, but he is apparently capable of realizing it is only metaphorically true. Vardaman is not. If Jewel's mother can be a horse, then Vardaman's can be a fish. But Vardaman also senses something wrong with this equation, since "Jewel is my brother," a recognizable human relationship. Thus, to preserve the familial bond, perhaps Vardaman's mother should be a horse too. Vardaman's compulsion is to substitute something living—a horse—for his mother. Darl attempts to reason with him by reminding him that he has a father ("Pa is your pa") and that Jewel's belief does not have to be his. The child does not understand and his simplicity has its point: are not Vardaman's mother and Jewel's the same? Yes, but their fathers are different, making Vardaman and Jewel different, a fact which complicates all the Bundren relationships. For his part, the child must struggle to keep straight his emotional and physical bonds: "Jewel is my brother"; "Darl is my brother."

Since Vardaman is not to identify his mother as fish or horse, he asks, "Then what is your ma, Darl?" "What" refers to something inhuman, perhaps an animal, and the present tense reiterates Vardaman's refusal to accept the fact of Addie's death. But Darl has no mother-substitute, and his answer is an attempt to precisely determine the temporal situation: "Because if I had one, it is *was*. And if it is *was,* it can't be *is*. Can it." Darl's choice of the impersonal pronoun is not accidental. Addie has become an "it"—a body. That body does not exist as a mother; it can't be the *is* that Vardaman wants it to be, because it has become the *was* of memory. The body can only be defined as something which *was* a human being, but "is not" now a human being. (Vardaman's uncertainty, of course, is partly understandable, for the body is, undeniably, an existent being of some sort. It now "is" a corpse, possessing the unfortunate properties of a corpse.)

But after defining this situation Darl still cannot make a determination of his own existence. He concludes that if Addie "is not," then he "is not"—that his being has been somehow obliterated, just as he believes happens during sleep. ("Then I am not, Darl said, am I.") Vardaman can simply not accept this. With all of a child's certainty, he *knows* he is, he knows Darl is his brother, and he knows they both exist. ("But you are, Darl.") Darl's answer avoids Vardaman's meaning and shifts from tense to number, time to space. He interprets Vardaman's "are" as referring to the family, and although it appears that he is refuting his definition of the time relationships, he is really only referring to the number of the verb. He is not "is" (singular) only because they "are" four Bundren children, "too many for one woman to foal."

The key to the passage is Darl's attempt to determine Addie's tense—the location of her humanity in relation to time. He is obsessed with the time-space relationships of death and he ponders them often. While at the river he interprets the space between himself and the other bank as "time: an irrevocable quality" (443). A quality is without spatial dimension, however, and Darl chooses a looping string as a metaphor for time-in-life: "It is as though time, no longer running straight before us in a diminishing line, now runs parallel between us like a looping string, the distance being the doubling accretion of the thread and not the interval between" (443). He returns to this metaphor when struggling with the idea of no-time-in-death: "How do our lives ravel out into the no-wind, no-sound" (491), and he wishes for something better: "If you could just ravel out into time. That would be nice. It would be nice if you could just ravel out into time" (492).

What appears to be a shifting metaphor here is really Faulkner postulating an unequivocal identification of existence: time is life, the only measure of being, and this identification is the thematic center of *As I Lay Dying*. It would be nice to ravel out into time, but it also is impossible. Man is not immortal; he must face an eventual human oblivion, the "is not" of human death, characterized by the loss of time. This is Addie's condition, a fact the Bundren family is reluctant to realize. Man's deepest wish may be for a perpetual "is," an immortality of raveling out into sound and wind, *into time,* but it can never happen; the smell of Addie's body proves that she no longer is "in time" as a human being. She has died into a condition that "is not" human, an oblivion which is irrevocable. Only the living, those who still hope for either immortality or a life after death, conceive of that oblivion in humanly existent terms.

The other Bundrens are affected by the idea of oblivion, but they, unlike Darl, preserve their sanity in the face of it. Dewey Dell has experienced a prefiguration of death while she was a girl and it frightened her badly:

> *When I used to sleep with Vardaman I had a nightmare once I thought I was awake but I couldn't see and couldn't feel the bed under me and I couldn't think what I was I couldn't think of my name I couldn't even think I am a girl I couldn't even think I nor even think I want to wake up nor remember what was opposite to awake so I could do that I knew that something was passing but I couldn't even think of time then all of a sudden I knew that something was it was wind blowing over me it was like the wind came and blew me back from where it was I was not blowing the room and Vardaman asleep and all of them back under me again and going on like a piece of cool silk dragging across my naked legs.* (423)

This passage is similar to Darl's "to be" reverie. Dewey Dell suffered a loss of personal identity ("I couldn't think I") but her more serious loss, like Darl's, was the loss of a sense of human existence: "I couldn't think what I was." Necessarily accompanying this loss was the loss of the sense of time ("I couldn't even think of time"), and only with the assertion of the wind was Dewey Dell returned to a feeling of life. Her experience of the wind is different from Darl's, for whereas he only heard it, she actually feels the wind, *knows* its presence physically "like a piece of cool silk." She has a more certain assurance of what she is, and thus confirmation *that* she is; she has an existence in time.

Faulkner's summary assertion in *As I Lay Dying,* the sum of the passages cited above, is that time is the measure of existence, and this is an idea often reiterated in his other work. In outline, his thesis is that one can only live in the present tense, that although the past may inform that present, or sometimes even explain a part of that present, it does not and must not "exist" in the present; it cannot be permitted to determine present reality. Charles Bon, writing to Judith Sutpen in *Absalom, Absalom!,* says: "We have waited long enough. . . . Because what WAS is one thing and now it is not because it is dead, it died in 1861, and therefore what IS. . . . What IS is something else again because it was not even alive then."[10] Bon's letter subsumes many of Faulkner's attitudes about the South and its past, but its chief value here is in Bon's acknowledgement of a necessary present. "Is" must be the determinant of existence. In *The Sound and the Fury* Quentin Compson awakens on June 2, 1910, from a state of being he thinks was outside of time ("and then I was in time again, hearing the watch"),[11] struggles with the enigma of being as he approaches the abyss of suicide, and finally defines the nonexistence which he is shortly to achieve, the falling outside of time for not just a night, but forever:

"A quarter hour yet. And then I'll not be. The peacefullest words. Peacefullest words. *Non fui. Sum. Fui. Non sum*" (192).

The same conceptions of time and being were expressed by Faulkner in the famous *Paris Review* interview. Speaking of his ability throughout the Yoknapatawpha saga to move his characters freely in time, he remarked: "There is no such thing as *was,* only is. If was existed there would be no such thing as grief or sorrow."[12] What he apparently meant was that all existence is a function of the present, that grief and sorrow are emotions of the living which may arise from a desire to reclaim the past, but which are irrevocably a part of the present. The boundaries of human existence are "is" and "is not"; the "was" of history does not "exist" in the present no matter how badly man desires to perpetuate the past with monuments or memories. In his conversations with Loïc Bouvard, Faulkner again confirmed this notion of time: "There is only the present moment, in which I include both the past and the future, and that is eternity."[13] Quentin Compson is told that "any live man is better than any dead man" (121), just as Harry Wilbourne in *The Wild Palms* makes clear that no matter how difficult, functions of the living are man's necessary choice; refusing to commit suicide with the cyanide offered him, he casts his lot with the living: "Between grief and nothing I'll take grief."[14] Faulkner consistently suggests that "nothing" is the oblivion that attends death, the loss of time that obliterates humanity.

In *As I Lay Dying* Faulkner's assertion of this necessary present is the primary reason for the ambiguity of the Bundren journey. Critical commentary on the book separates into two mutually exclusive camps: (1) those who believe that the Bundren struggle is a triumph of human will over incredible adversity, and (2) those who argue that it is all an absurd comedy proving the farcical nature of man's actions in a meaningless world.[15] It seems, however, that the journey is both; that it is an absurd triumph. The Bundrens perform absurdly and yet manage to make their performance astonishing. As Peabody labors to repair the damage to Cash's leg, his emotions are anger, wonder, shock, but chiefly awe. It is absurd to do what the Bundrens have done, but it is also incredible. They triumph by struggling with and mastering the forces of the present that seek to deny their journey, but their motive for the struggle is a senseless and foolish perpetuation of a promise of the past. Their actions are physically heroic and metaphysically absurd, like acts of warfare. They are particularly absurd because the Bundrens remain true to a past which no longer has relevance for their present lives; if it did, Anse could not so easily acquire a new wife, or Faulkner so easily mock our expectations of a purgative burial scene by substituting the account of the betrayal of Darl. Yet there is no question Faulkner is deliberately ambiguous about the Bundren motives. Each of them also has "other" reasons for going to town, and insofar as they are driven by these other motives, Faulkner approves of their journey. This is paradoxical, but only because Faulkner was apparently using the Bundrens to exhibit two different attitudes toward time. As a promise to the past, their trip is ultimately absurd. As a commitment to the present, their trip may be justified.

As I Lay Dying has frequently been considered a companion novel to The Sound and the Fury, illustrative of the same themes with a parallel set of characters at another economic level.[16] For the most part, the similarity is superficial, but at one point it is significant. Both novels reveal that the results of an obsession with the past will be either tragedy or absurdity. As I Lay Dying, however, also offers an alternative to these possibilities. The Bundrens are foolishly motivated in an absurd journey, but they do not perpetuate the past (i.e., their foolish commitment to the past) beyond the point of burial. Although the Bundrens are just as representative of the South as the Compsons, they are ultimately realists of the present, and they do, as Faulkner once remarked, cope rather well with their fate: "The father having lost his wife would naturally need another one, so he got one. At one blow he not only replaced the family cook, he acquired a gramophone to give them all pleasure while they were resting. The pregnant daughter failed this time to undo her condition, but she was not discouraged. She intended to try again, and even if they all failed right up to the last, it wasn't anything but just another baby."[17] Notice that Faulkner praises the Bundren actions after the burial, not their dedication to Addie's promise, or their heroics during the trip.

The Faulkner canon has perhaps been too often interpreted as an allegory of the Southern experience; nevertheless, it seems to me that As I Lay Dying is a kind of morality tale of Southern life, a symbolic prescription for the South's (or any man's) obsession with the past. Faulkner is saying that the South, like the Bundrens, must bury the past; that it cannot remain true—without courting tragedy or absurdity—to the promises given to dead ancestors or to the illusions of former glory. Faulkner's quarrel with the South was with its impossible wish to perpetuate historical illusion by substituting past fantasy for present reality. It was a lover's quarrel, filled with all the ambivalence that one expects from such a conflict, but it was a quarrel nonetheless, and one that often assumes importance in Faulkner's work. The Bundrens' true absurdity is in their journey, for their heroism there is ironically vitiated by the context of the heroics. As Faulkner said at the University of

Virginia, the real villain in the story is the Bundren's blind allegiance to convention—in other words, to the institutionalization of the past:

> If there is a villain in that story, it's the convention in which people have to live, in which in that case insisted that because this woman had said, I want to be buried twenty miles away, that people would go to any trouble and anguish to get her there . . . So if there was a villain it was the convention which gave them no out except to carry her through fire and flood twenty miles in order to follow the dying wish, which by that time to her meant nothing.[18]

It could be argued that Faulkner suggests here that the Bundrens had no choice, that convention becomes necessity; but it seems more likely that his novel itself is a protest against such a view, especially when it becomes clear, to Faulkner anyway, that the Bundren's true heroism is in their actions after the journey is over. They do cope with their fate rather well, but not because they are true to convention; indeed, the conventional response would demand a period of mourning. It does not seem unfair to conclude that Faulkner is implicitly suggesting that his beloved South must learn to cope with its fate, must learn to bury its dead and begin life anew. It must create new conventions designed to respond to the locus of human existence, the reality of the present tense. It must learn the lesson that Darl stumbles upon but does not recognize, "I am is." The fact that the Bundrens do not realize the lesson implicit in their experience is a consummate irony, but it is not necessarily reason to doubt that the moral is there.

Notes

1. William Faulkner, *The Sound and the Fury* and *As I Lay Dying* (New York, 1946), p. 396. All subsequent citations from *As I Lay Dying* refer to this edition and are included within parentheses in the text.

2. Avoidance takes several forms; Cleanth Brooks, in a long and valuable discussion of *As I Lay Dying,* does not treat the section at all; others gloss over the passage by calling it "poignant" (William Van O'Connor), "unsophisticated" (Ronald Sutherland), or "accidental" (Harry Campbell). See Cleanth Brooks, *William Faulkner: The Yoknapatawpha Country* (New Haven, 1963); William Van O'Connor, *The Tangled Fire of William Faulkner* (Minneapolis, 1954), p. 49; Ronald Sutherland, "*As I Lay Dying*: A Faulkner Microcosm," *Queens*

Quarterly, LXXIII (1966), 541–49; Harry M. Campbell, "Experiment and Achievement, *As I Lay Dying* and *The Sound and the Fury,*" *Sewanee Review,* LI (1943), 305–20.

3. See Olga Vickery, *The Novels of William Faulkner* (Baton Rouge, 1959), pp. 50–62; Michael Millgate, *The Achievement of William Faulkner* (London, 1966), p. 105; Melvin Backman, *Faulkner: The Major Years* (Bloomington, Ind., 1966), p. 55; and Irving Howe, *William Faulkner: A Critical Study* (New York, 1962), p. 179.

4. Robert Slabey, "*As I Lay Dying* as an Existential Novel," *Bucknell Review,* XI (1963), 12–23, has illustrated that Faulkner's language has important existential implications. Edmond Volpe has argued the same thing without the existential terminology: *A Reader's Guide to William Faulkner* (New York, 1964), pp. 126–40; and Calvin Bedient's recent article has brilliantly illustrated the validity of existential insights for both Darl's passage and *As I Lay Dying* as a whole: "Pride and Nakedness: *As I Lay Dying,*" *Modern Language Quarterly,* XXIX (March, 1968), 61–76. On the other hand, James M. Mellard has suggested that Faulkner's "existentialism" is not the real issue, but that the novel should be analyzed according to "the major questions of philosophy, the questions concerned with ontology—being and reality": "Faulkner's Philosophical Novel: Ontological Themes in *As I Lay Dying,*" *The Personalist,* XLVIII (1967), 509–23. My own reading of the novel is not "existential" in any formal sense, but it is indebted to these studies.

5. "La Theme de la Vie et de la Mort dans *As I Lay Dying,*" *Revue des Lettres Modernes,* V (1958–1959), 295.

6. One is hesitant to speak of Darl's "conclusions" for this implies a carefully reasoned, logical process of thought. Clearly Darl's passage is the stream of consciousness of a man on the verge of sleep, and although his mind does struggle with and come to a "conclusion" about the nature of existence, it is not arrived at by logical means, nor is Darl aware that a conclusion has been reached. Nevertheless, it is a "conclusion" that has important implications for the novel.

7. Bedient has suggested that Darl's reflections about sleep are disturbing to him because "by . . . equating being with consciousness which sleep annihilates, Darl removes from existence its stability, giving it the flickering reality of a dream" (p. 68). Contrast this with John Simon's assertion that Darl embodies the polarities of being and consciousness: "Darl dramatized the antithesis of subject and object, *I* and *he,* consciousness and being . . . .": "What are You Laughing at, Darl?: Madness and Humor in *As I Lay Dying,*" *College English* XXV (November, 1963), 104–10.

8. William Faulkner, *Intruder in the Dust* (New York, 1948), p. 30.

9. Peter Swiggart discusses at length the ambiguities of time in *As I Lay Dying,* arguing that "the dominant concept in . . . [*As I Lay*

Dying] . . . is that of human rage directed against a personified concept of time," and that the novel "is dominated by images suggesting the passage of time.": *The Art of Faulkner's Novels* (Austin, 1962), pp. 109, 123. Margaret Church's *Time and Reality: Studies in Contemporary Fiction* (Chapel Hill, 1963) also has an important discussion of time in the novel.

10. William Faulkner, *Absalom, Absalom!* (New York: Modern Library, 1951), p. 131.

11. William Faulkner, *The Sound and the Fury* and *As I Lay Dying* (New York, 1946), p. 95. Subsequent citations from *The Sound and the Fury* refer to this edition and are included within parentheses in the text.

12. Jean Stein, "William Faulkner: An Interview," *The Paris Review* (Spring, 1956), quoted in Frederick J. Hoffman and Olga Vickery, *William Faulkner: Three Decades of Criticism* (New York, 1960), p. 82.

13. Loïc Bouvard, "Conversation with William Faulkner," *Modern Fiction Studies,* V (Winter, 1959–1960), 362.

14. William Faulkner, *The Wild Palms* (New York, 1939), p. 324.

15. This question of absurdity vs. heroism is the most frequently debated issue in *As I Lay Dying* criticism. Brooks has probably made the strongest case for the essential heroism of the Bundren's journey, while Volpe argues persuasively for its absurdity. Other articles which treat the matter are William Rossky, "*As I Lay Dying:* The Insane World," *Texas Studies in Literature and Language,* IV (1962), 87–95; and Edward Wasiolek, "*As I Lay Dying:* Distortion in the Slow Eddy of Current Opinion," *Critique,* III (1959), 15–23.

16. See Swiggart, Campbell, and also Carvel Collins, "The Pairing of *The Sound and the Fury* and *As I Lay Dying*," *Princeton University Library Chronicle,* XVIII (1957), 114–23.

17. Stein, "An Interview," in Hoffman and Vickery, p. 81.

18. *Faulkner at the University,* ed. Frederick Gwynn and Joseph Blotner (New York, 1959), p. 112.

CHAPTER 5

"IF WAS EXISTED"
FAULKNER'S PROPHETS
AND THE PATTERNS OF
HISTORY

James G. Watson

Speaking on the subject "Faulkner and History" at a symposium in 1971, Cleanth Brooks, Michael Millgate, and James B. Meriwether agreed unanimously that, while Faulkner's novels are "drenched in history," history as a factual record of the past concerned him hardly at all.[1] Professor Millgate puts the matter most plainly in his remarks on *Absalom, Absalom!* He explains:

> *Absalom, Absalom!* seems to be chiefly concerned, not with accuracy of historical re-creation and representation, but with the act of historical interpretation in and of itself. The specific versions of history offered in the novel are important less for the light they throw upon the past than for the insight they provide into the respective interpreters. *Absalom, Absalom!,* that is to say, is not so much about Sutpen as about what the narrators, and expecially Quentin, make of the Sutpen legend—or even what the Sutpen legend makes of Quentin.[2]

Originally published in *Modern Fiction Studies*, Winter 1975.

Faulkner's concern, then, is not with the past alone but with the past and present together: with time, as he said, as "a fluid condition which has no existence except in the momentary avatars of individual people."[3] It is this conception of time which led him, in his remarks to Jean Stein in 1955 which I have been quoting, to insist that "there is no such thing as *was*—only *is*. If *was* existed there would be no grief or sorrow."[4]

Such wordplay with the verb *to be* is typical of Faulkner and may remind us of the terms in which Darl Bundren considers the state of his existence in *As I Lay Dying*. Lying "beneath rain or a strange roof, thinking of home," Darl muses:

> And since sleep is is-not and rain and wind are *was,* it [the wagon] is not. Yet the wagon *is,* because when the wagon is *was,* Addie Bundren will not be. And Jewel *is,* so Addie Bundren must be. And then I must be, or I could not empty myself for sleep in a strange room. And so if I am not emptied yet, I am *is.*[5]

Here, Darl's concern with his *is-ness* at the present moment and his fear of a time when he will become *was* suggest an equation of the dead past with an equally dead future. When he has emptied himself for sleep on the night of Addie's death, his body will be like her coffin, which "now slumbered lightly alive, waiting to come awake" (*AILD*, p. 75). When the empty coffin does metaphorically waken, it will be filled with death—the dead body of the Addie who *was*—and Darl foresees that he too will waken to *was-ness* from the emptiness of sleep. In creating this pattern of associations, he is not only a historian assessing his identity in terms of the history of his family but a prophet, whose clairvoyance allows him a vision of the future. That future is specifically apocalyptic. To his eyes, the log which upsets the wagon in the river *"surged up out of the water and stood for an instant upright upon that surging and heaving desolation like Christ"* (*AILD*, p. 141), and on the night he burns Gillespie's barn, he tells Vardaman that Addie is talking to God and that she wants Him "to hide her away from the sight of man" (*AILD,* p. 204). The Biblical Terrors of fire and flood, from which Addie herself has prophesied that Jewel will save her, are perfectly commensurate with Darl's vision of a personal apocalypse. It is an apocalypse, moreover, which will bring him no new life. His identity is utterly dependent upon Addie's, and her *was-ness* portends no *is-ness* for him in the future. Near the end of the funeral journey, Darl thinks, "How do our lives ravel out into the no-wind, no-sound, the weary gestures wearily recapitulant: echoes of old compulsions with no-hand on no-strings: in sunset we fall into furious attitudes, dead gestures of dolls" (*AILD*, pp. 196–97). In this light, the final scene in which he foams "Yes yes yes yes yes yes yes yes" (*AILD*, p. 244) may be seen as his affirmation of the fulfillment of his prophecy regarding himself. The Darl who was *is* is now *was,* and Cash laments, "This world is not his world; this life his life" (*AILD,* p. 250).

The figure of the prophet in Faulkner's fiction strongly suggests that there is another dimension inherent in his concern with history as a subject for interpretation: that of the future. What *was* reveals to what *is* is that which *will be*: in searching for the meaning of the past, the characters who interpret history arrive at personal visions of their own futures. They are not, then, simply *historians* but *historicists,* historian-prophets who discover in the past the laws of historical evolution which explain and predict historical phenomena. And this is particularly so when, like Quentin Compson in *Absalom, Absalom!,* they relate personally to the historical figures whose lives they examine. When Quentin becomes "Quentin-Henry" through the medium of the shared "heart and blood of youth,"[6] he is able to see his own future projected by Henry Sutpen's history as he has recreated it. Thus he says, "I am older at twenty than a lot of people who have died" (*AA,* p. 377). As Professor Millgate suggests, albeit without elaboration, it is not only what Quentin makes of the Sutpen legend that is at issue in the novel but also what the Sutpen legend, or Quentin's rendering of it, makes of Quentin. Significantly enough, Quentin's own death by water in *The Sound and the Fury* is the precise apocalyptic complement to Henry's death by fire in *Absalom, Absalom!*

The concept that historical knowledge is of two kinds, both past and future, is traceable to Hegel and Nietzsche, and, as Harvey Gross has recently demonstrated, it is a concept characteristic to writers of the modern period. Gross explains that at center is "the idea of process, the belief that history comprehends an order of antecedent cause and consequent effect; that this order moves purposively toward some goal; that this goal might also constitute an end to history—in theological language, an *eschaton.*"[7] An example of this impulse particularly relevant to Faulkner's conception of history is T. S. Eliot's poem "Gerontion," in which history is compared to a decayed house having "many cunning passages, contrived corridors / And issues." Interpreting history in terms of his own life, Gerontion prophesies an apocalypse in which he will be violently destroyed: "The tiger springs in the new year. Us he devours." In short, he sees an end to history in the hollow gestures of the inhabitants of his house, and when he declares that "Vacant shuttles / Weave the wind" he is prophesying much the same kind of end that Darl Bundren does when he hears "echoes of old compulsions with no-hand on no-strings" and prophesies his own fall, at sunset, into "furious attitudes, dead gestures of dolls." Ultimately, both Gerontion and Darl are immobilized by their historical knowledge not only of what *was* but also of what *will be:* each finds in his own version of history the portentous patterns which signify his own immanent destruction, patterns which are, in fact, already coming to fulfillment in the very process of being discovered.

The full scope of Faulkner's debt to Eliot has not yet been assessed, but it does seem certain that they shared a concern for the impact of historical knowledge of this kind on human lives. This impulse, in Eliot's early poetry, culminates with the reduction of blind Tiresias to a helpless voyeur, capable of knowing but not of acting. Speaking through Ezekial and Madame Sosostris, he prophesies ruin by fire and flood, warning against but unable to avert death "in a handful of dust" and "death by water." The culminating point of the impulse in Faulkner's work is *Absalom, Absalom!,* but like Eliot he had experimented widely with the theme prior to the publication of that book in 1936. In *Sartoris,* for example, Miss Jenny DuPre interprets and then imposes upon her grand-nephew, Bayard, the pattern of destruction in the Sartoris legend which Bayard re-enacts on horses and in automobiles to the moment of his violent death in a flaming airplane. In *The Sound and the Fury* there are several modifications on the historian-prophet figure. Although he does not interpret history, Benjy is a Tiresian figure, powerless to act yet holding in his timeless mind the pattern of Caddy's downfall which Miss Quentin re-enacts. In the Stein interview, Faulkner explained that the novel began with his picture of Caddy climbing the pear tree with muddy drawers and that that image gave way to "the one of the fatherless and motherless girl climbing down the rainpipe to escape from the only home she had, where she had never been offered love or affection or understanding."[8] To Benjy, past and present are synchronic, revealing by their juxtaposition in his mind profound patterns of historical recurrence which project the future and whose stages are marked by his otherwise unintelligible bellowing. The swing in which Miss Quentin entertains the circus man is the same in which Caddy once kissed Charlie, and the rainpipe down which Quentin flees her stunted childhood is the analogue of the tree which Caddy climbed to look on death. Dilsey too is both historian and prophet, and she too is immobilized by historical knowledge. She had seen Caddy in the pear tree in 1898 and, on Easter Sunday 1928, has witnessed Quentin's flight. Now, under the influence of the Reverend Shegog's sermon announcing the coming of Judgment Day, she announces an end to Compson history, saying, "I've seed de first en de last. . . . I seed de beginnin, en now I sees de endin."[9]

Her prophesy is supported in the course of the novel where, instead of Resurrection, the Compson sons, like Darl, "ravel out into time": Quentin knows that when Christ calls souls to Judgment only the flatirons with which he weights himself down will rise; Benjy is at the Christologic age of thirty-three but is castrated; Jason has the magic initials, J. C., but is impotent and he ends with "his invisible life ravelled out about him like a wornout sock" (*SF*, p. 391). As an addendum, it is interesting to note that in the Compson "Appendix," written in 1945, Dilsey is afflicted, like Tiresias, with blindness: she cannot see Melissa Meek's picture of Caddy and the German staff general.

Having established the historian-prophet as a seminal figure in *The Sound and the Fury*, it is not surprising that Faulkner returned to the Compson family, and in particular to Quentin, for the fuller development of his theme in *Absalom, Absalom!* In form the novel is actually fairly simple, consisting of two distinct sections, the first set on a September afternoon and evening in 1909 in Jefferson and the second on a January night in Quentin's Harvard room in 1910. In the first section two versions of the Sutpen legend are developed, Miss Rosa Coldfield's story in chapters 1 and 5 framing Mr. Compson's in chapters 2, 3, and 4. Each chapter works toward the interpretation of a moment in the legend which, for that narrator, is crucial. These cruxes derive from the narrator's own conception of the nature of history and, appropriately, proceed in chronologic order. To Miss Rosa, the house of history is circumscribed by her personal experience, the "unpaced corridor" of her childhood leading her "from one closed forbidden door to the next" (*AA*, pp. 144, 145). She defines the substance of remembering, furthermore, in terms which are personal and physical: "sense, sight, smell: the muscles with which we see and hear and feel—not mind, not thought: there is no such thing as memory: the brain recalls just what the muscles grope for: no more, no less: and its resultant sum is usually incorrect and false and worthy only of the name of dream" (*AA*, p. 143). For her Sutpen is physical proof that God has cursed her family, a curse to which she wakened at age three in 1848 when she first saw his "ogre-shape" (*AA*, p. 13) racing a carriage to church. In chapter 5, at the end of the frame, she reaffirms her interpretation that the Coldfields were "cursed to be instruments not only for that man's destruction, but for our own" (*AA*, p. 21) by describing herself as having "died" on the day in 1866 when Sutpen insulted her. Figuratively, his insult ended her life as his abruption into her consciousness had begun it; and her prophecy of a destructive curse, developed from her interpretation of history, is fulfilled when she actually dies after her December visit to

Sutpen's Hundred, thus justifying Quentin's apprehension of her in September as having "an air Cassandralike and humorless and profoundly and sternly prophetic out of all proportion to the actual years even of a child who had never been young" (*AA*, p. 22).

Within the frame, Mr. Compson develops his own version of the Sutpen legend in accordance with his conception of Southern history as an aristocratic and tragic drama whose events are foreordained by "pate, destiny, retribution, irony—the stage manager, call him what you will" (*AA*, pp. 72–73). His approach to history is not personal and prophetic, like Miss Rosa's, but objective and uninvolved. In the chronologic sequence in which he considers them, the cruxes of the legend are: Sutpen's bid for respectability by marrying Ellen Coldfield (1838); his performance of his duty as a Southerner by raising a Civil War regiment (1860); and Henry's murder of Charles Bon in 1865, when brother again kills brother against what Mr. Compson calls "that turgid background of a horrible and bloody mischancing of human affairs" (*AA*, p. 101). Born into a new era in the aftermath of the apocalyptic war, Mr. Compson sees himself not as a participant in the continuing drama of the South but as a member of the audience at an old play. Thus he finds in the Sutpen legend no portents for his own life or that of his family. Instead, he concludes that the relationship between Sutpen, Judith, Henry, and Charles Bon is like a "chemical formula" (*AA*, p. 101) in which one element is missing. That element is his own failure to empathize with the people whose lives he factually recreates, and it is symbolized in his ignorance of Bon's mixed blood, about which Quentin has to tell him. On the basis of his uninvolved view of history, he concludes:

> It's just incredible. It just does not explain. Or perhaps that's it: they dont explain and we are not supposed to know. We have a few old mouth-to-mouth tales; we exhume from old trunks and boxes and drawers letters without salutation or signature, in which men and women who once lived and breathed are now merely initials or nicknames out of some now incomprehensible affection which sound to us like Sanscrit or Chocktaw; we see dimly people, the people in whose living blood and seed we ourselves lay dormant and waiting, in this shadowy attenuation of time possessing now heroic proportions, performing their acts of simple passion and simple violence, impervious to time and inexplicable. (*AA*, pp. 100–101)

Together, the versions of the Sutpen legend set forth for Quentin by Miss Rosa and Mr. Compson in 1909 constitute two extremes of historical interpretation, the exclusively subjective and the exclusively objective, and each follows a chronologic sequence of cruxes central to that narrator. In January 1910, Quentin combines the two methods, transcending their individual limitations, and develops his own, truer version of history in which he finds a prophecy for his own future.

To the reader familiar with *The Sound and the Fury,* Henry Sutpen's incestuous love for his sister, Judith, and the idiocy of the last Sutpen heir, Jim Bond, will explain in part the course which Quentin's version of the Sutpen legend takes in the second section of *Absalom, Absalom!* Yet neither Caddy nor Benjy is mentioned in the later novel, where incest and idiocy are employed as supportive motifs in the development of what, for Quentin, is the crucial point in the legend: the moment when Henry murders his brother, Charles Bon, at the Sutpen gate in 1865. He says, "He (Quentin) couldn't pass that" (*AA*, p. 172), and his entire reconstruction of history builds through a series of related cruxes toward his own symbolic confrontation with Henry when he finds him at Sutpen's Hundred. Like Mr. Compson, who is possessed of "a few old mouth-to-mouth tales," Quentin and Shreve reconstruct a factual history out of "the rag-tag and bob-ends of old tales and talking" (*AA*, p. 303); and like Miss Rosa, they identify emotionally and physically with the characters they create, discarding facts which do not fit their preconceived formula "in order to overpass to love, where there might be paradox and inconsistency but nothing fault nor false" (*AA*, p. 316). Thus in the factual story of Sutpen's life as he told it to Grandfather Compson, the recurrence of "the boy-symbol at the door" (*AA*, p. 261) reveals to Quentin that history is cyclical: the pattern begun when Sutpen was turned away from the door of a Tidewater plantation is repeated when he turns Charles Bon away from the door of his own plantation and again when Henry murders Charles Bon at the Sutpen gate. Moreover, by his personal identification with Henry, Quentin is obliged to see himself as being caught up in the same pattern and to foresee, thereby, his own end in Henry's. In the scene in which he meets Henry, recounted in the final pages of the novel, Quentin himself becomes the boy-at-the-door: approaching the Sutpen mansion with Miss Rosa, he stands at the gate "thinking, wishing that Henry were there now to stop Miss Coldfield and turn them back, telling himself that if Henry were there now, there would be no shot to be heard by anyone" (*AA*, p. 364). What Quentin wants to avoid but cannot is the prophet's ultimate confrontation with his own future self. In announcing his immanent death to Quentin, Henry's words put an end to Quentin's future as surely as Henry's shot ended Charles Bon's life and his own future in the South. And by the time that Quentin describes this final episode in the events of September he is figuratively dead, immobilized in the "tomblike room in Massachusetts" (*AA*, p. 336) by historical knowledge of both *was* and *will be*.

Finally, it is possible to say that Quentin, like Eliot's Gerontion, conceives of his own life as an emblem of historical process. Gerontion's very situation is emblematic of both past and future, for he is "an old man in a dry month / Being read to by a boy, waiting for rain"; and Quentin, in September 1909, is "two separate Quentins," one a boy of twenty preparing for a future at Harvard and the other, bound in the past, "still too young to deserve yet to be a ghost, but nevertheless having to be one for all that" (*AA*, p. 9). And, like Gerontion's, Quentin's body becomes the house of history: he is "a barracks filled with stubborn back-looking ghosts" (*AA*, p. 12). His journey to Sutpen's Hundred with Miss Rosa, which he begins to recount in chapter 6 but does not conclude until chapter 9, leads him symbolically through the "cunning passages" and "contrived corridors" of the Sutpen legend and brings him at last to the actual corridors and passages of Sutpen's Hundred where he confronts what *was* in the specifically "corpse-like" figure of Henry Sutpen and discovers in their conversation the portents of what *will be* for him. The interview marks the culmination of the process by which Quentin is gradually absorbed into the historical cycles which he himself has discovered and with whose persona he has identified.

> *And you are ——?*
> *Henry Sutpen.*
> *And you have been here ——?*
> *Four years.*
> *And you came home ——?*
> *To die. Yes.*
> *To die?*
> *Yes. To die.*
> *And you have been here ——?*
> *Four years.*
> *And you are ——?*
> *Henry Sutpen. (AA, p. 373)*

This conversation, like history itself, proceeds according to a pattern of recurrent cycles, and at its center are the prophetic words, *"To die."*

Thus it is that in January, at the beginning of a new year, Quentin thinks on final things. Prompted by his father's letter of January 10, 1910, announcing the concomitant deaths of Miss Rosa and Henry in December, 1909, he recreates with Shreve a version of Sutpen history built upon a series of recurrent cruxes which mark not new beginnings but ends, and he finds in the end of the year 1909 the end of an era. Quentin cannot accept the hope expressed in his father's letter for an afterlife in which the ghostly figures which haunted Miss Rosa's life will become "actual people to be actual recipients of the hatred and the pity" (*AA*, p. 377). Instead, he finds what *will be* for the South symbolized in the idiot, Jim Bond, the last Sutpen heir, whom Shreve concludes will inherit the western hemisphere. Howling among the ruins of Sutpen's Hundred, Jim Bond is the last boy-at-the-door, turned away by history itself, and Quentin sees in him the end foretold in the cycles of the Sutpen legend; in Jim Bond is the conjunction of *was* and *will be*. "If *was* existed," Faulkner has said, "there would be no grief or sorrow," and in his letter to Judith at the end of the war Charles Bon says the same, writing *"what* WAS *is one thing, and now it is not because it is dead, it died in 1861, and therefore what IS . . . is something else again because it was not even alive then"* (*AA*, p. 131). By the end of *Absalom, Absalom!,* Quentin can accept the end of the South that was and grieve it. But what most torments him is his simultaneous, prophetic vision of his own immanent *was-ness*—a vision of a personal apocalypse; positing an *eschaton* or end to history; deriving from the discovery of recurrent historical patterns and intimate identification with historical persona. The Sutpen legend is an analogue not only for the South but for Quentin Compson's life as well. That he has revealed more of himself and of his visions than he knows is signified in Shreve's final pointed question, "Why do you hate the South?" and Quentin's reply is testimony to the agony of spirit attendant upon the prophet:

> "I dont hate it," Quentin said, quickly, at once, immediately; "I dont hate it," he said. *I dont hate it* he thought, panting in the cold air, the iron New England dark; *I dont. I dont! I dont hate it! I dont hate it!* (*AA*, p. 378)

Notes

1. The papers were presented at a symposium sponsored by the *Mississippi Quarterly* at the South Central Modern Language Association meeting, October 29, 1971. They are printed in the *Mississippi Quarterly,* 25 (Spring Supplement 1972).

2. Michael Millgate, "'The Firmament of Man's History': Faulkner's Treatment of the Past," *Mississippi Quarterly,* 25 (Spring Supplement 1972), 27.

3. James B. Meriwether and Michael Millgate, eds., *Lion in the Garden: Interviews with William Faulkner, 1926–1962* (New York: Random House, 1968), p. 255.

4. *Lion in the Garden,* p. 255.

5. *As I Lay Dying* (New York: Vintage, 1957), p. 76. Future references are in the text as AILD.

6. *Absalom, Absalom!* (New York: Vintage, 1964), p. 294. Future references are in the text as *AA.*

7. Harvey Gross, *The Contrived Corridor: History and Fatality in Modern Literature* (Ann Arbor: University of Michigan Press, 1971), p. 3.

8. *Lion in the Garden,* p. 245.

9. *The Sound and the Fury* (New York: Modern Library, 1956), p. 371. Future references are in the text as *SF.*

CHAPTER 6

ON LAMENTATION AND THE REDISTRIBUTION OF POSSESSIONS

FAULKNER'S *ABSALOM, ABSALOM!* AND THE NEW SOUTH

Rebecca Saunders

Lamentation is both a kind of language and a kind of time—a ritual language that claims a privileged relation to a singular, catastrophic moment. Like the fall of Jerusalem or the destruction of Troy—paradigmatic moments of lamentation in the West—lamentation is a moment when a social order has fallen, when structures of meaning have been shattered, when phenomena no longer fit into language, and when the world, radically remade, has become new, primeval, incomprehensible. And like the biblical "Lamentations of Jeremiah" which memorialize the fall of Jerusalem or the Euripidean laments of Hecuba that mourn the destruction of Troy, the language of lamentation, faced with the impossible task of responding to the inexpressible and incomprehensible, is, accordingly, a tentative, fragmented, indagatory language that even at its most literal is inevitably fantastic for the literal has become unbelievable.[1]

Originally published in *Modern Fiction Studies,* Winter 1996.

"Massive trauma precludes its registration," writes Dori Laub in *Testimony: Crises of Witnessing in Literature, Psychoanalysis, and History*; "the observing and recording mechanisms of the human mind are temporarily knocked out" (Felman and Laub 57). Thus catastrophe must be speculatively and belatedly (re)constructed, for knowledge of catastrophe like that recorded by the lamentation is "not simply a factual given that is reproduced and replicated by the testifier, but a genuine advent, an event in its own right" (62). This is to say that the moment and the language of lamentation are ultimately indistinguishable, for the catastrophic moment that conditions the language of lamentation also overwhelms and thwarts that language; and the language of lamentation thus overwhelmed cannot simply record catastrophe but must also speculatively construct it. Thus the moment of lamentation is simultaneously phenomenal and rhetorical—recorded and produced by the language of lamentation; and the language of lamentation is simultaneously representational and performative—both a record and the creation of the moment of lamentation.

It is from the tradition of lamentation, albeit from a more personal lament—of David for his son Absalom—that Faulkner draws his title for the novel *Absalom, Absalom!*:

> *O my son Absalom,*
> *my son, my son Absalom!*
> *would God I had died for thee,*
> *O Absalom, my son, my son! (2 Sam. 18:33, KJV)*[2]

While Faulkner's title invokes a narrative that resonates in the novel's father-son relationships, it also functions to place the novel in the tradition of lamentation. And such a placement seems apt enough for, as readers of *Absalom* have often remarked, the novel's plot is comprised of a relentless torrent of losses: the Old South, the Civil War, the Sutpen estate, the majority of the novel's characters, honor, pride, youth, and dreams are all ultimately lost, while the novel's main character falls from an Edenic origin, loses his "innocence," and subsequently embodies the Lost Cause. Meanwhile, narrators write elegies, allude obsessively to Greek and Shakespearean tragedy, render houses "mausoleums" and dorm rooms "tomblike." The thematic losses and mortuary allusions of *Absalom*, as well as the epistemological losses of its narrative structure, have occasionally led critics to speak of *Absalom*, justifiably if merely colloquially, in terms of lamentation.[3] Yet I wish to speak of lamentation in more specific terms—not merely as an expression of grief, but as a literary mode—and to read the appearances of that mode in *Absalom*. I wish, further, to focus on both a more specific aspect of the moment of lamentation and a more specific device of the language of lamentation.

The moment of lamentation is characterized not only by cognitive upheaval but also by the transfer of property, the redistribution of possessions, and the remapping of territorial boundaries. These transfers and redistributions include the redistribution of value, knowledge, and identity, as well as of material or "real" property. And the language of lamentation is not only characterized by the tentative and fragmented but also by a proliferation of privatives which rhetorically (re)enact dispossession.[4] Moreover, the phenomenal redistributions of the moment of lamentation and the rhetorical dispossessions of the language of lamentation follow that logic in which moment and language indissociably produce each other, in which, in this case, language both represents and effects a redistribution of possessions. I will argue that the narrators of *Absalom* deploy the lamentation's privative gestures to effect an interested redistribution of possessions, and I will thus be as much concerned with the ways in which the novel's narrators rhetorically construct catastrophe as with the way they represent the underlying thematic catastrophe of the Civil War.

Indeed I will further contend that if the privatives of *Absalom* reenact the historical moment of Civil War and Reconstruction, they also inscribe a subsequent moment that the novel only sketchily presents: that era between Charles Etienne's youth at Sutpen's Hundred and Quentin and Shreve's snowy night of storytelling at Harvard that we call the "New South." The rhetorical movement of the privative, I will argue, structurally corresponds to the social movement conceived by New South spokesmen during the period from about 1877 to 1913 when Southern journalists, educators, politicians, and preachers struggled to establish a new social and economic order. They did so, I will contend, by appropriating the rhetorical destructions of the lamentation—to produce newness, to construct desire, and, ultimately, to effect a redistribution of possessions. While thematically the period of the New South is only elliptically present in *Absalom*—glimpsed momentarily in Jim Hamblett's truncated speech to Charles Etienne (165), for example, or the Ku Klux Klan's visit to Sutpen's Hundred (130, 134)—it is rhetorically, I would argue, pervasively present.

I shall thus be tracing a triangular resemblance between the privative gestures of the lamentation, of Faulkner's narrators, and of New South spokesmen. The relation between these three discourses is, I would emphasize, not necessarily one of deliberate appropriation or influence but rather a structural resemblance between languages performing similar ideological tasks: rhetorically (re)enacting a redistribution of possessions. This specific argument about lamentation, *Absalom*, and the New South is also imbedded in two more general arguments: first, that deconstruction's attention to the rhetoricity of texts is not opposed, but rather highly relevant, to cultural studies' investigation of the worldliness of texts; and second, that a literary mode may manifest itself in small and inconspicuous rhetorical gestures but that such small appearances, empowered by the very cloak of their unnoteworthiness, may bear large significance.

The moment to which the narrators of *Absalom* respond is, like the moment to which a lamentation responds, characterized by the transfer of property, the redistribution of possessions, and the remapping of territorial boundaries: Sutpen's apparently extortionary acquisition of land from Ikkemottube; the subsequent transfer of "Sutpen's Hundred" to sharecroppers and, ultimately, to the state; Sutpen's obscene (and fateful) exchange of baubles for an heir; Judith's exchange of a store for a gravestone. Indeed a large portion of the narrative itself—that produced by Quentin and Shreve—is conditioned by the Compsons' exchange of a piece of property for a room at Harvard. Yet lamentation is a moment when ideological as well as material possessions are transferred, when, for example, value, knowledge, and identity are redistributed. Material and ideological property are not, of course, unrelated; on the contrary, they are inevitably collusive because possessions function as signs. Material property, that is to say, is often the procurer, and guardian, of ideological property; Sutpen, for example, acquires chairs, chandeliers, tapestry, slaves, and wife to be signs of respectability. Conversely, ideological possessions—what Bourdieu calls "cultural capital"—may be converted into material possessions, as Shreve's parodic lawyer systematically appraises the value of knowledge, records it in a ledger, and converts it into money; or as Rosa, bequeathing her knowledge and identity to Quentin, suggests that if he writes down her story, he might sell it to the magazines and buy his wife a new gown or a new chair for the house. Indeed, it is because the customary functioning of such significatory systems is advantageous to the preservation of both material privilege and fixed identities that it takes a catastrophe to effect a redistribution of possessions. In *Absalom*, the catastrophe of the Civil War effects transfers of real property that are simultaneously redistributions of identity: landowner becomes merchant, slave-holding heiress becomes landlord-employer, slave becomes freedperson, and (in the reverberations of that catastrophe a generation later) a college boy becomes inadvertent plenipotentiary of the South. And if it takes a catastrophe to redistribute possessions, New South spokesmen (in that later generation) would recognize that by engaging a language of catastrophe—by rhetorically redistributing value, identity, and knowledge—they might effect a redistribution of material possessions.

In the moment of lamentation, material possessions are, moreover, not only transferred but also transformed. Objects both acquire new meanings—as the shield of Hector, which once signified strength, valor, ἀρετή [arete], becomes, in Hecuba's lamentation, "a hateful thing to look at [that] means no love to me" ("Trojan Women" line 1158)—and take on new functions: they are literally remade. Judith, for example, by mid-war wears "the made-over dress which all Southern women now wore" and joins those other women "in the improvised hospital where (the nurtured virgin, the supremely and traditionally idle) they cleaned and dressed the self-fouled bodies of strange injured and dead and made lint of the window curtains and sheets and linen of the houses in which they had been born . . ." (99–100). In this moment, then, material possessions assume new identities because they must of necessity become other: like the Phrygian robes of Hecuba which become graveclothes for Astyanax or the children of Judah who, horrifyingly, become food, in the world of *Absalom*, rags become dresses, barns become hospitals, curtains become bandages, and boards from the carriage house become a coffin for Charles Bon. And this transformation is, moreover, a revaluation: an object's value as sign is replaced by its value as material. A dress or a curtain's value no longer inheres in its ability to function as sign—of taste, status, prosperity—but in its ability to function as material—with which to cover the body or a wound. This remade "property" of the lamentation is, further, no longer "proper" to its possessor. Such redistributions of identity, that is to say, effect an alienating disjunction—a *méconnaissance*—between a "possessor" and objects. Such, for example, is the disjunctive relationship between Rosa and the "botched over" dresses she wears, the secondhand ring she is offered by a secondhand husband, or, indeed, the alien deaths she makes over with her elegies.

Not only does the moment to which the narrators of *Absalom* respond mime the moment of lamentation, but the novel's incessant privatives, negations, and negative neologisms also mime, structurally and often semantically, the rhetorical dispossessions effected by the lamentation's privatives.[5] Because unhinged from an assertion a privative means nothing, because it must assert in order to negate, establish in order to destroy, the privative, in remaking value, identity, and knowledge, *reenacts* loss. Hence when Hecuba laments that she is "ἄπολις"[homeless] and "ἄτεκνος"[childless] ("Trojan Women" line 1186), she not only constructs an antithesis between the former possession of city and child and the subsequent absence of those possessions but also, linguistically giving and taking away, reenacts their loss. The privative, moreover, like the remade property of the lamentation, is by nature comparative, disjunctive, antithetical to itself. When Hecuba laments that she, as an old woman, will be forced in slavery to perform "ἀσυμφορώτατα" [*asumforotata*]—that which is most unfit, ill-matched, unmeet ("Trojan Women" line 492)—she illustrates the logic of the lamentation's affinity for privatives. For the privative "*asumforotata*" not only signifies disagreement but is a (structural) disagreement that mimes the disjunctive identity that Hecuba laments.

In the Greek lamentation, the a-privative linguistically performs the kind of dispossession we have described above: it not only describes the loss of material possessions (as in "ἄπολις" and "ἄτεκνος") but also designates the loss of value and identity concomitant to material loss. When, for example, Hecuba laments her torn robes—"πέπλων λακίσματ', ἀδόκιμ' ὀλβίοις ἔχειν [torn robes *unworthy* of that past blessedness]" ("Trojan Women" line 498; emphasis added)—the privative signals that as material possessions have become other, so has the worthiness, esteem, and honor that they signified. Indeed, the privative enacts in miniature the sentence's antithesis between the "ἀδόκιμα"—the base or mean—and "ὀλβίοις"—the blessed, happy, and prosperous. In similar fashion, the Faulknerian *via negativa* description designates and reenacts the loss of identity concomitant to the material losses of the war: "It was winter soon and already soldiers were beginning to come back—the stragglers, not all of them tramps, ruffians, but men who had risked and lost everything, suffered beyond endurance and had returned now to a ruined land, not the same men who had marched away but transformed . . ." (126). In this passage, the negations function first to distinguish those who have possessed and lost property from those who cannot be dispossessed ("tramps, ruffians") because they have never been entitled to possession in the first place, and second to mark the coincident contrariety ("not-sameness") of property and of identity: as a man's land has become other, or become the property of another, so has the man become other to his former self. Likewise, when Sutpen returns from war, he, like the ruined fields, fallen fences, and crumbling walls of his property, has become other, indeed has become alien to his own physical presence:

> He [Sutpen] rode up the drive and into our lives again and left
> no ripple save those [Judith's] instantaneous and incredible
> tears. Because he himself was not there, not in the house
> where we spent our days, had not stopped there. The shell of
> him was there, using the room which we had kept for him and
> eating the food which we produced and prepared as if it could
> neither feel the softness of the bed nor make distinction be-
> tween the viands either as to quality or taste. Yes. He wasn't
> there. . . . Not absent from the place, the arbitrary square of
> earth which he had named Sutpen's Hundred: not that at all.
> He was absent only from the room, and that because he had
> to be elsewhere, a part of him encompassing each ruined field
> and fallen fence and crumbling wall of cabin or cotton house
> or crib; himself diffused and in solution held by that electric
> furious immobile urgency and awareness of short time and the
> need for haste. (129)

Hence, just as the physical presence of the fence no longer possesses the characteristics of a fence—the ability to enclose space,
divide property, prohibit movement—so the physical presence of
Sutpen no longer possesses the characteristics of a self. The repeated negations of presence ("not there," "not in the house"), of
sentience (feeling and taste), of effect ("no ripple" save Judith's incredible tears), and subsequently of absence construct an identity
which, like the privative itself, is disjunctive from, and antithetical
to, the self—an identity figurally reinforced by the passage's alternative descriptions of Sutpen as a "shell" (which implicitly likens
Sutpen to the material alterity of the house),[6] as "diffused," and
as "in solution" (transformed beyond identifiability by and into a
dissimilar substance). These passages thus reenact that moment
of remade property and disjunctive identities that we call "Reconstruction," a term that, not coincidentally, also describes the remaking activity of the privative.

If lamentation is a moment of remaking, it is also a moment
when destruction has produced the radically new, when the world
has been "re-originated" through catastrophe. Indeed destruction
commonly functions as a sign of the new, and while the newly remade identities inscribed in the lamentation are, to be sure, alienating and aversive, this should not be allowed to obscure the fact
that newness is often positively marked. Destruction of existing
knowledge is, for example, closely associated with the production
of new knowledge, and indeed formulations of knowing itself—
revelation, disclosure, unconcealment—often rely on a primary act
of destruction (of cover or concealment). Thus the very act of de-

struction itself—however excessive, however independent of the legitimately new—is easily enough purveyed as the production of new knowledge. The fact that destruction may stand as a sign for the new begins to explain why Faulknerian narration often seems gratuitously destructive—narrators describe in more detail the knowledge they efface than the knowledge they affirm, employ privatives to construct suspiciously sophistic distinctions, and posit highly unlikely possibilities as if merely for the point of having something to negate.

Faulknerian privatives are, moreover, frequently imbedded in a "not . . . but" sequence that not only destroys knowledge but also functions to affirm a new knowledge. Mr. Compson, for example, explains that, when Sutpen first arrived in Jefferson, he looked like a man who had been sick, yet "not like a man who had been peacefully ill in bed and had recovered to move with a sort of diffident and tentative amazement in a world which he had believed himself on the point of surrendering, but like a man who had been through some solitary furnace experience which was more than just fever . . ." (24). Similarly, Shreve insists that Judith grew old "not as the weak grow old, either enclosed in a static ballooning of already lifeless flesh or through a series of stages of gradual collapsing whose particles adhere not to some iron and still impervious framework but to one another as though in some communal and oblivious and mindless life of their own like a colony of maggots, but as the demon himself had grown old" (151). Emerging from a frenzy of rhetorical destruction, such affirmations allow the Faulknerian narrator to lay claim to a radically new, and thus particularly valuable, knowledge: a pristine knowledge traditionally associated with purity of thought, with truth (ἀλήθειᾰ [*aletheia*], we should not forget, depends on a privative), and, later, with the originality that Romanticism valorized as authenticity.[7]

Even in those passages where narrators seem to be mired in a past that won't go away, in a legacy that threatens to eclipse the very possibility of a New South, the "not . . . but" structure of their discourse insistently produces newness. Picking up the narrative from Quentin and Shreve, the omniscient narrator, for example, describes

> the starved and ragged remnant of [the Confederate] army . . .
> swept onward not by a victorious army behind it but rather
> by a mounting tide of the names of lost battles from either
> side . . . battles lost not alone because of superior numbers
> and failing ammunition and stores, but because of generals
> who should not have been generals, who were generals not

through training in contemporary methods or aptitude for learning them, but by the divine right to say "Go there" conferred upon them by an absolute caste system. (276)

This pervasive destruction of knowledge in *Absalom*, customarily propadeutic to a new knowledge, structurally replicates that program which both urged and rhetorically enacted the destruction of old ideas, ideals, identities, in the interest of producing a New South. For the project advocated by New South spokesmen like Henry Grady of the Atlanta *Constitution* and Richard Edmonds of the *Manufacturers' Record* was contingent upon a series of destructions: of the South's single-crop system, its reliance on cotton, and its colonial raw-material economy, as well as of the leisure, manners, and elitism associated with the antebellum plantation. And such destructions, New South advocates wagered, would at once signify and produce newness: a South characterized not by plantation farming but by diversified agriculture, not by production of raw materials but by the manufacture of finished products, not by Northern and freedmen's governments but by Southern white supremacy—would effect, that is, a radical redistribution of both material and ideological possessions.[8]

To enact such a revolution and to produce the new—and because destruction functions as a sign of the new—New South spokesmen inevitably relied on a battery of rhetorical destructions, deploying not only the literal sort of privative we have signaled in the lamentation and in *Absalom* but also a particularly rich line of mortuary and burial imagery. On 21 December 1886 at Delmonico's restaurant in New York, Henry Grady rose to speak to a group of New England businessmen and, in what would become the New South's defining moment, began by quoting Georgia statesman Benjamin Harvey Hill: "There was a South of slavery and secession—that South is dead. There is a South of union and freedom—that South, thank God, is living, breathing, growing every hour" (*New South* 23).[9] Grady's opening statement at once structurally reproduces the Faulknerian "not . . . but" sequence, predicates a claim to newness on an event of destruction, and typifies the rhetorical construction of the New South. For just as Faulkner's narrators repeatedly perform acts of linguistic destruction to produce new knowledge, so did Grady and his colleagues repeatedly perform rhetorical destructions to produce the New South. *State Chronicle* correspondent Walter Hines Page, for example, in a similarly seminal phrase, rhetorically decimated a generation of politicians by labeling them "mummies," hoping thereby to bury "dead and now malodorous traditions" and make possible a new industrial school in North Carolina, to build a region distinguished not by unnatural preservation of already dead ideas and enterprises, but by "active and useful and energetic men" (11 Feb. 1886).

New South spokesmen often mined for rhetorical materials in the destruction effected by the Civil War, a destruction that, in New South terms, was less significant for the freedom it granted to blacks than the new order—and economic opportunity—it produced for whites. Frequent rehearsals of the destruction of slavery thus expediently functioned as both a conciliatory gesture toward the North and the destruction necessary for production of the new. In Grady's "New South" speech at Delmonico's, for example, the South became the enslaved rather than the enslaver and the war, accordingly, about the South's emancipation rather than its defeat: "The South found her jewel in the toad's head of defeat. The shackles that had held her in narrow limitations fell forever when the shackles of the negro slave were broken. . . . [The New South] understands that her emancipation came because through the inscrutable wisdom of God her honest purpose was crossed, and her brave armies were beaten" (*New South* 37–38). Rhetorically appropriating the destruction of war also allowed New South spokesmen to insert themselves into that logic of lamentation that simultaneously declares the past utterly destroyed and proclaims loyalty to it—a position not unlike Mr. Compson's insistence on the Old South as both "a dead time" and "larger, more heroic" than the "diffused and scattered" present (71).[10]

At once constructing, decimating, and eulogizing the Old South, the speeches and editorials of the New South thus routinely carried wrenching descriptions of either the dying confederate soldier or the surviving soldier who, like Sutpen, returns home to find "his house in ruins, his farm devastated, his slaves free, his stock killed, his barns empty, his trade destroyed, his money worthless, his social system, feudal in its magnificence, swept away" (*New South* 30). Such lamentations ratified the New South program with the affective potency of catastrophic loss and the reverence afforded the dead: men and women wept when Grady spoke. Thus harnessing the elegiac sensibilities of the South's Rosas and the tragic irony of its Compsons, New South spokesmen turned mourning to political advantage.[11] Grady, for example, concluding his Texas Fair speech, launched an excruciatingly long description of a wounded confederate soldier who, left by the surgeon to struggle for life until the following sundown, waited in "patient agony," dreaming of the South. Following the story's dramatic conclusion—in which, at long last, "the lanterns of the surgeons came and [the soldier] was taken from death to life"—Grady continued with an allegory:

The world is a battle-field strewn with the wrecks of government and institutions, of theories and of faiths that have gone
down in the ravage of years. On this field lies the South, sown
with her problems. Upon this field swings the lanterns of God.
Amid the carnage walks the Great Physician. Over the South
he bends. "If ye but live until tomorrow's sundown ye shall
endure, my countrymen." Let us for her sake turn our faces
to the east and watch as the soldier watched for the coming
sun. . . . [A]nd the Great Physician shall lead her up from
trouble into content, from suffering into peace, from death to
life. (*New South* 88–89)

In a single deftly conceived paragraph, Grady thus depicted catastrophic destruction; rhetorically replicated the production of the
new (transposing the Faulknerian "not . . . but" into a "from . . .
to"); transferred sympathy for the soldier's pain onto the South;
retrieved the South from identification with dead soldiers, lost
battles, and "wrecks of government"; and made the adherent to
New South ideology into a continuation of the confederate soldier—
watching as he watched for the coming sun, fighting as he fought
for the sake of the South.

This identification of the New South with a soldier fighting
the North also attests to the fact that the destruction most crucial
to the New South program was the destruction neither of slavery
nor of the Old South, but of *Reconstruction*. For in many Southern
whites' view, Reconstruction was primarily a vindictive punishment conceived by Northern radicals to humiliate the South, a moment Southern historians long interpreted as "an era of corruption
presided over by unscrupulous 'carpetbaggers' from the North,
unprincipled Southern white 'scalawags,' and ignorant freedmen"
(Foner xix),[12] a moment the novel describes as "the winter when
we began to learn what carpet-bagger meant and people—women—
locked doors and windows at night and began to frighten each
other with tales of negro uprisings" (130). New South spokesmen,
both sharing and constructing the Southern white community's
sense of terror and dispossession, thus customarily portrayed Reconstruction, rather than as a new society produced by the destruction of war (as did the Radical Republicans), as a continuation
of that destruction. In *Facts About the South*, for example, a book
which summarized editorials from the *Manufacturers' Record*, Edmonds's rehearsal of the devastation of war continued with the
assertion: "That was bad enough, but ten years of Reconstruction—
Destruction it should be called—with its unscrupulous swindling
and debauchery of legislation, its reign of terror greater than that

of 1860–1865, was equally bad if not worse" (12). Similarly, in his Texas State Fair address, Grady described Reconstruction's enfranchisement of freedmen, disfranchisement of rebels, military rule, and carpetbagger governments as an extension of the North's conquest of the South: "Not enough to have conquered our armies—to have decimated our ranks, to have desolated our fields and reduced us to poverty, to have struck the ballot from our hand and enfranchised our slaves—to have held us prostrate under bayonets while the insolent mocked and thieves plundered . . ." (*New South* 58).

By representing Reconstruction as loss—of ballot, power, and dignity—and by rhetorically negating Reconstruction and affirming Southern white power, Grady and his colleagues considerably fortified that process called, significantly, "Redemption."[13] Signifying at once a purification, a redistribution of property, and the recuperation of a lost object—a "but" retrieved from the "not"—"Redemption" named the Democratic overthrow of Reconstruction governments and the reestablishment of "home rule," strict segregation, and white supremacy. The degree to which the Redeemers' project was conceived as an act of destruction is evinced by the degree to which they defined their political platform *via negativa*; for as Edward Ayers notes: "The Democratic Redeemers defined themselves, in large part, by what they were not. Unlike the Republicans, the Redeemers were not interested in a biracial coalition. The Democrats would not seriously consider black needs, would not invert the racial hierarchy by allowing blacks to hold offices for which whites longed. Unlike the Republicans, too, the Redeemers would not use the state government as an active agent of change" (8). The conceptual negativity of Redemption, moreover, materialized: for Redemption was ultimately accomplished by a series of material destructions that, continuous with and legitimated by the Redeemer's rhetorical destructions, destroyed the bodies of blacks to affirm the identity of whites: the privative made flesh. During the "Redemption" of Faulkner's Mississippi, for example, white leagues murdered as many as 300 blacks in Vicksburg as well as a number of prominent blacks, including a state legislator, in Yazoo County; Republican officials resigned under threat of assassination.[14] *Absalom* alludes to this violence in Rosa's description of "the sheets and hoods and night-galloping horses with which the [KKK] discharged the canker suppuration of defeat" (134), and indeed the novel's climactic fire at Sutpen's Hundred might stand as a figure for the materially enacted privatives of the Democratic Redeemers: it is at once the culmination and an incarnation of the novel's privatives, a ritual purification, and the destruction of a black body.[15]

If the privatives of *Absalom* inscribe the rhetorical structure of the New South, so too does that indistinction between the phenomenal and the rhetorical that, as we shall see, characterizes not only the lamentation but Faulkner's novel as well. J. Hillis Miller has argued that *Absalom* dramatizes the necessity but incompatibility of constative and performative language in narration; he writes:

> If in one direction a storyteller tries to stick to the facts (the constative effort), and ends by inventing them (the performative element), in the other direction if a storyteller tries to invent a purely fictional story, wholly cut off from life, if he tries to absorb life into a perfect narrative design, he always ends by referring to life and to history, since the words he must use are after all referential. (167)

I wish to insist, however, that Miller's first "direction"—in which the constative slides into the performative—describes a situation particularly acute in catastrophe and thus particularly marked in the lamentation, and that his second "direction"—in which the performative inevitably "refer[s] to life"—describes not only a mere reference to, but a consequential construction of, life. Mr. Compson, for example, narrating the moment of Mississippi's Redemption, employs the privative to refigure the foreignness of Charles Etienne as unreal:

> . . . this child with a face not old but without age, as if he had had no childhood, not in the sense that Miss Rosa Coldfield says she had no childhood, but as if he had not been human born but instead created without agency of man or agony of woman and orphaned by no human being . . . but produced complete and subject to no microbe in that cloyed and scented maze of shuttered silk as if he were the delicate and perverse spirit-symbol, immortal page of the ancient immortal Lilith, entering the actual world not at the age of one second but of twelve years . . . (159)

This rhetorical emptying out of age, childhood, natural birth, mother, the vulnerability of the body, and indeed mortality itself is not without consequences, for it not only enacts a sustained and fantastic loss of being but also legitimates the novel's later constructions of Charles Etienne as insentient, as possessing "a strength composed of sheer desperate will and imperviousness to the punishment, the blows and slashes which he took in return and did not even seem to feel" (164). Indeed this rhetorical insentience solidifies into "knowledge" and, ratified by the deictic gesture of the demonstrative pronoun, becomes not only "that same fury and implacability and physical imperviousness to pain and punishment" (167) but, in a disturbingly eloquent elision of history, social conditions, and race, "that furious protest, that indictment of heaven's ordering, that gage flung into the face of what is" (164). The mutual contamination of constative and performative language of which Miller speaks thus allows a rhetorical construction of identity—such as the catastrophic loss of identity suffered by Charles Etienne—to pass for a representation, that is, for a disinterested record of the real. The gestures of a language that represents catastrophe may, such passages suggest, function to construct useful and interested catastrophe, for a reenactment and an enactment are disconcertingly difficult to distinguish.

In similar fashion, New South spokesmen, placing themselves like the narrators of *Absalom* at that site where the phenomenal and the rhetorical are indistinguishable, recorded as fact the very "New South" that they were in the act of rhetorically constructing. Grady opened his 1887 address at the Augusta exposition, for example, with a rhetorical destruction of desolation and poverty that, like the exposition itself, was less an accurate record of phenomena than a performance intended to enact them:

> We give thanks to-day that the Lord God Almighty, having led us from desolation into plenty, from poverty into substance, from passion into reason, and from estrangement into love—having brought the harvests from the ashes, and raised us homes from our ruins, and touched our scarred land all over with beauty and with peace permits us to assemble here to-day and rejoice amid the garnered heaps of our treasure. (*Harris' Life of Grady* 121–22)

Grady's negation of postwar conditions and affirmation of "heaps of treasure" illustrate the manner in which a new knowledge or a New South, which is less a representation of phenomena than a rhetorical construction of them, grants itself the status of a representation and thereby disguises its own interested production of the real: a reenactment and an enactment are disconcertingly difficult to distinguish.

Yet while such representations might well produce belief in a material heap of treasure, they did not, alas, always produce the material heap of treasure itself, a fact confirmed, for example, by the "carpetless room [in which Judith and Charles Etienne confer] furnished with whatever chairs and such which they had not had to chop up and burn to cook food or for warmth or maybe to heat water for illness from time to time" (167). Hence, at the Texas State Fair, while enlisting his customary series of performative destructions, Grady shrewdly combined his rhetorical destruction of the one-crop system and of raw material production with a description of loss of profits:

> with amazing rapidity [the South] has moved away from the one-crop idea that was once her curse. . . . With equal swiftness has she moved away from the folly of shipping out her ore at $2 a ton and buying it back in implements at from $20 to $100 per ton; her cotton at 10 cents a pound, and buying it back in cloth at 20 to 80 cents a pound; her timber at 8 per thousand and buying it back in furniture at ten to twenty times as much. (*New South* 79–81)

At the same time that Grady's constative language slides indistinguishably into the performative—precisely as the fair's "exhibits" were intended to do—his description of loss of profits compensates for the failures of rhetorical performativity by producing desire.

Desire is a kind of anticipatory loss: an anticipated possession and the (subsequent) lack of it. The lamentation produces desire—for a lost object, a forgotten past, a less aversive future—not only by chronicling loss but by employing the privative, for in (re)enacting loss the privative (re)enacts desire. It is thus no coincidence that *Absalom*'s primary site of desire—Bon's longing for the recognition of his father—is repeatedly constructed through privatives: "And he sent me no word? He did not ask you to send me to him? No word to me, no word at all?" (285). The very conception of the father and his signs (as anticipated possession) conditions both Bon's desire and his sense of perpetual "loss" of a father he has never possessed. "Thus desire for what is withheld," writes John T. Matthews, "is scarcely distinguishable from sorrow over what has been lost" (*Play* 60).

Just as the novel's rhetorical loss of the father produces Bon's incessant desire for the father, so does Grady's rhetorical loss of profits produce desire for profits. And the privatives employed by New South spokesmen routinely functioned to produce a desire that compensated for the failures of rhetorical performativity: if language itself did not remake society, perhaps desire for that remaking would. Benjamin Harvey Hill, for example, in a widely read article calling for educational reform, posited both a series of anticipated possessions and the lack of them and thus, enlisting the common technique of comparing the South's productivity with the North's, reenacts—and performatively enacts—desire:

> the persistent, pertinacious, persevering energy of the North has erected a hundred cotton factories where we have but one. . . . The facilities for manufacturing are all in our favor;

and it is owing to our own inattention and neglect that we are so immeasurably behind. . . . We became dependent upon the North for everything, from a lucifer match to a columbiad, from a pin to a railroad engine. A state of war found us without the machinery to make a single percussion cap for a soldier's rifle, or a single button for his jacket. (1: 3–9)

In similar fashion, in what came to be known as the "funeral oration," Grady cannily placed himself at the burial of a confederate soldier and, tapping the affective potency of the site of death, proceeded to describe not merely the loss of the soldier but a series of losses calculated to produce desire for precisely those industries he wished to promote—lumber, mining, textile mills:

They buried him in the midst of a marble quarry: they cut through solid marble to make his grave; and yet a little tombstone they put above him was from Vermont. They buried him in the heart of a pine forest, and yet the pine coffin was imported from Cincinnati. They buried him within touch of an iron mine, and yet the nails in his coffin and the iron in the shovel that dug his grave were imported from Pittsburg. They buried him by the side of the best sheep-grazing country on the earth, and yet the wool in the coffin bands and the coffin bands themselves were brought from the North. The South didn't furnish a thing on earth for that funeral but the corpse and the hole in the ground. There they put him away and the clods rattled down on his coffin, and they buried him in a New York coat and a Boston pair of shoes and a pair of breeches from Chicago and a shirt from Cincinnati . . . (*New South* 133)

Where rhetorical destruction failed to produce the New South, the privative thus offered the auxiliary function of formulating desire.

I have argued that the phenomenal redistributions of the moment of lamentation and the rhetorical dispossessions of the language of lamentation follow a logic in which moment and language indissociably produce each other, in which language both represents and effects a redistribution of possessions. And if the privatives of *Absalom* chronicle the rhetorical destructions of New South spokesmen—their production of newness and of desire—they also inscribe the redistribution of possessions that characterized the New South.

Both the New South spokesmen's explicit announcements—"a hundred farms for every plantation, fifty homes for every palace" (*New South* 38)—and their remarkable affinity for tabulating possessions—statistics, tables, charts, and graphs abound—testify to the fact that a redistribution of possessions was fundamental to the New South program. Because material and ideological possessions customarily condition each other, moreover, New South spokesmen often attempted to achieve a redistribution of material possessions by rhetorically redistributing ideological ones. Hill's argument for educational reform, for example, which redistributes value and aims to remake knowledge, transfers value to the manual labor, hard work, and utilitarian knowledge necessary to the production of material possessions: "We want . . . [a] plan of instruction, which will embrace the useful rather than the profound, the practical rather than the theoretic" (11).[16] Edmonds, likewise, rhetorically transfers value from the pleasures of material luxury to the hard labor and autonomy he believes will concomitantly transfer material possessions to the South: "a loaf, whether of bread or educational opportunity, won by hard and honest work, by the sweat of the brow, means more for manhood than a thousand dainties accepted as charity from those upon whom they have no claim" (*South's Prosperity* 7).

If the war remade the identity of the South, New South spokesmen, deploying a language of catastrophe and following the logic of their own privatives, attempted to remake the identity of the South once again, this time in the interest of attracting Northern capital. Edmonds, for example, in *Facts about the South*—a book distributed to hotel rooms and aimed, ostensibly, at traveling Northern investors—was at pains to remake the image of the Southern gentleman, the man of leisure and letters, into an image of a Southern businessman, a man of energy and enterprise. "But this is only a small part of the evidence available," he writes after a page of statistics on the South's antebellum progress in industry, "to conclusively prove that great energy and enterprise were displayed by the people of the South" (9); the census of 1860, he contends, proves that Southern peoples "were not slothful in the business of money-making" (11). Edmonds also wished to remake the identity of the South not as a place of monstrous social unrest but as a peaceful, secure place for investments. He thus advised newspapers to portray the South as "prosperous and contented, devoting her energies to the development of her unequalled resources, and to the education of her citizens, white and black." Editors, he urged, should "reduce to the minimum their record of local crimes and should demand that new suppliers send them other matters," especially "industrial information" (qtd. in Gaston 73).

Thus if the moment of lamentation is a moment when transfers of real property effect redistributions of identity, New South spokesmen bargained that by miming the moment of lamentation and remaking identity they might effect a transfer of real property. And while neither the causes of phenomena nor the effects of language are singular, to a certain degree they did. For such rhetorical redistributions of value and identity, subtly sliding from the constative to the performative, from "referring to" to constructing life, effected an actual, if not cataclysmic, redistribution of material possessions. The President of Emory College, Bishop Atticus Haygood, in his 1880 Thanksgiving Sermon entitled "The New South: Gratitude, Amendment, Hope," described such a redistribution, catalogued the new material possessions of the South, and, adopting the "then/now" structure of the lamentation, urged his parishioners to compare the new with the old:

> The houses built recently are better in every way than those built before the war. I do not speak of an occasional mansion, that in the old times lifted itself proudly among a score of cabins, but of the thousands of decent farm-houses, comely cottages that have been built in the last ten years. I know scores whose new barns are better than their old residences. Our people have better furniture. Good mattresses have largely driven out the old-time feathers. Cook-stoves, sewing machines, with all such comforts and conveniences, may be seen in a dozen homes to-day where you could hardly have found them in one in 1860. Lamps that make reading agreeable have driven out tallow dips, by whose glimmering no eyes could long read and continue to see. Better taste asserts itself: the new houses are painted; they have not only glass, but blinds. There is more comfort inside. There are luxuries where once there were not conveniences. Carpets are getting to be common among the middle classes. There are parlor organs, pianos, and pictures, where we never saw them before. (9)

Not an occasional mansion but scores of cabins, not old-time feathers but good mattresses, not tallow dips but electric lamps: while Haygood's list of possessions, characteristic of New South hyperbole, is no doubt comprised as much of commodities his parishioners were encouraged to desire as those they actually possessed, it nonetheless indicates the kind of redistribution of possessions that resulted, at least in part, from the rhetorical redistributions of New South spokesmen.

Moreover, many men and women in the New South enacted the structure of New South privatives and—like Judith, the mistress turned merchant—assumed remade identities: the planter became industrialist, the industrialist became merchant, the merchant became planter.[17] Many blacks, remaking their lives as freedpeople, acquired both a mobility and an opportunity to bargain for wages that allowed them to obtain material possessions; they were able, according to Ayers, "to acquire considerable amounts of clothes, furniture, musical instruments, bicycles, and buggies" (69–70). Many working-class whites moving from farm to the South's new mill towns, many women and children remaking themselves as factory workers, acquired education, material possessions, and a new sense of respectability.[18]

Thus if the war itself caused singular, cataclysmic transformations, New South boosterism brought about its own redistributions of knowledge, identity, and material property: less dramatic to be sure, but arguably more sustained. And if, as I have argued above, Faulknerian privatives reenact the loss of identity concomitant to the material losses of war, they also construct an even more pervasive and continuous loss of identity. Faulknerian privatives repeatedly construct identities antithetical to the "natural," the wholly familiar identities which, rather than being a disjunction from a temporally prior self, are a disjunction from the logically prior self posited (and subsequently negated) by the privative.[19] Charles Bon, for example, "must have appeared almost phoenix-like, full-sprung from no childhood, born of no woman and impervious to time and, vanished, leaving no bones nor dust anywhere" (58). Just as Bon is here dispossessed of childhood, mother, the marks of time, so are nearly all the characters of *Absalom* sooner or later described in terms of what they are not, as selves disjunctive from the natural or ordinary, from their environment, or, as in this passage, from the very materials through which identity is constructed.[20] Indeed, this disjunction, in Faulkner as in the lamentation, takes on fantastic proportions. When Hecuba laments that her life and duties will be *asumforotatos*, she laments not only that they will be unfit but that they will be most unfit, most ill-matched, most unmeet; she laments, that is, that while she once possessed tasks that were in agreement with her identity (*sumforos*)—such as holding the scepter of Priam, leading the choir and the dance—henceforth her duties, her activities, her environment will be not only disjunctive from her self (*asumforos*) but superlatively, fantastically disjunctive (*asumforotatos*). Many of the identities constructed by Faulknerian privatives are precisely of this superlative class of most ill-fitting identities—rhetorical constructions of the monstrous, the inhuman, and the fantastic, identities equivalent to sustained catastrophe.[21]

If the lamentation's privatives construct identities that are *asumforotata*, losses of and by knowledge effect an anti-knowledge which, like the fantastically disjunctive identity left by the privative, is antithetical to, and a negation of, that wholly familiar knowledge taken for the real, the natural, the believable. The initial privatives of Hecuba's lamentation for Polydorus, for example—a lamentation comprised of both a particularly dense constellation of a-privatives and an incantatory repetition, alliteration, and assonance that ono-matopoeically reenact the moment's overwhelming succession of losses—insist that the primary possession which she has lost is *be-lief* and, specifically, belief in that most intimate and secure of knowledges—the knowledge established by one's own senses:

> ἄπιστ' ἄπιστα, καινὰ καινὰ δέρκομαι
> ἕτερα δ' ἀφ ἑτέρων κακὰ κακῶν κυρεῖ
> οὐδέποτ' ἀστένακτος ἀδάκρυτος ἁ-
> μέρα ἐπισχήσει.

> *Unbelievable, unbelievable*, another and another woe I see
> Another after another evil of evil transpires
> Never *without* groan, *without* tear, *without* . . .
> a day shall pass.] ("Ἑκάβη" lines 689–92; emphasis added, translation mine)

These privatives perform, then, the ultimate revaluation of knowl-edge, in which that knowledge of the world taken for the "real"—the believed because sensorily perceived—is made over so dramatically as to be unbelievable, fantastic.

The Faulknerian privative, accordingly, repeatedly enacts a loss of knowledge that makes knowledge disjunctive from its own cus-tomary constituents. Mr. Compson's "It just does not explain" speech, for example, employs a series of privatives—incredible, incompre-hensible, impervious, inexplicable, indecipherable, inscrutable—that both describes the impossibility of constituting the past into knowl-edge and empties out the constituents of that knowledge, leaving, ultimately, "just the words, the symbols, the shapes themselves, shadowy inscrutable and serene" (80). Indeed, Faulknerian priva-tives routinely construct perceptions which, emptied out of certain knowledge and of the properties of the "natural," are *asumforotatos*, the most *not* in agreement with knowledge or with its "natural" con-stituents; Rosa's description of her arrival at Sutpen's Hundred follow-ing Henry's murder of Charles Bon is exemplary:

> Rotting portico and scaling walls, it stood, not ravaged, not invaded, marked by no bullet nor soldier's iron heel but rather as though reserved for something more: some desolation more profound than ruin, as if it had stood in iron juxtaposition to iron flame, to a holocaust which had found itself less fierce and less implacable, not hurled but rather fallen back before

the impervious and indomitable skeleton which the flames
durst not, at the instant's final crisis, assail. (108–9)

In this passage, then, privatives simultaneously establish and empty
out the "natural," causal relation between the activity of war and a
destroyed house, and leave but a residual anti-knowledge, an emptiness ("desolation") which can only be gestured towards negatively (as
not ravage, not invasion, not the result of bullet or iron heel), metaphorically ("as though"), and comparatively ("something more," "more
profound than ruin"). More generally, the privatives devalue that
knowledge that imputes destruction of the house of Sutpen to an active agency; indeed, the passage reinforces the passivity left over
from its initial privatives ("not ravaged, not invaded . . .") with a number of "figural privatives" ("rotting portico," "scaling walls," "skeleton")
and with a holocaust emptied out of its active properties both by a
privative ("not hurled but rather fallen back") and by the semi-privative
"less" ("less fierce and less implacable").

Moreover, in dispossessing the material world of its "natural"
constituents, the passage's privatives are likewise a dispossession
of that most certain of knowledges—the believed (because sensorily perceived) nature of the material world. Thus, house and body
(skeleton), ordinarily vulnerable to invasion by fire, are, according
to the passage's privatives, impervious and indomitable and have
a fantastic ability to resist the external and the active; likewise,
fire, which in ordinary circumstances actively and fearlessly overcomes passive materials of house or body, is here "less fierce and
less implacable," is "not hurled, but fallen back," and dares not assail. Yet this fantastic world where wood and flame are like iron,
where passivity is stronger than any activity, where house and
body are invulnerable and fire quails, is the site of a further perversion of the unbelievable beyond itself—a hyperfantastic. For if war
is already a perversion of "natural" peacetime, then Sutpen's Hundred is a hyperfantastic perversion of that perversion—a "something more," in the language of the passage. And if this passage
fantastically distorts the natural, the event (the revelation of)
which this description interrupts is a (hyperfantastic) distortion of
that (already fantastic) distortion. For unlike the fantastic body of
the house, Bon's body *has* been ravaged, invaded, marked by a bullet and indeed by the iron heel of a soldier's racist morality. Hence
while the description of the house may function as a wish-fulfilling
displacement, it also functions to cast the ostensibly natural (a body
vulnerable to a bullet) *as* the hyperfantastic. Likewise, this passage's
doubly duplicitous foreshadowing—this is not the final crisis, the
house will be assailed by fire—proleptically casts the novel's final

holocaust not as the "natural" result of setting a match to a "tinder-dry rotten shell" (300), but as a final, hyperfantastic permutation of the house's fantastic imperviousness.[22] Faulknerian privatives thus repeatedly construct the epistemologically *asumforotata*, the most ill-fitting of knowledges, a "knowledge" that indeed is often no knowledge at all, but the impossibility of knowledge.

In this manner, Faulknerian privatives chronicle, I would argue, the ill-fitting identities and fantastic knowledge of the New South. For while New South spokesmen rhetorically remade the identity of Southern whites into an energetic, enterprising, and industrious people, they simultaneously constructed an identity for blacks as an indolent, vagrant, deceitful, ignorant, and violent people. Many freedpeople thus came to bear identities that were, like Hecuba's, *asumforotatos* and to lead lives, like Charles Etienne's, equivalent to sustained catastrophe.[23] And with a conveniently circular justificatory logic abetted by the liaison between material and ideological possessions, blacks were often denied access to material possessions on the basis of their lack of ideological possessions: rhetorically made violent, blacks were excluded from the prosperity of mill towns where white women worked; rhetorically made deceitful and ignorant, educated blacks were excluded—with the help of fifty strikes against black labor between 1882 and 1900—from skilled jobs; rhetorically made indolent and prone to vagrancy, black laborers were excluded from many unskilled jobs as well.[24] Black farmers, moreover, who comprised the vast majority of black laborers, "not only worked the white man's land but," according to Woodward, "worked it with a white man's plow drawn by a white man's mule" (206).[25] Capturing both the shady calculations characteristic of the South's notorious lien system and the general redistribution of possessions in the New South, an African-American lyric of the period ran:

> Naught's a naught
> And five's a figger
> All for the white man
> And none for the nigger. (qtd. in Williamson 153)[26]

Similarly excluded from New South progress were white tenant farmers—the Wash Joneses of the South; for while New South spokesmen rhetorically constructed a South not of plantations but of diversified small farms, the material enactment of that negation and affirmation was not only a destruction of the old plantation but also a rise of the new lien system—a system in which small farmers not only did not possess any land but were soon dispossessed of both economic autonomy and freedom of movement.[27]

New South rhetoric, moreover, which continued to announce a fantastic progress, increasingly created a moment that was, like the moment of lamentation, characterized by a disruption of that most certain of knowledges—the believed because sensorily perceived—an incomprehensible moment in which the world no longer fit into language: not because the world had become fantastic and language was inadequate to describe it but because language had become fantastic and the world was simply inadequate to perform it. That very incomprehensibility, moreover, provided a rhetorical subterfuge behind which to conceal material conditions: "the magnitude of the investments made in Southern railroads . . . is almost beyond comprehension," declared Edmonds (*South's Redemption* 35); "the magnitude of the wealth of the South in coal is beyond computation" (*South's Redemption* 24); the impact of Southern iron and steel supremacy "is beyond our power at present to fully grasp" (*Facts* 27). Such assertions, which rhetorically obscure the real by declaring it unknowable, demonstrate how the gestures of a language that records confusion can likewise be used to construct confusion, to produce disbelief in the sensorily perceived conditions of the material world. For the incomprehensibility that inheres in the moment of lamentation—and that Faulknerian privatives repeatedly produce—increasingly functioned in the hands of New South boosters as obfuscation: a "can't-be-known" which concealed what must not be known.

Thus while the New South, from a number of perspectives, was a moment of dramatic change, those excluded from New South progress—particularly freedpeople and poor whites—testify to the degree to which a rhetoric that produces the appearance of newness may function to mask continuity. Indeed both New South spokesmen and Democratic Redeemers aspired to reestablish antebellum social relations in a new, industrial atmosphere.[28] And both the convict-lease system—which sold convicts to industries in need of labor and primarily affected blacks convicted on petty theft or vagrancy charges—and new codes of white supremacy—"vastly more complex than the antebellum slave codes or the Black Codes of 1865–1866" (Woodward 212)—effectively instituted a caste system that reproduced the social and economic dependency, and often the brutality, of slavery.[29] Ultimately excluded from New South progress was the South itself, for the language of New South boosters had neither the performative nor the motivational potency to enact the fantastic South to which it referred. Thus in 1913 the South remained a colonial dependent mired in a raw-material economy, a region of low-wage industries, and the poorest section of the nation; its railway system was in the hands of Northern investors—by 1890 more than half belonged to Northern companies; its mining industry was controlled by absentee owners; two-thirds of its lumber industry belonged to men in Chicago, Michigan, and Wisconsin.[30] Thus when Mr. Compson employs his customary privatives to describe Rosa "hearing and losing the knell and doom of her native land between two tedious and clumsy stitches on a garment which she would never wear and never remove for a man who she was not even to see alive" (61), his privatives alienate Rosa from the products of her own labor in a disjunction both structurally homologous to the "hearing and losing" of the passage and semantically homologous to the doom of the native land.

The New South program, for all its emphasis on progress, not only deployed enough nostalgia to rival any Faulknerian narrator but, through its very rhetoric of newness, disguised its continuity with that "lost" society on which *Absalom* so obsessively dwells. Conversely, if the narrators of *Absalom* seem thematically to resist New South optimism by dwelling on devastation and clinging to nostalgia, they are rhetorically as insistent on producing newness as any New South spokesman. The Faulknerian privative thus simultaneously marks the appearance of the mode of lamentation, refers to a fictional moment of catastrophe, and inscribes the historical moment of the New South. Those privatives record, that is, the production of newness and desire, the indistinction between the phenomenal and the rhetorical, the redistribution of material and ideological possessions, and the assertions of incomprehensibility characteristic of both the lamentation and New South discourse: for in this most unprepossessing of rhetorical gestures lies capacities for remaking the world.

Notes

1. On the Lamentations of Jeremiah see Westermann; Hillers; Gottwald; Mintz chapter 1; and Landy. Lamentations of Hecuba are found in Euripides' "Hecuba" and "The Trojan Women." On Greek lamentation see Alexiou, Seremetakis, and Holst-Warhaft.

2. Distinguishable communal, individual, and funeral lament forms exist in Hebrew, though the forms often overlap and personal laments often express the intensity of grief over a loved one as catastrophe—as an entire world passed away. See Gottwald chapters 1 and 2 and Hillers introduction. On the relation of *Absalom* to the biblical tragedy of Absalom see Ross; Behrens 29–31; and Irwin 148ff.

3. On the thematic losses of *Absalom* see Mortimer chapter 3; on Faulknerian language and loss see Matthews, *Play*; on the relation of the novel to Southern mourning and melancholy see Moreland 28ff; on uncertainty and the narrative structure of *Absalom* see Brooks chapter 11, Robert Dale Parker chapter 5, Snead chapter 5, and Miller; on loss and Faulkner's creative process see Irwin.

4. Grammatically, a privative designates an affix that expresses negation or privation; as an adjective the word means having the quality of depriving, tending to take away, characterized by the loss or want of some quality (*OED*). It is precisely the relation between these two meanings that I am exploring below. I use the term in its strict grammatical sense as well as to name both words formed by privatives and other forms of linguistic negation.

5. A helpful catalog of Faulknerian negating patterns can be found in Slatoff 122–27. Two recent studies of negation in *Absalom* appear in *Faulkner's Discourse: An International Symposium*: Winfried Herget's "The Poetics of Negation in Faulkner's *Absalom, Absalom!*," which argues that negations are an "expression of unfulfilled expectations" and "an index of the presuppositions and prejudices of the cultural context in which they operate" (34); and François Pitavy's "Some Remarks on Negation and Denegation in William Faulkner's *Absalom, Absalom!*," which reads Rosa's negations psychoanalytically as denial; I would contend, in opposition to Pitavy, that negation is a textual symptom too widespread to be localized in the psychopathology of a single character. See also Mortimer 77–78.

6. See the description of the house as "a shell marooned and forgotten in a backwater of catastrophe—a skeleton giving of itself in slow driblets of furniture and carpet, linen and silver . . ." (105). See also 108, 111, and 173.

7. On purity in Greek thought see Robert Parker and Burkert 75–84. See also Ricoeur's analysis of the word *katharos* (25–46) and its equivalence with "the essential purification, that of wisdom and philosophy" (38). On Quentin's struggle to possess authority through authoring narrative see Irwin 113ff. On Faulkner's production of newness in modernism see Moreland's discussion of "revisionary repetition" 4–5.

8. On the period of the New South see Ayers and Woodward. On the program of New South spokesmen see Gaston. On the New South era in the Mississippi Delta see Cobb chapters 3–6. On the relation of Faulkner to New South ideology see Morris chapter 5. On *Absalom*, the Southern Agrarians, and the New South see Moreland, especially 24, 75n10, and 87. On the New South and nostalgia see Sundquist 98ff. On the life of the Faulkner family in the New South see Williamson chapters 1–5.

9. Grady's speech, which followed an address by General Sherman and a rendition of "Marching through Georgia" by the band, made

a strong appeal to national unity and garnered considerable sympathy for the New South program. Generations of southern schoolboys, including, no doubt, William Faulkner, were required to memorize it. See Gaston 87–90.

10. Such a logic explains the apparently paradoxical fact that, as Woodward puts it, "one of the most significant inventions of the New South was the 'Old South'" (155). The United Confederate Veterans, the cult of the confederacy, town monuments to confederate soldiers, and the plantation romance are all products of the New South era.

11. On *Absalom's* vacillations between nostalgia and irony see Moreland, especially 27, 77–79, and 94.

12. The phrase is drawn from Foner's description of the Dunning School's position on Radical Reconstruction (1867–77).

13. Grady wrote his first article entitled "The New South" on the occasion of Georgia's Redemption; Edmonds entitled his 1890 book on the New South *The South's Redemption*. On Redemption see Foner chapter 12 and Woodward chapter 1.

14. According to Foner, the 1875 campaign, which sealed Mississippi's Redemption, "quickly degenerated into a violent crusade to destroy the Republican organization and prevent blacks from voting" (558). When the state legislature assembled, it completed Redemption by first impeaching black Lieutenant Governor Alexander K. Davis (to prevent him from succeeding to the governorship) and then compelling Governor Ames to resign and leave the state. On Mississippi Redemption see Foner 558–63.

15. However, if it is Clytie that we witness being "destroyed" in this scene, Henry is ostensibly consumed by the fire as well, while the partly black Jim Bond escapes.

16. Along similar lines, William S. Speer, in *The Law of Success*, declared:

> The educator of the future . . . will teach his pupils what will pay best. He will teach them the art of thinking, which, for the purpose at hand, I may define to be the art of turning one's brains into money. He will not teach dead languages, obsolete formulas, and bric-a-brac sciences . . . which are never used in the ordinary transactions of the forum, the office, the shop, or the farm. (qtd. in Gaston 111)

On education in the New South see Woodward 61–64 and 153–54 and Ayers 417–26.

17. A disproportionate quantity of the South's material possessions was, however, transferred into the hands of a new elite, which consisted primarily of merchants, industrialists, and planters. According to Woodward, "A strong tendency early asserted itself for

merchant and planter to become one—that is, for the merchant to acquire the farms of the hapless landowner, and for the more fortunate planters to move to town and become supply merchants" (184)—a tendency encouraged by the lien laws and lowered land levies of Redeemer governments.

18. On southern mill towns see Ayers chapter 5 and Woodward 222–27.

19. This reading follows and extends Herget, who reads negation as an "interplay of norms and deviations" (34), and Pitavy, who argues that negations "function as referential indexes" ("Some Remarks" 27).

20. See *via negativa* descriptions of Bon, 100, 120; of Rosa, 55, 57, 61, 116; of Ellen, 84; of Judith, 95; of Sutpen, 184, 199. This disjunction is thematically reinforced by "the two separate Quentins now talking to one another in the long silence of notpeople in notlanguage" (5).

21. While Slatoff draws his thesis primarily from thematic readings, and while I would contend that there is more at stake in the construction of the *asumforotatos* than merely Faulkner's temperament, my rhetorical reading is, nonetheless, in many ways consistent with Slatoff's notion of the "polar imagination": "a deep-seated tendency in Faulkner to view and interpret experience in extreme terms and to see life as composed essentially of pairs of warring entities" (79).

22. This reading is in the spirit of Slatoff, who argues that "it was as though even the extremes were insufficient, as though Faulkner were seeking somehow to go even beyond the extreme, to give the screw a turn or even several turns beyond the final turn" (81). On the fantastic and gothic elements of *Absalom* see also Sundquist 98ff; Vickery 88ff; and Pitavy, "Gothicism."

23. A number of widely read works of the period—such as *The Negro a Beast*; *The Negro, A Menace to American Civilization*; and Thomas Dixon's *The Clansman*—constructed a monstrous, "unnatural" identity for freedpeople much like the selves constructed by Faulknerian privatives. On racial identity and race relations in the New South see Ayers chapter 6 and 426–37; Woodward chapter 13; and Foner chapter 12.

24. On labor relations, see Ayers 67–72 and 431.

25. The census of 1880 indicates that, in thirty-three Georgia counties, not more than one in one hundred black farmers owned land; seventeen Mississippi counties reported the same proportion; "twelve others reported not one in twenty, and many not one in fifty" (Woodward 205). By 1900, blacks in the cotton South owned a smaller percentage of land than at the end of Reconstruction (Foner 597).

26. Whites were often outraged when blacks did acquire material possessions, precisely because they functioned as signs of social

equality. "Just generally," a black woman from South Carolina tes-tified, "if you were black, you were not supposed to have either time or money, and if you did, you ought not to show it. Some of them did think colored people oughtn't to have a certain nice thing, even if they had money enough to buy it" (qtd. in Ayers 88). Klansmen, who functioned as the police force of Redeemer gov-ernments, often killed blacks' livestock in an effort both to deny blacks' right to own material possessions and to make them more dependent upon their white employers.

27. Tenant farmers pledged future crops to merchants to obtain sup-plies; and since merchants determined both the interest rate and the cost of the supplies, tenant farmers at the end of the season, more often than not, had not "paid out." Once indebted to a mer-chant, no competitor would grant the farmer credit, and the farmer was thus obligated to contract again with the same merchant to pay off his debts. Woodward writes of the tenant farmer:

> From this time until he has paid the last dollar of his indebt-edness, he is subject to the constant oversight and direction of the merchant. Every mouthful of food he purchases, every implement that he requires on the farm, his mules, cattle, the clothing for himself and family, the fertilizers for his land, must all be bought of the merchant who holds the crop lien, and in such amounts as the latter is willing to allow. (180)

On the lien system see Woodward chapter 7; Foner 594–96; and Ayers chapter 8.

28. Matthews, in "The Rhetoric of Containment in Faulkner," makes a similar point about the political unconscious of *The Sound and the Fury*:

> What seems to be the simple passage from old to new turns out to be in *The Sound and the Fury* the disguised reinvigora-tion of the dominant ideology. Mercantile capitalism obscures its affinity with the exploitative mechanism of agrarian, slave-holding capitalism precisely because it rests on the same foundation of economic and racial exploitation. (60)

29. On the convict lease system see Woodward 212–15, 232–34, and 424–25; and Ayers 154–55.

30. On railroad industry see Ayers chapter 1 and Woodward 120–24, 292–99, and 379–84; on mining industry see Ayers chapter 5; on lumber industry see Ayers 123–31 and Woodward 115–20.

Works Cited

Alexiou, Margaret. *The Ritual Lament in Greek Tradition*. Cambridge: Cambridge UP, 1974.

Ayers, Edward L. *The Promise of the New South: Life after Reconstruction.* Oxford: Oxford UP, 1992.

Behrens, Ralph. "Collapse of Dynasty: The Thematic Center of *Absalom, Absalom!*" *PMLA* 89 (1974): 24–33.

Brooks, Peter. *Reading for the Plot: Design and Intention in Narrative.* New York: Vintage Books, 1984.

Burkert, Walter. *Greek Religion.* Trans. John Raffan. Cambridge: Harvard UP, 1985.

Cobb, James C. *The Most Southern Place on Earth: The Mississippi Delta and the Roots of Regional Identity.* Oxford: Oxford UP, 1992.

Edmonds, Richard H. *Facts About the South.* Baltimore: Manufacturers' Record, 1902.

———. *The South's Prosperity Its Danger: Strength of Character Needed as Never Before.* Baltimore: Manufacturers' Record, 1907.

———. *The South's Redemption: From Poverty to Prosperity.* Baltimore: Manufacturers' Record, 1890.

Euripides. "Ekavbh." Trans. A. S. Way. *Euripides.* Vol. 1. 4 vols. Loeb Classical Library. Cambridge: Harvard UP, 1978. 243–349.

———. "Hecuba." Trans. William Arrowsmith. *Euripides III. The Complete Greek Tragedies.* Ed. David Grene and Richmond Lattimore. Chicago: U of Chicago P, 1958. 1–68.

———. "Trwiavdež." Trans. A. S. Way. *Euripides.* Vol. 1. 4 vols. Loeb Classical Library. Cambridge: Harvard UP, 1978. 351–459.

———. "The Trojan Women." Trans. Richmond Lattimore. *Euripides III. The Complete Greek Tragedies.* Ed. David Grene and Richmond Lattimore. Chicago: U of Chicago P, 1958. 121–75.

Faulkner, William. *Absalom, Absalom!* New York: Random House, 1986.

Felman, Shoshana, and Dori Laub, M.D. *Testimony: Crises of Witnessing in Literature, Psychoanalysis, and History.* New York: Routledge, 1992.

Foner, Eric. *Reconstruction: America's Unfinished Revolution 1863–1877.* New York: Harper & Row, 1988.

Gaston, Paul M. *The New South Creed: A Study in Southern Mythmaking.* New York: Knopf, 1970.

Gottwald, Norman K. *Studies in the Book of Lamentations.* SCM Press, 1954.

Grady, Henry Woodfin. *The New South and Other Addresses with Biography, Critical Opinions, and Explanatory Note by Edna Henry Lee Turpin.* New York: Maynard, Merrill & Co., 1904.

Harris, Joel Chandler, ed. *Joel Chandler Harris' Life of Henry W. Grady Including His Writings and Speeches.* New York: Cassell Publishing Company, 1890.

Haygood, Atticus G. D.D. "The New South: Gratitude, Amendment, Hope. A Thanksgiving Sermon for November 25, 1880." Oxford, GA, 1880.

Herget, Winfried. "The Poetics of Negation in Faulkner's *Absalom, Absalom!*" *Faulkner's Discourse: An International Symposium.* Ed. Lothar Hönnighausen. Tübingen: Max Niemeyer Verlag, 1989. 33–37.

Hill, Benjamin Harvey. "Education." *The Land We Love.* 1.1 (May 1866): 1–11; 1.2 (June 1866): 7–91.

Hillers, Delbert R. *The Anchor Bible Lamentations.* New York: Doubleday, 1972.

Holst-Warhaft, Gail. *Dangerous Voices: Women's Laments and Greek Literature.* New York: Routledge, 1992.

Irwin, John T. *Doubling and Incest/Repetition and Revenge: A Speculative Reading of Faulkner.* Baltimore: Johns Hopkins UP, 1975.

Landy, Francis. "Lamentations." *The Literary Guide to the Bible.* Ed. Robert Alter and Frank Kermode. Cambridge: Harvard UP, 1987. 329–34.

Matthews, John T. *The Play of Faulkner's Language.* Ithaca: Cornell UP, 1982.

———. "The Rhetoric of Containment in Faulkner." *Faulkner's Discourse: An International Symposium.* Ed. Lothar Hönnighausen. Tübingen: Max Niemeyer Verlag, 1989. 55–67.

Miller, J. Hillis. "The Two Relativisms: Point of View and Indeterminacy in the Novel *Absalom, Absalom!*" *Relativism in the Arts.* Ed. Betty Jean Craige. Athens: U of Georgia P, 1983. 148–70.

Mintz, Alan. *Hurban: Responses to Catastrophe in Hebrew Literature.* New York: Columbia UP, 1984.

Moreland, Richard C. *Faulkner and Modernism: Rereading and Rewriting.* Madison: U of Wisconsin P, 1990.

Morris, Wesley, with Barbara Alverson Morris. *Reading Faulkner.* Madison: U of Wisconsin P, 1989.

Mortimer, Gail L. *Faulkner's Rhetoric of Loss: A Study in Perception and Meaning.* Austin: U of Texas P, 1983.

Page, Walter Hines. *Raleigh, North Carolina State Chronicle.* 4 Feb. 1886; 11 Feb. 1886.

Parker, Robert. *Miasma: Pollution and Purification in Early Greek Religion.* Oxford: Clarendon P, 1983.

Parker, Robert Dale. *Faulkner and the Novelistic Imagination.* Urbana: U of Illinois P, 1984.

Pitavy, François. "The Gothicism of *Absalom, Absalom!*: Rosa Coldfield Revisited." *A Cosmos of My Own: Faulkner and Yoknapatawpha, 1980.* Ed. Ann J. Abadie and Doreen Fowler. Jackson: UP of Mississippi, 1981. 199–226.

———. "Some Remarks on Negation and Denegation in William Faulkner's *Absalom, Absalom!*" *Faulkner's Discourse: An International Symposium.* Ed. Lothar Hönnighausen. Tübingen: Max Niemeyer Verlag, 1989. 25–32.

Ricoeur, Paul. *The Symbolism of Evil.* Trans. Emerson Buchanan. Boston: Beacon P, 1968.

Ross, Stephen. "Faulkner's *Absalom, Absalom!* and the David Story: A Speculative Contemplation." *The David Myth in Western Literature.* Ed. Raymond-Jean Frontain and Jan Wojcik. West Lafayette: Purdue UP, 1980. 136–53, 203–4.

Seremetakis, C. Nadia. *The Last Word: Women, Death and Divination in Inner Mani.* Chicago: U of Chicago P, 1992.

Slatoff, Walter J. *Quest for Failure: A Study of William Faulkner.* Ithaca: Cornell UP, 1960.

Snead, James. *Figures of Division.* New York: Metheun, 1986.

Sundquist, Eric J. *Faulkner: The House Divided.* Baltimore: Johns Hopkins UP, 1983.

Vickery, Olga. *The Novels of William Faulkner: A Critical Interpretation.* Baton Rouge: Louisiana State UP, 1964.

Westermann, Claus. *Lamentations: Issues and Interpretation.* Trans. Charles Muenchow. Minneapolis: Fortress P, 1994.

Williamson, Joel. *William Faulkner and Southern History.* Oxford: Oxford UP, 1994.

Woodward, C. Vann. *Origins of the New South 1877–1913.* Vol. 9 of *A History of the South.* Ed. Wendell Holmes Stephenson and E. Merton Coulter. 10 vols. Baton Rouge: Louisiana State UP, 1951.

CHAPTER 7

"SO I, WHO HAD NEVER HAD A WAR ..."
WILLIAM FAULKNER, WAR, AND THE MODERN IMAGINATION

Donald M. Kartiganer

So I, who had never had a sister and was fated to lose my daughter in infancy, set out to make myself a beautiful and tragic little girl.

—William Faulkner, "An Introduction to *The Sound and the Fury*"

There were three wars at work in the mind of William Faulkner: the American Civil War, World War I, and World War II. He did not fight in any of them, nor did he write about them, if by writing we mean an account, factual or fictional, of what occurs or is likely to occur during military engagement. They are all there—in novels, short stories, essays, and letters—and yet not there: wars fantasized as reckless adventure, wars recalled as part of a legendary past or foretold as apocalyptic future, wars that have paused and are about to begin again, but never the plausible, violent reality of actual battle.

Originally published in *Modern Fiction Studies,* Autumn 1998.

With very few exceptions, war for Faulkner is an occasion for gesture, a decisive event that—in the fighting of it, in the telling and the fullest understanding of it—demands something other than concrete involvement: a figurative rather than a literal action, dramatic rather than strategic effect, the miming of battle. As for territory won or lost, casualties suffered or inflicted, prisoners captured, planes downed—these are not the purpose (although occasionally they are the result) of military action in Faulkner. What counts is the manner of engagement, however irrelevant to the war's ultimate outcome, which usually turns out to be of small importance. "What the devil were you folks fighting about, anyhow," asks Old Bayard of a Civil War veteran in *Flags in the Dust*, and Will Falls answers, "damned ef I ever did know" (252).

Surrounding Faulkner's accounts of his own experience in war and the portrayal of it in his fiction is a curious, in some ways unique, gathering of literary, regional, and biographical contexts: late nineteenth-century literary movements in France and Great Britain; shifts in the American Southern cultural background, ranging from a paradox in turn-of-the-century Southern manners to the historical and psychological factors that were to contribute to the Southern Renaissance in the 1920s; and, finally, the specific crises of Faulkner's individual and family history. Together they comprise a series of modernist movements that pervade Faulkner's fiction, assuming a distinctive resonance in his treatment of the wars that preoccupy him throughout his career.[1]

Faulkner's introduction to literary modernism began under the tutelage of his fellow townsman, Phil Stone, in 1914 and continued more or less for over a dozen years. Unusually well read from the ancients to the modern poets, Stone supplied Faulkner with books and journals containing the work of the writers and theorists who were in the process of creating the modern age: Swinburne, Housman, Yeats, Pound and the Imagists, Eliot and Joyce, Frazer, Croce, Clive Bell.

Of particular importance to Faulkner as a poet—originally his preferred literary mode—were the French Symbolists, whom, like many of his British and American contemporaries, he probably first encountered in Arthur Symons's *The Symbolist Movement in Literature*, the 1919 edition of which also contained a large selection of poetry in English translation.[2] Here he could read not only the poems he would himself translate as some of his earliest published work, but also Symons's summary and interpretation of the theories lying behind French symbolism. Faulkner seems to have been particularly impressed by Symons's discussion of Mallarmé, which emphasized his commitment to the suggestiveness of allusion rather than to the detailed, realistic account of scene or situation:

To evoke, by some elaborate, instantaneous magic of language, without the formality of an after all impossible description. . . . Remember his principle: that to name is to destroy,
to suggest is to create. Note, further, that he condemns the
inclusion in verse of anything but, "for example, the horror of
the forest, or the silent thunder afloat in the leaves; not the
intrinsic, dense wood of the trees." (Symons 195–96)[3]

In 1955, during an interview at the Nagano seminar in Japan when
he was asked to describe his "ideal woman," Faulkner responded,
apparently recalling these lines of Mallarmé:

Well, I couldn't describe her by color of hair, color of eyes,
because once she is described, then somehow she vanishes.
That the ideal woman which is in every man's mind is evoked
by a word or phrase or the shape of her wrist, her hand. . . .
And every man has a different idea of what's beautiful. And
it's best to take the gesture, the shadow of the branch, and
let the mind [that is, the reader's mind] create the tree. (*Lion*
127–28)[4]

Reading elsewhere in Symons, Faulkner would have come across
what would be regarded as some of the central statements of modern poetry: "Description is banished that beautiful things may be
evoked, magically; the regular beat of verse is broken in order that
words may fly, upon subtler wings" (Symons 8), and this passage
from Mallarmé: "I say: a flower! and out of the oblivion to which my
voice consigns every contour . . . musically arises, idea, and exqui-
site, the one flower absent from all bouquets" (qtd. in Symons 199).
    Explicit here and in Symons's discussion generally is the sense
of an alchemical magic and miraculism in symbolist poetry that the
High Modernists, and especially their later New Critical interpreters,
found compelling: part of what distinguished the language of poetry
from the words of the tribe and the truths of literature from those
truths available to the more common uses of language.[5] A significant aspect of the current reappraisal of modernism is a reconsideration of the French Symbolists, Mallarmé in particular, which abandons magic, what Symons referred to as "that spiritualising of the
word . . . that confidence in the eternal correspondences between
the visible and the invisible universe, which Mallarmé taught" (202–
3). Such theorists as Michel Foucault and Julia Kristeva continue to
regard the Symbolists—especially Mallarmé—as responsible for
what Kristeva terms a "revolution in poetic language," based on
their quite secular attempt to reduce the control of established linguistic and social constraint over the word. The present emphasis is

not on an Absolute or One, capable of being sounded by the poetic word, but rather on the notion that symbolist poetry restores to language a solidity, a corporeality that allows it to resist its role as a transparent vehicle of external meaning and achieve some degree of autonomous presence.

For Foucault, the upshot is nothing less than "the reappearance . . . of the living being of language," an unexpected reversal of the principle of "representation" that dominates ideas of language in the seventeenth and eighteenth centuries: "all language had value only as discourse. The art of language was a way of 'making a sign'—of simultaneously signifying something and arranging signs around that thing; an art of naming" (43). In the nineteenth century, by means of "suggestion" rather than precise naming, literature recovers for language a thickness of being that it had sacrificed to its representational function, giving up its own substantiality in order to transmit a significance not inherently its own. In its insistent remoteness from the materiality of "the intrinsic, dense wood of the trees," literature frees itself from a complete, totalizing sign system, within which the word is the passive servant of its referent. According to Foucault, literature "leads language back from grammar to the naked power of speech, and there it encounters the untamed, imperious being of words" (300).[6]

Kristeva's version of the Symbolist revolution focuses on Mallarmé's use of language so as to reveal more fully what she calls its semiotic force. The semiotic, an energy linked to Freudian primary processes and which exists prior to the formation of the subject, ultimately joins with the Lacanian "symbolic" (which functions virtually in opposite ways from the poetry of the Symbolist movement) to form "the *signifying process* that constitutes language" (*Revolution* 24). Within that union the semiotic, in its articulated form of a *chora*—an articulation Kristeva describes as "essentially mobile and extremely provisional" (*Revolution* 7)—can assume a creative, revisionary role. While avoiding the psychosis that results from a total resistance to the formation of the Symbolic Order, the semiotic modality—particularly "in so-called poetic practice" (62)—can enact a transgression, a "breach" of the symbolic. Whatever its disruption of the socially, ideologically constrained order of the symbolic, however, the poetic "maintains a *signification*. . . . All its paths into, indeed valorizations of, pre-symbolic semiotic stases, not only require the ensured maintenance of this signification but also serve signification, even when they dislocate it" (65). The result is not the abandonment of meaning or that Symbolic Order which insists on it, but a renewal, a pluralization of meaning.

Central to Kristeva's focus on language—"meaning not as a sign-system but as a *signifying process*"—is her emphasis on a semiotic and symbolic in continual tension, energy at once released and articulated, "constrained by the social code yet not reducible to the language system" ("System" 28). The practice of signification involves "the acceptance of a symbolic law together with the transgression of that law for the purpose of renovating it" (28–29).

Language, in other words, because of the necessary relationship between the semiotic and the symbolic, remains an agent of possible revisionary signification within the context of the various constraints of grammar, society, and the paternal law. The transgressive nature of the semiotic, which Mallarmé invokes by his flight from precise naming to suggestion, has the power to renovate the symbolic; the semiotic remains possessed of what Kristeva calls a "negativity—drive-governed, but also social, political and historical—which rends and renews the social code" ("System" 33). Whatever the extremity of some of Mallarmé's lyrics, in which the word seems to strive for complete self-referentiality, in his theory, poetic language ultimately reengages the world. Poetry "remakes an entire word, new, unknown to the language, and as if magical, attains this isolation of speech" (Symons 200); but, as *"Crise de Vers"* continues, *"en même temps que la réminiscence de l'objet nommé baigne dans une neuve atmosphère* [at the same time the recollection of the object named bathes in a new atmosphere]" (Mallarmé 368). Literature recreates the world of the real through the "suggestion" that has seemed to reject it.

The impact of Mallarmé and the French symbolists on Faulkner was to coincide with attitudes he derived from other sources. Chief among these were the historical, social, and psychological conditions that belonged to him by virtue of his birth and upbringing in the South at the beginning of the twentieth century.

In 1906, in *The Independent*, a New York weekly, there appeared an article by Mrs. L. H. Harris entitled "Southern Manners," exploring the role of dramatic gesture in the social behavior of contemporary white Southerners. Allusion, Harris insists, is the Southerners' central bodily and verbal currency, for they are caught, particularly the male, in the condition of being "himself and his favorite forefather at the same time" (322).[7] They inhabit "two characters . . . one which condemns us, more or less downtrodden by facts to the days of our own years, and one in which we tread a perpetual minuet of past glories" (321–22). The condition to which Harris refers is the familiar one of the post-Reconstruction, Southern white man, Lost-Cause ridden and suffering what Faulkner would later call, while describing Percy Grimm in *Light in August*, "the terrible tragedy of having been born not alone too late but not late enough to have escaped first hand knowledge of the lost time" (*Light* 450).

The heart of Southern manners for Harris is the need to exist in the discrepancy between Southern past (or at least what Southerners take to be Southern past) and Southern present, a need that calls for theatrical gesture, the adoption of a "pose . . . [behind which] he sits and watches the effect of his own mannerisms with all the shrewdness of a dramatic critic. . . . [H]e feels the part, sees himself in the eyes of the other and enjoys the performance as much as if he were himself observing a good actor. And he is always a good actor; every Southern man and woman must be that" (Harris 322). In other words, the Southerner acts out, in full consciousness, a theatrical imitation of inherited social codes—with all the differences that theater requires: "[W]e carry our sword next to our manners, not literally, but figuratively—we have been compelled to substitute much that is figurative for what was once literal in our conduct" (322). And yet that "figurative" behavior must continue to convey the power of its former literal expression. "Nothing is more offensive to Southern men," Harris continues, "than to intimate that every man-jack of them is not as dangerous today as when his favorite ancestor wore ruffles, knee buckles and a sword tied in his sash" (324). In the exchange of the literal and the figurative nothing need be lost; men must "preserve their honor" by practicing—and perhaps all the more perfectly for the empty scabbard at the hip—what Harris calls the "sword-point manner" (324). Mallarméan "suggestion" becomes a discipline of "gesture," in which the "intrinsic, dense wood" of violence is performed in bloodless pantomime.

The gesture need not be empty, a mere reference to another, more powerful form of behavior that is no longer feasible. Rather, it is a "new word," a revisionary act that accomplishes a comparable but not identical effect. Allusion has acquired a self-sufficiency beyond nostalgic representation: "Thus the Southern man continues to resent an insult with a challenge or the threat of one. But he never really fights a duel. It would be a scandal and an outrage for the friends of the prospective belligerents to allow them to go this far" (Harris 323).

Harris's evocation of the Southerner who is "himself and his favorite forefather at the same time" captures on the social level the divided condition that Allen Tate, on the literary level, refers to decades later as a "double focus, a looking two ways" (*Memoirs* 33). For Tate the double focus characterized the generation of Southern intellectuals of which Faulkner, born in 1897, was such a prominent member. "After the war the South again knew the world," Tate recalls in 1942, "but it had a memory of another war. With us, entering the world once more meant not the obliteration of the past but a heightened consciousness of it" (32–33). One of the two ways a Southerner looked was backward to the past of the Old South, which by 1900 had evolved into a complex mix of fact and myth. Young Southerners had come to regard it as an era of tranquility and elegance, an agrarian civilization of aristocratic refinement and high-mindedness, its slave economy either ignored or more or less justified by its alleged benevolence: all in all, an exemplary mode of existence which, moreover, had defended itself in the War between the States with extraordinary heroism and sacrifice.

The other way they looked was forward to a new freedom that was exhilarating precisely because it threatened everything that the previous age considered to be of lasting value. This was the modernist, urban, industrial, free-market world of intellectual as well as financial speculation, a world of universal questioning, fathered, in Paul Ricoeur's term, by the "masters of suspicion" (213)—Marx, Nietzsche, and Freud—and marked by a new order of economic, social, and aesthetic movements, all of which were determined, one way or the other, to, in Pound's phrase, "make it new."

For Faulkner's Southern generation the traditional and the modern clashed powerfully, even traumatically; the two perspectives not only looked in opposite directions, they looked at each other, and with equally subversive effect. On the one hand, under modernist probing, the Old South revealed its flaws: a glaring inequality among classes, the crude origins and highly questionable rise of the so-called planter "aristocracy," the squandering, irresponsible behavior of that planter class both in peacetime and in war, and a system of chattel slavery whose fundamental inhumanity was undeniable. On the other hand, to a traditional Southern perspective, modernism seemed to be, economically, the victory of Northern industry and its rampant materialism, and culturally, a revolutionary stance without a program, one that raised questions but gave few answers, exchanging a flawed but stable order for chaos.

For Southern writers the competing visions of the Old South and the modern world could become a fresh version of what Tate regarded as the most harrowing, yet aesthetically fertile, historical examples of cultural conflict: the clash of feudalism and the Reformation on the eve of the Elizabethan Age; and the clash of Puritanism and transcendental individualism on the eve of the American Renaissance. At these moments, as with the Southern Renaissance about to begin, there occurred what Tate called that "curious burst of intelligence that we get at a crossing of the ways" (*Essays* 583).

The choice for the Southerner seemed to be either, on the one hand, a single-minded commitment to the Old or New South—that is, a life of principled yet impotent nostalgia or one of vital yet vulgar materialism—or, on the other hand, clear-eyed acceptance of the conflict itself, that is, the double focus as the necessary stance of the fully aware individual. "Looking two ways" could be a psychological torment, even a form of generational neurosis: to harbor two utterly opposed ego ideals at the same time. And yet, as Tate was keenly aware, it could also be the painful provocation for the most comprehensive thinking and the greatest writing: "the perfect literary situation" (*Essays* 292). The writer caught up in this conflict yearned for the past, yet was morally troubled by it; embraced the excitement of the new, yet feared it; was drawn in opposing directions and could resolve them, or at least address them, more comprehensively in language than in life.

The Southern version of modernism thus contains a unique dialectic: not merely the tension between old and new central to the language of any modernism, but one that compels the new, to a greater extent than usual, to inscribe itself within the forms, the received conventions, of the old. One of the results of that need, at least in the case of Faulkner, is to apply the Mallarméan credo of suggestion and allusion to a kind of theatrical historicism: a "gestural" mode of behavior and writing in which one's acts and one's words define themselves as the repetition of an older cultural code still present, yet no longer viable—a code to be acknowledged, indeed faithfully performed, but as a form of allusion, in the half-parody of pantomime. However faithful the performance, the effect is to rewrite the code so that gesture becomes bodied with meanings its model never dreamed of, becomes the new word, "unknown to the language," that alters everything.

War in Faulkner's life and fiction is one of his central points of entrance into this cultural and aesthetic network of gesture and indirection. The story of his war experiences—which is essentially the story of his imaginative reconstruction of those experiences—has been well told by his biographers, although perhaps not always with the humor that it deserves and may have been designed in part to elicit, or with awareness of that reconstruction as a kind of representative cultural text, one of the ways Faulkner had of being "himself and his favorite forefather at the same time." As a Southerner born in 1897, and as the great grandson of William C. Falkner, a decorated officer in the Civil War, Faulkner never ceased to regard war as a kind of quintessential experience for men, yet one that always seemed to have a strong aesthetic component: war as the epitome of Keatsian oxymoron, filled, as he would later put it in *Flags in the Dust*, with "glamorous fatality" and "needless and magnificent violence" (94).

As David Minter was the first to point out, Faulkner's inclination to theatricality took the form of his incessant role-playing. He presented himself to the world in a series of impersonations, variously playing the parts of the English Dandy, the bohemian poet, the town bum, the Southern aristocrat, the ex-bootlegger and gunrunner, the romantic suitor, the cynical father of illegitimate children, and eventually the hard-working farmer who happened to do some writing on the side. (See also Grimwood 17–21.) But his greatest role, the one he played the longest and most consistently, and which represents his deepest personal involvement in the clash of Old South and modernist forces, is that of the World War I aviator. Within this masquerade Faulkner not only invoked the Southern nostalgia for heroic action; he also introduced, through comic exaggeration, an element of parody, as if he were at once reenacting and ridiculing the bold deeds that were a crucial part of the folklore surrounding the Civil War. That is to say, in performing verbally what was already a mythologized inheritance—claiming, of course, his poses were authentic—he also began the literary act of revising both the myth and its meaning: as Kristeva puts it, to "rend . . . and renew . . . the social code" ("System" 33).

When the United States entered World War I in April 1917, Faulkner was not yet twenty years old, and, according to the Selective Service Act of May 1917, still not eligible to serve without his parents' permission. Subsequent events, however, indicate that Faulkner's ultimate failure to see active duty in the war was not merely the result of parental concern. Reading about the bizarre measures he and his partner in fantasy, Phil Stone, concocted in their attempts to get to "the show," one gets the impression that Faulkner's romantic requirements for war largely ruled out any actual involvement in it.

From the outset, Faulkner made it clear that he had no intention of merely enlisting in the army as a private. Apparently more important than his actual participation in the war was the manner of that participation: he wanted to go as his great grandfather had gone to the Civil War, as an officer, and even more, as an aviator. As eventually he would supply himself with a wholly apocryphal war record, Faulkner seems also to have fabricated tales even of his attempts to enlist as well as of his eventual experiences in pilot training school. Presumably concerned about minimum height and weight requirements, he claimed that before appearing at the United States Army's Signal Corps recruiting station he ate as many bananas and drank as much water as he could, on the grounds that the bananas, in combination with water, would swell, adding bulk to his relatively small stature. Evidently the strategem didn't work, yet, according to Joseph Blotner, Army Air Service records contain no evidence that Faulkner ever tried to enlist, nor do they specify any height and weight requirements (60).

In 1918, having joined Phil Stone in New Haven, where the latter was at Yale working on his second law degree, both Faulkner and Stone decided to try for the British or Canadian services— Faulkner for the RAF, Stone for the Royal Artillery—by passing themselves off (quite unnecessarily) as Englishmen. They began to practice English accents and to assemble enough documentation of their British birth, Stone would later say, "to have put us in Leavenworth for the rest of our lives" (Snell 107). Using a stolen notary public seal, Faulkner became a native of Finchley, in the county of Middlesex, born in 1898 rather than 1897, complete with a sterling character reference from someone named the Reverend Edward Twimberly-Thorndyke. Faulkner's new English mother, oddly enough, turned out to be living in, of all places, Oxford, Mississippi. Apparently Faulkner's family romance had its limits.

Despite his elaborate credentials, however—at least according to a story he told his younger brother John—when Faulkner finally presented himself at the RAF recruiting office on Fifth Avenue in New York, he was rejected as being too short; at which point, "Bill got mad and told them he was going to fly for someone and he guessed if they didn't need him the Germans would take him. They needed flyers too. He asked them the way to the German embassy"—whereupon the RAF recruiter, no doubt alarmed at the prospect of Faulkner on the opposing team, relented and accepted him as an applicant for flight training in the RAF-Canada (John Faulkner 34–35).

Some of these pranks were ingenious, some were doubtless imaginary, and probably none was necessary—if Faulkner's intention were simply to get to the European front. Several Americans who would later write about the war, Hemingway and Dos Passos, of course, among them, volunteered for the Red Cross ambulance corps. A good deal closer to home was the experience of Faulkner's younger brother Jack, who, while Faulkner was bloating himself with bananas and inventing a hyphenated English vicar, quietly enlisted in the United States Marine Corps while still only eighteen years old. By September 1918 he was with American ground forces moving across France toward Germany; on November 1 he suffered serious leg and head wounds in the Argonne Forest, and eventually he returned, a decorated war hero (Murry C. Falkner 91–101).

As for William Faulkner, he was a competent RAF cadet for the five months he spent in Canada while "the biggest thing that will happen in your lifetime" took place elsewhere (*Selected Letters* 165–66).[8] He never got to Europe and it is virtually certain that he never flew a plane during his service, in fact may never have even been in a plane that was not sitting safely on the ground. But it hardly mattered. While in training, Faulkner began writing his parents of solo flights; of flying in such severe weather that "I came down the other day, so cold that I had to be lifted out of the machine, could scarcely stand" (*Thinking of Home* 133). A month after the Armistice, having been "discharged in consequence of being Surplus to R.A.F. requirements (Not having suffered impairment since entry into the Service),"[9] Faulkner purchased a British officer's uniform, complete with overseas cap, Sam Browne belt, and wings on his tunic, and returned to Oxford, where he immediately began the process of turning himself into a comic folk hero of the skies.

There had been spectacular training-camp crashes, one of which ended with his plane inside a hangar, dangling from the rafters, with Faulkner drinking from a bottle of bourbon, while all three—the plane, Faulkner, and the bourbon—were upside down. He developed a limp and complained of headaches from a steel plate in his head (oddly imitating Jack's genuine wounds). Eventually he shifted the sites of his exploits to the European theater, where he claimed he had crashed twice during aerial combat, once in France, once in Germany. By the time he was done, Faulkner had his war: the best of all wars, pure fiction.[10]

Faulkner's pose as combat veteran continued through the 1930s and World War II. Although he took pains to see to it that Malcolm Cowley would delete his fantasized exploits from the introduction to *The Portable Faulkner*, the fact is he never confessed the truth of his war experiences (Cowley 82). The brief biography he supplied to *Forum* magazine, for example, which published "A Rose for Emily" in 1930, included this information: "War came. Liked British uniform. Got commission R.F.C., pilot. Crashed. Cost British gov't £2000. Was still pilot. Crashed. Cost British gov't £2000. Quit. Cost British gov't $84.30. King said, 'Well done'" (*Selected Letters* 47).

What was he doing, and why did he feel it necessary, or useful, to maintain the pose for a lifetime? He remained a player of roles, certainly; next to silence and indifference, it was his customary way of relating to the world. But the role of combat veteran was of a different order. Beginning with the apocryphal antics of his attempts to enlist, he gradually constructed an elaborate fable miming the war tales he had heard as a boy, the romantic quality of which he probably catches accurately in *Flags in the Dust*, in his description of Aunt Jenny's story of the death of her brother Bayard in 1862: "[A]s she grew older the tale itself grew richer and richer, taking on a mellow splendor like wine; until what had been a hair-brained prank of two heedless and reckless boys wild with their own youth, was become a gallant and finely tragical focal-point" (14). Over the years, in his life and fiction, the war experience Faulkner never had became a point of reference, a history he could call upon in order to impress a lover, wish a war-bound nephew well, console a friend in grief, or make a political or moral point.

On the one hand, all of this can be seen as Faulknerian gesture, comic yet complex versions of a willingness to adopt for his life what Mallarmé had advised for poetry, to turn from the mundane details of his reality to the "silent thunder" of his fantasies. On the other hand, Faulkner also realized, possibly through Symons's example of Mallarmé, that ultimately his life and language must replenish our vision of the world, not merely dismiss it. "The world," Symons writes, "which we can no longer believe in as the satisfying material object it was to our grandparents, becomes transfigured with a new light" (202).

Faulkner's warrior pose became a not quite reconciled meeting between emulation and parody, as if he were struggling to construct a gesture with a solidity of its own: an imaginary stance that yet casts a shadow, remakes the meaning of war from within an already intact Lost-Cause oral and literary tradition. Throughout Faulkner's creation of a war record, it is important to note, he never claimed to be a genuine hero, downing enemy planes, knocking out vital targets, saving lives. On the contrary, his tales celebrate the rashness of combat rather than its strategic aims, consisting of a series of extravagant comic episodes that belong more to the genre of the tall tale than to military history or realistic war fiction.

Faulkner "in war" is a man playing at being in war. In his play he invokes the stories he had heard of the Civil War, yet performs them, simultaneously, in the opposing modes of repetition and ridicule. He is honoring the combatants of that war through the flattery of imitation and yet also mocking the mythology that had attached itself to them. He confines his own deeds to comic flamboyance, in which courage is limited to the casualness—which is also the measure of the boldness—with which he confronts danger. Faulkner's war consists of zany theatrics, gallant pratfalls: gestures so empty of serious military content that they become at once farcical and heroic. Ultimately, this double-edged performance becomes the key to the wars he described in his fiction, wars that reflect, with increasing complexity, the characteristic Southern conflict of "looking two ways."

Beyond the dual aims of imitation and parody, I suspect Faulkner believed that in some strange way he had successfully appropriated the war—not only as a civilian by eventually learning to fly but more by the sheer power of his imaginative empathy. There is a passage in *Absalom, Absalom!* which perhaps describes Faulkner's conviction that his war masquerade held a knowledge that transcended his lack of authentic experience. Quentin Compson, in his own Southern limbo of belatedness, envisions an episode from the war:

> It seemed to Quentin that he could actually see them: the ragged and starving troops without shoes, the gaunt powder-blackened faces looking backward over tattered shoulders, the glaring eyes in which burned some indomitable desperation of undefeat . . . he could see it; he might even have been there. Then he thought *No. If I had been there I could not have seen it this plain.* (154–55)

For Faulkner, even more than for Quentin—whose gestural existence cannot replace the heroic past denied him—the "real" war he had missed was an accident of time and circumstance that could hardly withstand the urgency of his need or the depth of his talent.

Faulkner's pose as combat veteran reaches its climax in two letters written during World War II. The first, written 3 April 1943, is to his nephew Jimmy Falkner, who was training as a pilot and would eventually see action in the Pacific. It combines some practical advice—if, given the source, of limited value—about foolhardiness and fear, with a by now characteristic paragraph of comic posturing that, under the circumstances, seems inappropriate at best:

> I would have liked for you to have had my dog-tag, R.A.F., but I lost it in Europe, in Germany. I think the Gestapo has it; I am very likely on their records right now as a dead British flying officer-spy.
>
> You will find something else, as you get along, which you will consider your luck. Flying men always do. I had one. I never found it again after my crack-up in '18. But it worked all right, as I am still alive. (*Selected Letters* 170)

The second letter, written 1 July 1943, is not at all comic, and its implicit claim of veteran status sinks from inappropriateness to the level of indecency. He wrote the letter to Robert Haas, his former publisher, when Haas's son, a naval torpedo-bomber pilot, was killed in action:

Bob, dear boy,

Of course you dont want letters. They dont do any good. Besides, the sympathy is already yours without letters, from any friend, and some of the pride belongs to all the ex-airmen whom time has altered into grounded old men, and some of the grief is theirs too whose blood flies in this war. My nephew, 18, is about to be posted to carrier training. He will get it too. Then who knows? the blood of your fathers and the blood of mine side by side at the same long table in Valhalla, talking of glory and heroes, draining the cup and banging the empty pewter on the long board to fill again, holding two places for us maybe, not because we were heroes or not heroes, but because we loved them. (*Selected Letters* 175)

Faulkner does not quite claim to be among the "ex-airmen," but the possibility is surely open, and a letter three years earlier to Haas clearly implies it (*Selected Letters* 125). Nor does he identify himself as hero or not-hero, but he will likely be at that long table in Valhalla, for all the world like one of his invented Sartorises, sharing the wine and talk of "glory and heroes." Was there no other prose available to him to console Haas for this terrible loss, except the fabulous language of his own self-aggrandizement? Is this bombast the sign of an astonishing insensitivity or of a shyness so deep it cannot express affection unarmed? Is he simply claiming their common blood—"the blood of your fathers and the blood of mine"? (Haas was Jewish, a fact that Faulkner had well in mind, as a letter written two days later indicates.) Or did he truly believe that he had so mastered the gestures of war that his failure to experience it hardly mattered—that he could say, with at least the authority of Quentin Compson, "*No. If I had been there I could not have seen it this plain*"? Indeed, did he believe that if he had been there, he could not have more genuinely fought it?

The move from biography to fiction is always perilous, especially when so much of the biography is also fiction. In Faulkner's case one link between the two is that war, as the violent engagement of armies or individual soldiers in what we take to be a plausible account of combat, is not only missing from the life but also rarely occurs in the fiction, virtually never in the novels (Gresset 15–16). And like his general public stance, so often characterized by impersonation, Faulkner's fictional wars are steeped in gesture.

Flags in the Dust (the original novel from which *Sartoris* was extracted and published in 1929) provides vivid scenes of both the Civil War and World War I, yet invariably they focus on acts of pure individual recklessness, as irrelevant to war as Faulkner's tales of his own experiences. Aunt Jenny's account of her brother's absurdly gallant ride behind enemy lines in order to capture a supply of anchovies from a Union officers' commissary tent—resulting in his being shot in the back by a cook—replicates itself three generations later in World War I, with Johnny Sartoris's foolish or drunken insistence on engaging in grossly uneven aerial combat with a German fighter plane. This scene, as his brother Bayard narrates it, concludes with Johnny climbing out onto the wing of his burning plane: "Then he thumbed his nose at me like he always was doing and flipped his hand at the Hun [who has just riddled his plane with bullets] and kicked his machine out of the way and jumped" (280). Such heroics signify a war essentially without pain, without blood or shattered bone, and unblemished by any mention of a cause to justify the loss of life. Their supposed glory lies in their very pointlessness: "deaths of needless and magnificent violence" (94).

In Bayard's memory, the war is a cosmic event, of gods who continue their glorious dying eternally, their exploits surviving whatever motives may have once driven them: "[H]e fell to talking of the war. Not of combat, but rather of a life peopled by young men like fallen angels, and of a meteoric violence like that of fallen angels, beyond heaven or hell and partaking of both: doomed immortality and immortal doom" (*Flags* 133).

Much of the problem with this early novel lies with its erratic tone. The novel vies between, without adequately controlling, a celebration of Old South heroics and a criticism of their irrelevance. Certainly the war scenes Bayard and Aunt Jenny narrate are both characterized by the absence of any sense of the abiding gap between the gesture and its material core. This is not a case, as Edmund Wilson put it in his early discussion of symbolism, of "metaphors detached from their subjects" (21), but of metaphors that have no subjects at all. The manner of Johnny's death does not so much remake its subject—the violence of war—or reveal its hidden truth, as simply ignore it.

A possible consequence is the collapse of Tate's double focus or Harris's subtle distinction between the literal and figurative versions of an action. *Flags in the Dust* may be an example of the Southern text that avoids the tension of "looking two ways" by committing itself wholly to a nostalgic rehearsal of an already mythologized past: gesture is all there is. Johnny's repetition of Sartoris's bravado is thus empty of the ironies of the interval between "himself and his favorite ancestor" because there is no difference between them. In Kristevan terms, gesture here is absent of the tensions of which any genuine "signifying *practice*" is made, absent of "the moment of transgression" of the Symbolic Order ("System" 29). As a result, the possibly unintended point of the novel may be that Sartoris's gesture has no meaning: it rests, as Mr. Compson says in *The Sound and the Fury*, "symmetrical above the flesh" (177).

One of the major differences between *Flags in the Dust* and *Light in August* is the latter's deep and consistent probing of a mind determined to see the virtue of war as rooted in its remoteness from any object whatsoever, a version of Kant's "purposiveness without purpose" (77). The death of Hightower's grandfather, following the burning of the Union storage depot in Jefferson, becomes *for Hightower* the height of superfluous gesture—and this is its beauty. Its status as such does not necessarily lie in the grandfather's behavior but rather in the grandson's reading of it. The point of that reading is to recreate war as a substitution of art for life and then use it as a model and justification for present behavior. Hightower's obsession with his own vision of his grandfather's death is an instance of Lost-Cause nostalgia perfectly aware of, indeed priding itself on, its irrelevance.

The raid on the Jefferson stores—based on General Earl Van Dorn's raid on Holly Springs in 1862, although placed by Hightower in 1865—was by no means a mere gesture, but an extremely effective military action.[11] Hightower's refusal to acknowledge this—like his shifting of the date to a point in time when any Southern triumph could be little more than gesture—betrays his preference for the act unmarked by strategic significance: "A handful of men . . . performing with the grim levity of schoolboys a prank so foolhardy that the troops who had opposed them for four years did not believe that even they would have attempted it. . . . Boys. Because this. This is beautiful" (*Light* 483).

Consistency being as inconsequential as fact, Hightower is not bothered by the contrary versions he has heard of his grandfather's death. In one, the grandfather is shot from his horse during the raid itself; in the other he is killed, following the raid, stealing chickens. Hightower prefers the second story (without acknowledging the contradiction) precisely because of its implausibility and its pointlessness:

> They didn't know who fired the shot. . . . It may have been a woman, likely enough the wife of a Confederate soldier. I like to think so. It's fine so. Any soldier can be killed by the enemy in the heat of battle, by a weapon approved by the arbiters

and rulemakers of warfare. Or by a woman in a bedroom. But not with a shotgun, a fowling piece, in a henhouse. (*Light* 485)

Crucial to Hightower is the fact that his own commitment to un-truth becomes a dismissal of reality commensurate with, perhaps surpassing, the act itself (which may not have occurred): "And I believe. I know. It's too fine to doubt. It's too fine, too simple, ever to have been invented by white thinking. A negro might have in-vented it. And if Cinthy did, I still believe. Because even fact cannot stand with it" (484).

The Unvanquished is a major transitional text in Faulkner's treatment of war. To be sure, the Civil War scenes of the novel are predictably far-fetched, focusing on John Sartoris's boundless ca-pacity to outwit superior Yankee forces—although his skill hardly results in any significant victories. In one episode, he escapes cap-ture on his own front porch through the ruse of pretending to be a demented old man; in another, with the help of two teenage boys, his son and a slave, he disarms and disrobes an encampment of sixty Yankee soldiers, without losing—or killing—a man.

The concluding story, however, "An Odor of Verbena," written in 1937, seriously alters Faulkner's understanding of the possibili-ties of gesture. Not a war story, "An Odor of Verbena" nevertheless climaxes in a duel in which gesture not only replaces violence, it appropriates its power—and yet without sacrificing its own meta-phoric nature. Bayard Sartoris (grandfather of Johnny's brother Bayard in *Flags in the Dust*) is determined to confront the killer of his father, John Sartoris, yet he refuses to repeat literally his boy-hood act during the Civil War of vengeance against the profiteer Grumby, which would be the behavior consistent with the prevail-ing social code. Instead, Bayard enters Redmond's office without a weapon, his unarmed presence figuring the armed, his refusal of violence becoming its theatrical equivalent. So skillful is Bayard's performance that he compels Redmond to participate in the play: Redmond misses twice with his pistol and then leaves town—the literal succumbing to the power of gesture.

What has happened is that allusion has taken on body; Bayard's unarmed stance simulates the armed, enfolds itself within the estab-lished code in order to transgress it. He remains within the classic Southern paradox of "himself and his favorite forefather at the same time," yet also writes Mallarmé's new word ("*un mot total, neuf, étranger à la langue*" (*Oeuvres* 368) ["an entire word, new, unknown to the language" (Symons 200)]). Redmond, like Bayard, may also be ready to forego violence; note that when Redmond raises his pistol, Bayard thinks, "I could see the foreshortened slant of the barrel and

I knew it would miss me" (*Unvanquished* 248). Yet when Redmond realizes that Bayard has no gun at all, not even in order to miss intentionally, he becomes aware of a new sign and is shaken by its revisionary power. He rises "with a convulsive motion . . . one arm extended as though he couldn't see and the other hand resting on the desk as if he couldn't stand alone . . . he blundered along the wall and passed me and reached the door and went through it" (249).[12]

Upon returning home, Bayard receives the same confirmation (and scolding) from Aunt Jenny that would have come from his literal violence: "'So you had a perfectly splendid Saturday afternoon, didn't you? Tell me about it.' . . . [A]nd suddenly the tears sprang and streamed down her face . . . 'Oh, damn you Sartorises! . . . Damn you! Damn you!'" (253–54). Aunt Jenny, accustomed to earlier forms of Sartoris bravado, is unable (or unwilling) to draw any distinction between pure gesture and gesture complicated with moral cause. Perhaps her anguish is justified, given the genuine risk Bayard has taken. Even in its revised form, the duel betrays Faulkner's continued attachment to the old bravado, which allows Bayard to retain the approval of the community, even as he violates—or at least seriously revises—one of its most cherished conventions.

Following *The Unvanquished*, Faulkner's representation of war shifts again. Not only does he still avoid any attempt to portray war in terms of credible military action, but also he begins to eliminate battle scenes of any sort. He takes us to a point that is virtually outside time, poised within an expanded prelude to war or a period of delay—war figured as a fantasy of postponement, as about to happen or prevented from happening, as imminent, portentous, yet almost magically forestalled, like a film image suddenly frozen on the screen.

In *Intruder in the Dust*, a memorable speech (by Gavin Stevens, spoken to his nephew Chick Mallison) invokes the moment before the tide-turning battle of the Civil War:

> For every Southern boy fourteen years old, not once but whenever he wants it, there is the instant when it's still not yet two oclock on that July afternoon in 1863, the brigades are in position behind the rail fence, the guns are laid and ready in the woods and the furled flags are already loosened to break out and Pickett himself with his long oiled ringlets and his hat in one hand probably and his sword in the other looking up the hill waiting for Longstreet to give the word and it's all in the balance, it hasn't happened yet, it hasn't even begun yet . . . (194)

Hovering above the long-settled outcome is an abiding potentiality. Knowing and fully registering the disastrous ending, "every Southern boy fourteen years old" can yet recover the exhilaration and hope that must have preceded, can harbor the double vision that gathers its power of possible reversal from the very battle it holds back:

> [I]t not only hasn't begun yet but there is still time for it not to begin against that position and those circumstances . . . yet it's going to begin, we all know that, we have come too far with too much at stake and that moment doesn't need even a fourteen-year-old boy to think *This time. Maybe this time* with all this much to lose and all this much to gain. (194–95)

With *A Fable*, Faulkner's massive World War I novel, deferral moves beyond even the complexities of Southern memory. At its center is the moral act of soldiers bringing war to a halt by refusing to mount an attack. But that deferral, despite the three-day peace that descends on the front as a result, is also no more (and no less) than gesture designed to accomplish nothing, altering neither the inevitable resumption of war nor its enduring necessity. Gesture is the refrain of *A Fable*, appropriated by those who would continue the war—and the status quo it protects—as much as by those who stop it. Thus the particular engagement halted by the mutiny was itself purely gestural, an attack calculated to fail, the regiment to be sacrificed to an undisclosed military expediency. Moreover, the second mutiny of the novel, the one inspired by the model of the first, only succeeds in bringing to a climax, and terminating, the three days of peace.

Led by the Sentry, the Runner, and the Reverend Sutterfield, a British battalion climbs out of the trenches, and begins to run, weaponless, across the battlefield, towards a unit of German soldiers which has also emerged, unarmed:

> [T]he two of them running toward each other now, empty-handed, approaching until he could see, distinguish the individual faces but still all one face, one expression, and then he knew suddenly that his too looked like that, all of them did: tentative, amazed, defenseless, and then he heard the voices too and knew that his was one also—a thin murmuring sound rising into the incredible silence like a chirping of lost birds, forlorn and defenseless too. (*Fable* 321)

But the mutiny is doomed, the men of both forces merely running toward the artillery barrages that have already been launched from both sides: "[A]nd then he knew what the other thing was even before the frantic uprush of the rockets from behind the two wires, German and British too" (321).

Of the practical pointlessness of this second mutiny the runner at least is aware. The generals of both sides, anticipating the plan, have colluded to prevent it from spreading: "Then they will shoot at us, both of them, their side and ours too—put a barrage down on all of us. They'll have to. There wont be anything else for them to do" (313). Such is the gestural quality of the action of the whole novel: the hope of men "to have done with it, be finished with it, quit of it" (317); of the Corporal to overthrow the war culture over which the Old General, the Corporal's father, presides; or, for that matter, of the Old General to tempt his son away from his martyrdom—they are all acts whose meaning has nothing to do with their realization in the world, or even the expectation of it.

And yet *A Fable* builds its theme of the irrelevant act into a vision of a potentiality that never subsides, that maintains the power of possibility even though completion is inconceivable. Faulkner accomplishes this by bringing together something of the magical quality that Symons identified in the French Symbolists—"that confidence in the eternal correspondences between the visible and the invisible universe" (203)—and the metaphysical mystery inherent in the Christian story he has chosen as the narrative core of the novel: the gesture that redeems even as it awaits fulfillment. In Karl Löwith's description of the event of Incarnation, "Invisibly, history has fundamentally changed; visibly, it is still the same . . . the time is already fulfilled and yet not consummated. . . . [E]verything is 'already' what it is 'not yet'" (Löwith 188).

If *A Fable* contains a tragic view opposite to that of the New Testament—the recognition that potential and actual redemption will never coincide—it also contains the hope implicit to the fact that they will never relax their tension: "[W]e are two articulations," the Old General says to the Corporal, "two inimical conditions . . . I champion of this mundane earth . . . you champion of an esoteric realm of man's baseless hopes and his infinite capacity—no: passion—for unfact" (*Fable* 347–48). Fact and gesture, father and son, law and mutiny, Symbolic and semiotic, "the intrinsic, dense wood of the trees" and "the silent thunder afloat in the leaves"—Faulkner balances them against each other, confirming an essential tension of his career, in this novel unwilling to advance them beyond a static equilibrium.

For the fullest account of the theme of gesture (and much else) I conclude with Faulkner's greatest novel, *Absalom, Absalom!* War in *Absalom, Absalom!* is generally peripheral to the main action: the rise of Thomas Sutpen and the ultimate destruction of his family, and the retelling of that history by four narrators in the present. Yet the novel's climactic scene takes place in an encampment of Confederate soldiers, shortly before the end of the war, when the outcome is inevitable.

Quentin and Shreve, still talking in their freezing Harvard dormitory, create the scene—the action of which has less factual support than any other in the novel—and in doing so reach the greatest point of intimacy with each other and with the two men whom they have recreated as brothers: "Because now neither of them was there. They were both in Carolina and the time was forty-six years ago, and it was not even four now but compounded still further, since now both of them were Henry Sutpen and both of them were Bon . . ." (280).

For the setting, they have chosen central North Carolina in 1865, where two warring armies have also come together, on the eve of the end of their four years of battle. Invisible but for the camp fires, the combatants are close enough to begin to talk across the coming doom that divides and unifies them:

> [T]he two picket lines so close that each could hear the challenge of the other's officers passing from post to post and dying away; and when gone, the voice, invisible, cautious, not loud yet carrying:
> Hey, Reb.
> Yah
> Where you fellers going?
> Richmond
> So are we. Why not wait for us?
> We air. (280–81)

The tragedy of scene and setting is that all the talking can only lead to one end: for Quentin and Shreve, it is their final interpretation that Charles Bon is part black and therefore had to die; for the armies, it is the culmination of the war in the South's total defeat. And yet, as Faulkner freezes the entire scene of some seven pages in the italics of the possible, there is a sense of fact faltering before the imaginary. As long as Quentin and Shreve keep recreating the past, they remain virtual brothers inventing the brotherhood of Henry and Bon. As long as the interpretive play lasts, metaphor will disarm reality; words rob time of its destiny. As long as the soldiers around the fires keep talking, the war will not come down.

It is as if Faulkner were holding back the war, holding back history, holding back the murder whose meaning he wants to explore forever, in the artist's delusion that, supremely rendered, the real will give way to gesture, the body to the imaginative power—as if what Symons called the Symbolist desire to "evade the old bondage of exteriority" (8) could achieve its complete reversal.

Within the scene the great cultural conflict of Faulkner's life and work receives its most intense depiction. Here, at the edge of ultimate defeat, is the pinnacle of Old South heroism—"*Why not wait for us? We air*"—that provided Faulkner's generation with its most daunting challenge; and yet here also emerges the novel's grandest example of modernist imaginative intervention. The narrators too late for the war nevertheless strive to explain it, join themselves to the past by bringing to bear on it meanings only the present can dare to take hold of. They take the leap no teller of the story, no actor in the story, has ever made: that the destruction of the Sutpen family, the destruction of the South, is a tragedy of race: the white man murders the black man who is his brother.

The majesty of the Symbolist dream so central to Faulkner's literary development found uncanny resonance in the Southern contexts central to his life: a war that ended more than thirty years before his birth, the war of his own time he could not experience while keeping his double consciousness intact. His response was the imaginative power that at once reflects the real and rewrites it through the gesture that, almost magically, unfolds reality's unknown possibility: demonstrating in "failed" novel after novel just how dangerous he was, how much the prose gestures of his life and his writing could perfect "the sword-point manner" that enabled him not only to possess but also to revise the reality he had only missed in ordinary time. "*No. If I had been there I could not have seen it this plain.*"

Notes:

1. See Gresset for a list of Faulkner's novels and stories (approximately twenty-five) that concern themselves with war.

2. See Kreiswirth, whose examination of Faulkner's translations of Verlaine provides convincing evidence that Faulkner consulted the 1919 edition of *The Symbolist Movement*—certainly by 1920 when the translations were published.

3. Symons's quotations are from *"Sur l'Evolution litteraire,"* an 1891 interview, and *"Crise de vers,"* written 1886–96, first published in full in 1897. Throughout this essay I use Symons's translations of Mallarmé's prose, since they are very likely the ones with which Faulkner was familiar.

4. See Minter (283n21) for a comment on the similarity of Faulkner's statement to Mallarmé.

5. See Kermode's chapter on Symons, which emphasizes the element of the occult in symbolism: "Symbols are, simply, images with this essential magical power" (Kermode 112).

6. See the discussion of Foucault in Bürger 48–54.

7. For further discussion of Harris, see Banta 208–9.

8. The quote is actually Faulkner's comment in a letter to his stepson Malcolm A. Franklin (5 December 1942), complimenting him on his desire to enlist in the service.

9. I am grateful to Panthea Reid, who provided me with a copy of Faulkner's discharge papers. Under the category "Casualties, Wounds, Campaigns, Medals, Clasps, Decorations, Mentions, etc." the papers bear the stamp "NIL."

10. See Anderson's story, "A Meeting South," based on Faulkner's supposed war injuries (103–21).

11. Combined with an action by Nathan Bedford Forrest, Van Dorn's raid on Holly Springs forced Grant—his supply lines cut—to delay his advance on Vicksburg. See McPherson 578.

12. See the discussion of this scene in Hinkle and McCoy 205. There is a similar scene in *Absalom, Absalom!*, when Sutpen "subdues" the Haitian natives: "[H]e just put the musket down and had someone unbar the door and then bar it behind him, and walked out into the darkness and subdued them, maybe by yelling louder, maybe by standing, bearing more than they believed any bones and flesh could or should" (204–5).

Works Cited

Anderson, Sherwood. "A Meeting South." *Sherwood Anderson's Notebook*. New York: Boni & Liveright, 1926. 103–21.

Banta, Martha. "The Razor, the Pistol, and the Ideology of Race Etiquette." *Faulkner and Ideology*. Ed. Donald M. Kartiganer and Ann J. Abadie. Jackson: UP of Mississippi, 1995. 172–216.

Blotner, Joseph. *Faulkner: A Biography*. New York: Random House, 1984.

Bürger, Peter. *The Decline of Modernism*. Trans. Nicholas Walker. University Park: Pennsylvania State UP, 1992.

Cowley, Malcolm. *The Faulkner-Cowley File: Letters and Memories, 1944–1962*. New York: Viking, 1966.

Falkner, Murry C. *The Falkners of Mississippi: A Memoir*. Baton Rouge: Louisiana State UP, 1967.

Faulkner, John. *My Brother Bill: An Affectionate Reminiscence*. New York: Trident, 1963.

Faulkner, William. *Absalom, Absalom! The Corrected Text*. 1936. New York: Vintage, 1990.

———. *A Fable*. New York: Random House, 1954.

———. *Flags in the Dust*. 1973. Ed. Douglas Day. New York: Vintage, 1974.

———. *Intruder in the Dust*. New York: Random House, 1948.

———. *Light in August. The Corrected Text*. 1932. New York: Vintage, 1990.

———. *Lion in the Garden: Interviews with William Faulkner 1926–1962*. Ed. James B. Meriwether and Michael Millgate. New York: Random House, 1968.

———. *Selected Letters of William Faulkner*. Ed. Joseph Blotner. New York: Random House, 1977.

———. *The Sound and the Fury. The Corrected Text*. 1929. New York: Vintage, 1990.

———. *Thinking of Home: William Faulkner's Letters to His Mother and Father, 1918–1925*. Ed. James G. Watson. New York: Norton, 1992.

———. *The Unvanquished. The Corrected Text*. 1938. New York: Vintage, 1991.

Foucault, Michel. *The Order of Things*: *An Archaeology of the Human Sciences.* 1966. New York: Vintage, 1973.

Gresset, Michel. "Faulkner's War with Wars." *Faulkner and History*. Ed. Javier Coy and Michel Gresset. Salamanca: Ediciones Universidad de Salamanca, 1986.

Grimwood, Michael. *Heart in Conflict: Faulkner's Struggles with Vocation*. Athens: U of Georgia P, 1987.

Harris, L. H. "Southern Manners." *The Independent* 9 Aug. 1906: 321–25.

Hinkle, James, and Robert McCoy. *Reading Faulkner: The Unvanquished.* Jackson: UP of Mississippi, 1995.

Kant, Immanuel. *Kritik of Judgment*. 1790. Trans. J. H. Bernard. London: Macmillan, 1892.

Kermode, Frank. *Romantic Image*. New York: Vintage, 1964.

Kreiswirth, Martin. "Faulkner as Translator: His Versions of Verlaine." *Mississippi Quarterly* 30 (1977): 429–32.

Kristeva, Julia. *Revolution in Poetic Language*. Trans. Margaret Waller. New York: Columbia UP, 1984.

———. "The System and the Speaking Subject." *The Kristeva Reader.* Ed. Toril Moi. New York: Columbia UP, 1986. 25–33.

Löwith, Karl. *Meaning in History*. Chicago: U of Chicago P, 1949.

Mallarmé, Stephane. *Oeuvres Completes*. Ed. Henri Mondor and G. Jean-Aubry. Paris: Gallimard, 1945.

McPherson, James M. *Battle Cry of Freedom: The Civil War Era.* New York: Oxford UP, 1988.

Minter, David. *William Faulkner: His Life and Work*. Baltimore: Johns Hopkins UP, 1980.

Ricoeur, Paul. *The Philosophy of Paul Ricoeur*: *An Anthology of His Work.* Ed. Charles E. Reagan and David Stewart. Boston: Beacon, 1978.

Snell, Susan. *Phil Stone of Oxford: A Vicarious Life*. Athens: U of Georgia P, 1991.

Symons, Arthur. *The Symbolist Movement in Literature*. New York: Dutton, 1919.

Tate, Allen. *Essays of Four Decades*. New York: William Morrow, 1970.
——. *Memoirs and Opinions 1926–1974*. Chicago: Swallow, 1975.
Wilson, Edmund. *Axel's Castle: A Study in the Imaginative Literature of 1870 to 1930*. New York: Scribner's, 1931.

CHAPTER 8

ACCOUNTING FOR SLAVERY
ECONOMIC NARRATIVES IN MORRISON AND FAULKNER

Erik Dussere

[A]ccounting is no longer to be regarded as a neutral device that merely documents and reports "the facts" of economic activity. Accounting can now be seen as a set of practices that affects the type of world we live in, the type of social reality we inhabit . . . the way in which we administer the lives of others and ourselves.
　　　　—Peter Miller, "Accounting as Social and Institutional Practice: An Introduction"

　　The critical pairing of Toni Morrison and William Faulkner has received a great deal of scholarly attention in the last few years, although the affinity between the two writers has long been a topic of discussion.[1] At the 1985 *Faulkner and Yoknapatawpha* conference in Mississippi, Morrison described her interest in Faulkner as a concern with writing history in the novel: "My reasons . . . for being interested and deeply moved by all his subjects had something to do with my desire to find out something about this country and

Originally published in *Modern Fiction Studies,* Spring 2001.

that artistic articulation of its past that was not available in history" (Morrison, "Faulkner" 296). In this essay, I am concerned especially with the ways in which Faulkner's and Morrison's books are constructed in relation to texts and practices which have shaped the history of slavery and its telling. I argue that both writers encounter slavery as a set of ideological, formal, and historical discourses, formed by and formulated through economic terms. Thus, the oeuvres of both writers represent crucial moments in the ongoing engagement of American—and particularly African-American—literature with what Houston Baker calls the "economics of slavery."[2] I begin with a discussion of the ledger, and of the accounting system in which it is employed, in order to open up a series of questions about the way that Faulkner and Morrison write about the movement of their characters out of slavery and how the legacies of slavery linger in the lives and actions of these characters.

It is only in the past two decades that scholars, working in the field of "critical accounting," have begun to examine the historical importance of bookkeeping not just as a commercial tool but as a social, legal, rhetorical, and narrative practice.[3] Although its development dates back at least five hundred years, the system of double-entry bookkeeping underlies any system of modern accounting, and it continues to have effects in the modern world—most notably its broad diffusion as an organizational principle in nineteenth-century American commerce. Double-entry bookkeeping provides a system by which merchants and businesses can account for the value of their holdings and transactions over a given period of time. For a brief and nontechnical explanation of the double-entry system, I defer to Mary Poovey, who writes:

> In addition to the ledger, the double-entry system consisted of an inventory, in which a merchant's stock was described in considerable detail; a memorial, which recorded complete accounts of daily business transactions; and a journal, in which the narrative accounts contained in the memorial were translated into numbers, which signified prices recorded in a single currency, the money of account. From the journal, which consisted mostly of numbers, it was but a short step to the ledger, where those numbers were simply rewritten and rearranged. ("Accommodating" 2–3)

The innovation and cornerstone of double-entry bookkeeping is the ledger. The ledger serves as the master-book in which all the transactions of the year are recorded finally, in matching columns on facing pages, one side representing credits and the other, debits.

By the time these commercial events have passed through inventory, memorial, and journal, each one has been reduced to its most concise form, most of the narrative description having been converted to numbers. In the ledger the assessment of accounts can be made quickly and easily, as it displays that the balance has been kept. This balance is the powerful and necessary fiction of the ledger; as Poovey demonstrates in her study of sixteenth-century merchants, at the end of the year an imaginary sum of money must be entered in the ledger (whether as credit or debit, depending on which is lacking) in order to force the books to balance, a practice which demonstrates the importance of the balance as a formal element. Insisting that its narrative is factual, the ledger asserts that within its pages experience has been translated into a language transparent, objective, and concise, and the visual balance of the accounts testifies that the books are honest and accurate ("Accommodating" 1–2).

The ledger's status as a book is crucial, since it highlights the relationship between double-entry accounting and writing as an institutional practice. Keith Hoskin and Richard Macve write that the ledger "turns events into writing" (68), indicating that it is specifically a narrative form, a means of organizing past occurrences into a particular framework. Accounting is, above all, a discursive act; as James Aho notes, an account "can be a descriptive reckoning of an act, a systematic explanation of the act, or a justification for it" (21). The complete account is concerned with telling or narrating an event or action, with all the descriptive, explanatory, and ethical elements that the process of narration entails.

The ledger, then, is a written mode of narrating past events, and like any mode of narrative writing it is defined by certain generic characteristics. Within the linked cluster of figural practices that define the ledger as a form of narrative, the central idea is that of balance. The first assumption of the double-entry system is that, at the end of the day, at the moment of reckoning, the books will be balanced, which contributes to the ledger's claim to represent events objectively. Poovey argues that this characteristic of the ledger is central to the creation of "natural laws"—and, ultimately, the creation of the "modern fact"—the social constructs which present themselves as natural and logical: "[L]awfulness could be so privileged only because of the development of representational systems that made phenomena that might otherwise be viewed as incommensurate seem to be alike in some fundamental way. . . . [T]he development of [double-entry bookkeeping] permitted early modern English merchants to conceptualize experiences that were heterogeneous by nature as comparable in kind ("Accommodating"

1–2).[4] This assertion of equivalency, or "quantification of qualities," is crucial: speaking primarily in numbers and abbreviations, the ledger asserts its language to be both objective and transparent, and in that language renders all things comparable since each can be assigned a financial value in the form of a numeric sign. The assumption of objective transparency masks the narrative work that is necessary in order to perform this quantification of qualities; the appearance of accuracy becomes valuable, while eloquence, which fails to disguise the fact that it is a form of rhetoric, is perceived as suspect. By contrast, numeric representation and brevity, the style of no apparent style, become the very model for what is considered factual, and thus truthful. These qualities form the basis for what I will call the discourse of the ledger.

Poovey points out that the result of this formal logic is to assert and justify—while effacing the assertion and justification of—an autonomous and law-governed domain known as "the market" ("Accommodating" 15–17). Rendering all experience that falls outside of exchange inessential, the double-entry style naturalizes the practice of commerce. Book of books, the ledger implies the ethicality of commerce and also provides a model for justice and moral practice. As a narrative of past events, the ledger insists not only that those events have been recorded accurately and honestly, but that they have literally been "done justice," that the form in which those events have been recorded and displayed ensures a just and balanced conclusion. Thus accounting posits the economic domain of the market as ethical and, indeed, as a model for justice, a paradigm of right and proper action.

The ledger's logic takes on a special significance for America in the nineteenth century, and in particular for the institution of slavery. Hoskin and Macve argue that despite the double-entry system's early modern origins, it is only in nineteenth-century America that accounting takes on its modern significance, as double-entry bookkeeping becomes broadly diffused and institutionalized. Arguing that this diffusion constitutes an epistemic shift, Hoskin and Macve trace accounting's new focus on "productivity, performativity, and profitability . . . an approach which simultaneously analyzed both financial and *human* performativity, rendering the interrelated but separable values of products and persons jointly calculable" (80). If the ledger implies an autonomous rule-governed market, at the moment of its diffusion the ledger makes those rules applicable generally for the governing of people, so that one's selfhood becomes linked to one's place within the economic sphere: "accounting . . . has become one particularly privileged way of measuring and restructuring man as the 'calculable person'" (70).

In this nineteenth-century American context, slavery provides a crucible in which the economic analysis of narrative takes on special urgency. The epistemological foundation of slavery is the ability to see other human beings as property to be bought and exchanged and recorded in the account book, the transformation of people into monetary value. Slavery is in fact predicated upon the joint calculability of persons and products. Within the slave system, the ledger's capacity to posit equivalency, to assert the likeness of unlike things within the universal language of financial value, is indispensable. Slavery insists precisely upon the equivalency of humans and animals, humans and objects; that equivalency is at the heart of the slave system and the violence perpetrated by that system against its victims, the epistemic violence from which the most contentious legacies of slavery flow. It is on this ground that Morrison and Faulkner create their respective fictional engagements with the economics of slavery. Encountering this economics through the representative figure of the ledger, itself a narrative form, both authors are forced to alter and recreate the form and style of their narratives in order to articulate their very different responses to the movement of African-Americans from slavery into the economic sphere.

The centerpiece of *Go Down, Moses*, "The Bear," is also in many ways the central text in Faulkner's collected works, and it is certainly the text in which he copes most explicitly with the idea of the ledger and its relationship to the Southern slave system. At twenty-one, Ike McCaslin inherits the family plantation, and as he reads the family ledgers that record the plantation's accounts through the years, his inheritance becomes more complicated and burdensome. This scenario introduces the narrative function of accounting: because the account books record what has been bought and sold on the McCaslin property, they contain a disjunctive but essential history of the slaves who have lived and died there. Through careful reading, Ike learns with creeping horror that his grandfather Carothers McCaslin first raped one of his slaves, Eunice, and had a child by her, then eventually raped that child—his daughter, his slave—and had a child by *her*. Although the ledgers are tools of a system that converts humans into property, they are also the only historical record of the McCaslin slaves: "a chronological and much more comprehensive though doubtless tedious record than he would ever get from any other source, not alone of his own flesh and blood but of all his people, not only the whites but the black one too" (268).[5]

For Faulkner, Ike's story is paradigmatic; the history of the McCaslin family and their slaves—the subject both of the ledgers and of *Go Down, Moses*—stands in for the history of the South itself. The ledger with its parallel columns is a chronicle which was a whole land in miniature, which multiplied and compounded was the entire South . . . that slow trickle of molasses and meal and meat, of shoes and straw hats and overalls, of plowlines and collars and heel-bolts and buckheads and clevises, which returned each fall as cotton— the two threads frail as truth and impalpable as equators yet cable-strong to bind for life them who made the cotton to the land their sweat fell on. (293–94)

The story that the ledger tells is not limited to the grand horror of Old Carothers McCaslin's rape and incest; the everyday items listed here provide the contours of the lives of the slaves: what they ate, what they wore, the tools of the work they were forced to perform. As Ike reads on, the slaves themselves "took substance and even a sort of shadowy life with their passions and complexities too as page followed page and year; all there, not only the general and condoned injustice and its slow amortization but the specific tragedy which had not been condoned and could never be amortized" (265–66). Faulkner suggests the extent to which the ledger books provide a model for justice through the lens of commerce, by mingling discourses of justice and debt: "injustice" must be "amortized." As historical documents, the account books provide a connection between past and present, affirming the role of the slaves in the making of the South, even as Faulkner's novel extends this insight by tracing the roots and branches of the McCaslin interracial family tree, a genealogy that stands in for the history of America itself.

Knowing *what* the ledger records, we are forced to return to the question of *how* it tells the story. In *Go Down, Moses*, the ledger appears not only as a figure but as an alternative narrative of events. The work of Faulkner's text is hermeneutic: for Ike and his cousin Cass Edmonds the ledgers are historical texts of slavery, and their argument over the interpretations of these texts becomes the occasion for a larger dispute over the nature of property. But this interpretive frame is also an alternative narrative of events in that Faulkner relates the McCaslin history in the ledger's terms and in his own as well. As Ike talks to Cass, he turns over the pages of the plantation's ledger that are photographically imprinted on his memory. In this way we are actually introduced to the discourse of the ledger, its dry descriptions and curt cadences, the eccentric abbreviations used by Ike's father and uncle, the flattening of experience into figures, dates, and notations. These are the characteristics Poovey attributes to the ledger, the "quantification of qualities" by which human experience is translated into a language of numerical worth.

There is a parodic edge to Faulkner's use of the ledger form here, an implicit suggestion that the language of accounting is ill suited to the work of representing and understanding the enormous complexity of history. These passages recall the section of *Absalom, Absalom!* in which Shreve imagines a cynical and opportunistic lawyer's description of the events of the novel recorded in a ledger:

> Today Sutpen finished robbing a drunken Indian of a hundred miles of virgin land, val. $25,000. At 2:31 today came up out of swamp with final plank for house. val. in conj. with land 40,000. 7:52 p.m. today married. Bigamy threat val. minus nil. unless quick buyer. (301)

References to subjects such as the "drunken Indian" or the "Bigamy threat" let us know that Faulkner is working in a parodic register, asserting the absurdity of representing or mediating human passions and relationships in terms of monetary value and accounting. Such passages indict the ledger as a reductive and amoral form of narrative, but the fact that it has such a privileged role in these books testifies to the power and persistence of that narrative mode.

In the fourth section of "The Bear," Faulkner highlights the moral and formal inadequacy of accounting language by juxtaposing the curt official language of the ledger with his longest, most baroque, most outraged and emotive sentences. Consider this passage concerning one of the McCaslin slaves:

> *Thucydus Roskus @ Fibby Son born in Callina 1779. Refused 10acre peace fathers Will 28 Jun 1837 Refused Cash offer $200. dolars from A.@ T. McCaslin 28 Jun 1837 Wants to stay and work it out*
> and beneath this and covering the next five pages and almost that many years, the slow, day-by-day accruement of the wages allowed him and the food and clothing—the molasses and meat and meal, the cheap durable shirts and jeans and shoes and now and then a coat against rain and cold—charged against the slowly yet steadily mounting sum of balance (and it would seem to the boy that he could actually see the black man, the slave whom his white owner had forever manumitted by the very act from which the black man could never be free so long as memory lasted, entering the commissary, asking permission perhaps of the white man's son to see the ledger-page which he could not even read, not even asking for the white man's word, which he would have had to accept for the reason that there was absolutely no way under the sun

for him to test it, as to how the account stood . . .) on to the double pen-stroke closing the final entry:

3 Nov 1841 By Cash to Thucydus McCaslin $200. dolars Set Up blaksmith in J. Dec 1841 Dide and burid in J. 17 feb 1854 Eunice Bought by Father in New Orleans 1807 $650. dolars. Marrid to Thucydus 1809 Drownd in Crick Cristmas Day 1832. (266–67)

While the rest of "The Bear" and even of *Go Down, Moses* is written in a relatively straightforward narrative style, this fourth section is in the eloquent, overfull style we call "Faulknerian," a style that strains to render the fullness and detail of history in a language that is equally rich. Faulkner offers his own narrative structures as alternatives to the succinct formulations of the ledger, the fever-pitch breathlessness of those endless sentences making an attempt to force the violence and suffering of slavery off the pages of the ledger and into the foreground. This is the language of excess, an inefficient, wasteful, inclusive prose that is the very opposite of Poovey's description of the ledger's economical style, with its strict elision of "irrelevant" information.

The resonant language Faulkner employs in this section draws directly upon the cadences of the King James Bible. *Go Down, Moses* takes its title from a slave spiritual based on the biblical story of Moses, and both the language and themes that Faulkner introduces in opposition to the language of the ledger are themselves biblical. At the core of this chapter is the understanding that God has placed a curse, a blight, upon the white South and even upon the land itself because of the sin of slavery, which Ike considers merely the logical conclusion of property ownership.[6] This bold and encompassing theme finds expression in Faulkner's excessive prose; in its grandiloquence and baroque constructions, this prose takes on a prophetic tone which is enhanced by the repetition of highly charged, vaguely anachronistic words: "relinquishment," "accursed," "bequeathing," and so on. The effect of these devices is to create an echo of both the biblical themes and of the eloquence of the King James edition,[7] as when Ike describes the divine plan:

> He made the earth first and then peopled it with dumb creatures, and then He created man to be His overseer on the earth and to hold suzerainty over the earth and the animals on it in His name, not to hold for himself and his descendants inviolable title forever, generation after generation, to the oblongs and squares of the earth, but to hold the earth mutual and intact in the communal anonymity of brotherhood. (257)

But even while this grand, expressive language is placed in counterpoint to the ledger's prosaic brevity, the two narrative modes are thematically linked.

The ledger becomes a stand-in for the Bible in "The Bear," as the two systems of order which these two books represent come to look strikingly similar. Critics have observed that the McCaslin family history, which one would expect to be recorded in the family Bible, is actually recorded on the pages of the family ledger. There are a number of references to the physical presence of the ledger as a book, sitting on the shelf, and as the conversation goes on, the ledger becomes itself the Book which records earthly doings and provides some measure of divine justice:

> To [Ike] it was as though the ledgers in their scarred cracked leather bindings were being lifted down one by one in their fading sequence and spread open . . . upon some apocryphal Bench or even Altar or perhaps before the Throne Itself for a last perusal and contemplation and refreshment of the Allknowledgeable before the yellowed pages and the brown thin ink in which was recorded the injustice and a little at least of its amelioration and restitution faded back forever into the anonymous communal original dust. (261)

This sense of a divine ledger and the final reckoning of accounts that it implies, the linking of divine justice to accounting, recalls again Shreve's parodic ledger in *Absalom, Absalom!*, in which God is referred to explicitly as "the Creditor." Both Bible and ledger assert themselves as models for justice through their insistence upon balance: the scales or columns in which events and experiences are weighed or recorded must always be made equal at the end of the day.[8]

This equivalence of biblical justice with (re)distributive justice is also present in the spiritual "Go Down, Moses," which insists that God will free the enslaved Israelites and punish the enslaving Pharaoh: "'Thus spake the lord,' Moses said / 'Let my people go / If not I'll strike your first-born dead.'" The Bible story is transformed by the spiritual into an imperative to justice in the form of repayment, but there is no material payment that can be offered for the debt owed by whites to blacks. The only true justice that can be offered, or even imagined, would come through divine intervention. Thus Ike's theological interpretations must posit a complex and long-brewing divine plan—culminating in Ike's repudiation of his inherited property—which would even things up and clear the ledger, the book which holds the record of injustice and the unrealized possibility for remuneration. Faulkner's narrative knows that this is ultimately a false hope, and so its biblical cadences become joy-lessly parodic as it thunders on, bearing in its breathless rush the always imminent promise of salvation, redemption, repayment, which can never arrive.

Describing Ike's recognition that he cannot escape his grand-father's legacy, Faulkner creates a language that runs in place, slowing time down while accelerating the flow of language:

> he couldn't speak . . . even to explain his repudiation, that which to him too, even in the act of escaping (and maybe this was the reality and the truth of his need to escape) was her-esy: so that even in escaping he was taking with him more of that evil and unregenerate old man who could summon, be-cause she was his property, a human being because she was old enough and female, to his widower's house and get a child on her and then dismiss her because she was of an inferior race, and then bequeath a thousand dollars to the infant be-cause he would be dead then and wouldn't have to pay it, than even he had feared. (294)

The overlong interrupting clause ("who . . . pay it"), which reiter-ates the history Ike is trying to escape, represents the impossibil-ity of his plan to balance the books, to offer repayment for slavery; at the moment that he tries to escape and move forward, he is dragged back by both history and grammar. "The Bear"'s darkly comic parody of the ledger is mirrored by a profound and despair-ing self-parody in which Faulkner's prose recognizes its own inabil-ity to enact or even forecast the justice that both Bible and ledger insist upon. Ike's plan to balance the books through his own repu-diation of property is ultimately an empty gesture, a failure. The land continues to be owned (by his cousin), and no one seems to benefit except perhaps Ike, who attends to his own conscience by washing his hands of all ownership.

In this irony we can read the central anxiety expressed in "The Bear." While *Go Down, Moses* is the book in which Faulkner explic-itly seeks to write about the history of black life in the South, at its heart—in "The Old People," "The Bear," and "Delta Autumn"—is the dilemma of a young white man, Ike McCaslin. Faulkner's novels dealing with race and slavery, for all their force and insight, return again and again to the analysis, the concerns and sufferings and dispossession, of white male characters. "The Bear" is a parable of the failure of white male selfhood, an identity which had tradition-ally been defined through possession, through patriarchal power exercised over women, heirs, owned things, and in particular owned slaves. For Faulkner, the engagement with economic figures, the attempt to disrupt or negate the narrative provided by the ledger, is a problem posed for his white characters as a means to deal with *their* suffering, the crushing weight of their inherited sin and debt.

As a correlative, Faulkner is unable to imagine the appropriation by blacks of the economic facts and figures that have enslaved them as a path to liberation. The disparate stories that form the novel *Go Down, Moses* are linked not only by their focus on the Mc-Caslin family tree, but also by their concern with and horror of the entry of blacks into the marketplace. Although this horror proceeds from a Faulknerian distrust of the economic sphere, there is a disturbing quality to this fear of black economic success, as if the real horror was the specter of a moneyed class of African-Americans.

The economic sphere is represented throughout the novels as inevitably corrupting, in both humorous and tragic registers, and any attempt by a Faulkner character to enter into the world of accounting, calculation, ownership of property, or accumulation of wealth as a means to social mobility results in disaster, vilification, or both. This is true for white characters as well as black. Two of Faulkner's arch-villains, Jason Compson and Flem Snopes, are also arch-accountants. Thomas Sutpen makes his life the stuff of Greek tragedy when he grasps the nature of Southern class oppression and responds by accumulating the wealth and property to make himself part of the planter class. Even Faulkner's most likable and unassuming characters are brought low when they begin to speculate, as happens to Ratliff in *The Hamlet* when he believes there is buried treasure at the Old Frenchman's place.

But for black characters, the entry into the economic sphere is a particularly disturbing corruption, because to Faulkner blacks are "pure"—as the sufferers rather than the perpetrators of slavery, they are as yet untainted by the curse that lies over the South, haunting its whites, poisoning the pores of its rich earth. Thus the economic problem articulated in the narrative of "The Bear" is played out thematically in the other stories of *Go Down, Moses*, which depict black characters who accumulate wealth, or try to, as corrupted by the endeavor. Although their historical presence and suffering must be accounted for, blacks are not to become accountants themselves; their purity is to be preserved and protected by Southern whites. In the final story, "Go Down, Moses," Samuel Beauchamp has gone north and been corrupted by wealth, which is apparently the real reason he must be executed, since he claims not to have committed the murder for which he is convicted. Asked for his occupation by the jailhouse census-taker, he replies "Getting rich too fast," and the narrative describes his elegant clothing in a detail and tone that suggest that no decent (black) man should own it (his

voice is "anything under the sun but a southern voice or even a negro voice"): "He wore one of those sports costumes called ensem-
bles in the men's shop advertisements, shirt and trousers matching
and cut from the same fawn-colored flannel, and they had cost too
much and were draped too much, with too many pleats" (369–70).

Although Faulkner's work asserts the necessity of the ledger
in constructing a revisionary historical form for representing slavery and race, it is unable to envision, or even consider, the liberatory possibilities of such a form. Because his focus remains on the
responses of white Southerners to the problems posed by the persistence of the ledger form, his narratives assert that the ledger
cannot simply be exploded or negated or parodied, but for these
white characters that persistence remains a tragedy, a curse. The
only move left open to Ike is absolute rejection, absolute repudiation of the ledger and its structures of meaning, but Faulkner's text
knows from the beginning that this rejection will fail. This is one
form of the unique and powerful tragedy Faulkner creates; his
characters have no choice but to reject the ledger, but they know
even before they reject it that it will persist.

This focus on white suffering and black innocence puts Faulkner
at odds with the critical approach to these issues articulated in
texts by Hortense Spillers and Houston Baker. Both Spillers and
Baker suggest that African-American literature itself always exists
in some relation to the "economics of slavery," but they argue that
African-American characters are always engaged in a struggle with
that economic legacy. In *Blues, Ideology, and Afro-American Literature*, Baker provides readings of classic slave narratives—by Olau-
dah Equiano (Gustavas Vassa), Frederick Douglass, and Harriet Jacobs (Linda Brent)—that foreground the narratives' appropriation of
economic terms. He notes the "ledger-like detail" Vassa employs in
his narrative, and sums it up as "a work whose protagonist masters
the rudiments of economics that condition his very life. It can also
be interpreted as a narrative whose author creates a text which inscribes these economics as a sign of its 'social grounding'" (33). In
each narrative, freedom is achieved or enabled by the author's
mastery, through refiguration, of economic tropes that have been
the source of the slave's oppression. Vassa acquires property in
order to escape being property; Douglass "*publicly* sells his voice in
order to secure *private* ownership of his voice-person"; Brent responds to the conjunction of patriarchy and property in her experience of slavery by "convert[ing] the fruit of her womb (rather than
the skill of her hand or the capital of a husbanded store) to mer-
chandise" (54). In each case, the slave narrator takes the primary
economic function of slavery—the conversion of human beings into

commodities, ledger entries—and makes it work for her or him, refiguring the master's tools in order to escape the master's house.

Spillers takes a more radical approach than Baker in suggesting that the (accounting-style) discourse of slave codes and legislation concerning slavery represents a particular "American grammar." Reading an article of Maryland slave legislation, she writes:

> we are stunned by the simultaneity of disparate items in a grammatical series: "Slave" appears in the same context with beasts of burden, *all* and *any* animal(s), various livestock, and a virtually endless profusion of domestic content from the culinary item to the book. . . . That imposed uniformity comprises the shock, that somehow this mix of named things, live and inanimate, collapsed by contiguity to the same text of "realism," carries a disturbingly prominent item of misplacement. To that extent, the project of liberation for African-Americans has found urgency in two passionate motivations that are twinned—1) to break apart, to rupture violently the laws of American behavior that make such *syntax* possible; 2) to introduce a new *semantic* field/fold more appropriate to his/her own historic movement. (79)

For Spillers, the project of social liberation for blacks takes place at least in part as an attempt to reject the economic terms of slavery, the oppressive American grammar. Within their common claim that African-American literature frequently takes the form of an engagement with the economics of slavery, Baker and Spillers provide two different models for this engagement: appropriation and refiguration on the one hand, disruption leading to a radically new semantics on the other. As we have seen, Faulkner's text negotiates these two models without actually performing either one. "The Bear" refuses appropriation, instead representing its own failure to achieve the grand and absolute rejection of the ledger for which Spillers calls. Nonetheless, Faulkner, Baker, and Spillers share a common belief that literature is the site on which the history of slavery must be represented, and that to represent its force the narrative must respond formally to the writing of the ledger.

Although Morrison's meditations on economics and liberation have none of Faulkner's grand gestures, she is engaged in a similar attempt to find the narrative form that will represent the power of these economic issues in the lives of her characters. Throughout her novels Morrison is concerned with the connection between slavery's economic structure and twentieth-century black individuals and communities, but she deals most explicitly with issues surrounding slavery in *Beloved*. Trudier Harris catalogues *Beloved*'s ubiquitous use of monetary and debt-based imagery, which, she suggests, implies a disturbing persistence of the slave past within the present moment of the narrative: "At striking jolts in the narrative, Morrison reverts our attention to the buying and selling of human beings by inserting images of monetary units to describe physical features and to convey states such as frustration and remorse. . . . Monetary images also become the language of desire in the novel, as characters express their greatest wants in financial terms" (333). Denver perceives Beloved's bottomless desire as "a palm held out for a penny" (*Beloved* 118), which recalls the Sambo coin-holder she notices at the Bodwins' house, his mouth clogged with loose change; the story of her birth "made her feel like there was a bill owing somewhere and she, Denver, had to pay it" (77); Paul D, who as a slave learned his actual dollar value, speaks of "paying for an afternoon in the coin of life to come" (129); a memory of Stamp Paid's burns him "like a silver dollar in a fool's pocket" (170).

Harris concludes that this consistent, free-floating imagery of coins and payment signals the residual, haunting presence of slavery in the lives of these ostensibly free women and men: "Ultimately, these monetary images succeed in sending mixed messages about how well the characters in *Beloved* have succeeded in transcending slavery. If black people are indeed free of slavery, then why burden them with evocations of that condition?" (338–39). Indeed, much of the novel seems to be focused on that very ambivalence, that insertion of uncertainty, that appearance of unfinished business at the moment of apparent liberation. Continuing to figure history in economic terms, Morrison's characters believe that they have, if not transcended, then at least *paid* for whatever debts they may have accumulated during slave times. Yet the book is forever insisting that the attempt to figure these debts and payments on a ledger will not hold up: at the moment when an ex-slave believes he or she has offered the final, absolute *over*payment that will settle past business, another creditor arrives at the door. Stamp Paid believes that he has settled all accounts through the "gift" of allowing his wife to be raped by their master without killing her or himself: "With that gift, he decided that he didn't owe anybody anything. Whatever his obligations were, that act paid them off" (185). But by the end of the novel, Stamp finds himself wondering if his name is appropriate after all, or if there is yet more to be required of him. It is this ongoing, outrageous impossibility of clearing one's accounts that Paul D responds to in his anguished question: "Tell me something, Stamp. . . . Tell me this one thing. How much is a nigger supposed to take? Tell me. How much?" (235). If liberation is to be had at all for ex-slaves, it is not through the paying of debts or the balancing of books; Morrison deliberately denies the notion of justice implied by such acts.

The dangers of economic logic are made clear in Morrison's own chillingly parodic version of the ledger, the chart which the slave owner, schoolteacher, asks his students to keep concerning the slaves. Overhearing her name from inside the classroom one day, Sethe stops to listen as schoolteacher corrects a student's work: "No, no. That's not the way. I told you to put her human character-istics on the left; her animal ones on the right. And don't forget to line them up" (193). The form of this written chart, with its precision and balanced columns, recalls the ledger—a quantitative, clinical, and objective means of describing human action and being. By hav-ing schoolteacher delineate Sethe's supposed human and animal attributes, Morrison renders explicit the ability of accounting to as-sert equivalencies between human slave and animal livestock; the "imposed uniformity" Spillers describes is accomplished via Poovey's "quantification of qualities."

Given such a set of accounts, Morrison creates her narrative specifically out of the knowledge that the books can never be bal-anced. The impossibility of exchange which troubles Stamp and Paul D is also the point of origin for the book's plot; Sethe's first "rememory" is of how she had to barter her body in exchange for the inscription on her daughter's tombstone—the inscription which gives her the name "Beloved":

> Ten minutes for seven letters. With another ten could she have gotten "dearly" too? . . . But what she got, settled for, was the one word that mattered. She thought it would be enough, rutting among the headstones with the engraver, his young son looking on. . . . That should certainly be enough. Enough to answer one more preacher, one more abolitionist and a town full of disgust.
>
> Counting on the stillness of her own soul, she had for-gotten the other one: the soul of her baby girl. Who would have thought that the little old baby could harbor so much rage? Rutting among the stones under the eyes of the en-graver's son was not enough. (5)

Once again, the final, seemingly most outrageous, barter which is offered by each ex-slave is never "enough." Sethe hopes that the pain and humiliation of these ten minutes will buy some peace for her and her daughter by providing a memorial, an epitaph. Instead, it only agitates the baby ghost; and when Beloved returns, she is utterly unappeasable. Murdered by her own mother, she returns as the embodiment of the debt that cannot be repaid, the expense that cannot be balanced.

This is not to say that the economic sphere bears the same inevitable aura of corruption and curse that Faulkner's novels indicate. Despite the fact that in *Beloved* exchange is represented as impossible, an ongoing burden, money is not always poison to Morrison's characters. In the final rememory offered by Paul D, Morrison does pose a possible connection between money and liberation. At the book's denouement, as Paul D returns to 124 to reconcile with Sethe, he recollects the years after slavery, ending with an epiphany in New Jersey:

> Then came the miracle. Standing in a street in front of a row of brick houses, he heard a whiteman call him . . . to help unload two trunks from a coach cab. Afterward the whiteman gave him a coin. Paul D walked around with it for hours. . . . Finally he saw a greengrocer selling vegetables from a wagon. Paul D pointed to a bunch of turnips. The grocer handed them to him, took his one coin and handed him several more. Stunned, he backed away. Looking around, he saw that nobody seemed interested in the "mistake" or him, so he walked along, happily chewing turnips. . . . His first earned purchase made him glow, never mind the turnips were withered dry. That was when he decided that to eat, walk and sleep anywhere was life as good as it got. (269–70)

Paul D's release from slavery is realized and symbolized through his first purchase, his first coin earned for labor and his subsequent exchange of the coin for goods, events which are equated with being able to "eat, walk and sleep anywhere." The irony of Faulkner's freed slave who receives his legacy from Old Carothers' will "twenty-one years too late to begin to learn what money was" (*Go Down* 269) appears in altered form here as a freed slave who learns that he is free through his entry into the marketplace.

But Morrison is not positing a narrative of progress—a Horatio Alger tale of self-realization or an argument for racial uplift through economic success. Paul D's "miracle" leads us directly to the heart of Morrison's fictional project precisely because her books are dedicated to working through the problem of (Northern) black communities and individuals who seek economic success and yet are confronted endlessly by the dangers of such success. Morrison's characters who achieve wealth or assume a place in the middle class are invariably prey to the dangers of co-optation by or replication of the white patriarchy, losing contact with personal and collective histories and with any larger vision of African-American solidarity.[9] One of Morrison's remarkable accomplishments is her refusal to posit any sacred space or unexamined piety—community, family, mother, agrarian South—which is not in its turn revealed to be problematic or even deadly, which is not held up for a novelistic investigation. I am suggesting that one crucial theme through which she investigates these difficult issues is the double-edged dilemma of economic success for blacks in twentieth-century America. And as *Beloved* indicates, this theme is rooted in an engagement with the economics of slavery.

The theme of imbalance, which *Beloved* explores so powerfully in considering the immediate aftermath of slavery, persists in the twentieth century in *Sula*, a novel that enacts the ledger's imbalance within the prose itself. In writing about *Sula* critics have often focused on the relationship and the opposition between the characters of Sula Peace and Nel Wright. But to consider the issues of exchange and liberation that the novel raises, it is necessary to examine the dichotomy between Sula and her grandmother, Eva.[10] The matriarch of the Peace household—its "creator and sovereign"—Eva presides magisterially over her family. She gives names to her subjects and receives callers haughtily, but the real source of her power and mystique is in her missing leg. At the moment of her family's greatest poverty, with no income, her children young and sick and her husband having left her, Eva simply leaves town for eighteen months, returning with a missing leg but apparently affluent. Although the circumstances are mysterious, what is clear is that an exchange has been made, whether actual or symbolic: the leg for the cash. Sula, who has inherited her grandmother's fierce unconventionality, shows a similar willingness to mutilate herself to get what she wants, when she frightens away a gang of bullies by slicing the tip of her own finger off.

But Eva and Sula justify their actions in profoundly different ways. Although Eva lives outside of respectability, her life is still organized according to a ledgerlike sense of ultimate, distributive justice. In her role as sovereign and namer, her extreme generosity is balanced by the extreme demands she makes upon her subjects. When she can no longer bear the self-destructive behavior of her best-loved child, she burns him alive while he sleeps. Although she sets the terms of exchange, her relations with people are nonetheless predicated on the fairness, however unconventional, of the exchange, the balance that will be shown at the final reckoning of accounts. Eva seems to represent, in simplified form, the model offered by Houston Baker: she appropriates and reshapes the economic terms that have made her suffer, and makes them work for her. That she does so at the cost of a leg recalls the specter of slavery, human flesh exchanged for cash, and suggests that in order to take control of one's life one must be willing to make that exchange in one way or another.

This appropriation of economic terms, although it refuses to conform to the terms of middle-class behavior and concerns, is still alien to Sula, whose project of self-liberation is predicated upon an absolute rejection of the conventional—and the economic. If Eva follows a strategy described by Baker, then Sula takes on the challenge offered by Spillers, the negation of the "syntax" provided by the ledger and the positing of an entirely new and disruptive grammar, a way of being that is discontinuous with the opportunities for being which are available. Sula's life is radically disconnected from the economic sphere, founded upon disruption and the very principle of imbalance. While Eva sacrifices her leg for money to live and feed her family on, Sula cuts off her fingertip for the sheer effect of it; while Eva's exchanges are practical, Sula's are excessive. Uninterested in money, she scorns Eva for "[selling her] life for twenty-three dollars a month" (93). What the town—and often the reader—finds unforgivable in Sula's behavior is its absolute refusal to acknowledge the rules of balance; in her relations with people she shows no feeling of obligation to be responsible or fair; there is no exchange. Eva's generosity to her—raising her, sending her to college, sending her money—is "repaid" flatly by Sula when she returns to town and puts Eva in a home, taking over the Peace house for herself. When she sleeps with all the men of Medallion, her transgression is not balanced against the providing of a kind of social service, as it was in the case of her mother Hannah: "Hannah had been a nuisance, but she was complimenting the women, in a way, by wanting their husbands. Sula was trying them out and discarding them without any excuse the men could swallow. So the women, to justify their own judgment, cherished the men more, soothed the pride and vanity Sula had bruised" (115). Although the town finds ways to account for Sula, to explain her in ways that support the community's views, her actions in themselves remain unjust, unaccountable.

The remarkable and puzzling prose of the book, deceptively smooth and fluid, mirrors the imbalance and injustice of Sula's life, literalizing her search for a "new syntax." We see an early example of Sula's character in the scene of her mother Hannah's self-immolation: "[Eva] rolled up to the window and it was then she saw Hannah burning. The flames from the yard fire were licking the blue cotton dress, making her dance. . . . Hannah, her senses lost, went flying out of the yard gesturing and bobbing like a sprung jack-in-the-box" (75–76). During this horrific scene, while others are galvanized into action, Sula stands watching. Although the townspeople attribute her behavior to something understandable, paralyzed horror, Eva remains convinced "that Sula had watched Hannah burn not because she was paralyzed, but because she was interested"—and, with her belief in balance and justice, distrusts Sula thereafter (78). Meanwhile, the language Morrison employs to describe the burning seems to take Sula's position—aloof, interested, undisturbed. Lyrical and steady, the narrative rolls right over this incident without a hint of shock or horror. This is not to say that the reader remains undisturbed; the shock and horror are registered precisely by the narrative's calm, which is contrasted with the textual details surrounding the incident. Once the fire is put out, Hannah "lay there on the wooden sidewalk planks, twitching lightly among the smashed tomatoes, her face a mask of agony so intense that for years the people who gathered 'round would shake their heads at the recollection of it" (76). It is this very contrast that the novel foregrounds: the horror which we feel, but which is not felt in the rhythms of the language.

The same is true of the incident that convinces Sula that not only are others undependable, but there is also "no self to count on" (119)—her accidental killing, at the age of twelve, of the young boy Chicken Little:

> Sula picked him up by his hands and swung him outward then around and around. His knickers ballooned and his shrieks of frightened joy startled the birds and the fat grasshoppers. When he slipped from her hands and sailed away out over the water they could still hear his bubbly laughter.
>
> The water darkened and closed quickly over the place where Chicken Little sank. The pressure of his hard and tight little fingers was still in Sula's palms as she stood looking at the closed place in the water. . . . The water was so peaceful now. There was nothing but the baking sun and something newly missing. (60–61)

In a book full of pain and of seemingly disturbing and disruptive deaths—Hannah, Chicken Little, Plum burned to death by his mother, the soldier whose decapitation Shadrack witnesses, the many who die in a cave-in during a liberatory march on National Suicide Day— the language absorbs them all and refuses to mark their passing with a change of tone. Like the unaccountably serene water that closes over Chicken Little's head, the narrative does not even ripple, let alone splash; it maintains a plain, poetic, and faintly nostalgic tone. In this it seems to echo Sula's approach to life: pain and suffering and death are not registered as unjust or balanced against Faulknerian crescendos of language. The smooth surfaces of the text present asymmetrical representations of the horrors described, creating not a style that is the opposite of the ledger's—as Faulkner does in "The Bear"—but rather a stylistic refutation of the ledger, of the claim that justice can be enacted through a quantitative balance.

Faulkner and Morrison construct their novels at a particular juncture of economic and historical narrative, a juncture whose terms are set but not settled by the social and legal conditions of slavery in America. In *Sula* we see how Morrison's prose, so different in its calm eloquence from Faulkner's adjectival gush, nonetheless suggests a similar sense of imbalance, a sense that the American novel must strive to articulate the legacies of slavery, even if it cannot provide a final accounting for or reckoning with those legacies. Both Morrison and Faulkner bear witness to the importance and persistence of economic discourse in our thinking about race in America. They offer a range of formal narrative and stylistic responses to the written narrative and style of the ledger, all of which engage in some way with the economics of slavery, whether through appropriation or disruption, refiguring or repudiation.

Throughout her work, Morrison continues to consider these crucial terms and questions, which are posed in different forms, in different contexts, by Faulkner's novels. While Faulkner's writing evokes the drama of whiteness, of white characters who can neither escape nor ameliorate their inherited and debt-laden pasts, Morrison creates a language to explore the lives of her equally but differently conflicted black characters, who in working toward liberation from their pasts are forced again and again to recall them. If the shape of Morrison's engagement with the economics of slavery is illuminated by the way that *Go Down, Moses* constructs a narrative relationship to the ledger as a formal concern, the exploration of the conflicting possibilities for black economic success in *Beloved* and *The Bluest Eye* makes possible a reading of Faulkner's anxiety about such success. The alternating current of this analysis flows not only through the works of these two authors, but through all literary work which seeks to make sense of the cultural history of race in America, to balance the books or to articulate the impossibility of that balance.

Notes

1. Two comparative studies, a book by Philip Weinstein and a collection of essays edited by Kolmerton, Ross, and Wittenberg, have

appeared recently, and others are forthcoming. At the same time, Faulkner/Morrison panels have begun to appear regularly at major conferences, and undergraduate courses and graduate seminars designed specifically to study the two authors together have appeared at a number of universities. In introductions to separate collections of critical essays on Morrison, both Harold Bloom and Henry Louis Gates Jr. have claimed Faulkner as the central "influence" or "ancestor" to which her work can be connected. In January 1998, even *Time* magazine got into the action, however obscurely, with a cover reading "The Sound and the Fury of Toni Morrison" and an article by Paul Gray entitled "Paradise Found." This work has not emerged out of a vacuum—it is perhaps common knowledge by now that Morrison wrote her MA thesis at Cornell on themes of alienation in Faulkner and Virginia Woolf. A few stray articles linking the two writers have appeared in the last twenty years: see Willis, Cowart, and Duvall. The Duvall essay is a good starting point for research into the issues raised by dealing with Faulkner and Morrison together.

2. The relationship between literature and economics is an enormous topic, and this essay claims only to be a very particular intervention within that general field. For a broad exploration of the formal connections between literary figuration and economic figures, see Marc Shell's two ambitious studies. Walter Benn Michaels provides readings of classic American literary texts using discourses of money and property as a point of entry. The most extended treatment of economic forms, especially exchange, in Faulkner's fiction occurs in Snead.

   The most complete discussions of the ledger as a figure in Faulkner's work appear in Brooks, *Reading for the Plot,* and in Kauffman. Brooks suggests that a plot ending with no loose ends mirrors an account-book with no remainders or unexplained costs, whereas in Faulkner, "[t]he narrative ledger cannot be cleared by a neat calculation; the tale can never be plotted to the final, thorough, Dickensian accounting" (309). Kauffman argues that the ledger represents a "patriarchal economy" or "the logic of the phallus. . . . The ledger's columns and computations of spending and getting, its list of Negroes bought, bred, and sold—all reveal how fundamental the equation of sex and money is in the false economy of . . . the entire South" (661). This "ledger mentality," she argues, is opposed in *Absalom, Absalom!* by the figure of the loom, representing a female principle of interdependence and plenitude which "is the opposite of the debit-credit mentality of niggardly economy" (667). While Kauffman's identification of the ledger figure with patriarchal structures is important, I remain skeptical of her glib opposition between dystopian patriarchal economy and utopian disruptive female plenitude.

3. The 1994 collection *Accounting as Social and Institutional Practice* presents the best sampling of this work. There is also a journal, *Accounting, Organizations and Society*, devoted to this topic.

4. Here I have also drawn on Poovey's *A History of the Modern Fact*, in which she elaborates on and clarifies the argument of "Accomodating Merchants: Double-Entry Bookkeeping, Mercantile Expertise, and the Effect of Accuracy." While the essay asks us to see the connection between accounting and the "natural laws of gender," the book shifts its focus to the (much more convincingly argued) role of accounting and double-entry bookkeeping in the historical process which has created the "modern fact": "the relation between accounting and theorizing about wealth and society constitutes a chapter in the uneven process by which the status hierarchy that characterized ancient society was gradually replaced by modern, functionally differentiated domains" (31).

5. This narrative function of plantation ledgers is expressed particularly well in McDonald. The primary texts of McDonald's book are the ledgers of sugar plantations, which he uses to construct a history of the slaves—their living conditions and their culture—that would otherwise be unavailable.

6. Thadious Davis writes that "at the base of the novel and [the novel's black-white] relationships is the concept of property as it relates to human rights and the rights of the individual." She continues: "The ideological context inspiring Faulkner's novel stems mainly from the existence of chattel slavery in the South rather than from philosophical treatises on property" (138). Davis's remarks suggest that the existence of slavery in America is for Faulkner the defining instance of ownership. See Davis for more on the ledger as a model for biblical redistributive justice, and for more on the novel's relation to the spiritual "Go Down, Moses."

7. Faulkner's use of this particular style is relevant to his use of "excessive" prose which challenges the abbreviated, factual style of the ledger. The "Authorized" English translation of the Bible was published in 1611. Thus its famous style—grand, eloquent, elaborate—epitomizes the Renaissance emphasis on *copia*, the style that seeks to demonstrate humanist learning in prose. It is precisely this style that, according to Poovey, the discourse of the ledger replaced. She suggests that writings by merchants such as Thomas Mun represent a shift from the conventions of Renaissance humanism and the rich erudition of Erasmian style—with its emphasis on *copia*—to a style which resembles that of the ledger: literal, arranged, numbered, and abbreviated, drawing its authority from its own evidence rather than from classical sources ("Accomodating" 9–11).

8. The force of the ledger as a model for narrative itself is most vivid in *Absalom, Absalom!*, a reading that Peter Brooks gestures toward in *Reading for the Plot*. Like the numbers that must be imported into the ledger in order to maintain the fictional balance, Quentin's "knowledge" that Charles Bon is part black has no factual basis but is imported into the narrative because it allows Quentin to construct his narrative of how the racial divisions created by the South have ultimately destroyed it. As Shreve says, there are "some

things that just have to be whether they are or not, just to balance the books, write *Paid* on the old sheet so that whoever keeps them can take it out of the ledger and burn it, get rid of it" (260). However, the racial mixture ultimately forces the inconsistencies in this ledger-narrative to the surface, in the form of Jim Bond, the mixed-race Sutpen who, like Morrison's Beloved, is both remainder and reminder that the books can never be balanced.

9. Valerie Smith writes that "Morrison consistently problematizes what it means to be black and privileged" (52). Susan Willis presents a more fully developed Marxist reading of Morrison's novels as responses to the situation of African-Americans in the era of late capitalism. She writes that "Morrison's writing . . . represents a process for coming to grips with historical transition. Migration to the north signifies more than a confrontation with (and contagion of) the white world. It implies a transition in social class . . . a number of black Americans will criticize her problematizing of Afro-American culture, seeing in it a symptom of Morrison's own relationship to white bourgeois society as a successful writer and editor" (264). Willis points out that each of Morrison's novels deals with a historical moment in African-American history at which "social and cultural forms underwent disruption and transformation" (265). At each of these moments, she argues, the problem confronting Morrison's characters is the alienation they experience from white bourgeois culture, an alienation disrupted by the liberatory potential of "funk."

10. The dichotomy between Sula and Eva is foregrounded by the economic and historical concerns that are central to my essay, but of course this is not to disregard the relationship of Sula and Nel, which figures crucially in many readings of the novel. Throughout *Sula*, the "dangerous freedom" explored is that of a world where men and certainly patriarchal authority are radically absent. This novelistic experiment, and Nel's final cry of sorrow at having missed Sula rather than Jude, have had a remarkable impact in the reading of literature by women. Barbara Smith reads *Sula* as a lesbian novel, while Margaret Homans reads Nel's final "howl" as the radical possibility of identification between women and of "unborrowed women's language" (192). These critical works suggest the remarkable impact Morrison's novel has had, and in particular its importance in the emergence of black feminist criticism.

Works Cited

Aho, James. "Rhetoric and the Invention of Double-Entry Bookkeeping." *Rhetorica* 3:1 (1985): 21–43.
Baker, Houston A. *Blues, Ideology, and Afro-American Literature*. Chicago: U of Chicago P, 1984.
Benn Michaels, Walter. *The Gold Standard and the Logic of Naturalism*. Berkeley: U of California P, 1987.

Bloom, Harold, ed. *Toni Morrison: Modern Critical Views*. New York: Chelsea House, 1990.

Brooks, Peter. *Reading for the Plot*. Cambridge: Harvard UP, 1984.

Cowart, David. "Faulkner and Joyce in Morrison's *Song of Solomon*." *American Literature* 62:1 (1990): 87–100.

Davis, Thadious M. "Crying in the Wilderness: Legal, Racial, and Moral Codes in *Go Down, Moses*." *Critical Essays on William Faulkner: The McCaslin Family*. Ed. Arthur F. Kinney. Boston: Hall, 1990. 137–53.

Duvall, John N. "Doe Hunting and Masculinity: *Song of Solomon* and *Go Down, Moses*." *Arizona Quarterly* 47:1 (1991): 95–115.

Faulkner, William. *Absalom, Absalom!* New York: Modern Library, 1964.

——. *Go Down, Moses*. New York: Vintage, 1973.

——. *The Hamlet*. New York: Vintage, 1964.

Gates, Henry Louis, Jr., and K. A. Appiah, eds. *Toni Morrison: Critical Perspectives Past and Present*. New York: Amistad, 1993.

Gray, Paul. "Paradise Found." *Time* 19 January 1998: 63–68.

Harris, Trudier. "Escaping Slavery but Not Its Images." Gates and Appiah 330–41.

Homans, Margaret. "'Her Very Own Howl': The Ambiguities of Representation in Recent Women's Fiction." *Signs: A Journal of Women in Culture and Society* 9:2 (1983): 186–205.

Hopwood, Anthony G., and Peter Miller, eds. *Accounting as Social and Institutional Practice*. Cambridge: Cambridge UP, 1994.

Hoskin, Keith, and Richard Macve. "Writing, Examining, Disciplining: The Genesis of Accounting's Modern Power." Hopwood and Miller 67–97.

Kauffman, Linda. "Devious Channels of Decorous Ordering: Rosa Coldfield in *Absalom, Absalom!*" *Feminisms*. Ed. Robyn Warhol and Diane Price Herndl. New Brunswick: Rutgers UP, 1991. 644–70.

Kolmerton, Carol, Stephen Ross, and Judith Bryant Wittenberg, eds. *Unflinching Gaze: Morrison and Faulkner Re-Envisioned*. Oxford: UP of Mississippi, 1997.

McDonald, Roderick A. *The Economy and Material Culture of Slaves: Goods and Chattels on the Sugar Plantations of Jamaica and Louisiana*. Baton Rouge: Louisiana State UP, 1993.

Miller, Peter. "Accounting as Social and Institutional Practice: An Introduction." Hopwood and Miller 1–40.

Morrison, Toni. *Beloved*. New York: New American Library Penguin, 1987.

——. "Faulkner and Women." *Faulkner and Women*. Ed. Doreen Fowler and Ann J. Abadie. Jackson: UP of Mississippi, 1986. 295–302.

——. *Sula*. New York: NAL Penguin, 1982.

——. [Chloe Ardellia Wofford]. "Virginia Woolf's and William Faulkner's Treatment of the Alienated." Master's thesis. Cornell U, 1955.

Poovey, Mary. "Accommodating Merchants: Accounting, Civility, and the Natural Laws of Gender." *Differences* 8:3 (1996): 1–20.

——. *A History of the Modern Fact: Problems of Knowledge in the Sciences of Wealth and Society*. Chicago: U of Chicago P, 1998.

Shell, Marc. *The Economy of Literature*. Baltimore: Johns Hopkins UP, 1978.

———. *Money, Language and Thought: Literary and Philosophic Economies from the Medieval to the Modern Era.* Baltimore: Johns Hopkins UP, 1993.

Smith, Barbara. "Toward a Black Feminist Criticism." *The New Feminist Criticism: Essays on Women, Literature, and Theory.* Ed. Elaine Showalter. New York: Pantheon, 1985. 168–85.

Smith, Valerie. "Black Feminist Theory and the Representation of the 'Other.'" *Changing Our Own Words: Essays on Criticism, Theory, and Writing by Black Women.* Ed. Cheryl A. Wall. New Brunswick: Rutgers, 1989. 38–57.

Snead, James A. *Figures of Division: William Faulkner's Major Novels.* New York: Methuen, 1986.

Spillers, Hortense. "Mama's Baby, Papa's Maybe: An American Grammar Book." *Diacritics* (Summer 1987): 65–81.

Weinstein, Philip M. *What Else But Love? The Ordeal of Race in Faulkner and Morrison.* New York: Columbia UP, 1996.

Willis, Susan. "Eruptions of Funk: Historicizing Toni Morrison." *Black Literature and Literary Theory.* Ed. Henry Louis Gates, Jr. London: Methuen, 1984. 263–84.

GENDER AND RACE:

AFFECT, THE BODY, AND IDENTITY

CHAPTER 9

FAULKNER'S GARDEN
WOMAN AND THE
IMMEMORIAL EARTH

Karl E. Zink

Life, for Faulkner, originates in and is limited to the mysteriously living surface of the Earth. This basic assumption has seldom been recognized or admitted in discussions of Faulkner's work. He has had little, if anything, to do with ultimate causes, phrasing instead the necessity for the acceptance of suffering, evil, and responsibility. Very few of his characters reveal a concern for an afterlife, though it is apparent that time and immortality dominate his art. The purpose of living, Addie Bundren said in *As I Lay Dying,* is to get ready to stay dead a long time. The mysterious, enduring process of Life seems to be for Faulkner the primary reality.

Faulkner records external nature with the loving and exact eye of a naturalist, but his backgrounds serve as much more than static or conventional settings. Nature invariably moves or sounds, through graphic reference disclosing life and ceaseless activity. It is always dynamic and palpable, and it is a constant and deliberate frame of reference for human behavior. The living earth is, in the Faulkner novel, the ultimate stage of Life. Even in his first novel, *Soldiers' Pay* (1926),[1] it is apparent that Man is not alone on a cardboard stage but is, instead, a passionate organism within a great and throbbing web of life. Here, from that novel, is a familiar transcript of natural night

Originally published in *Modern Fiction Studies*, Autumn 1956.

sounds that will be heard throughout Faulkner's later work: "Tree-frogs shrilled in the trees, insects droned in the grass. . . . When he moved they fell silent . . . when he became still again, they released the liquid flute-like monotony swelling in their throats" (p. 162). Only Man's motion, not his presence, disturbs the life in the leaves and the grass and the woods. In this novel, Faulkner speaks explicitly of "the hushed myriad life of night things," using one of his favored adjectives, "myriad," to its best advantage to connote the incessant "seethe" of life on the earth. Man is alert to this dynamic ground through all of his senses. Lying sleepless on her bed, Cecily Saunders heard "the hushed sounds of night, smelled the sweet scents of spring and dark and growing things: the earth, watching the wheel of the world, the terrible calm, inevitability of life, turning through the hours of darkness" (p. 169).

When Quentin Compson, in *The Sound and the Fury,* discovers that his sister Caddy has taken a lover, he runs through rain and fog and night sounds to the branch to find her. His emotionally charged report of the total scene includes references to Nature which acknowledge its usual minute dynamism: ". . . then I was running in the grey darkness it smelled of rain and all flower scents the damp warm air released and crickets sawing away in the grass pacing me with a small travelling island of silence . . . I ran down the hill in that vacuum of crickets . . . I could smell the honeysuckle on the water gap the air seemed to drizzle with honeysuckle and with the rasping of crickets a substance you could feel on the flesh" (p. 168).

The odor of flowers, the sounds of insects, the feel of the dew or the rain—all serve as a kind of chorus. And time and again in Faulkner's stories self-conscious human action is juxtaposed against this ceaselessly dynamic ground—whether it be the insects outside the distressed Hightower's window in *Light in August* or the locusts beyond the courthouse windows of *A Fable,* or the persistent gnats of the protracted drinking scene behind Suratt's barn in *Sartoris,* or the noisy sparrows and pigeons of every Faulkner courthouse square.

In "outdoor" novels, like *The Hamlet, The Wild Palms, Light in August,* and *Go Down, Moses,* the ancient struggle between right and wrong, between responsible and irresponsible behavior, occurs directly on the oldest stage of all, the mother earth, or within her primeval woods. And the earth is teeming—for this, *fecund* is the favored word. In "Delta Autumn" (*Go Down, Moses*), it is "the rich black land, imponderable and vast, fecund up to the very doorsteps of the negroes who worked it and the white men who owned it." The earth is female—in "Old Man" (*The Wild Palms*), it is specifically "mare" to the "stallion sun." And the earth is wet. Eula Varner of *The Hamlet* is asserted (in Rabelaisian caricature) as a lush earth or fertility goddess: "her entire appearance suggested some symbology out of the old Dionysic times—honey in sunlight and bursting grapes, the writhen bleeding of the crushed fecundated vine beneath the hard rapacious trampling goat-hoof" (p. 107); and, again: "a face eight years old and a body of fourteen with the female shape of twenty, which on the instant of crossing the threshold brought into the bleak, ill-lighted, poorly-heated room dedicated to the harsh functioning of Protestant primary education a moist blast of spring's liquorish corruption, a pagan triumphal prostration before the supreme primal uterus" (p. 129).

In the eyes of Labove, her tortured monk/faun lover, Eula actually becomes the fecund earth in a reverie which anticipates her later sterile union with Flem Snopes:

> He could almost see the husband which she would someday have. He would be a dwarf, a gnome, without glands or desire, who would be no more a physical factor in her life than the owner's name on the fly-leaf of a book . . . the crippled Vulcan to that Venus, who would not possess her but merely own her by the single strength which power gave, the dead power of money, wealth, gewgaws, baubles, as he might own, not a picture, a statue: a field, say. He saw it: the fine land rich and fecund and foul and eternal and impervious to him who claimed title to it, oblivious drawing to itself tenfold the quantity of living seed its owner's whole life could have secreted and compounded, producing a thousandfold the harvest he could ever hope to gather and save. (pp. 134–35)

These passages illustrate well Faulkner's preoccupation with the Earth as ancient, as living and life-giving, as eternal. And they introduce the important identification of Earth and Woman, which we shall examine.

In *The Hamlet* and in "Old Man" and other stories, the sun serves conventionally as a clear symbol of potency, a male sex symbol correlated with the wild power and freedom of the stallion. But the sun is honorific only in conjunction with the moist and fertile earth. When Eula departs from Frenchman's Bend with her sterile husband, Flem Snopes, the sun is merciless: the drought that follows, which gives the section called "The Long Summer" its name, is intense and prolonged beyond record in the folk mind; it is followed by an unusually harsh winter: "the windless iron cold came down upon it [the snow] without even a heatless wafer of sun to preside above a dead earth cased in ice" (p. 300). Only with Eula's return, like Persephone, the following spring, does the dessicated land know release and respond normally to the plow: "Then even that winter was over at last. It ended as it had begun, in rain, not cold rain but loud fierce gusts of warm water washing out of the earth the iron enduring frost, the belated spring hard on its bright heels and all coming at once, pell mell and disordered, fruit and bloom and leaf, pied meadow and blossoming wood and the long fields shearing dark out of winter's slumber, to the shearing plow" (p. 302).

But Nature is not always gentle or merely quietly busy. Ultimately, Nature is, to use Faulkner's words, "savage," "implacable," and, particularly, "oblivious." In "Old Man," for example, the convict reflects in constant terror upon the swollen river's prodigious indifference to his frantic efforts to survive. The flux that is Nature's common denominator inheres in the literal and symbolic torrents of *The Wild Palms, Requiem for a Nun,* and *A Fable.* "Old Man" is more than an authentic picture of the Mississippi River in full, raging flood, as it is so often described. The meaning of the story depends almost wholly on the symbolism of *torrent.* For half the length of the story, the foreground is dominated by the convict's hectic search for some surface, more stable than the bottom of the bounding skiff, on which the woman may give birth. She is gripped by a parallel force every bit as powerful and inexorable as the great flood on which both she and the convict float helplessly: "When he looked upon the swelling and unmanageable body before him it seemed to him that it was not the woman at all but rather a separate demanding threatening inert yet living mass of which both he and she were equally victims" (p. 154). In the grip of her necessity, she is as oblivious of the flood as the flood is of them.

Another remorseless flood occurs in *Requiem for a Nun.* This, of course, is the steady, impersonal flux of human events in Time (rationalized by some as Progress, but not by Faulkner) in which change, obsolescence, and death are merely inevitable. The tone of poignant regret for the loss of old values which dominates the prose sections of this structurally unique novel derives from a compulsive and sustained sense of torrent. An intense syntactical continuum, which never resolves, contributes a physicial impression of constant movement which gives the prose sections their distinctive form and flavor. Because of this syntax, it is almost useless to seek short representative quotations. However, a strong impression of both the movement of the prose and the torrent of change may be found in "The Golden Dome" section. The passage begins: "The rich deep black alluvial soil which would grow cotton taller than the head of a man on a horse, already one jungle one brake one impassable density of briar and cane and vine. . . ." (p. 101).

The wave, or the flood, is also one of the governing symbols of *A Fable,* especially as it dramatizes the blind and irresistible momentum of crowds of people dominated by a single purpose or fear. This image of torrent dominates the entire first chapter of *A Fable.* Almost an entire city begins early in the morning to stir and then quickly to take the shape of an irresistible wave of humanity pouring blindly into the *Place de Ville* to witness the arrival of the lorries carrying the mutinied regiment—their husbands and brothers and sons: "hovel and tenement voiding into lane and alley and nameless *cul-de-sac,* and lane and alley and *cul-de-sac* compounding into streets as the trickles became streams and the streams became rivers, until the whole city seemed to be pouring down the broad boulevards converging like wheel spokes into the *Place de Ville,* filling the *Place* and then, pressed on by the weight of its own converging mass, flowing like an unrecoiling wave up to the blank gates of the *Hotel* where the three sentries of the three co-embattled nations flanked the three empty flagstaffs awaiting the three concordant flags" (p. 4). When the same group later rushes out of the city across a plain toward the compound where the prisoners were kept, their movement is again compared in detail to the blind, powerful wave: "They had no plan: only motion, like a wave; fanned out now across the plain, they—or it—seemed to have more breadth than depth, like a wave, seeming, as they approached the compound, to increase in speed as a wave does nearing the sand, on, until it suddenly crashed against the wire barrier, and hung for an instant and then burst, split into two lesser waves which flowed in each direction along the fence until each spent itself" (p. 130).

Occasionally, in this heavy novel, Faulkner uses his established symbols and distinctive style rather perfunctorily and gratuitously, but this massed crowd of life, with its tremendous potentials of power, its constant massed movement, its noisy muteness and loud silences, demonstrates the underlying preoccupation with flux.

But Nature is more than such literal and symbolical assertions of flux as torrents and crowds, or the small noises of insects and the earth itself seething with life. Man himself, but especially Woman, is a manifestation of Nature. Faulkner's deep commitment to flux and change helps explain his unusual women. Old women, like Granny Sartoris of *The Unvanquished,* Aunt Jenny Du Pre of *Sartoris,* or humorous portrayals like Mrs. Littlejohn of *The Hamlet,* are more or less authentic, conventional characters, appropriate to a time or social class or place. But his young, married or marriageable women share so many generalized traits that despite their individuating features, they all seem the same woman. Such women seldom appear exclusively as romantic or as sexual objects; instead, they are usually already pregnant, wed or unwed—channels for the more obvious natural processes, obliviously coming to fruit. The traits they share are honorific: endurance, acceptance, practicality, devotion, love, strength, patience, emotional maturity. Some of these women are anonymously, but all are more or less placidly pregnant: Lena Grove of *Light in August,* Eula Varner Snopes of *The Hamlet,* Caddy Compson of *The Sound and the Fury,* Laverne Shumann of *Pylon,* Dewey Dell Bundren of *As I Lay Dying,* and especially the woman of "Old Man," who is not named. Despite her central role in the story, and other than her more or less typical woods reticence and taciturn speech, she has no individuating traits—she is merely but profoundly Woman: pregnant. Despite the fact that so many of these women are unmarried, they are good women; they have an integrity that conventionally respectable women in the novels consistently do not have. These women, more than their men, are akin to the "fecund" earth, like the earth itself potential sources for renewal and development, for physicial continuity within the continuous process of Nature. The birth scene of "Old Man" graphically dramatizes woman as the biological channel and vehicle for the continuation of human life. The woman, not the convict, performs the Promethean service of fire on the snake-infested Indian mound in order to heat the river water. She carries matches preserved in two telescoped shotgun shells. She has little, if any, control over the force working irresistibly within her. In giving birth she surrenders to it and becomes its instrument or agent. Process, Faulkner would say, is her "doom." Those few women in the novels who have repudiated or resisted this responsibility have not been symbolic sisters of this group. For example, Charlotte Rittenmeyer (*The Wild Palms*) abandoned her children, attempted to abort when she became pregnant, and died horribly. Caroline Compson's self-centered failure as a mother is the source of the evil which destroys her family. Joanna Burden's fanatic dedication to the abstraction, Sin, rather than to honest sexual gratification contrasts vividly with the placid, normal behavior of Lena Grove as woman and mother.

In *Light in August,* when Byron Bunch discovers Lena in labor and hears her cries, she seems to him to be speaking "to something in a tongue which he knew was not his tongue nor that of any man." Lena "lives" of and by and with "the old earth." Gripped suddenly by one of her pangs, "her face has drained of color, of its full, hearty blood, and she sits quite still, hearing and feeling the implacable and immemorial earth, but without fear or alarm. 'It's twins at least,' she says to herself, without lip movement, without sound"

(p. 26). An organic part of the old earth, Lena's very chemistry is closer than that of men to old, abiding, mysterious rhythms.[2]

When Lena stops to "listen" to herself, she echoes another related symbolic pattern in which Faulkner's strange women are sometimes cast, that of the "musing maiden." This is the young girl who, for a magical time between puberty and full maturity, exists in an oblivious state of listening bemusement which relates directly to the obliviousness of Nature. These girls are strange paradoxes of apparent spirituality and frankest physicality. Little Belle Benbow of *Sanctuary* is such a creature. Judith Sutpen of *Absalom, Absalom!* is one, Cecelia Farmer of *Requiem for a Nun* another, Eula Varner of *The Hamlet* another, and hers is by all odds the fullest and longest analysis, although the shorter study of Judith Sutpen is the most poetic. Faulkner's description of Judith's musing maidenhood is as fullthroated as it is for structural reasons. This naturally happy "suspension" of the young Judith parallels her later, grimmer, spiritual suspension—when she has endured the war and taken the shock of Charles Bon's death, and at thirty is penurious, weathered, taciturn, ungrieving. But for all its poetry it faces graphically the essentially physical, sensual condition:

> . . . and Judith gone even further than that—into that transition stage between childhood and womanhood . . . that state where, though still visible, young girls appear as though seen through glass and where even the voice cannot reach them; where they exist (this the hoyden who could—and did—outrun and outclimb, and ride and fight both with and beside her brother) in a pearly lambence without shadows and themselves partaking of it; in nebulous suspension held, strange and unpredictable, even their very shapes fluid and delicate and without substance; not in themselves floating and seeking but merely waiting, parasitic and potent and serene . . . (p. 67)

Like Lena, these girls listen to their own maturation—turned wholly inward, away from the immediate actuality they share with others. Their remoteness suggests the egocentric, dynamic isolation of the foetus. With Judith Sutpen, the relationship is explicit: "the young girl who slept waking in some suspension so completely physical as to resemble the state before birth" (p. 70). In *The Hamlet* the description of the young Eula Varner repeats the listening quality and the basic sensualness of the state, adding, however, another exclusively female trait—a "wisdom" that is inherent in their very natures: "She seemed to be not a living integer of her contemporary scene, but rather to exist in a teeming vacuum in which her days followed one another as though behind sound-proof glass, where she seemed to listen in sullen bemusement, with a weary wisdom heired of all mammalian maturity, to the enlarging of her own organs" (p. 107). It is surely no man's language they hear.

Faulkner's females know an innate affinity for sex; they are born with a "knowledge" the male learns only by hectic experience. Woman's more organic identification with the mysterious compulsions and forces of her destiny underlies the frequent assertions of her superior knowledge of life, compared with which men are innocent. "You men," Mrs. Beard says to Byron, in *Light in August,* "It aint a wonder womenfolks get impatient with you. You cant even know your own limits for devilment. Which aint more than I can measure on a pin, at that. I reckon if it wasn't for getting some woman mixed up in it to help you, you'd ever one of you be drug hollering into heaven before you was ten years old" (p. 396).

In the "Eula" section of *The Hamlet,* Labove's passionate reverie anticipating his futile attempt at seduction rather caricatures the male's frustration in the presence of woman's mysteriously superior knowledge:

> It would now be himself importunate and prostrate before that face which, even though but fourteen years old, postulated a weary knowledge which he would never attain, a surfeit, a glut of all perverse experience. He would be as a child before that knowledge. He would be like a young girl, a maiden, wild distracted and amazed, trapped not by the seducer's maturity and experience but by blind and ruthless forces inside herself which she now realized she had lived with for years without even knowing they were there. He would grovel in the dust before it, panting: "Show me what to do. Tell me. I will do anything you tell me, anything, to learn and know what you know." (pp. 135–36)

Labove is blocked from consummation, as he knows, by words, by his tendency to intellectualize all experience. But the source of his feeling is a kind of awe akin to fear, which is partially explained in another of his intense reflections on the girl's compulsive attraction: "an eleven-year-old girl who, even while sitting with veiled eyes against the sun like a cat on the schoolhouse steps at recess and eating a cold potato, postulated that ungirdled quality of the very goddesses in his Homer and Thucydides: of being at once corrupt and immaculate, at once virgins and the mothers of warriors and of grown men" (p. 128).

Sensitive young males like Jack Houston of *The Hamlet,* Joe Christmas of *Light in August,* and Quentin Compson of *The Sound and the Fury* betray an initial delicacy and recalcitrance that is affronted to the point of hatred by the inexorable fact of the female's organic functionalism. The male feels no such deep responsibility to organic process; he knows innately a sense of freedom and irresponsibility—Jack Houston is "not high-spirited so much as possessed of that strong lust, not for life, not even for movement, but for that fetterless immobility called freedom" (p. 236). This male recalcitrance is graphically dramatized in *The Hamlet* by the short story of Houston, a flashback which rejoins the present as Mink Snopes bushwhacks him. It is the account of Houston's hatred and fear and love for the dove-quiet Lucy Pate, from whom he fled in terror, and who waited—"tranquil, terrifying"—for twelve years for him to return and marry her. Part of the money he borrowed for his marriage he spent on a beautiful stallion. And it is quite clear that Houston feels the stallion represents what he himself has sacrificed to marriage: "He bought the stallion too then, as if for a wedding present to her, though he never said so. Or if that blood and bone and muscles represented that polygamous and bitless masculinity which he had relinquished, he never said that. And if there were any among his neighbors and acquaintances—Will Varner or Ratliff perhaps—who discerned that this was the actual transference, the deliberate filling of the vacancy of his abdication, they did not say it either" (p. 246). Six months later the stallion killed Lucy, and Houston, having shot the stallion, grieved for her for four years "in black, savage, indomitable fidelity."

Quentin Compson betrayed this male delicacy and refused sexual maturity; he was repelled by the menstrual blood and morbidly associated the cloying odor of honeysuckle and the dull, neutral color of gray with sexuality. He sought futilely to deny Caddy's sexual knowledge and even her pregnancy by verbalizing frantically the myth of their incest. His father tried to explain to him that if any human being knows physical chastity it is the male, women being the mysteriously informed creatures they are: "Women are never virgins. Purity is a negative state and therefore contrary to nature. It's nature hurting you not Caddy and I said That's just words and he said So is virginity and I said you dont know" (p. 135).

Joe Christmas exemplified the male delicacy too, and something of Houston's recalcitrance, in his adolescent experiences with the compliant Negro girl brought to the mill shed by a group of boys, and with his first love, the whore Bobbie. He refuses the girl in the shed not because she is Negro but because she is female[3]—as Faulkner has it: "womanshenegro." Joe senses that this composite "encloses" him. He smells the Negress and strikes and kicks her, and then fights with the other boys in the shed, smelling now not the "she" but only "male." The change is like a wind blown among them "hard and clean." A companion's description of the menstrual cycle so outrages Joe that he kills a sheep and ritualistically wets his hands in its blood to purchase "immunity" from that terrible knowledge of women.[4] When Joe's innocence forces Bobbie to explain her "sickness" to him, he strikes her and flees, appropriately, into the woods, where in his sick fantasy, the trees assume the "suave" female shape of urns, vessels, each of which is broken:

> He went on down the road fast and turned from it and sprang over a fence, into plowed earth. Something was growing in the furrows. Beyond were woods, trees. He reached the woods and entered, among the hard trunks, the branch-shadowed quiet, hardfeeling, hardsmelling, invisible. In the notseeing and the hardknowing as though in a cave he seemed to see a diminishing row of suavely shaped urns in moonlight, blanched. And not one was perfect. Each one was cracked and from each crack there issued something liquid, deathcolored, and foul. He touched a tree, leaning his propped arms against it, seeing the ranked and moonlit urns. He vomited. (pp. 177–78)

Joe's revulsion from what he conceives as imperfect, death-related, and foul recalls Quentin's championship of virginity, an interpretation which he imposed on the essentially positive and dynamic condition of Nature. When Joe does take Bobbie, a week later, he literally drags her back to this same place, "among the growing plants, the furrows, and into the woods, the trees" (p. 178). At this sensitive time for the boy he intuitively and ritualistically associates sex with Nature and natural process. But his recognition is blundering and agonizing.

It is hardly coincidental that with Joe and others the object of love is also the object of hate or fear. The paradox is implicit in the male's innocence. And in *Light in August* Joe's experience is paralleled by old Hightower's early, and lost, "love" of darkness and Nature: "He hears now only the myriad and interminable insects, leaning in the window, breathing the hot still rich maculate smell of the earth, thinking of how when he was young, a youth, he had loved darkness, of walking or sitting alone among trees at night. Then the ground, the bark of trees, became actual, savage, filled with, evocative of, strange and baleful half delights and half terrors. He was afraid of it. He feared; he loved in being afraid" (p. 300). This passage goes on to explain that Hightower came to hate Nature, and that in hating Nature he also lost the habit of prayer, turning instead to a sterile and thoughtless reading of

Tennyson: "the gutless swooning full of sapless trees and dehydrated lusts begins to swim smooth and swift and peaceful. It is better than praying without having to bother to think aloud. It is like listening in a cathedral to a eunuch chanting in a language which he does not even need to not understand" (p. 301). However, years later, with the experience of delivering Lena's baby, he experiences a comprehensive spiritual renewal. His visits to her cabin take him through the woods, where he recalls his long lost sensuous awareness of Nature: "'I must do this more often,' he thinks, feeling the intermittent sun, the heat, smelling the savage and fecund odor of the earth, the woods, the loud silence. 'I should never have lost this habit, too. But perhaps they will both come back to me, if this itself be not the same as prayer'" (pp. 384–85).

It is also in the woods and fields, intimately exposed to raw nature, that Joe Christmas knows his apocalyptic moment: "The air, inbreathed, is like spring water. He breathes deep and slow, feeling with each breath himself diffuse in the neutral grayness, becoming one with loneliness and quiet that has never known fury and despair. 'That was all I wanted,' he thinks, in a quiet and slow amazement. 'That was all, for thirty years. That didn't seem to be a whole lot to ask in thirty years'" (p. 313). He discovers there the peace and resignation—the timeless *ataraxia*—that enables him to face arrest. He leaves the woods immediately. But while he was one with a Nature which knows no despair he had lost "the old habit" of keeping track of the days; leaving the woods resolved to surrender, he must first reorient himself in time. He must ask the first person he meets what day it is. Christmas and Hightower, both of these tormented males, come in time to a moment of illumination in which they recognize and acknowledge the simple but awesome implications of Lena's "implacable and immemorial earth."

In the early *Soldiers' Pay*, the quiet of night and physical contact with the earth, "the gracious earth," brings to George Farr a similar deeply felt sense of peace, a oneness with the earth:

The turned flower bed filled the darkness with the smell of fresh earth, something friendly and personal in a world of enormous vague formless shapes of greater and lesser darkness. The night, the silence, was complete and profound: a formless region filled with the smell of fresh earth and the measured ticking of the watch in his pocket. After a time, he felt soft damp earth through his trousers upon his thighs and he sat in a slow physical content, a oneness with the earth, waiting a sound from the dark house at his back. He heard a sound after a while but it was from the street. . . . Soon the night was again vague and vast and empty.

Again he became one with the earth, with dark and silence, with his own body . . . with her body, like a little silver water sweetly dividing . . . turned earth and hyacinths along a veranda, swinging soundless bells. . . . (p. 165; Faulkner's ellipses)

Not only does this very early passage assert the mystical oneness which can be absorbed from the earth, but here also Earth and Woman are identified; the union with the earth becomes in Farr's mind sexual union with Cecily Saunders; and the damp earth is echoed in the "little silver water" of the female.

A very few characters cannot respond to Nature in the novels, and they contrast dramatically with those who enjoy the regenerating experience. Such a person is the wildly frustrated Burch of *Light in August,* who rejects both Lena and his child. Significantly, he behaves in flight from his responsibility like "an animal fleeing alone, desiring no fellowaid, clinging to its solitary dependence upon its own muscles alone and which, in the pause to renew breath, hates every tree and grassblade in sight as if it were a live enemy, hates the very earth it rests upon and the very air it needs to renew breathing" (p. 410). People who actually hate the earth are few, but Burch is one. In a later story, "Delta Autumn" (*Go Down, Moses*), another father will offer the mother of his child and the baby nothing but money when he rejects them, the hollowest of all compensation. We see this man, Roth Edmonds, force himself through an empty ritual in the elemental woods, shooting does for camp meat—a symbolic restatement of his treatment of the mother and child.

Faulkner casts the human condition against fundamental processes, the raw common denominator of life on Earth, and it is quite possible that the male's ambiguous fear and hatred and love of woman must be explained in terms of his fear and hatred and love of the old Earth itself, to which Woman is so disturbingly related.

Notes

1. I have taken all quotations from the following editions of Faulkner's novels: *Soldiers' Pay* (New York, 1951); *The Sound and the Fury & As I Lay Dying* (New York, 1946); *The Hamlet* (New York, 1940); *The Wild Palms* (New York, 1939); *Requiem for a Nun* (New York, 1951); *A Fable* (New York, 1954); *Light in August* (New York, 1932); *Absalom, Absalom!* (New York, 1951).

2. Many of Faulkner's Negroes share with his women (either white or Negro) this *ataraxia*. The women have it because they are more obviously tied to the rhythms and drives of natural process. Despite their poverty and depressed status, the Negroes have a spiritual equilibrium as people who live on and by the old earth, cherishing their families, protecting the young. Dilsey's innate serenity contrasts with the frustration of the Compson men and the morbid respectability of Caroline Compson to give *The Sound and the Fury* its remarkable thematic resolution in the fourth section. The extended studies of Lucas Beauchamp in both *Go Down, Moses* and *Intruder in the Dust,* Nancy Mannigoe of *Requiem for a Nun,* and the Reverend Tooleyman (*Tout le Monde*) of *A Fable* provide other examples of the serenity of the Faulkner Negro. The recurrent fact that his Negroes and his women bear or bear with children placidly and that they love and protect them further indicates Faulkner's preoccupation with the continuity of life.

3. The point should be made that Joe's mature sex life is entirely normal, vigorous, healthy. Symbolists like Richard Chase ("The Stone and the Crucifixion: Faulkner's *Light in August,*" *Kenyon Review* X, Autumn 1948) who read homosexuality into Joe's troubles might remember the following comment in *Light in August* by the author: "His own life," Faulkner says, referring to Joanna's complete corruption, "for all its anonymous promiscuity, had been conventional enough, as a life of healthy and normal sin usually is" (p. 246).

4. Joe's bloody ritual, although it continues the theme of male delicacy, gains complexity from its function in the religious framework of the story, the culmination of which endows him with immortality through his ritual castration.

CHAPTER 10

"THE BEAUTIFUL ONE"
CADDY COMPSON AS HEROINE OF *THE SOUND AND THE FURY*

Catherine B. Baum

William Faulkner's statement that *The Sound and the Fury* is "a tragedy of two lost women: Caddy and her daughter"[1] indicates that he intended Caddy Compson to be both a central and a tragic figure in the novel. None of the critics, however, emphasizes the role of Caddy as much as Faulkner does, and even those who do consider her life a unifying force in the novel have not thought of the novel as her tragedy. Lawrence Bowling points out that Caddy is "the essential center of the main action . . . the primary obsession with Benjy and Quentin and Jason throughout the first three sections of the book,"[2] yet he treats her life as but one aspect of the "theme of innocence"[3] he finds in the novel, thus ignoring her role as tragic heroine. Similarly, Olga Vickery sees Caddy as a center of action, but she thinks Caddy's importance is primarily technical, rather than thematic: "Within the novel as a whole it is Caddy's surrender to Dalton Ames which serves both as the source of dramatic tension and as the focal point for the various perspectives."[4] Caddy's function, Miss Vickery believes, is to provide an opportunity for each of the brothers to react to her and thereby to reveal his own character. In view

Originally published in *Modern Fiction Studies*, Spring 1967.

of Faulkner's remarks, however, it seems just as likely that the reverse is true—that the main function of the other characters is to reveal something about Caddy.

Because no one of the Compsons has a complete and unbiased view of Caddy, there is an obscurity surrounding her character, but it is not an impenetrable obscurity. In fact, a main aim of the novel is to allow the reader to piece together information and derive for himself a true picture of Caddy. Faulkner's technique in *The Sound and the Fury* is very much like that he used in *Absalom, Absalom!,* of which he said: "It was . . . thirteen ways of looking at a blackbird. But . . . when the reader has read all these thirteen different ways of looking at the blackbird, the reader has his own fourteenth image of that blackbird which I would like to think is the truth."[5] Similarly, the reader can see several distorted ways of looking at Caddy, but through careful reading and discernment, he will be able to derive that fourteenth image, the truest picture of Caddy.

That Caddy's life is a cohesive force in the novel can easily be seen. She is the central concern of each brother, and the telling of her story is the common purpose of each section. She causes the other characters to speak out. She is the only human factor in Benjy's life which gives it meaning, for the other things he loves are inanimate objects—the fire, the pasture, the red and yellow cushion, the blue bottle, and the jimson weed. Caddy is also the main interest of her brother Quentin. His thoughts turn ceaselessly from the present—his trip on the bus, his walk on the bridge, his adventure with the Italian girl—to the past, and the past for Quentin *is* Caddy. His thoughts revolve around her pregnancy, her wedding, and the question of honor, which to him is inextricably bound up with Caddy. She likewise is important to Jason, her antagonist, as the ruination of his plans for the future.

Many explanations have been offered for the arrangement of the four sections of the novel, but no one has noticed the most simple and probable one: a logical and traditional ordering based on the chronology of Caddy's life, her childhood, adolescence, and maturity. Because the past is as immediate to Benjy as the present, he reveals Caddy's personality as a child, and his section logically comes first. With an ever-present concern about chastity and honor, Quentin is best suited to tell of Caddy's adolescence and loss of innocence. His section therefore follows Benjy's. Since Jason is interested not in morals, but in money, he is concerned about Caddy only as she affects his financial welfare; for this reason, she impinges on his consciousness only after her divorce from Herbert, which costs Jason his promised job. She is again of interest to him when he can appropriate to himself the money she sends Quentin. Jason then, fittingly enough, tells the story of Caddy's adulthood, her divorce and her relationship with her daughter. The climax of the novel is Caddy's defeat at the hands of Jason, who leaves her stammering, helpless, and broken, as she acknowledges, "'I have nothing at stake. . . . Nuh-nuh-nothing. . . .'"[6]

The final section of the novel comments on life without Caddy and the love she represents. As Dilsey says, "'I seed de beginnin, en now I sees de endin'" (p. 313). The events of this day, as Quentin, "the extension of Caddy,"[7] runs away, mark the disintegration and the "endin" of the Compson family. Without the warmth of Caddy's love, everything seems cold and dying. The house is "decaying" (p. 301) and "rotting" (p. 313), and the word "cold" is used repeatedly to describe the weather, the house, the meals, Jason, and Mrs. Compson. Benjy's sorrowful moans have the effect of a Greek chorus crying "woe." As "the grave hopeless sound of all voiceless misery under the sun" (p. 332), these cries furnish an appropriate dirge for the loss of Caddy.

All that remains of Caddy is her "white satin slipper . . . yellow now, and cracked and soiled" (p. 332). This slipper is a touching and effective symbol of Caddy's life, which once was clean and shining too, but now is spoiled and dirty like the slipper.

In addition to its structural significance, Caddy's life also thematically represents love, compassion, pity, and sacrifice in a family which is destroying itself through its lack of these qualities. This most important role is also the most neglected by the critics. Before one can understand Caddy's unselfish love, one must understand her character, and it is here that many critics seem to have gone astray, apparently accepting at face value Jason's and Quentin's evaluations. To Charles Anderson, Caddy is only a promiscuous nymphomaniac;[8] to Carvel Collins, she represents the libido, and "her development as charted in the novel is a twisting of the libido's normal development toward full sexuality";[9] to Bowling, "Caddy is essentially like Jason in that she is a naturalist and never rises above her natural state."[10] Powell speaks of "the darkness of her soul,"[11] and Foster describes her as "a sensitive, beautiful girl, but given to bitchery from her early teens."[12] Certainly there is some basis for these feelings. Caddy has affairs with several men, becomes pregnant, and marries a man she does not love in order to give her unborn child a father.

To judge her solely on the basis of these facts, however, is to distort her character completely. Faulkner in 1957 remembered her as "the beautiful one, she was my heart's darling. That's what I wrote the book about and I used the tools which seemed to me the proper tools to try to tell, try to draw the picture of Caddy."[13] And he adds, "Caddy was still to me too beautiful and too moving to reduce her to telling what was going on."[14] Thus to Faulkner, Caddy is not only central, but also beautiful and moving.

Caddy's most important and distinctive quality is unselfish love. She is the only Compson who loves without thought for self and with a genuine desire for the happiness of others, especially for her two innocent brothers, Benjy and Quentin. Caddy offers the care that Benjy needs, "the tenderness," Faulkner says, "to shield him in his innocence."[15] She gets into bed with him to help him go to sleep, she is concerned about him when his hands are cold, and she tries to make him happy by telling him about Christmas: "Santy Claus, Benjy. Santy Claus" (p. 27). She has the ability to sense what he wants and the initiative to get it for him: "'You want to carry the letter.' Caddy said. 'You can carry it'" (p. 32); "He wants your light-ning bugs, T.P. Let him hold it a while" (p. 55). She knows that Benjy likes the red and yellow cushion and that "if you'll hold him, he'll stop [crying]" (p. 82). These are things the other members of the family either do not know or do not care about.

The beauty of Caddy's love becomes especially prominent when seen against the background of the other characters' lack of concern for Benjy's happiness. Quentin never hurts Benjy, but nei-ther does he show any affection for him. Jason pesters and teases Benjy by cutting up his paper dolls; Luster impishly whispers "Caddy" in his ear to make him cry (p. 74); Mrs. Compson's words to Benjy are usually sharp and chilled—"You, Benjamin" (p. 60)—or they are admonitions to the rest of the household to keep him quiet. Mr. Compson and Dilsey both seem to care about Benjy, but they are either too busy or too preoccupied to do anything for him. Mr. Compson's "Well, Benjy. . . . Have you been a good boy today" (p. 83) shows some distracted interest, but he does not play an active role in Benjy's life. Dilsey tries to protect Benjy from Luster's teas-ings (p. 74), but she is kept too busy by her work around the house and the whining demands of Mrs. Compson. Only Caddy is actively interested in his welfare.

The reaction of Caddy's daughter, Quentin, to Benjy height-ens the effect of Caddy's tenderness by contrast. Quentin feels only disgust and repugnance for Benjy and his repulsive table man-ners (p. 89), whereas Caddy had solicitously and patiently fed him. When Benjy was distressed at finding Caddy and Charlie in the swing, Caddy ran to comfort Benjy and gave up Charlie (p. 67). On the other hand, when Benjy finds Quentin with her boyfriend in the swing, Quentin calls him an *"old crazy loon"* (p. 67) and runs to the house, not to comfort Benjy, but to complain to Dilsey.

Caddy has other qualities as admirable as her selfless love. In the first section of the novel she is an active and curious little girl. She is the one who asks many questions about Damuddy's funeral and who finds an ingenious way of getting around her father's orders that the children go to bed immediately after supper:

> "Your pa say for you to come right on up stairs when you et supper. You heard him."
> "He said to mind me." Caddy said. (p. 46)

While Jason tags along saying "I'm going to tell . . ." (p. 46) and while Quentin obediently stays behind on the kitchen steps (p. 47), Caddy leads the way to the tree outside the parlor window so that she can see what's going on inside. She is the one, as Faulkner put it, "brave enough to climb that tree to look in the forbidden window."[16] Although Caddy disobeys her father's instructions, still her behavior is better than Quentin's excessive obedience which keeps him from participating in life, and it is an indication of her independence and spirit.

Only Caddy knows her brother Jason for what he is. When he makes one of his numerous threats to "tell," Caddy defies him: "Let him tell. . . . I dont give a cuss" (p. 39). When Jason destroys Benjy's dolls, Caddy's fierce protectiveness reveals the intensity of her love:

> "He cut up all Benjy's dolls." Caddy said. "I'll slit his gizzle."
> "Candace." Father said.
> "I will." Caddy said. "I will." She fought. Father held her. She kicked at Jason. He rolled into the corner, out of the mirror. (p. 84)

Caddy's tone here suggests her youthful confidence that she can handle anything. The poignancy of the scene, however, is that Jason cannot be destroyed so easily.

The qualities Caddy evinces before her loss of innocence—her self-reliance, courage, independence, and especially her love—are attributes that certainly make her "beautiful and moving,"[17] and Benjy's section of the novel serves largely to reveal these traits. That Caddy loses these qualities is her tragedy, and the remainder of the novel depicts the tragic changes as the world finally destroys her courage and her love.

Caddy is doomed, Lawrence Bowling points out, by "the general state of lovelessness into which all the Compson children were born without any choice on their part."[18] The lack of guidance from her father, the coldness of her mother, the vengefulness of Jason— all contribute to her downfall. More than this, she is doomed by society itself for violating its mores and by the attitude of men like Dalton who consider women only "bitches" (p. 179).

One cannot, however, place all the blame on circumstances or the Compson family. A large part of the reason for Caddy's damnation is found in herself. Ironically enough, those qualities in her character that are admirable are the ones which lead to her fall: her complete selflessness, which leads her to be indifferent to her virginity and to what happens to her; her willingness to put the other person's interests first; and her great desire to communicate love. She is too selfless for the world she is in, because all that the world, in the form of Jason and Dalton, knows how to do is take advantage of that selflessness. What Cash said of Darl in *As I Lay Dying* is applicable also to Caddy: "this world is not his world; this life his life."[19] This world is not "the right place for love"[20] for Caddy. In a family which needs tenderness and compassion as urgently as do the Compsons, the destruction of such a capacity for love is a terrifying waste.

By the end of *The Sound and the Fury,* Caddy has changed from a loving, innocent girl to a feverish, anxious woman who, as Jason said, looked "like some kind of a toy that's wound up too tight and about to burst all to pieces" (p. 227). In the novel's appendix, published in 1946, it is evident that she has changed even more: she has become the mistress of a German staff general, and she has become "ageless and beautiful, cold serene and damned" (p. 12). Now, as the librarian Melissa Meek believes, *"Caddy doesn't want to be saved hasn't anything anymore worth being saved for nothing worth being lost that she can lose"* (p. 16). If the older Caddy is impervious now to harm from the world, she is also completely and irrevocably damned. Quentin believes "temporary" is the saddest word (p. 197), but for Caddy the saddest thing is the permanence of her doom.

Caddy's constant and selfless love for others makes it momentarily difficult to understand her coldness when she is with the Nazi. Yet the change has been prepared for in the novel, and her coldness years later is only the logical culmination of forces working against her earlier. The dramatic alteration of her character can be traced in stages through her relationships with the seven men important in her life: Benjy, Charlie, Dalton, Quentin, Herbert, Jason, and the Nazi general. Mr. Compson can be omitted because he does not delineate any particular segment of her life; his influence on her is a more general one.

In her childhood relations with Benjy, Caddy is self-confident, warm, and innocent. Then the beginning of Caddy's sexual experience and her loss of innocence is marked by the episode with Charlie in the swing. But she is still in control of her feelings and is able to give up Charlie for Benjy's sake. When she meets Dalton, however, she loses her mastery over herself:

> he's crossed all the oceans all around the world
>   then she talked about him clasping her wet knees her face tilted back in the grey light the smell of honeysuckle. . . . (p. 169)

She is a childlike Desdemona in her wonder at knowing someone who has seen "all the oceans." She seems still innocent mentally and spiritually, if not physically.

When Quentin asks Caddy if she loves Dalton, she does not declare her love in words:

> Caddy you hate him dont you dont you
>   she held my hand against her chest her heart thudding
> I turned and caught her arm
>   Caddy you hate him dont you
>   she moved my hand up against her throat her heart was hammering there. (p. 169)

Her pounding heart should prove her love more than words could, but Quentin cannot understand. "Incapable of love" (p. 10), he must hear the word to comprehend it. To Quentin, love is just a word, as Addie Bundren puts it, "a shape to fill a lack."[21] To Caddy, who knows the meaning of love and who has loved, the word is not necessary.

Caddy's interest in men is a natural part of growing up, like her playing with the perfume and the hat. Since she should not remain as much a child as Benjy, it is wrong to condemn her interest in Dalton. What one could censure her for, however, and what the world *does* censure her for, is that she gives herself completely and without reserve to Dalton. She loves Dalton and wishes to communicate her love, and the lack of love in the Compson household drives her to seek it outside the family. Robert Penn Warren writes that the only real villains in Faulkner are "those who deny the human bond"[22]—like Jason, Quentin, and Mrs. Compson. Caddy fights to assert the human bond. Her love for Dalton is not passive, but active; she did not *"let"* him kiss her, she *"made"* him (p. 152).

Caddy's giving herself to Dalton reveals not only her love, but also her selflessness. Love to her is more important than morality, and she has been taught no good reason for preserving her chastity. All her mother cares about is the appearance of virtue, and Caddy places no value on her maidenhood, which means "no more than a hangnail" (p. 10) to her. What does matter to her is the communication of love. Mr. Compson perhaps best expresses Caddy's attitude toward virginity when he says it is "contrary to nature" (p. 135), or, as Olga Vickery says, it is "an artificial isolation of the woman."[23] Virginity, therefore, is just one of the "high dead words."[24]

Caddy's loss of mental and spiritual innocence comes towards the end of her affair with Dalton. Thinking Dalton has hurt Quentin, she tells him to go away. Then she realizes Quentin is not hurt, and she is anxious to go to Dalton. Her words indicate her growing awareness of his true feeling toward her:

> let me go Ive got to catch him and ask his let me go Quentin please let me go let me go
>> all at once she quit her wrists went lax
>> yes I can tell him I can make him believe anytime I can make him . . . anytime he will believe me. (pp. 181–82)

The repetition of "let me go" and "anytime I can make him believe me" seems to indicate an increasing desperation on Caddy's part and a fearful realization that she might not be able to make Dalton believe her. Caddy does not say what it is she can make him believe, but a probable answer is that she is afraid she is pregnant and is apprehensive about whether or not he will believe he is the father. She seems to know that Dalton is not as close to her as she would like to think.

In her relationship to Quentin after her affair with Dalton, Caddy's sense of despair is evident in her willingness for Quentin to kill her or commit incest with her (pp. 170–71). It makes no difference to her which alternative he chooses: "yes Ill do anything you want me to anything yes" (p. 175). Her own well-being is a matter of no concern to her, and her independence seems to have disappeared. Her affair with Dalton, she knows, hurts both Quentin and Benjy. Quentin she pities because he cannot understand what it is to love: "poor Quentin . . . youve never done that have you" (p. 170). The sad thing for Quentin is that he has never done anything. As T. S. Eliot has pointed out, ". . . it is better, in a paradoxical way, to do evil than to do nothing; at least we exist."[25] In these terms, Caddy's fall is better than Quentin's innocence.

That Benjy is hurt by Caddy's actions is evident in his bellowings and pulling at her dress when she comes in after having been with Dalton (pp. 87–88). Quentin notices that when Caddy is near Benjy now, her eyes are "like cornered rats" (p. 168). Torn as she is between her love for Benjy and her new love for Dalton, she has good cause to feel despair.

The men in Caddy's life after Dalton appear only vaguely in *The Sound and the Fury,* and one can only speculate about Caddy's motives in going with them. There is no evidence that she loved them as she had Dalton, but her indifferent attitude toward virginity and her need to give and receive love may explain her giving herself to them.

Just before her marriage to Herbert, Caddy tells Quentin, "*I died last year I told you I had but I didnt know then what I meant I didnt know what I was saying. . . . But now I know I'm dead I tell you*" (pp. 142–43). Even with Dalton she had half suspected that he would not "believe" her and might betray her. Since then, she has evidently learned that she can trust no one. When she becomes pregnant and is forced to face the consequences of her actions, she knows that she is dead.

In her marriage to Herbert, Caddy is willing to assume responsibility for her actions. She cares nothing for Herbert, but her concern for Benjy and her father has convinced her that marrying Herbert is the only thing she can do. When Quentin says, "*we can go away you and Benjy and me where nobody knows us where . . . ,*" Caddy's answer shows both her realism and her ever-present concern for Benjy: "*On what on your school money the money they sold the pasture for so you could go to Harvard dont you see you've got to finish now if you dont finish he'll have nothing*" (p. 143). When Quentin tells Caddy to think of Benjy and her father and not to marry Herbert, Caddy's interest in the welfare of others is still predominant: "*What else can I think about what else have I thought about . . . Father will be dead in a year they say if he doesnt stop drinking and he wont stop he cant stop since I since last summer and then they'll send Benjy to Jackson I cant cry I cant even cry . . .*" (pp. 142–43). Her love for her father is also revealed in the broken, rushed way she speaks of him. By marrying Herbert, Caddy hopes she will enable her father to stop worrying about her and to stop drinking. Then he will not die in a year, and Benjy will not have to be sent to Jackson. So, although Slatoff castigates Caddy for "abandon[ing] Benjy,"[26] the marriage is really one of her most selfless acts; it will, she hopes, benefit Benjy in the long run.

Caddy's compassion for Benjy and reluctance to leave him are seen on her wedding day. When she hears Benjy crying, she rushes out to him and hugs him (pp. 59, 101). She has not stopped loving Quentin either, for as Herbert tells Quentin, "Candace talked about you all the time up there at the Licks . . . she couldnt have talked about you any more if you'd been the only man in the world . . ." (pp. 126–27). In her eagerness to have Quentin promise to take care of Benjy and Mr. Compson, she not only expresses her heartfelt concern for them but also seeks to divert Quentin's mind from the shattering fact of her pregnancy. Although he tenaciously tries to find out about her pregnancy, her own situation is of such slight importance to her and the well-being of Benjy and her father are of such major importance that she brushes off his questions in order to extract his promise:

> *Have there been very many Caddy*
> *I dont know too many will you look after Benjy and Father*
> *You dont know whose it is then does he know*
> *Dont touch me will you look after Benjy and Father.* (p. 134)

After her marriage and subsequent divorce from Herbert, Caddy sends her daughter back to Jefferson with Mr. Compson. At first, this act seems heartless, but it is almost the only thing she could do. In entrusting Quentin to her father, Caddy probably hoped that things would turn out well for her, and at any rate, as Jason pointed out later to her, Caddy had no way to provide for her. When Mrs. Compson coldly refused to let Caddy come home in spite of Mr. Compson's pleas that she be allowed to do so (p. 228), she practically determined Caddy's fate. Thrown entirely on her own, Caddy could do little but become a mistress or a prostitute, and she did not want her daughter to become part of such a life.

Caddy did not forget her daughter, however, and Jason remarks that she would come back once or twice a year to see her (p. 228). The first time she came back, Jason allowed her only a passing glimpse of Quentin, and he noticed that "Caddy saw her and sort of jumped forward" (p. 223). The involuntary movement shows love for Quentin and eagerness to have her back. The only way Jason can keep her from going out to see Quentin is by attacking her in her most vulnerable spot, her love for Benjy: "So the next time I told her that if she tried Dilsey again, Mother was going to fire Dilsey and send Ben to Jackson and take Quentin and go away" (pp. 225–26). This threat seems to have been effective, for there is no evidence of Caddy's again trying to go to the house.

Slatoff criticizes Caddy for her attitude toward Quentin: "We learn that she is concerned about her daughter Quentin's welfare, but not concerned enough to do anything serious about it."[27] What Slatoff ignores is that Caddy is so hamstrung by the maneuverings of Jason and the unforgivingness of Mrs. Compson that she is powerless to do anything more for Quentin than send her money. Caddy is cut off almost entirely from communication with the Compson household: Jason censors her letters to Quentin (p. 208), she learns of her father's death only by accident (p. 220), and Jason tells her, "We dont even know your name at that house" (p. 221).

The most important reason for Caddy's not taking Quentin away is again her love. She does not want Quentin to become a mistress or a prostitute, and Jason knows it. When she offers Jason a thousand dollars to let her have Quentin back, he mocks her:

> "And I know how you'll get it," I says, "You'll get it the same way you got her. And when she gets big enough—" Then I thought she really was going to hit at me. . . .
>
> "Oh, I'm crazy," she says, "I'm insane. I can't take her. Keep her. What am I thinking of." (p. 227)

Now like a wound-up toy (p. 227), Caddy is completely frustrated and broken down by her lifelong antagonist, Jason. He notes that "her hands were hot as fever" and that she is making a strange noise: "she begun to laugh and to try to hold it back all at the same time. 'No. I have nothing at stake,' she says, making that noise, putting her hands to her mouth, 'Nuh-nuh-nothing,' she says" (p. 227). This is a terrifying picture of the collapse of her spirit.

Still, Caddy is anxious about Quentin; even though she realizes that Jason has not "a drop of warm blood" in him (p. 226), she pleads with him to take care of Quentin. Her broken and incoherent sentences indicate her highly emotional state and her sense of helplessness: "Just promise that she'll—that she—You can do that. Things for her. Be kind to her. Little things that I cant, they wont let . . ." (p. 226). By this time Caddy has lost her self-confidence and her innocence; she is reduced to pleading with the brother she knows will not help her. The only quality Caddy has not lost is her love, for she still cares about Quentin.

But in Faulkner's appendix to the novel, when Caddy is seen with the Nazi, even the love is gone, and destruction is complete. Yet even though Caddy's final position with the Nazi represents spiritual damnation, it seems to be, ironically enough, one of worldly success. The picture of Caddy which the librarian finds is "filled with luxury and money and sunlight—a Cannebière backdrop of mountains and palms and cypresses and the sea, an open powerful expensive chromiumtrimmed sports car, the woman's face hatless between a rich scarf and a seal coat, ageless and beautiful, cold serene and damned . . ." (p. 12).

The description of Caddy here resembles that of Eula Varner riding out of Frenchman's Bend with her impotent bridegroom: "The beautiful face did not even turn as the surrey drew abreast of the store. It passed in profile, calm, oblivious, incurious. It was not a tragic face: it was just damned."[28] The coldness and serenity isolate and protect the two women from the world. Yet there is an important difference between Caddy and Eula. Eula's face is not tragic, just damned: she had had nothing to lose; Caddy had much to lose, and her face is both tragic and damned. Although she gains the "luxury and money and sunlight" (p. 12), she loses *"anything . . . worth being saved for,"* as the librarian Melissa Meek pointed out, and she now has *"nothing worth being lost that she can lose"* (p. 16). Caddy is damned because she has become cold, empty-eyed, and passionless like Eula Varner. She has lost her capacity for love, and Dilsey's comment "What a sinful waste . . ." (p. 109) is the most apt summary of her tragedy. Even selfless love can result in the destruction of the person who practices it. The wasteful loss of Caddy's great capacity for compassion and sacrifice makes her fate the most unbearable and tragic doom in *The Sound and the Fury*.

Notes

1. Jean Stein, "William Faulkner," *Writers at Work, The* Paris Review *Interviews,* ed. Malcolm Cowley (New York, 1958), p. 130.

2. Lawrence Bowling, "Faulkner and the Theme of Innocence," *Kenyon Review,* XX (1958), 475.

3. Bowling, p. 466.

4. Olga Vickery, *"The Sound and the Fury:* A Study in Perspective," *Publications of the Modern Language Association,* LXIX (1954), 1017.

5. Frederick L. Gwynn and Joseph L. Blotner, eds., *Faulkner in the University* (Charlottesville, Virginia, 1959), p. 274.

6. William Faulkner, *The Sound and the Fury* (New York, 1946), p. 227. Subsequent references, which appear in the text, are to this edition.

7. Bowling, p. 475.

8. Charles Anderson, "Faulkner's Moral Center," *Etudes Anglaises,* VII (1954), 57.

9. Carvel Collins, "A Conscious Literary Use of Freud?" *Literature and Psychology,* III, iii (1953), 3.

10. Bowling, p. 476.

11. Sumner C. Powell, "William Faulkner Celebrates Easter, 1928," *Perspective,* II (1949), 208.

12. Ruel E. Foster, "Dream as Symbolic Act in Faulkner," *Perspective,* II (1949), 181.

13. Gwynn and Blotner, p. 6.

14. Gwynn and Blotner, p. 1.

15. Robert A. Jellife, *Faulkner at Nagano* (Tokyo, 1956), p. 104.

16. Gwynn and Blotner, p. 31.

17. Gwynn and Blotner, p. 1.

18. Bowling, p. 479.

19. William Faulkner, *As I Lay Dying* (New York, 1946), p. 532.

20. Robert Frost, "Birches," *The Poems of Robert Frost* (New York, 1946), p. 128.

21. Faulkner, *As I Lay Dying,* p. 464.

22. Robert Penn Warren, *William Faulkner and His South,* The First Peter Rushton Seminar in Contemporary Prose and Poetry, No. 16 (unpublished essay, Univ. of Virginia, Charlottesville, Virginia, 1951), p. 14.

23. Vickery, p. 1026.

24. Faulkner, *As I Lay Dying,* p. 467.

25. T. S. Eliot, "Baudelaire (1930)," *Selected Essays 1917–1932* (New York, 1932), p. 344.

26. Walter J. Slatoff, *Quest for Failure: A Study of William Faulkner* (New York, 1960), p. 151.

27. Slatoff, p. 151.

28. William Faulkner, *The Hamlet* (New York, 1940), p. 270.

CHAPTER 11

DEVIOUS CHANNELS OF DECOROUS ORDERING

A LOVER'S DISCOURSE IN *ABSALOM, ABSALOM!*

Linda Kauffman

There is something in the touch of flesh with flesh which abrogates, cuts sharp and straight across the devious intricate channels of decorous ordering, which enemies as well as lovers know because it makes them both— touch and touch of that which is the citadel of the central I-Am's private own.

Language (that meager and fragile thread . . . by which the little surface corners and edges of men's secret and solitary lives may be joined for an instant now and then before sinking back into the darkness where the spirit cried for the first time and was not heard and will cry for the last time and will not be heard then either).

Critics of *Absalom, Absalom!* have concentrated so exhaustively on the relation of history to myth in the novel that they have

Originally published in *Modern Fiction Studies*, Summer 1983.

wholly overlooked the relation of myth to love and the rhetoric of the lover's discourse in Faulkner's masterpiece. Lovers' discourses have their roots in such myths as Ariadne's lament to Theseus, who promises to marry her if she gives him the thread to escape from the labyrinth but instead deserts her and marries her sister. In Ovid's *Heroides*, a series of forlorn female figures write to the men they love, men who either are absent or have abandoned them: Ariadne writes to Theseus, Penelope to Odysseus, Helen to Paris, Dido to Aeneas. In another epistolary discourse, the seventeenth-century French classic *Letters Portugaises (Letters of a Portuguese Nun)*, the nun first beseeches the French chevalier who seduces and abandons her to return, then dedicates herself to the recreation of her passion in her letters. The influence of *Letters Portugaises* on French and English fiction before Richardson was so enormous that a new literary genre emerged; the "Portugaises" became a generic term referring not only to the scores of imitations, translations, and sequels to the original text but to any work of intense subjectivity written in the moment of disordered passion. Despite the antiquity of its origins, the lover's discourse defies simple classification. It frequently appears as a subgenre within a larger, more conventional genre. Alexander Pope's *Eloisa to Abelard* (1717) is a heroic epistle, for example, but Eloisa's lament is also a lover's discourse strongly influenced by *The Letters of a Portuguese Nun*.[1] The most recent example is Roland Barthes's *A Lover's Discourse: Fragments*, which presents a persona and tells a story but is not a novel. The text cites a variety of authorities, but it is not a treatise. It moves toward no climax, yet it is moving and dramatic. It invites the reader to participate and to identify, but there is no moral, no plot. It is arranged alphabetically. The text defies definition in terms other than those of a lover's discourse.

The difficulty with categories and definitions is not only generic but philosophic, for the lover is a linguistic orphan in philosophic solitude. Barthes's lament in *A Lover's Discourse* is directed as much toward modern systems of thought as toward the absent beloved, for no system, no language, no philosophy validates the experience of the lover. Instead the lover is an embarassment, an anachronism—sentimental, irrelevant, or mad. Barthes protests that both philosophy and language consistently oppress and repulse him, but I believe that the female lover faces even greater oppression and repulsion. She has been reduced to a few well-worn clichés: the Seduced Maiden-Victim (the Portuguese nun); the Frigid Martyr (Clarissa); the gullible Plain Jane (Jane Eyre); the Repressed Madwoman (the governess in *The Turn of the Screw*); the Frustrated Spinster (Rosa Coldfield). The female lover, indeed, is frequently regarded merely as a madwoman, a figure of fury and frigidity. No system of discourse seriously considers her suffering, her passion, or the remarkable range and resourcefulness of her imaginative powers.

My focus, therefore, is on the fluctuations of states of mind (despair, frustration, rage, loneliness, yearning, nostalgia) and on conditions of being (isolation, exile, imprisonment), for without such states, the text would not exist. Subjectivity is the subject. There is thus a traditional rhetoric in lovers' discourses that links such disparate texts as *The Heroides* and *The Letters of a Portuguese Nun* to such contemporary works as *Absalom, Absalom!* and Barthes's *A Lover's Discourse.*

Why this rhetorical tradition has been overlooked in *Absalom, Absalom!* is a matter of speculation. It is related, I think, to what Barthes calls the philosophic solitude of the lover, which arises, he suggests, because no modern system of thought accounts for love or considers the lover:

> Christian discourse . . . exhorts him to repress and to sublimate. Psychoanalytical discourse . . . commits him to give up his [beloved] as lost. As for Marxist discourse, it has nothing to say. If it should occur to me to knock at these doors in order to gain recognition *somewhere* . . . for my "madness" (my "truth"), these doors close one after the other; and when they all shut, there rises around me a wall of language which oppresses and repulses me.[2]

This protest of Barthes's has a special relevance to literary criticism, for despite all the "systems of thought" that have been employed to explicate *Absalom, Absalom!*, the lover's discourse woven into the fabric of the novel still remains unrecognized. No one has noticed how frequently the language of the lover's discourse is invoked in the novel, nor has anyone identified the character who is the real lover, the one who draws most consistently on the rhetoric of the lover's discourse. It is not Quentin, recreating his passion for his sister in his imaginative reconstruction of the relationship between Henry and Judith Sutpen. Or Mr. Compson, lingering lovingly on the sensuousness of Charles Bon's octoroon mistress. Or even Charles himself, writing love letters to Judith while waiting on his destiny. The character who seeks recognition of her "truth" is the one who has been dismissed as mad: Rosa Coldfield is the Lover-as-Artist in *Absalom, Absalom!*, endlessly naming her pain and sustaining her passion in weaving her narrative.

Most critical commentaries, however, focus on Rosa not as a passionate but as a pathetic creature: they emphasize her grotesqueness, her Gothicism, her thwarted and bitter life. The critical perceptions of Rosa demonstrate the validity of Barthes's assertion that modern systems of thought refuse to recognize the lover and instead define the lover as repressed, disturbed, or mad. Cleanth Brooks describes Rosa's language as a "dithyramb of hate . . . [a] shrill, tense voice . . . [of] Norn-like frenzy."[3] Albert Guerard's assessment is also characteristic:

> Her ornate, often sexualized rhetoric and rhythms of almost insane intensity . . . admirably convey a particular disturbed personality . . . [her] ranting [is] controlled by exquisitely timed . . . sentences . . . [in a] hysterical narrative . . . of wild rhetoric.[4]

Guerard is representative of all those critics whose "systems" of discourse—psychoanalytic or otherwise—have failed to recognize Rosa. Guerard is particularly provocative because he *senses* that there is a language in *Absalom, Absalom!* that he can neither define nor assimilate, for he notes that "all the narrators share Faulkner's ironic love of hyperbole and paradox, of absurd oxymoron and analogy drawn from an alien area of discourse."[5] My aim is to show the close connection of Rosa's narrative to the traditional rhetoric of lovers' discourses and, in so doing, to make that form of discourse a little less alien.

Lovers' discourses have striking similarities in mood and motif, tone and technique. Their abiding themes are love and hate, seduction and betrayal, desire and despair. They frequently combine elements of the classic tragic tirade with the intense subjectivity of the epistolary form or the monologue. Of all the narratives in *Absalom, Absalom!*, Rosa Coldfield's has the most personal immediacy and the most passionate intensity. Far more than Quentin, she is the one who is most actively engaged in her narrative. Yet she has been dismissed as a "frustrated spinster," as if those two words were simply redundant. Although Rosa has much in common with such grand obsessives as Dickens' Miss Havisham in *Great Expectations* and Mrs. Clennam in *Little Dorrit*, she is far more complex than the stereotypical jilted lover. This distorted perception of her is wholly shaped by Mr. Compson, Quentin, and Shreve, none of whom ever really sees Rosa as anything but a warped, bitter, outraged, pathetic old woman. Rosa is a text they all misread.

It is one thing to indulge in imaginative reconstructions of the long-dead Sutpen, Henry, Bon, and Judith. But Rosa is not remote— she is a living, breathing woman whose relations with Quentin and Mr. Compson are far more personal, immediate, and intimate. The Sutpens are ghosts; she is not. Yet both men try to make Rosa as

well into a ghost. When Quentin asks his father why he must answer Rosa's summons, for instance, Mr. Compson replies, "Years
ago we in the South made our women into ladies. Then the War
came and made the ladies into ghosts. So what else can we do, being gentlemen, but listen to them being ghosts?"[6] They try to distance themselves from her by thus reducing her complexity. But if
they cannot even comprehend the living woman in front of them,
what hope is there of comprehending the long-dead Sutpens? This
is what Shreve implies when he confronts Quentin at the end by
saying, "You dont even know about the old dame, the Aunt Rosa. . . .
You dont even know about her" (p. 362). Rosa resists reduction,
however, as Shreve senses when he reflects that "She refused at
the last to be a ghost." She refuses to allow herself to be reduced
to some stereotypical figure of mere pathos and fury.

Female fury, indeed, is one of the obsessions that pervades
the consciousness of males in the novel. The reductive view of
Rosa, moreover, may stem from a fundamental uneasiness among
characters *in* the novel and critics *of* the novel with the idea of
female fury. "The dread and fear of females," after all, is something
men draw in "with the primary mammalian milk" (p. 265). The
words here are Grandfather Compson's, but the idea reverberates
throughout the novel. What is fascinating is that Faulkner juxtaposes the complex with the reductive view of female anger by creating not one but two outraged women in *Absalom, Absalom!* The
second is Eulalia Bon, the Creole wife whom Sutpen abandons, who
is wholly invented by Quentin and Shreve. The Gothic is actually
more pervasive in their imaginations than in Rosa's, for Eulalia resembles another Creole from the West Indies who is probably the
most famous figure of fury in fiction: Bertha Mason, Rochester's
mad wife in *Jane Eyre.*[7] Bertha's heritage is tainted by hereditary
madness; Eulalia's is allegedly "tainted" by Negro blood.

Rosa Coldfield's narrative is no mere diatribe by a mad woman,
for she is a figure not of simple pathos but of considerable passion.
Because Mr. Compson, Quentin, and Shreve all describe her as "an
old lady that died young of outrage" (p. 174), it is difficult to imagine
her as young, much less passionate. Quentin, for example, wonders
if Rosa's voice "had even been a cry aloud once . . . long ago when
she was a girl," but he immediately rejects the possibility, thinking,
"but not now: now only the lonely thwarted old female flesh embattled for forty-three years" (p. 14). Quentin's reaction fulfills the
prophecy contained in my second epigraph, for Rosa's cry was not
heard the first time when she was young, nor is it heard now, at the
last. It is also difficult to see her narrative as a lover's discourse
because it contains so much rage. But hatred is as much a form of

passion as love, and outrage is a major characteristic of lovers' discourses from Ariadne's lament to Theseus to *The Letters of a Portuguese Nun*. Whenever the lover is abandoned, in fact, the tone of the discourse is frequently furious, characteristically wavering between hope and despair, fury and fortitude. These are precisely the polarities that shape Rosa's narrative. Her character and imagination reflect multiple conflicts between love and hate, forgiveness and revenge, pity and despair. In the epigraph with which I began, she says that touch makes enemies as well as lovers. Rosa herself is both an enemy and a lover. The object of her worship is Charles Bon; the object of both her desire and her enmity is Thomas Sutpen.

Whereas she invests Charles with all the qualities of courtly romance, Sutpen is the focus of her fury. Rosa's very name symbolizes the duality in her character between courtly love (*La Roman de la Rose*) and frigid fury. I draw quite consciously on the language of literature because Rosa herself is so self-consciously literary. She transforms her passion into art by telling and retelling her story. She wants to preserve her passion while exorcising its object. This impulse is also characteristic of lovers' discourses: the abandoned lover frequently writes to separate her passion from its object. The Portuguese nun tells her lover, for example, that in the process of writing about her passion, "I discovered it was not so much you as my own passion to which I was attached; it was remarkable how I suffered while struggling with it even after you had become despicable to me through your wretched behavior."[8] I think the Portuguese nun's reflections reveal more about Rosa's motives and attitude than the psychoanalytic language of repression and frustration has yet revealed.

Writing and speaking of passion is frequently a process of exorcism. This is why Rosa's narrative so often sounds like an incantation—the evocation of a ghost in order to exorcise it. This process, moreover, is a peculiarly literary one—self-conscious and theatrical. The betrayed lover creates her own theater and her own audience. Cleanth Brooks has noted Rosa's "sense of the histrionic. She is conscious of the fact that she is acting a part, and . . . she actually refers to herself in the third person as if she were a character in a play."[9] What has been overlooked, however, is the role of language as enchantment and the close connection, as in Rosa's speech on the "devious intricate channels of decorous ordering," of love to hate, memory to revenge, presence to absence.

In *A Lover's Discourse*, Roland Barthes defines language as enchantment. Consider the issues of language, structure, and Rosa's character in relation to Barthes's observation that in the Christian West, until today, all strength passes through the Interpreter, as a type (in Nietzschean terms, the Judaic High Priest). But the strength of love cannot be shifted, be put into the hands of an Interpreter; it remains here, on the level of language, enchanted, intractable. Here the type is not the Priest, it is the Lover. . . . Historically, the discourse of absence is carried on by the Woman . . . It is Woman who gives shape to absence, elaborates its fiction . . . she weaves and she sings; the Spinning Songs express both immobility . . . and absence. . . . (Myth and utopia: the origins have belonged, the future will belong to the subjects *in whom there is something feminine.*) (*ALD*, pp. 13–14, 23–24)

Barthes's ideas here illuminate the relation of myth to love. They also help to explain why Rosa seems at once intractable and enchanted, why she seems to be under an enchanted spell as she speaks. The passage also points up the connection of spinning thread and the narrative line, a connection I shall discuss further.

Now Rosa is not the only one who waits in *Absalom, Absalom!* All the women whose men go to war are waiting. (Judith, moreover, is poignantly contrasted to other women, for she waits not only "not knowing for what, but . . . not even knowing for why" after Henry repudiates his birthright and departs with Charles.) But it is Rosa—intractable and implacable—who remains to interpret events in the end. It is Rosa who summons Quentin. It is Rosa who conjures up the past and is the catalyst for the entire plot. She embodies the classical "figure" of absence—its textuality.

In view of the current preoccupation with absence in texts, let me explain why absence so affects the tone and texture of lovers' discourses. Simply stated, fulfilled lovers have no need of writing because they have each other. Only those who have been rejected or abandoned turn to art, to "devious channels of decorous ordering," to sustain something or someone who no longer exists. Lovers' discourses are eternal monologues. Thus, nullification is a chief characteristic of the discourse of passion. The discourse is predicated on the absence of the beloved. From abandonment, then, comes the birth of language. Loss is the structure. Although I am concentrating exclusively on Rosa, her experience replicates that of the others in the novel; indeed loss is what structures the lives of all the characters in *Absalom, Absalom!*: Sutpen's loss of innocence at Pettibone's door; Eulalia's loss of Sutpen; Charles Bon's search for the lost father; Judith's unmarried widowhood. And looming over all these losses is the loss of the Civil War. Loss, lack, absence are the structures.

Rosa Coldfield "gives shape to absence and elaborates its fiction" from the very first page of the novel: once listening reneges and hearing-sense-self-confounds, "the long-dead object of her impotent yet indomitable frustration would appear, as though by outraged recapitulation evoked, quiet inattentive and harmless, out of the biding and dreamy and victorious dust" (pp. 7–8). There are multiple ironies in Sutpen's being "inattentive"; what I wish to point out is how it reinforces the sense of nullification that has been the fundamental pattern of Rosa's existence. From birth, her very presence is predicated on her mother's absence: "She was born, at the price of her mother's life and was never to be permitted to forget it" (p. 59). Her entire childhood is described in terms of lack: her aunt serves not only as mother but also as father to her; her sister, she is taught, "vanished not only out of the family and the house but out of life too" (p. 60); her childhood is marked by the absence of play and is passed "in that aged and ancient and timeless *absence of youth* which consisted of a Cassandralike listening beyond closed doors, of lurking in dim halls" (p. 60, italics mine). She is ignored by her father, excluded from her cousins' company, ridiculed by her sister, Ellen, when she offers to teach Judith to cook. She describes herself as a "small plain frightened creature whom neither man nor woman had ever looked at twice" (p. 141). As in Roland Barthes's *Discourse,* Rosa's narrative arises from extreme silence and solitude. As she tells us: "*instead of accomplishing the processional and measured milestones of the childhood's time I lurked, unapprehended as though, shod with the very damp and velvet silence of the womb, I displaced no air, gave off no betraying sound, from one closed forbidden door to the next*" (p. 145).

Indeed, an astonishing number of forbidden doors, gates, and corridors appear in *Absalom, Absalom!*: Goodhue Coldfield nails the attic door shut; Henry stops Bon at the gate; Clytie stops Rosa on the stair; Sutpen forbids Wash entrance; there is a door in Quentin's consciousness through which he cannot pass. All of these images contribute to the sense of the novel as a labyrinth and to the narrative line as a thread. Many of these images replicate Sutpen's humiliation at the door of Pettibone's mansion, which in turn is a reenactment of the psychic shock Pip in *Great Expectations* suffers at the door of Satis House. (Satis: desire seems to increase in direct proportion to humiliation and rejection, as in Dostoevsky's *Notes from Underground* and in Rosa's narrative.) The connection of humiliation to narration and naming can be seen by comparing the reactions of young Pip at Satis House and young Thomas Sutpen at Pettibone's door. Just as Thomas "couldn't get it straight yet . . . he was seeking among what little he had to call experience for something to measure it by, and he couldn't find anything" (p. 233), Pip describes himself a being "so humiliated, hurt, spurned, offended, angry, sorry—I cannot hit upon the right name for the smart—God knows what its name was . . . As I cried, I kicked the wall . . . so bitter were my feelings, and so sharp was *the smart without a name,* that needed counteraction" (*Great Expectations,* Book I, chapter 8, italics mine). Rosa Coldfield's own efforts to name her pain are similarly related to humiliation and to the frustration of desire.

Rosa's obsession with Charles Bon is clearly the result of lack, of silence and solitude. She does not love Bon himself but what Barthes calls "the Image-repertoire," which is not a person but the correspondence between an object of desire and her image of him. She retains the "Image-repertoire" long after the living man departs. Bon is an absence to which Rosa gives shape, as she herself explains:

> There must have been some seed he left, to cause a child's vacant fairy-tale to come alive . . . even before I saw the photograph I could have recognized, nay, described, the very face. But I never saw it. I do not even know of my own knowledge that Ellen ever saw it, that Judith ever loved it, that Henry slew it: so who will dispute me when I say, Why did I not invent, create it? And I know this: if I were God I would invent out of this seething turmoil we call progress something . . . which would adorn the barren mirror altars of every plain girl who breathes with such as this . . . this pictured face. It would not even need a skull behind it; almost anonymous, it would only need vague inference of some walking flesh and blood desired by someone else even if only in some shadow-realm of make-believe. (pp. 146–47)

This passage clearly demonstrates that Rosa is aware of the fictive endeavor in which she is engaged. She sees herself as the highly self-conscious Lover-as-Artist, worshipping her own imaginative powers and her "Image-repertoire." She worships not Bon but the idea of Bon and his very absence: his footprint obliterated by a rake; the fading sound of his breathing; "*his foot, his passing shape, his face, his speaking voice, his name: Charles Bon, Charles Good, Charles Husband-soon-to-be*" (p. 148).

The Keatsian and Shakespearean ordering of the images with which she endlessly recreates her passion for Bon also illuminates Rosa's attachment to her "Image-repertoire." She does not love Bon but the idol she constructs, the receptacle of all her hopes and illusions. Rosa draws repeatedly on the traditional language of lovers' discourses when she refers to worshipping Bon, erecting an altar, making sacrifices to her idol. Not only is the Portuguese nun's rhetoric nearly identical, but it further illuminates Rosa's actions, motives, and attitude:

> A heart is never more deeply affected than when it is first made aware of the depths of feeling of which it is capable. All its emotions are centered upon the idol which it builds for itself. Its first wounds are neither to be healed nor to be effaced. The passions which come freely to the heart's aid and give it power to express and satisfy itself afford it a profound emotion that is never to be recaptured. All the pleasures which it seeks, though without true desire to find them, serve only to show that nothing is so dear to it as the remembrance of past sorrows.[10]

This, of course, is the great theme of Romantic poetry, which is one of the formative influences on Rosa's imagination. John Irwin maintains that Rosa can never become Bon's lover, not even by identifying herself vicariously with Judith, because Judith never becomes Bon's wife.[11] But Irwin's formula literalizes and thus reduces Rosa's remarkable imagination. My point is just the opposite of Irwin's: Rosa sees herself as a more perfect lover precisely because her emotions are centered on the idol she has built for herself. Just as unheard melodies are sweeter in Keats's "Ode," Rosa's love for Bon is ideal because it comes from the imagination. Her Keatsian allusions are perhaps most pronounced when she speaks of all those unfulfilled urges that are "*more globed and concentrate and heady-perfect*" (p. 144) precisely because they remain to be fulfilled. (I shall return to examine this image in another context presently.)

Barthes's description of desire further illuminates Rosa's desire for Bon:

> It is my desire I desire, and the loved being is no more than its tool. I rejoice at the thought of such a great cause, which leaves far behind it the person whom I have made into its pretext . . . I sacrifice the image to the Image-repertoire. And if a day comes when I must bring myself to renounce the other, the violent mourning which then grips me is the mourning of the Image-repertoire itself: it was a beloved structure, and I weep for the loss of love, not of him or her. (*ALD*, p. 31)

From *The Heroides* onward, a frequent contrast in lovers' discourses is between the absent male at war for his country and the abandoned female warring with her passions; Bon and Sutpen battle in the Civil War while Rosa remains embattled at home. The heroine's single-minded obsession with her passion, with her own imaginative powers, and with the private theater of her emotions supercedes all other concerns.[12] The result is precisely the kind of passionate intensity that makes Rosa so memorable. Subjectivity and style are the dual motives for and subjects of her discourse.

If Bon is the receptacle of Rosa's illusions, Sutpen is the one who shatters them. Here again, loss is the structure: the loss of Rosa's illusions about the possibility of salvaging something of *"the old lost enchantment of the heart."* What is striking is that Sutpen is as much a figure of absence as Bon is. Rosa's experience with Sutpen consists of repeated nullification, for she never really exists to him despite the fact that he is her foe (according to Mr. Compson) from the time she is ten: his is "the face of a foe who did not even know that it was embattled" (p. 63). As usual, he is "inattentive." She cannot even say how often she sees Sutpen as a child, "for the reason that, waking or sleeping, the aunt taught her to see nothing else" (p. 63). He is the constantly present absence. Even after he "proposes," Rosa realizes that *"My presence was to him only the absence of black morass and snarled vine"* (p. 166).

Yet once their marriage is planned, she allows herself to hope anew, to believe that *"he was not oblivious to me but only unconscious and receptive"* (p. 167). Sutpen not only is a symbol of a megalomaniacal male principle, but, in the terms of lovers' discourses, he is the Other, inaccessible and unknowable. (His incomprehensibility, indeed, is one reason all the characters in *Absalom, Absalom!* are obsessed with him.) The Other always has a life structure to which the lover does not belong, from which the lover is excluded. This is why René Girard says that the birth of passion coincides with the birth of hate: the person who is the object of desire is transformed into a magical Other who holds the keys to the edifice but denies the lover access.[13] The Portuguese nun, for example, addresses her absent lover saying, "What would I do, alas, without so much hate and without so much love which fills my heart?"[14] The word she uses in French is "remplir": to fill up; to fill in a gap, a space; to occupy. In Rosa's discourse, born of absence, repetition and recollection signal all that is lost and all the gaps, the voids, the haunted silences she is trying to fill.

Repetition and circularity are trademarks of lovers' discourses; the heroine realizes that she is neither the first to be seduced nor the last to be abandoned by her lover. This realization recurs throughout *The Heroides*; Ariadne, for instance, is supplanted by Phedre, who compares her own fate to Ariadne's. Phyllis, who loves Theseus' son, similarly sees the son's betrayal as a repetition of Theseus' betrayal of Ariadne. The suffering is always new, always individual, always unique, yet always the same.

The idea of the magical Other helps to explain why Rosa transforms Sutpen into an ogre, a djinn, a Bluebeard. With Sutpen as with Bon, Rosa is "elaborating her fictions," but where she draws on Keats, Shakespeare, and romance in her recreation of Bon, with Sutpen her sources are the Old Testament, Milton, and the Brothers Grimm. In one poetic passage, full of Miltonic cadences, she describes Wash Jones as

> *that brute progenitor of brutes whose granddaughter was to supplant me, if not in my sister's house at least in my sister's bed to which (so they will tell you) I aspired—that brute who (brute instrument of that justice which presides over human events which, incept in the individual, runs smooth, less claw than velvet: but which, by man or woman flouted, drives on like fiery steel and overrides both weakly just and unjust strong, both vanquisher and innocent victimized, ruthless for appointed right and truth) brute who was . . . to preside upon the various shapes and avatars of Thomas Sutpen's devil's fate. (p. 134)*

Such self-conscious theatricality is characteristic of lovers' discourses. In the absence of the beloved, lovers invent scenes, poses, situations to occupy themselves. They have, after all, only words to play with. "Absence becomes an active practice, a business. There is the creation of a fiction which has many roles (doubts, reproaches, desires, melancholies)." The lover, says Barthes, is always inventing scenes of "pathos which I imagine and by which I am moved . . . this theater, of the stoic genre magnifies me, grants me stature. By *imagining* an extreme solution . . . I produce a fiction, I become an artist, I set a scene, I paint my exit" (*ALD*, pp. 15–16, 142). Rosa's discourse is simlarly marked by a theatricality of which she is well aware—with Bon as well as with Sutpen. When she describes her frequent forays into Judith's room to look at Bon's picture, for instance, she does so "*not to dream . . . but to renew, rehearse, the part as the faulty though eager amateur might steal wingward in some interim of the visible scene to hear the prompter's momentary voice*" (p. 147).

The necessity of invention helps to explain why Rosa dedicates herself to hating Sutpen. It is not simply because he proposes that they breed first and marry later. Outrageous as the proposition is, I think Rosa reacts with such vehemence for two reasons. First and foremost, Sutpen's proposition is a reenactment of the fundamental trauma of Rosa's existence. Because she has been nullified over and over since birth, Sutpen's obliteration of her as an individual at this point has far more cumulative force than it would otherwise have. And because nullification has been the pattern of her life, I think she dedicates herself to hating Sutpen in a final attempt to break the pattern. She combats nullification by mythologizing Sutpen and herself, transforming her experience into what Barthes calls "a myth of grief" (*ALD*, p. 182). Like many lovers' discourses, Rosa is in the process of creating the language with which to name her pain, to sustain her passion, to reorder experience and to make it comprehensible. She reconstructs her desire while deconstructing its object, Sutpen. Her narrative is an effort at comprehension and, simultaneously, an acknowledgment of the futility of that effort. One source of her frustration, indeed, is that no telling can express the meaning of her tale; it has to be traced and retraced, just as Theseus must retrace Ariadne's thread in the labyrinth.[15] She is aware of her compulsion to repeat, as she tells Quentin:

> I will tell you what he did and let you be the judge. (Or try to tell you, because there are some things for which three words are three too many, and three thousand words that many words too less, and this is one of them. It can be told; I could take that many sentences, repeat the bold blank naked and outrageous words just as he spoke them, and . . . leave you only that Why? Why? and Why? that I have asked and listened to for almost fifty years.) (pp. 166–67)[16]

Given the utter incomprehensibility of Sutpen as the Other, hatred is Rosa's way of making him more accessible. There is, after all, a kind of knowledge in hating, as Quentin points out: "*Maybe you have to know anybody awful well to love them but when you have hated somebody for forty-three years you will know them awful well so maybe it's better then, maybe it's fine then because after forty-three years they cant any longer surprise you or make you either very contented or very mad*" (p. 14).

Rosa's narrative, then, is a defiant effort to break the pattern of nullification that has plagued her throughout her life. But no matter what she says, she knows she is perceived as a "*warped bitter orphaned country stick . . . Rosie Coldfield, lose him, weep him, caught a man but couldn't keep him*" (p. 168). No matter how she embroiders and elaborates, she remains trapped in the flesh, in the system she knows she has constructed, and in the perceptions of those around her. Barthes has a similar lament:

> All the solutions I imagine are internal to the amorous sys-
> tem: I order myself to be still in love and to be no longer in
> love. This kind of identity of the problem and its solution pre-
> cisely defines the *trap*: I am trapped because it lies outside
> my reach to change systems: I am "done for" twice over: in-
> side my own system and because I cannot substitute another
> system for it. This double noose apparently defines a certain
> type of madness. (*ALD*, p. 143)

Rosa reveals a similar awareness of the *trap* and the systems which
imprison her when she reflects:

> *There are some things which happen to us which the intelli-
> gence and the senses refuse just as the stomach sometimes
> refuses what the palate has accepted but which digestion can-
> not compass—occurrences which stop us dead as though by
> some impalpable intervention, like a sheet of glass through
> which we watch all subsequent events transpire as though in
> a soundless vacuum, and fade, vanish; are gone, leaving us
> immobile, impotent, helpless; fixed, until we can die. That was
> I.* (pp. 151–52)

Lovers' discourses characteristically are a series of no exits. The
only way out is death. By dying, Sutpen escapes his obsessions,
whereas Rosa remains trapped in hers. She rages because she
cannot disentangle herself from the threads of memory, frustration, and desire, whereas Sutpen has "kicked himself loose of the
earth" like Conrad's Kurtz. This is ultimately what she cannot forgive: for Sutpen the rest is silence; for Rosa there is no rest, only
recollection, reflection, repetition.

Faulkner's use of the thread as a metaphor for language reinforces the motif of doubling and repetition and connects the thread
to the narrative line. In the myth of Ariadne, as in the novel, laby-
rinthine doubling takes many forms: in one version of the myth,
Ariadne becomes pregnant; in another, she hangs herself with the
thread. In other versions, she is either married to or abducted by
Dionysus. Their relations with men make the parallels between
Rosa and Ariadne particularly provocative, for the doubling of Ariadne's relation to Theseus and Dionysus is compressed in *Absalom,
Absalom!* into one male figure: Sutpen. Sutpen's traits, moreover,
are specifically associated with threads on a spool, signifying conflicts in his character. One thread on the spool contains Theseus'
characteristics: shrewdness, courage, will, rationality. The other
thread contains Dionysian elements of nature, impulse, unpredict-
ability. When Sutpen tries to discover where he made his "mis-

take," for instance, he goes to Grandfather Compson and explains how eminently rational and judicious he was when he abandoned his first wife and son:

> I was faced with condoning a fact which had been foisted upon me without my knowledge during the process of building toward my design, which meant the absolute and irrevocable negation of the design; or in holding to my original plan for the design in pursuit of which I had incurred this negation. I chose, and I made to the fullest what atonement lay in my power for whatever injury I might have done in choosing, paying even more for the privilege of choosing as I chose than I might have been expected to, or even (by law) required. (p. 273)[17]

Mr. Compson ironically calls this "*the old logic, the old morality which had never yet failed to fail him*" (pp. 279–80). It fails him because there are so many Dionysian forces that cannot be reduced and constrained by control, intellect, and rationality, by a "code of logic and morality, his formula and recipe of fact and deduction" (p. 275).

The Dionysian facets of Sutpen's character create internal and external pressures. His insulting proposition to Rosa, for instance, is an unpremeditated act of sheer impulse, as Rosa admits: "*He had never once thought about what he asked me to do until the moment he asked it because I know that he would not have waited two months or even two days to ask it*" (p. 166). His drunken bouts in the scuppernong arbor with Wash further connect him to the god of wine, who was also known as the sufferer who grieves for his own pain. Dionysus, moreover, is the vine pruned so severely that it seems incapable of producing again; during the battle in the West Indies, we recall, one wound "came pretty near leaving him that virgin for the rest of his life" (p. 254). Potency and fertility, of course, are the roots of Sutpen's obsession: "*he was past sixty and . . . possibly he could get but one more son, had at best but one more son in his loins, as the old cannon might know when it has just one more shot in its corporeality*" (p. 279).

While evoking the images of loom, thread, and spool, Faulkner makes it clear that Sutpen weaves nothing from these threads of Theseus and Dionysus within his character. Instead, the images represent the thwarting of desire and the coming of death: "*The thread of shrewdness and courage and will ran onto the same spool which the thread of his remaining days ran onto and that spool almost near enough for him to reach out his hand and touch it*" (p. 279). Unlike Rosa, Sutpen creates nothing. Instead, like Dionysus,

he is the "ambiguous seducer-rescuer in a family romance involving defeat or death for the father figures, and a complex role for
the female figures as murderous mothers, as self-slaying victims,
and as transfigured mates for the god" ("AT," p. 65). In Faulkner's
family romance one thinks of Eulalia Bon as the murderous mother,
Clytie as the self-slayer, and Milly Jones as the mate for Sutpen.
Defeated or dead father figures also abound: Goodhue Coldfield,
Charles Bon, Wash Jones, and Sutpen himself. Therefore, the multiplication of images of the phallus at the end (Sutpen's horse, his
whip, the rusty scythe, the butcher knife) merely inscribes its loss
("AT," p. 76).

Like Persephone, Dionysus dies with the coming of cold, reduced to a gnarled stump. The connection of Sutpen to the god of
the vine may also give us an added insight into Rosa's preoccupation with wisteria, snarled vines, and roots. She affirms her own
potential for love and the urge of her own desire by comparing herself to a "warped chrysalis of what blind perfect seed: for who shall
say what gnarled forgotten root might not bloom yet with some
globed concentrate more globed and concentrate and heady-perfect
because the neglected root was planted warped and lay not dead
but merely slept forgot?" (p. 144). In the imagery of Keatsian ripe-
ness and ecstasy ("heady-perfect"), Rosa affirms the potential her
sexuality had to be fuller, more vital, more "concentrate," precisely
because her desires had been so long deferred. Sutpen, in contast,
is obsessed with the waste and loss of potency, with "th' expense of
spirit in a waste of shame." If Sutpen resembles Dionysus dying of
cold, Rosa sees herself as the sun and believes he is "unconscious
and receptive like the swamp-freed pilgrim feeling earth and tasting
sun and light again and aware of neither but only of darkness' and
morass' lack—who did believe there was that magic in unkin blood
which we call by the pallid name of love that would be, might be sun
for him" (pp. 167–68).

Rosa's responses to Sutpen are thus remarkably varied and
complex. Shreve's and Quentin's repeated emphasis on Rosa's hatred must not overshadow her pity and compassion for Sutpen.
Rosa manages to make a remarkable imaginative leap in vanquish-
ing her childhood vision of Sutpen as an ogre. When he returns
from the war, she sees him not as "the ogre; villain true enough,
but [as] a mortal fallible one less to invoke fear than pity . . . victim . . . [of] solitary despair" (p. 167). Now Rosa knows something
about both solitude and despair, and I see her ability to empathize
with Sutpen as a remarkable imaginative achievement. Sutpen's
proposition is most devastating, finally, because he makes no effort
to reciprocate. What is outrageous, ultimately, is the utter disparity

between how Rosa thought Sutpen saw her (as a source of sunlight and hope) and his actual view of her (as no more than a mare). (His mare's name, not so incidentally, is Penelope.)[18] There is thus great poignancy in Mr. Compson's reflections upon Rosa's death. He hopes that she gains a bourne where there are actual people to be recipients of her "outrage *and* her commiseration, her hate *and* her pity" (p. 377, italics mine). These words signal again the duality of all lovers' emotions and also reveal that reciprocity is the key, for the recognition of desire is bound up with the desire for recognition.[19] Traditionally in lovers' discourses, the abandoned lover prefers anything—even the beloved's active animosity—to his indifference. This is why the Portuguese nun says, "I would have endured your hatred and all the pangs of jealousy which your affection for another woman might have aroused in me. Then, I would at least have had some passion to combat, something real to contend with, but your indifference to me is insupportable."[20]

Indifference is also insupportable to Rosa, for active hatred involves engagement, as she well knows. I think this sense of "engagement" is what Faulkner had in mind when Shreve describes Rosa as "irrevocably husbanded . . . with the abstract carcass of outrage and revenge" (p. 180). What moves lovers to rage is the beloved's utter indifference, the lack of recognition. This lack has far-reaching ramifications not only in terms of Sutpen's relations with women but in terms of his refusal to recognize Charles Bon as well. Reciprocity is the vital ingredient missing in Sutpen's recipe for morality, in his grand design, and in all his relations.

Rosa Coldfield is thus well fitted for the role of Lover-as-Artist: she writes nearly a thousand odes to the Confederate dead and becomes the entire region's poetess laureate of "poems, ode, eulogy and epitaph, out of some bitter and implacable reserve of undefeat" (p. 11). She becomes the chronicler of the time, the one who records births, deaths, and disasters not only in the family Bible but in the imaginations of a younger generation. Like Ariadne, she is the One Who Waits, who gives shape to absence and weaves its fictions. Faulkner finally makes Rosa's relation to Ariadne explicit when he juxtaposes Rosa's sewing with the slow unravelling of the South in the War. She steals the cloth from her father's store and spends her days and nights

> sewing tediously and without skill on the garments which she was making for her niece's trousseau and which she had to keep hidden not only from her father but from the two negresses, who might have told Mr Coldfield—whipping lace out of raveled and hoarded string and thread and sewing it onto

garments while news came of Lincoln's election and of the fall of Sumpter, and she scarce listening, hearing and losing the knell and doom of her native land between two tedious and clumsy stitches on a garment which she would never wear and never remove for a man whom she was not even going to see alive. (p. 78)

Thus, what J. Hillis Miller has said about Ariadne's thread seems to me to be particularly relevant to *Absalom, Absalom!*, for the image of the thread is an analogue for the narrative line, dependent on doubling and tedious repetition to form a pattern ("AT," pp. 71–74). Yet in his absorption with (in?) the labyrinth of interpretation, Miller wholly forgets Ariadne herself—her role, her fate, her feelings before and after the betrayal. Indeed, in another essay he reveals his close identification with Theseus, for he compares his own essay to Theseus' impossible attempts at mastery: the "dance of the too rational Theseus . . . marked out ever-changing, winding figures . . . compulsively retracing the labyrinth in an always frustrated desire to master it. . . . The present essay is one more execution of the dance of Theseus."[21] What has happened to Ariadne in these few lines? She has disappeared, despite Miller's nominal title, despite the fact that it is *her* thread that literally saves Theseus' life and figuratively becomes a source of creative inspiration not just for Theseus but for *herself.* She, also, is frustrated by desire, but her frustration has nothing to do with reason and everything to do with passion. Thus, in charting Theseus' quest, Miller replicates his crime.

By focusing on Sutpen's quest, critics have consistently done the same thing to Rosa Coldfield. The critical preoccupation with the obliteration of origins, beginnings, entrances, and exits sometimes leads to the obliteration of the female as well. Not only is it the female who weaves and spins, but she is aware of the connection of this creative impulse to identity, as Judith Sutpen explains:

You are born at the same time with a lot of other people, all mixed up with them, like trying to, having to, move your arms and legs with strings only the same strings are hitched to all the other arms and legs and the others all trying and they dont know why either except that the strings are all in one another's way like five or six people all trying to make a rug on the same loom only each one wants to weave his own pattern into the rug. (p. 127)

This vision of interdependence is what Sutpen never manages to comprehend. That is why he creates nothing, despite the fact that his design, his very life, and all the lives his touches draw on the imagery of loom, thread, and spool. In contrast, Judith, Clytie, and Rosa form a *"triumvirate":* they are the three fates who are like *"one being, interchangeable and indiscriminate, which . . . spun thread and wove the cloth"* (p. 155). When Quentin confronts Henry at the end, he sees Clytie as "the one who owns the terror" (p. 369). But the drama of the telling belongs to Rosa; she is the one who articulates not only the doom, the curse, and the fatality of Sutpen's downfall but the sorrow and the pity of it as well. As Miller has shown, "the language of narrative is always displaced, borrowed. Therefore any single thread leads everywhere, like a labyrinth made of a single line or corridor crinkled to and fro" ("AT," p. 74). (Dis: apart, from; *discurre*: to run to and fro [*ALD*, p.4].) By identifying the origins of Rosa's borrowed language, I hope it has become a little less "the alien area of discourse" that puzzled Albert Guerard. Rosa's narrative establishes a pattern that is but one of many on the loom, one with a complex texture of love *and* hatred, romance *and* fury. She dedicates herself to what Barthes calls the Loquela: "The flux of language through which the subject tirelessly rehashes the effects of a wound or the consequences of an action: an emphatic form of the lover's discourse" (*ALD*, p. 160). In the absence of the touch of flesh with flesh, Rosa gives shape to lack and elaborates the fictions of loss which structure all the lives around her. She makes her presence felt by transforming passion into art, weaving and reweaving through "devious intricate channels of decorous ordering."

Notes

1. For the influence of *The Letters of a Portuguese Nun* on French and English fiction, see Robert Adams Day, *Told in Letters: Epistolary Fiction Before Richardson* (Ann Arbor: University of Michigan Press, 1966), pp. 32–40. On the "Portugaises" as a genre, see Charles E. Kany, *The Beginnings of the Epistolary Novel in France, Italy, and Spain* (Berkeley: University of California Press, 1937), p. 116. Although it is unlikely that Faulkner was familiar with *The Letters of a Portuguese Nun*, both his poetry and his prose reveal his familiarity with the rhetoric of the lover's discourse. Joseph Blotner points out that, in Faulkner's poetry, "the world-weariness of the poet complaining of his unrequited love would frequently be his subject, as might the languid fatal woman who did not return his passion." *Faulkner: A Biography* (New York: Random House, 1974), p. 185.

2. Roland Barthes, *A Lover's Discourse: Fragments*, trans. Richard Howard (New York: Hill and Wang, 1978), p. 211. Further references will be made parenthetically in the text as *ALD.*

3. Cleanth Brooks, "The Poetry of Miss Rosa Canfield [sic]," *Shenandoah*, 21 (Spring 1970), 199–206.

4. Albert Guerard, *The Triumph of the Novel: Dickens, Dostoevsky, Faulkner* (New York: Oxford University Press, 1976), pp. 323, 329.

5. Guerard, p. 321.

6. William Faulkner, *Absalom, Absalom!* (New York: Random House, 1964), p. 265. Further references to this edition will be made parenthetically in the text.

7. Michael Millgate mentions the similarities between the plot of *Absalom, Absalom!* and *Jane Eyre* in *The Achievement of William Faulkner* (New York: Random House, 1966), pp. 162–64, but he overlooks the extraordinary similarities in characterization, particularly between Rochester and Sutpen. They are both evasive, manipulative, and self-deceptive and pride themselves on their rationality. See note 17.

8. F. Deloffre and J. Rougeot, eds., *Letters Portugaises, Valentins, et autres Oeuvres de Guilleragues* (Paris: Garnier 1962), p. 62. My translation, here and elsewhere.

9. Brooks, p. 204.

10. *Lettres Portugaises,* p. 64.

11. John T. Irwin, *Doubling and Incest/Repetition and Revenge* (Baltimore, MD: Johns Hopkins University Press, 1975), pp. 74–75.

12. In *Love in the Western World,* Denis de Rougemont lists some of the common themes of the French troubadors. Their rhetoric includes motifs that are nearly identical to Rosa's lover's discourse: passion "sets one apart from all others"; one "dies of not being able to die"; one "complains of an ill that is yet prized more than every joy and worldly good." *Love in the Western World,* trans. Montgomery Belgion (London: Faber and Faber, 1940), p. 154. For the influence of the troubadors on Faulkner, see Richard P. Adams, "Faulkner: The European Roots," in *Faulkner: Fifty Years After* "The Marble Faun," ed. George H. Wolfe (University: University of Alabama Press, 1976), pp. 21–41. Among Faulkner's early poetry, moreover, is a poem entitled "Aubade. Provence. Sixth Century." See Blotner, p. 185.

13. René Girard, *Deceit, Desire, and the Novel,* trans. Yvonne Freccero (Baltimore, MD: Johns Hopkins University Press, 1965), pp. 40–41.

14. *Lettres Portugaises,* p. 54.

15. Although J. Hillis Miller never mentions Faulkner, I am indebted to his essay, "Ariadne's Thread: Repetition and the Narrative Line,"

Critical Inquiry, 3 (Autumn 1976), pp. 57–77. Further references to this essay will be made parenthetically in the text as "AT."

16. Rosa's words here echo another motif common in lovers' discourses: "to deplore that words should betray an 'ineffable' emotion which nevertheless demands to be avowed." *Love in the Western World,* p. 154.

17. The similarity between Sutpen's rhetoric and Rochester's in *Jane Eyre* is startling not only because each is trying to defend himself for abandoning a West Indian wife but because each stresses the legality of his actions and ignores the morality. Like Sutpen, Rochester prides himself on being the eminently rational man. To justify bigamy to Jane, he reasons, "Imagine yourself in a remote foreign land; conceive that you there commit a capital error. . . . Mind, I don't say a *crime*; I am not speaking of shedding of blood or any other guilty act, which might make the perpetrator amenable to the law: my word is *error.* The results of what you have done become in time to you utterly insupportable; you take measures to obtain relief: unusual measures, but neither unlawful nor culpable." Charlotte Brontë, *Jane Eyre: An Autobiography*, ed. Richard J. Dunn (New York: W. W. Norton, 1971), p. 191.

18. In the short story "Wash," similarly, Sutpen's mare is named Griselda. The names Penelope and Griselda are ironic allusions to the figure of the Woman Who Waits.

19. Jacques Lacan, "The Insistence of the Letter in the Unconscious," *Yale French Review*, No. 36–37 (1966), pp. 112–47.

20. *Lettres Portugaises*, p. 62.

21. J. Hillis Miller, "The Figure in the Carpet," *Poetics Today*, 1 (1980), 107–18.

CHAPTER 12

LINDA SNOPES KOHL
FAULKNER'S RADICAL WOMAN

Keith Louise Fulton

I

Faulkner's *Snopes* trilogy is not generally regarded as a radical critique of America. More commonly critics discuss ethical or aesthetic concerns that are rooted, as American political rhetoric is, in eighteenth-century ideas of universality and the individual. In both the eighteenth century and Faulkner's fiction, that individual is male; his experience is represented as culture. Faulkner's women also have a tradition in the texts, criticism, and Western civilization: they are nature. This mythology is set forth comically in *The Hamlet* and further subverted in *The Town* and *The Mansion*. The alternate vision of America is embodied finally in Linda Snopes Kohl, who walks out of the mansion and closes the door on the American dream of a patriarchal dynasty after achieving what no other female or male character in Faulkner's fiction achieves, an act of justice that settles her conflicts with the past and empowers her move into the future. Simone de Beauvoir would call it transcendence.

"Nigger Lover . . . Communist, Jew": the taunts scrawled on the sidewalk outside Linda's home name the radical causes that she represents as well as the role of the historical scapegoat she

Originally published in *Modern Fiction Studies,* Autumn 1988.

plays. Linda is doubly radical, however, for she is also a woman who shuns marriage, who arranges for the murder of her "father," and who avenges her mother's death by using the gallant liberalism of a family friend. Critics have not responded positively to her.[1] Linda, however, provides a timely although fictional way out of Faulkner's impasse between his liberal civil rights stance and his privileged position as male and white.[2] Moreover, Linda recalls the lives of other real American women who have been fighting a civil war different from the one the South lost.[3]

The trilogy tells the story of the Snopeses who take over the hamlet of Frenchman's Bend and then graze up the town of Jefferson and the positions of conservative power and respectability: bank president and U.S. senator. Flem Snopes makes his move from hamlet to town with the wealth he acquires by marrying the pregnant Eula Varner, a "loose girdled bucolic Lilith" (*Town* 319). When the child Linda is nineteen, Eula kills herself in an effort to protect her daughter from the shame of illegitimacy. Nineteen years later Linda petitions for the release of a relative, Mink Snopes, from the penitentiary where he has spent 38 years because his kinsman Flem would not help him: she accepts the moral responsibility for what she knows he will do—kill Flem.

Linda's experiences call into question the values of the American South and of the patriarchal civilization on which it is modeled. Faulkner embodies in her what David Mintner calls "the drama of longstanding dissatisfactions . . . with his region and his family" (239), a drama which Faulkner's own identity as white, privileged, and male prevented him from resolving. Critical responses to Linda, however, espouse values that she challenges and that entrap her in judgments, ironically opposite of what Faulkner does in the text.

II

Snopes is about origins and the process of history. To consider the relationships among women, men, and the land in terms of origins is to see them as transhistorical: the way they are is explained by their origin, their nature, and not by the process of historical change (Lerner 37). The trilogy begins as a comedy of transhistorical origins and concludes with a realization of historical change.

We can see what Faulkner had in mind in 1938 from the notes on his projected plot and titles: "The Peasants," "Rus in Urbe," and "Ilium Falling" (*Selected Letters* 107–8). Evidently the trilogy was planned as an epic cycle, traditionally the story of a nation. Faulkner's comic epic ostensibly recounts the battle between the Snopeses and the non-Snopeses they dispossess, but he did not follow his unrealistically hopeful plan where the victorious Snopeses breed themselves out of power, the last "scion of the family" a worthless boy (*Selected Letters* 108). Instead he dramatizes another conflict through the foregrounding of narrative and narrators, this one between the non-Snopeses who do the scrutinizing and telling and the inscrutable Snopeses who are successful "by means of the single rule and regulation and sacred oath of never to tell anybody how" (*Town* 107). Instead of the genetic dead end Faulkner had planned, the trilogy he wrote concludes in the tension between the unknowable Snopeses and the knowing narrators. Linda destroys Flem Snopes, not through biological nature, but through her growth in consciousness and her courage to act. The epic ends with the dramatization of historical change and the limits of the narrators' knowledge.

In Eula and Linda, Faulkner creates an alternative to those limits. Just as Helen was not the cause of the Trojan War, Eula and Linda are not the source of the conflict between Snopeses and non-Snopeses. But like Helen, they have become symbols. Their transformation into symbol (as woman, as nature) disempowers them as human creatures and masks the real problem of male dominance and greed. The male power that transforms mother and daughter into symbols also transports them from the center of human community to the margins of male discourse. Female abundance, fertility, is commodified in symbols, ultimately in the Snopeses' symbol of value and respectability: the dollar. As mother and daughter become symbols, the living Eula and Linda become scapegoats whose existence justifies and excuses the men who act for them. Eula and Linda are triply subjugated: by their blood kin, the Varners; by their legal kin, the Snopeses; and by their friends, the narrators who tell their stories.

It is not hard to find evidence of their subjugation by blood kin: old Will Varner, whose name Will punningly suggests his strength, trades them along with the deed to the Old Frenchman's Place to Flem in return for his nominal paternity and the respectability whose rules regarding daughters even the tomcatting Varner follows. Will marries his pregnant daughter to Flem. Flem's legal subjugation of Eula is more complicated. His power is not physical (he is impotent) but social and economic. Flem parlays into a bank presidency Eula's eighteen-year-old love affair with De Spain by blackmailing Eula, De Spain, and Varner with the threat of exposing Eula's adultery and Linda's illegitimacy. Since his marriage, Flem has been prevented from such an action by Varner's will in favor of Eula and her daughter Linda. Flem's real evil is that he trades on

Linda's need to love a father, her need to see his restrictions on her as his love for her, which seems to be proven when, after two years, he finally allows her to go to the university at Oxford. In the flush of gratitude for her escape, Linda has a will drawn up bequeathing whatever she might inherit from her grandfather through her mother to her "father" Flem. Needing nothing more from her now, Flem can use the threat to expose her as a bastard and her mother as a whore and an adulteress to gain voting control of Varner's and De Spain's bank stock. The only way Eula can stop Flem is suicide. Before she kills herself, however, she appeals to Gavin to marry Linda, to give her the name and home that Flem's disclosure would take from her.

Although perhaps Gavin is right not to marry where he feels such ambivalence, his conversational method of handling the conflict between his feelings and his notion of respectability exemplifies the subjugation of Eula and Linda by the narrators, who make them characters in their stories. Mother and daughter are like the Snopeses, their other topic of discussion, in being unknowable to the narrators, but they are unlike the Snopeses in that they are named and thought to be understood. They are the subjects of stories in which their own consciousness plays no part. The narrators in *The Town*, Gavin Stevens, his nephew Charles, and friend Ratliff, who tell the life stories of Eula and Linda, present themselves as friends and are seemingly the only allies these women have. The alliance is deceptive. Ratliff in *The Hamlet* admits that Eula's marriage to Flem is a "waste . . . intrinsically and inherently wrong by any economy" (161), yet when he looks at her face on the departing train he sees behind it "only another mortal natural enemy of the masculine race" (151). More than Charles and Gavin, Ratliff recognizes the barter context for the struggle between men and women; neither Gavin nor Charles understands even the struggle. Both adopt the self-serving and exploitative chivalrous stance which Kate Millett calls the "game the master group plays in elevating its subject to pedestal level" (50). Although Gavin is attracted to both mother and daughter, he toys with them from within the safety of his respectability. Gavin not only carries out his desires for the adolescent Linda under the avuncular guise of "forming her mind" (which fools only Linda), he ambushes her as she tries to get home unseen before a planned tryst, holds her by the wrist, and demands his right to know whose idea it was to dress her as a woman.

Although subjugated, Eula is the energy at the center of *The Hamlet* and *The Town*. After Eula's death Linda comes into her own womanhood—motherless, fatherless, and confused by the double message of Gavin's friendship. While Faulkner was revising *The Town*, he wrote in a letter, "I still think it is funny, and at the end very moving; two women characters I am proud of" (*Selected Letters* 399–400). Faulkner was justly proud; in these characters he has embodied an intuition about women and history and the problems in the American South.

III

The Hamlet reenacts the defeat of the fertility goddess, Eula. Even as an eleven-year-old girl, she is "the drowsing maidenhead symbol's self . . . tranquilly abrogating the whole long sum of human thinking and suffering which is called knowledge . . . at once supremely unchaste and inviolable" (114–15). None of the comedy Faulkner supplies dissuades us from a real sense of her power. When the school master Labove (whose name suggests what he is, above love) attacks her, she sends him sprawling: "Stop pawing me . . . You old headless horseman Ichabod Crane" (122). Faulkner places her physical development in the context of the art that has drawn on her. As a young child, Eula refuses to walk, so her mother has her carried by their Negro manservant, "staggering slightly beneath his long, dangling, already indisputably female burden like a bizarre and chaperoned Sabine rape" (96). As young wife to Flem, Eula appears in the window: "to those below what Brunhilde, what Rhinemaiden on what spurious river-rock of papier-mâché, what Helen returned to what topless and shoddy Argos, waiting for no one" (306). Apparently, because no amount of the cardboard that Faulkner exposes in the two-dimensional constructions of romance will challenge the self-deceiving fictions held by peasant and reader alike, they may see behind the staged symbolism to the barter at the heart of *The Hamlet*, where the fertility of the female is exchanged for the respectability and social power of the male. That exchange seals his right to own and to bequeath. The right to exchange stories, horses, and land (so important in the trilogy) sets him off from the woman, for it is a right she does not have. In the "Sabine rape," the "Ichabod Crane," the "Rhinemaiden" is the evidence that male art and literature have enshrined his right in culture, no matter if it is made of papier-mâché.

Gerda Lerner's analysis of the political and economic benefits one family achieved by placing a daughter as bride in a rival or even enemy family alerts us to another of Will Varner's possible motives. Flem has already shown himself master of Varner's methods of squeezing tenants; what better way could Varner protect his interests than by making Flem a son-in-law always in hope of his wife's inheritance. Lerner writes that the "customary right of male

family members . . . to exchange female family members in marriage antedated the development of the patriarchal family and was
one of the factors leading to its ascendancy" (110–11). Certainly
this transaction increases the power of both Varner and Snopes.
Ironically, but appropriately, Eula's own power is mystified as
symbolic woman while she is made a material object of trade.

In *The Town* Faulkner dramatizes the process of mystification
in the storytelling of Ratliff, Gavin, and Charles, who together seem
the American small town equivalent of a celibate priesthood. Ratliff
has the oral wisdom of the storyteller; Gavin has the Harvard law
degree and the Heidelberg doctorate. The "knowledge" they create
is passed to the next generation in Charles, whose position is conspicuously different from Linda's (although she is a child as he is).
What the narrators do not know is as important as what they do
know. Flem, like Varner, will need respectability; Gavin does not
know that in the town of Jefferson he himself will be Flem's model,
teacher, and accomplice. He will teach Linda to value love whether
it exists or not, and Flem will trade on that "love" to obtain her inheritance. Gavin will see to it that the suicide Eula is buried re-
spectably, covering in her death the cause of it. When he commis-
sions a marble medallion from Italy to mark Eula's grave, he blocks
in marble the woman Flem had bought and cashed in (although he
does so in part because that is the price to be paid for Linda's freedom). The inscription—"A Virtuous Wife is a Crown to Her Husband
/ Her Children Rise and Call Her Blessed"—is chosen by Flem, but it
could have been selected by Gavin. An accomplice to Flem's rise
through his need to cover realities in fine words, Gavin is also an
accomplice to Flem's death—although he intends neither. He contributes to a patriarchy he does not understand but benefits from.
Gallantly consistent, Gavin insists to Linda from the beginning that
Flem is her father. When she finally discovers that he is lying for
her, it is after she has been victimized—in part because he has lied
to her. Child that she was, she put real feeling into a false story of
kinship and love.

The "marble lie" marking Eula's grave also marks the end to
the illusion of timeless story (*Mansion* 420); the events of history
that invade Jefferson in *The Town* have a subtle impact on our
understanding. Although the name Faulkner chooses for the town
reminds us of Thomas Jefferson's passion to "liberate the human
mind from tyranny, whether imposed by the state, the church, or
our own ignorance" (Murphy 607), the small-town forms of democracy in Faulkner's Jefferson are unequal to the imperialist and racist aggression in Europe and the Snopish greed and legalism at
home. The Great War changes Gavin's perception of the world as

completely as Eula's death changes Linda's. For both, the process is a demystification of wishes. Gavin reassesses "them splendid mystical ideas" of Germany, and Linda goes off to Greenwich Village where she abandons the love poems and lives with a sculptor, Barton Kohl, who is not only a Jew but a Communist; together they arrange to go to Spain to fight for the Loyalists. The message from the *ad hoc* church of misfit World War Two veterans who help Mink after his release from Parchman Penitentiary is "Trust in God without depending on him."

In the years between the writing of *The Hamlet* (1940) and *The Town* (1957), Faulkner himself became politically active, using his abilities to represent the State Department abroad and to mediate in the civil rights struggle in the South. Convinced that the only way America could win the cold war was for the country to make real the democratic rhetoric of freedom and to eliminate racial oppression at home, Faulkner tried to persuade Southerners to accept integrated education before the federal government forced it on them. Otherwise, Faulkner warned, the South might "wreck and ruin itself twice in less than a hundred years, over the Negro question" (*Essays* 151). Like Linda, Faulkner was called a "nigger lover" (Mintner 244).

In the fictional Linda, however, Faulkner could present an analysis of the cold war and the racial struggle more radical than in his interviews, letters, and speeches because, unlike them, it could deal with "the impasse of the emotional conflict" (*Essays* 219). After a year in Spain Linda returns to Jefferson widowed and deafened; she forms a Communist cell with two Finns and tries to improve the education of the Negroes. Like the early feminists, her passion as an adolescent was for education. Now like the early feminist abolitionists who identified with the enslaved and oppressed Negroes, Linda begins teaching black children. Whereas Faulkner debated the civil rights issues publicly in language he hoped both sides would accept (a clue perhaps to his art), Linda enters the classrooms. Asked to leave by the Negro principal and forced out by the board of supervisors, she begins meeting children each Sunday at one of the Negro churches, "where she read aloud in the dry inflectionless quacking, not the orthodox Biblical stories perhaps but at least the Mesopotamian folklore and the Nordic fairy tales which the Christian religion has arrogated into its seasonal observances, safe now since even the white ministers could not go on record against this paradox" (*Mansion* 229). Thus Linda keeps alive in the children traces of culture before the Old Testament, which said they were "doomed to be inferior" (*Essays* 99).

A reader of the Old Testament, Faulkner would know of the references to the culture that the Israelite tribes supplanted by their own. Faulkner's early title for the Snopes stories, "Father Abraham," shows his interest in the patriarchy; Lerner's historical work with the Mesopotamian culture illuminates connections among slavery, the subordination of women, and the difficulties of democracy that Faulkner caught artistically. Lerner traces the historical creation of patriarchy in the civilization that commodified the fertility of women who "themselves became a resource, acquired by men much as the land was acquired by men" (212). The metaphoric association of women and land predates the Old Testament; in older mythologies than the Christian, the male seed is implanted in the furrows of the female womb. In a Sumerian poem, Inanna asks, "who will plow my vulva, who will plow my field?" (Lerner 189). The metaphor was still in use in 1915 when an American educator used it to argue against feminism and the higher education that Linda wants so passionately in 1922. He proclaimed "the farmer that uses his land for golf-links and deer preserves instead of for crops has but one agricultural fate; the civilization that uses its women for stenographers, clerks and school-teachers instead of mothers has but one racial fate" (Clinton 131).

In the story of Varner's marrying off the pregnant Eula to the capitalist Flem Snopes, Faulkner has seized a political metaphor at the center of patriarchal state and family, one that is pertinent to the civil rights struggle Faulkner was trying to ease. The assumed right of men to dominate women, to acquire, own, and plow the field, was historically the basis of Aristotle's metaphoric argument justifying slavery. "It is clear," Aristotle writes, "that the rule of the soul over the body, and of the mind and the rational element over the passionate, is natural and expedient . . . the male is by nature superior, and the female inferior" (Lerner 208, 281). The husband's rule over his slaves is as natural as his rule over his wife and children. "And indeed the use made of slaves and of tame animals is not very different; for both with their bodies minister to the needs of life" (Lerner 208). Linda's Mesopotamian folklore goes behind the Aristotelian tradition and gives to the black children knowledge of a time when humans first created and internalized the idea of slavery, first of women and then of other peoples. A condition that has not always been need not always be.

The Mesopotamian reverence for the Great Mother would also solace a woman whose own mother died in the patriarchically created impasse between respectability on the one hand and nurturance and passionate love on the other. That Linda has not forgotten the mother she does not talk about is clear from her patient weaving of events and motives. When Flem's death is accomplished, each person—Mink, Gavin, Linda, Ratliff, and even Flem—is doing what is most essential to the self, yet only Linda is realistically aware of all the others. Her understanding is sophisticated, grounded in a knowledge of what humans are.

Linda has the complexity of mythological thought and yet represents a twist to our comprehension of mythology. Whereas *mythos* derives from Greek words relating to mouth, speech, and oral storytelling (Weigle 295), Linda's own voice is damaged, "a dry, lifeless . . . duck's quack" (*Mansion* 238). The mythologies we are familiar with tell of the extraordinary and the heroic, the underworlds and the upperworlds. Linda's, however, is the world of the mundane which *mythos* and the codifiers of myth have devalued. Faulkner's characterization of Linda continues the process of demythologizing women that he began in the Eula of *The Town*, recovering these women from the fixed status of symbols. Although the idealized Helen might not have left "one recorded word of hers anywhere in existence" (*Mansion* 133) according to Gavin, Eula does have a woman's voice, although it is one Gavin does not hear because, as Ratliff tells him, "by that time you were already talking again" (*Town* 229). Ratliff, however, has talked with Eula and trusts her with the secret of his initials: V. K. stand for Vladimir Kyrilytch. This American storyteller and moralist is a Russian! If his identity were known, Ratliff, like Linda, would be the victim of the easy bigotry that is the flip side of Gavin's idealism.

When the men return from World War Two and take their jobs away from the working women, Linda comes back from the shipyards of Pascagoula where she worked as a riveter and lives with Flem in the De Spain mansion. But the tables are turned now that Flem must defend his respectability. Finally a bank president, Flem cannot disown Linda and must walk to his bank over the words NIGGER LOVER and COMMUNIST JEW KOHL. Linda is undeterred by scapegoat labels just as she is unfrightened by Flem's theft of her party card—"They will send me another one I suppose" (*Mansion* 240). The conclusions that Faulkner gives to the stories of mother and daughter focus on the ground Linda has gained. Whereas Eula dies out of the story, the fate of so many strong women in fiction before the twentieth century, Linda drives out in a car she has ordered herself.

IV

Eula reminds Gavin of Lilith: "the one before Eve herself whom earth's Creator had perforce in desperate and amazed alarm in person to efface, remove, obliterate, that Adam might create a progeny to populate it" (*Town* 44). In the *Kabbalah*, Lilith defies the idea of legitimate birth and the oppression of the marriage contract. Transformed from the Sumerian goddess, "the hand of Inanna," Lilith becomes the first wife of Adam who is, like him, made of the dust of the earth but who leaves him for her own life when he insists she lie beneath him (Stone 127–28). In *The Hamlet* the rape of the land is paralleled by and figured in the rape of the goddess; both become property.

Linda's avenging of Eula's death revises Aeschylus' *Oresteia*, which has been interpreted as the last defense of Mother Goddess power against patriarchy (Lerner 205, Millett 158–62). There Apollo tries to settle the argument between Orestes and the Furies who are pursuing him for killing his mother Clytemnestra, his own blood. Apollo defends Orestes and asserts the patriarchal claim:

> *The mother is not the parent of the child*
> *Which is called hers. She is the nurse who tends the growth*
> *Of young seed planted by its true parent, the male. . . .*[4]

The goddess Athena supports Apollo, "No Mother gave me birth. Therefore the father's claim and male supremacy in all things . . . wins my whole heart's loyalties." Without knowing it, the adolescent Linda—like Athena—names the father when she has a will drawn up in Flem's favor. Linda lives, however, to honor in her patient revenge the memory of her mother. Knowing that Mink will kill Flem, she arranges for his release from prison on humanitarian grounds.

Critical responses to Linda have not met the brilliance of Faulkner's reversal of Aeschylus. In the *Oresteia*, Athena, by a combination of fine rhetoric and threat, persuades the Furies to turn their power of revenge against the killers of kin over to the courts of Zeus's laws, for she knows that "freedom can survive only if it is balanced by the existence of a force that can punish crime" (Lloyd-Jones 6). In *Snopes*, however, Faulkner dramatizes the reality that in American society the law cannot punish such crimes as Flem's, for his crime is in essence the crime of legitimacy and the hegemony it allows him over the lives of mother and daughter. Linda protects social freedom (as the Furies did) from the threat of either tyranny or chaos by taking the power back from the impotent courts; she avenges the death of her "true parent," her mother, through the arranged murder of the man who is only her legal father. The punishment is appropriate to the crime. Eula's death is matched by Flem's, and Gavin's responsibility in Eula's suicide is matched by his complicity in Flem's murder. Respectability is no proof against guilt.

Where Faulkner acknowledges the power of the Furies by giving Linda a white Jaguar, critics have blocked her in their judgments just as Gavin and Flem do Eula. Michael Millgate writes, "Linda's share of the guilt for Flem's murder is in a real sense greater than Mink's, in that she acts deliberately, whereas Mink operates almost instinctively from a deep-rooted sense of what he *must* do if he is to remain a man" (131). The sexism of Millgate's evaluation of Linda's action is evident in his language; if we say that Linda acts from a deep-rooted sense of what she must do if she is to remain a man, we catch him out. Linda is not preserving a stronghold of identity. She is acting from a wellspring of her own values. Is that action less human for being brought to consciousness? Apparently so, for Millgate continues, the "deterioration of Linda as a human being is further indicated by her purchase of the white Jaguar" that makes clear her "determination to cast off not only Flem but Jefferson and Gavin Stevens as well" (248). Noel Polk quotes Millgate's judgment of Linda approvingly and adds, "It is not at all a pretty thing she does to Stevens" (131). Gary Lee Stonum, too, focuses on Linda's betrayal of Gavin's trust, on her "furtive complicity" in Flem's murder (188).

But Linda is not furtive as her last meeting with Gavin makes clear: "she stood looking at his face out of the dark blue eyes. . . . They were not secret: intent enough yes, but not secret . . ." (*Mansion* 424). Linda leaves Jefferson because there is nothing there for her, as Gavin has insisted all along. Her mother is dead, and he himself is married. She must make her own life as Gavin knows and maintained nineteen years before when he refused Eula's plea that he marry Linda: "Don't you see, that's what I'm after: to set her free of Jefferson, not to tie her down to it still more, still further, still worse, but to set her free?" (*Town* 226–27).

According to Simone de Beauvoir's existentialist ethics, a human "achieves liberty only through a continual reaching out toward other liberties" (xxxiii). Our last view of Linda is through Gavin's eyes after his fictions about her have failed; he sees her look at him: "no faint smile, no nothing: just the eyes which even at this distance were not quite black" (*Mansion* 426). Her situation is that of woman as de Beauvoir describes her, "a free and autonomous being like all human creatures—nevertheless [who] finds herself living in a world where men compel her to assume the status of Other" (xxxiv). In contrast to interpretations by his narrators and his critics, Faulkner creates Linda as a human creature with the strength to reach out "toward other liberties." Her status as Other is as useful to Faulkner, however, as the real existence of women like her, for there he can locate a power and hope grounded in something stronger, more patient, than the "ancient subterrene atavistic ethnic fear" (*Mansion* 227) that defeated his hopes to see human freedom in the American South.

Whereas Linda's singular existence dramatizes the power of the patriarchy to isolate women from their mothers, from each other, and even from their mates, and while her bomb-deafened ears and quacking voice evidence the dehumanizing, desexualizing, and silencing assault she has survived, her strength and vision are the powers that Faulkner imagines will not only outlast the letter-of-the-law rapacity of the titular fathers and the respectable although self-serving guardianship of the timid uncles but destroy and transcend them.

How did Faulkner come up with the character of Linda? Perhaps he was aware of the other "civil war" being fought by women, a civil war against the authority of the fathers. Perhaps Faulkner had learned from the young women in his life, Jean Stein and Joan Williams, something of their power and determination ultimately not subject to his control (Mintner 244). Perhaps Linda was Faulkner's last in a long line of strong female characters, an antiauthor whose life is beyond the text that marginalizes her and whose purpose and understanding outstrip the authority of words. David Mintner writes that in *The Mansion* Faulkner makes "not only a culmination of the Snopes saga but a revision of his kingdom" (243). In the subversive ways of fiction, it may be that Faulkner not only revised his kingdom but ended it. Although he gives the novel's last words to describing Mink's death, in Linda he almost seems to realize a transformative power that would allow her to escape from story and emerge into life. In the tradition of male writers investing female characters with qualities precluded by their ideas of masculinity, Faulkner creates a female survivor, an Athena, whose quacking voice offers no rhetorical justification of the law and whose actions name the mother. Linda is not born solely from the head of her creator but, like the warrior Athena, transformed from earlier figures (Spretnak 97); women fighting for freedom and equality are perhaps Faulkner's hope and our own. In Linda, his fictional vessel of life, Faulkner sends his radical vision out of story and into the future. Although Linda leaves Gavin, she carries her creator with her as she struggles for a world beyond the patriarchy of Father Abraham.

Notes

1. See Patricia E. Sweeney (ix–xi, xv–xix, 319–39).

2. For a different argument, see Walter Taylor, "Faulkner used . . . Linda, just back from Greenwich Village, to show why liberals ought to 'Go Slow'" (185).

3. See Catherine Clinton.

4. As quoted by Kate Millett (160–61) from Philip Vellacott's translation for the Penguin Edition of the Oresteian trilogy.

Works Cited

Beauvoir, Simone de. *The Second Sex*. 1952. Trans. H. M. Parshley. New York: Vintage, 1974.

Clinton, Catherine. *The Other Civil War: American Women in the Nineteenth Century*. New York: Hill, 1984.

Faulkner, William. *Essays, Speeches & Public Letters*. Ed. James B. Meriwether. New York: Random, 1965.

——. *The Hamlet*. 1940. New York: Vintage, 1956.

——. *The Mansion*. 1959. New York: Vintage, 1965.

——. *Selected Letters*. Ed. Joseph Blotner. New York: Random, 1977.

——. *The Town*. 1957. New York: Vintage, 1961.

Lerner, Gerda. *The Creation of Patriarchy*. New York: Oxford UP, 1986.

Lloyd-Jones, Hugh, trans. *The Eumenides*. By Aeschylus. Englewood Cliffs: Prentice, 1970.

Millett, Kate. *Sexual Politics*. 1969. New York: Ballantine, 1978.

Millgate, Michael. *The Achievement of William Faulkner*. Lincoln: U of Nebraska P, 1978.

Mintner, David. *William Faulkner: His Life and Work*. Baltimore: Johns Hopkins UP, 1980.

Murphy, Francis, ed. *The Norton Anthology of American Literature*. 2nd ed. Vol. 1. New York: Norton, 1985. 2 vols.

Polk, Noel. "Faulkner and Respectability." *Fifty Years of Yoknapatawpha: Faulkner and Yoknapatawpha*. Eds. Doreen Fowler and Ann J. Abadie. Jackson: UP of Mississippi, 1980. 110–33.

Spretnak, Charlene. *Lost Goddesses of Early Greece: A Collection of Pre-Hellenic Myths*. 1978. Boston: Beacon, 1984.

Stone, Merlin. *Ancient Mirrors of Womanhood: A Treasury of Goddess and Heroine Lore from Around the World*. 1979. Boston: Beacon, 1984.

Stonum, Gary Lee. *Faulkner's Career: An Internal Literary History*. Ithaca: Cornell UP, 1979.

Sweeney, Patricia E. *William Faulkner's Women Characters: An Annotated Bibliography of Criticism 1930–1983*. Santa Barbara: Clio, 1985.

Taylor, Walter. *Faulkner's Search for a South*. Urbana: U of Illinois P, 1983.
Weigle, Marta. *Spiders & Spinsters: Women and Mythology*. Albuquerque: U of New Mexico P, 1982.

CHAPTER 13

FAULKNER'S RETURN TO THE FREUDIAN FATHER

SANCTUARY RECONSIDERED

Doreen Fowler

"Who is your father?" "I know not / surely. Who has known
his own engendering?"
— Homer, *The Odyssey*

The co-ordinates [of the Freudian myth of Oedipus]
amount to the question . . . "What is a Father?" "It's the
dead Father," Freud replies, "but no one listens."
— Lacan, *Écrits: A Selection*

Faulkner's disclaimer that he was "not familiar with" Freud
(*Faulkner in the University* 268) often has been regarded skepti-
cally by scholars. John T. Irwin, for example, identifies Freudian
allusions in *Mosquitoes* (1927) and wryly observes that "if the author of the novel was not familiar with Freud, his characters certainly were" (*Doubling* 5). Possibly Faulkner meant that he had not
formally studied Freud since he readily admitted that he had been
exposed to Freudian ideas: "Everybody talked about Freud when I
lived in New Orleans, but I never read him" (*Lion* 251). Alternatively,

Originally published in *Modern Fiction Studies,* Summer 2004.

we could interpret Faulkner's statement as a Bloomian denial of influence. Irwin theorizes that Faulkner may have actively resisted acknowledging Freud's work "to avoid the threat to his own creative energy and enterprise that might be posed by a sense of his own work having been anticipated by Freud's" *(Doubling* 5). Of course, Faulkner himself subscribed to the view that all such speculation is irrelevant since the artist can intuit the psychic paradigms that the scientist analyzes: "a writer don't have to know Freud to have written things which anyone who does know Freud can divine and reduce into symbols. And so when the critic finds those symbols, they are of course there. But they were there as inevitably as the critic should stumble on his own knowledge of Freud to discern symbol" (*Faulkner in the University* 147). Faulkner's understanding of the creative process mirrors Freud's, who frequently stated that poets often "discover" what philosophers and scientists theorize about many years later. However we choose to read Faulkner's acquaintance with Freud—whether as a direct influence or as an independent, parallel investigation of similar psychic processes—as countless critics have demonstrated, the texts of his novels reveal a persistent, even obsessive, engagement with Freudian motifs. In particular, in *Sanctuary* he compulsively revisits and refashions a centerpiece of Freudian thought, an image out of the unconscious mind that Freud called the primal scene.

Freud came across the primal scene when he was seeking to discover a real, early event that was the origin of his patient's neurosis (Laplanche and Pontalis 331); however, at the origin, he found, not an actual event, but an imagined one. Beginning with a terrifying early childhood dream of white wolves sitting in a tree, then following one memory trace after another, Freud, together with his twenty-four-year-old patient, whom he termed the "Wolf Man" after the dream, pieced together a reconstruction of the child's own conception, a scene of parental intercourse allegedly witnessed by the child, which, in the later stages of analysis, Freud recognized to be a fantasy image.[1] Undaunted by the unreality of the primal scene, Freud insisted that his patient's fantasy is "absolutely equivalent to a recollection" because "the memories are replaced (as in the present case) by dreams the analysis of which invariably leads back to the same scene and which reproduce every portion of its content in an inexhaustible variety of new shapes" (17: 51). Citing Freud's alignment of fantasy and recollection, Ned Lukacher argues that the primal scene is a substitute formation for an unrememberable origin, which "comes to signify an ontologically undecidable intertextual event that is situated in the differential space between historical memory and imaginative construction, between archival

verification and interpretive free play" (24); consequently, Lukacher claims, Freud's origin theory is comparable both to Derrida's deconstructive strategy and to Lacan's notion of the absent
center.

Working from the premise that the primal scene is, in Lukacher's words, "a narrative reconstruction" (37), my project is to
read this narrative in conjunction with Faulkner's *Sanctuary* and
with two other accounts of an original psychic trauma: Freud's essay "The Dissolution of the Oedipus Complex" (1924) and Lacan's
theory of the rise of subjectivity in loss. I do *not* mean to use
Freudian principles to analyze Faulkner's novel; rather, I intend to
read the narratives of Freud, Lacan, and Faulkner as analogous
texts and to propose that Faulkner's representation of the origin
story revises the phallocentric biases of Freudian and Lacanian
theory.

What does the primal scene signify? This fantasy image of the
original constitutive event can be variously interpreted. As construed by Freud, it seems to become a dramatization of his theory
of male identity-formation in castration anxiety. Following Freud,
my outline of his theory traces male, not female, development,
since, for reasons Freud finds "incomprehensible," his "insight into
these developmental processes in girls is unsatisfactory, incom-
plete and vague" (19: 178).[2] In "The Dissolution of the Oedipus
Complex," Freud proposes that the key event in the development
of male identity occurs when "the boy's Oedipus complex is destroyed by the fear of castration" (19: 179). The threat of castration is made real for the boy by the sight of female genitalia, which,
Freud asserts disturbingly, occasions a "recognition that women
were castrated" (19: 176). Out of a fear of suffering the mother's
fate, the boy represses Oedipal desire and performs a symbolic
self-castration; he "preserve[s] the genital organ," Freud writes, by
"paralyz[ing] it—remov[ing] its function," and, "if [the repression]
is ideally carried out," it accomplishes "an abolition of the Oedipal
complex" (19: 177). Juliet Mitchell explains the importance of this
development: "Together with . . . the Oedipal complex . . . the castration complex governs the position of each person in the triangle
of father, mother and child; in the way it does this, it embodies the
law that founds the human order itself" (14).[3]

For Freud, the primal scene seems to be the symbolic analogue for the developmental processes described in "The Dissolution of the Oedipus Complex"; that is, it poses the castration threat
that drives the boy to turn away from the mother and to subordi-
nate himself to the father. Ignoring narrative leads provided by the
Wolf Man that suggest a fear of maternal incorporation—for exam-

ple, the tale of "Little Red Riding-Hood," in which a wolf disguised as a *grandmother* threatens to eat a child, and the tale of "The Wolf and the Seven Little Goats," in which six goats are eaten by the wolf and later removed from his stomach—Freud focuses on a threat of castration from the father. For example, he deduces that the parental intercourse must have been performed *a tergo* (from behind), "the man upright, and the woman bent down *like an animal*" (17: 39; emphasis added). He insists on these postures because only these positions would afford the child the opportunity "to see his mother's genitals as well as his father's organ" and to make the same observation that precipitates the dissolution of the Oedipal complex, that is, to "discover the vagina and the *biological significance* of masculine and feminine." For Freud, this biological significance is evident: "He understood now that active was the same as masculine while passive was the same as feminine" (17: 47; emphasis added). Arguably, at this juncture, Freud is imposing on biology— the difference between male and female genitalia—cultural assumptions of male ascendancy.

To this interpretation of the witnessed scene of parental intercourse, Freud's patient, who would later assert that he could never recall having witnessed his parents engaged in intercourse (Obholzer 35), adds an observation that also fosters the notion of the father's total mastery of a "castrated" mother:

> When the patient entered more deeply into the situation of the primal scene, he brought to light the following pieces of self-observation. He assumed to begin with, he said, that the event of which he was a witness was an act of violence, but the expression of enjoyment which he saw on his mother's face did not fit in with this; he was obliged to recognize that the experience was one of gratification. What was essentially new for him in his observation of his parents' intercourse was the conviction of the reality of castration—a possibility with which his thoughts had already been occupied previously. . . . For he now saw with his own eyes the wound of which his Nanya had spoken, and understood that its presence was a necessary condition of intercourse with his father. (17: 45–46)

In the patient's reading, the father is so powerful that, contrary to all reason, he is able to satisfy his desire and the mother's desire even as he castrates her. This self-observation appears to be a child's wish-fulfillment fantasy projected on the father: the child desires both to master the mother and also to gratify her sexually. This construction of the scene of witnessed parental intercourse as an image of paternal domination and maternal victimization has become the standard interpretation of the primal scene; and, because this reading is so widely accepted, feminist readers, like Maria Ramas, have denounced the primal scene as our culture's "dominant patriarchal sexual fantasy." In the primal scene, Ramas writes, "ultimately and always, a woman is being degraded" (157).

In *Sanctuary*, the primal scene is repeatedly depicted, and these successive depictions point to the fraudulence of the Freudian father. While Faulkner's initial representations of the scene seem to conform to the Freudian model, these versions are revised by later ones, which counter Freud's alignment of power with masculinity and inscribe an image of an unstable paternal prohibition threatened by a desire for maternal incorporation.[4] I identify as a primal scene a witnessed sexual act, wherein the couple engaged in intercourse or its equivalent assume the roles of parents, and the observer, who is barred from participation in the scene enacted before him/her, represents the alienated, subordinated child. My reading reflects the Lacanian tenet that the mother, father, and child in the Oedipal triangle are roles or positions, which are variously occupied.

Temple Drake is placed at the center of an Oedipal drama when an inebriated Gowan Stevens wrecks their car and she is stranded at Frenchman's Bend, where lawless bootleggers grotesquely configure a family (Matthews 156). Temple is the Oedipal prize, whose sexual conquest denotes ascension to the father's position. Gowan, Temple's date, finds himself not "big enough" to occupy that position (66): when Van gropes Temple, a scuffle ensues, and Gowan is knocked unconscious and laid on a bed beside Temple. These events contextualize the first reprise of the primal scene. Hidden in the darkness, Ruby and Tommy observe as Popeye enters the room where Temple and Gowan lie and, as Temple later tells Horace, "fiddl[es] around" inside her knickers with his "nasty little cold hand" (218). Faulkner's narration focuses not on the sexual act, which is withheld from the reader, but the observation of the act by the feeble-minded, "child"-like Tommy (42): "Tommy's pale eyes began to glow faintly, like those of a cat. The woman could see them in the darkness when he crept into the room after Popeye, and while Popeye stood over the bed where Temple lay. They glowed suddenly out of the darkness at her . . . with a quality furious and questioning and sad" (77). In this first reenactment, Temple is the daughter-substitute for the desired mother, and Popeye assumes the role of father, whom Tommy, along with Ruby, watches helplessly. This reprise appears to conform to the Freudian model: both Temple, who lies like a passive victim beneath Popeye's probing hand, and Ruby, who appears to be unable to prevent the violation of her daughter-double, seem to personify the notion of female castration. This scene serves as a prelude to Popeye's rape of Temple, which is also configured as a primal scene, with Popeye again positioned as father, Temple as the mother-figure, and Tommy as the murdered child-witness. Once again, the observation of the unrepresented sexual scene is critical, as Popeye kills Tommy, posted as Temple's lookout, for watching:

> "Didn't I tell you about following me?"
> "I wasn't following you," Tommy said. "I was watching him," jerking his head toward the house.
> "Watch him, then" Popeye said. Tommy turned his head and looked toward the house and Popeye drew his hand from his coat pocket. (102)

Because the nature of the rape and Popeye's nature are withheld from us, at this point in the text, Popeye's violent sexual assault on Temple and his murder of Tommy seem to confer on him the dread aspect of the father in Freud and the Wolf Man's primal scene. Temple's wounded vagina, conspicuously marked by her flowing blood, figures the castration that the child-witness imagines he/she witnesses; and this sexual assault appears to induce castration anxiety in a distant witness to the scene, Lee Goodwin, who hears the shot that killed Tommy. Before the rape of Temple and the murder of Tommy, Goodwin, as the leader of the men and the father of Ruby's child, seemed to assume the father-position in the Oedipal triangle. But now he refuses to allow Horace to divulge Popeye's presence at the scene of the murder: "'let me just open my head about that fellow,' he says to Horace, 'and there's no chance to it. I know what I'll get'" (132). Like the Wolf Man, who imputes to the father unchallengeable power, Goodwin assumes that he has "no chance" against Popeye.

Subsequent inscriptions of the primal scene dismantle Freud's image of the invincible father-figure. Like the child outside his or her parents' locked bedroom door, like Clarence Snopes, who, on his knees, peeks through the keyhole of Temple's locked door at the brothel, we want to see and know the scene of desire enacted behind the barred door. Late in the novel, the scene we voyeuristically have anticipated is reported by Miss Reba: "Yes, sir, Minnie said the two of them would be nekkid as two snakes, and Popeye hanging over the foot of the bed without even his hat took off, making a kind of whinnying sound" (258). This configuration of the primal scene, which is withheld until nearly the novel's end, reveals that the positions of father and son are not fixed or natural as

Freud implies. Here Red, who "look[s] like a college boy" (235), assumes the father's role. Popeye, fully dressed even to his hat, is marked as a spectator, not a participant, in the sexual drama enacted before him, and his "whinnying sound" suggests an infantile cry of frustrated desire. Miss Reba's image of Popeye "hanging over the foot of the bed" also identifies him as the child-observer by invoking a correspondence to another child-witness of another primal scene in the novel. Ruby expects to pay Horace for his lawyering by copulating with him, but her baby would have to accompany them, a witness to their sexual act. Appalled, Horace imagines the scene: "You mean with him at the foot of the bed, maybe? perhaps you holding him by the leg all the time so he wouldn't fall off?" (276). The verbal echoes pair Popeye with Ruby's sick baby, and this coupling is further reinforced by another correspondence that is withheld until the novel's conclusion: Popeye, we learn in the novel's coda, is the product of a syphilitic union as presumably is Ruby's chronically ill child. This doubling invokes the scene of his engendering, when his father infected him and his mother with syphilis. In the context of the primal scene, syphilis functions as a trope of the father's fraudulence.

Sanctuary's successive representations of the primal scene anticipate a Lacanian perspective of the founding event and expose the myth of the omnipotent father, which Freud's reading codified. Freud interprets the primal scene literally and reads castration as an act and the father as a person. In Lacan's revision of Freud, castration is a function, and the father is a position or role, which can be variously occupied. According to Lacan, his substitution of the status of paternity for the biological father is a crucial distinction since to make of the father a referent, as Freud does, is to fall into an ideological trap: "the prejudice which falsifies the conception of the Oedipus complex from the start, by making it define as natural, rather than normative the predominance of the paternal figure" (Feminine Sexuality 69). The father in the primal scene stands for what Lacan calls the phallus, a difficult concept because the term suggests meanings that Lacan does not mean. While the male sexual organ is one of many figures for the phallus, the phallus is not the penis. Rather the phallus "is a signifier" that "forbids the child the satisfaction of his or her own desire, which is the desire to be the exclusive desire of the mother" ("Les formations" 14). The phallus is a way of naming the function of the father in the primal scene, the breaking of the imaginary mother-child dyadic relation. As James M. Mellard explains, for Lacan, "castration is the symbolic function within the Oedipal complex that establishes the position of father" (29). Variously enacted, the father is the site of prohibition: he forbids access to the mother's body, and, because the father stands between us and our desire, the father or phallus seems to signify the fulfillment of all desire; but, according to Lacan, the actor in the primal scene who plays the father does not possess the satisfaction he forbids, and this is a crucial (and often overlooked) difference between Freud's father as referent and Lacan's father as symbolic role. In Lacan's narrative of identity, the fulfillment that we seek and that Freud imputes to the father in the primal scene is lacking as a condition of our induction into culture or what Lacan calls the symbolic order. While the function of alienation is real, the "father" in the primal scene, like a stop sign, represents the law, but is not the law. On this issue of figurization, Lacan, frequently obscure, is unambiguous: "when the legislator (he who claims to lay down the Law) presents himself to fill the gap, he does so as an imposter. But there is nothing false about the Law itself" (*Écrits: A Selection* 311).

Lacan's notion of the phallus as a signifier that only masks lack seems to be personified in *Sanctuary*'s Popeye. Initially, Popeye assumes the role of phallic father in the primal scene; subsequently, he is exposed as "an imposter." Disease-ridden, child-like, and impotent ("he will never be man, properly speaking," a doctor says of him [308]), he exemplifies the Lacanian notion that all subjects experience lack as the condition of subjectivity and that any subject can enact the role of "father," but they do so only as a signifier; that is, like the phallic symbols he relies on—the gun, the corn-cob, and even, eventually, Red—Popeye is only another in a long line of symbols that merely represent an always absent final authority.

Even as *Sanctuary* demythologizes the father as phallus, it also revises the role of the forbidden, "castrated" mother. *Sanctuary* reflects a poststructuralist understanding of the troubling notion of "female castration," which anchors Freud's reading of the primal scene. For Freud, a woman's lack of a penis is tantamount to castration, and the recognition that "women were castrated" drives the child to separate from the mother and to accept subordination. For Lacan, on the other hand, men and women alike experience privation (symbolic castration) as the price of human subjectivity, and the possession of a penis is not enabling: "what in reality [the male] may *have* that corresponds to the phallus . . . is worth no more than what he does not" (*Écrits*: *A Selection* 289). At the same time, however, Lacan observes that *within culture* gender roles are assigned on the basis of the presence or absence of a penis, and culture identifies the penis with phallic authority, a bias that Freud's reading of the primal scene reflects; that is to say, women are not castrated, but they are inscribed within culture as castrated to invent a phallic distinction. Woman, Jacqueline Rose writes, "is defined purely against the man (she is the negative of that definition— 'man is not woman')" (49). Ultimately, according to Lacan, the logic of this binary supports the notion that on woman's denigration rests male ascendancy: "For the [male] soul to come into being, she, the woman, is differentiated from it . . . called woman and defamed" (*Écrits* 156). In a move that seems to intuit poststructuralist thought, *Sanctuary's* representation of gender identity also suggests that woman is not biologically inferior but rather that she is culturally subordinated. Popeye's horrific rape of Temple, for example, literalizes this cultural derogation: the violent rending of Temple's vagina enacts a desire to castrate her. Powerfully figured by rape, the novel's dominant trope, the impulse to designate gender difference and female subordination by "castrating" women is compulsively reenacted in Faulkner's novel. Popeye, for example, in the aftermath of the rape, puts into words the objective of the sexual violation: "Aint you ashamed of yourself?" (139). Similarly, when Ruby defies her father and tries to run away with her lover, her father attempts to objectify the notion of female castration by killing the lover and then saying to her: "Get down there and sup your dirt, you whore" (58). And again when Ruby acts to prevent Lee from violating Temple, he signifies female subordination by slapping her until she falls to her knees and then saying: "That's what I do to them" (95). All such gestures perform a cultural inscription of the same meaning that Freud finds encoded in the primal scene: they inscribe women as the castrated coordinate in a male/female dialectic.[5]

The notion of female castration, which Freud embraced so readily, is, according to Lacan, an image out of the unconscious mind for the breaking of the mother-child dyad that introduces gender differentiation. The image of the castrated mother presupposes an earlier, phallic mother, whom the child imagines possesses all, including the child and the phallus, within herself. As Jane Gallop explains, the mythic phallic mother is a psychic representation for the inmixed existence prior to the mother's displacement, which Lacan calls the imaginary: "The imaginary might be characterized as the realm of non-assumption of the mother's castration. In the imaginary, the 'mother' is assumed to be still phallic, omnipotent and omniscient, she is unique" (147). Freud's primal scene configures the suppression of an early psychic identification with the mother in terms of the "castration" of the phallic mother;[6] *Sanctuary's* final inscriptions of the primal scene, on the other hand, subliminally suggest that a desire for the mother of the imaginary stage is not so easily banished as the Freudian paradigm suggests.[7]

Both the original and revised texts of *Sanctuary* leak forbidden Oedipal desire.[8] As John T. Matthews observes, both texts chart "Horace's regressive career" (257), an undoing of primary repression that is initiated by leaving his wife, Belle—who, in Lacanian terms, represents the *petit objet a*, that is, a substitute for the banished maternal body—and returning "home" to his elder sister, another substitute. The desire for a lost, prohibited mother-child relation is perhaps most strikingly evoked in a series of dreams that Faulkner deleted from the revised text. In one of these dreams Horace awakes "calling his mother's name" and feeling "that he had irrevocably lost something" (60). Faulkner removes this trace of a desire to return to an early, identificatory stage; however, disguised and displaced, this desire plays out in the revised novel as, in anticipation of Derridean theory, the text exposes the instability of the boundary-making process that generates identity. Derrida states that the prohibition on which the cultural order rests is "a pure, fictive and unstable, ungraspable limit. One crosses it in attaining it . . . before the prohibition, it is not incest; forbidden, it cannot become incest except through the recognition of the prohibition" (267). The father's prohibition imaged in the primal scene marks a border, but, as Derrida directs us to see, borders are inherently porous; while they designate discrete identities, they are also the site where oppositions run together, where identity dissolves. *Sanctuary*'s final inscriptions of the primal scene evoke it as the site where a desire for maternal incorporation meets paternal prohibition and where the father's prohibition is unveiled as mere cultural artifice charged with governing an inchoate material existence identified with the primal, or phallic, mother.

Disguised images of forbidden desire attend the representation of the novel's long deferred, central primal scene, the rape of Temple Drake, which the reader finally observes in the form of Horace's fantasy image of the event. Late in the novel, Horace visits Temple in Miss Reba's brothel, and she rehearses the story of her rape in a series of substitute formations (Pettey 80). In effect, Horace witnesses the sexual scene, and, after leaving Temple, Horace imaginatively recasts the rape in a series of scrambled images that encode a desire for incorporation. This desire is initially signified as Horace studies a photograph of Little Belle, his stepdaughter, another displaced mother-figure, which, in a transgressive gesture, he has taken out of its frame. At this moment, the long-withheld scene of Temple's rape is represented in a series of fusional images.[9] As Horace gazes at Little Belle's picture, he is overcome by nausea, and, as he vomits, he merges with Popeye as he sexually assaults Temple: "he gave over and plunged forward and struck the lavatory and leaned upon his braced arms while the shucks set up a terrific uproar beneath her thighs." Leaning on his braced arms, Horace assumes the position of a man engaged in intercourse: his spewing vomit simulates an ejaculation. Concomitantly, Horace identifies with Temple. As he fantasizes the rape, the pronoun "he" gives way to "she," and the "she" who "watched something black and furious go roaring out of her pale body" (223) refers not only to Temple, who sees the bloody cob withdrawn from her vagina, but also to Horace, who watches vomit gush from his mouth. These identifications invoke another, with Horace's dead mother, who, in a dream sequence deleted from the revised text, opens her mouth to reveal "a thick, black liquid welled in a bursting bubble that splayed out upon her fading chin" (60). More identifications follow as Temple's rape coalesces with Lee Goodwin's lynching. As Horace fantasizes the rape, the female victim is "bound naked on her back on a flat car," like Goodwin bound to planks and boards in the center of the blaze; and Horace's image of "living fire" is identical with the "blazing mass" of fire that contains Goodwin's living flesh. Temple's rape merges as well with Popeye's hanging, as the female figure of Horace's fantasy "swing[s] faintly and lazily in nothingness." This breakdown of symbolization in an identificatory moment moves to an inexorable denouement, a scarcely disguised image for a return to the origin. Horace envisions a flat car speeding "through a black tunnel." The car's trajectory seems to trace the upward slanting path of the vagina through the birth canal to the womb/uterus: "The car shot bodily from the tunnel in a long upward slant, the darkness overhead now shredded with parallel attenuations of living fire, toward a crescendo like a held breath, an interval in which she would swing faintly and lazily in nothingness, filled with pale, myriad points of light" (223). The primal scene images the moment of prohibition, when identity, particularly gender identity, arises out of repression of a regressive instinct; and, for Freud, the paternal interdiction accomplishes not only a repression but "a destruction and an abolition of the complex" (19: 177). The latent content of *Sanctuary*'s inscription suggests that the very image of phallic authority, the primal scene, is disrupted and challenged by the prohibited desire, which is both a desire for incest and a desire to return to an origin identified with the matrix or mother.

The instability of the father's prohibition is the disguised subtext of another configuration of the primal psychodrama, Lee Goodwin's lynching. While a lynching is not a scene of observed

parental intercourse, in the manner of the unconscious, it imaginatively recasts these events. A lynching is an observed scene of always symbolic and often literal castration, performed before spectators, to enforce prohibition. In the post–Civil War South, black
men were lynched in appalling numbers either for allegedly raping
or for being suspected of desiring a white woman. In these lynchings, the white lynch mob assumes the role of father or law, who
forbids merging; the black community, who watch, terrified, in hiding, represent the observing child-witnesses; and the lynched black
man performs the mother's role—like the female other, he is the
racial other whose alienation and presumed castration function as
the fictive grounds on which racial difference depends. In a racially
segregated culture like Faulkner's South, race inflects the primal
scene. For example, in the American South, with its history of racial
slavery, the prohibition against miscegenation replaces the prohibition against incest; and a difference in skin pigmentation provides a
token by which the members of the white mob distance themselves
from the role of child-spectator; that is, their whiteness betokens
an identification with the white lynchers, not with the lynched black
man.[10]

Of course, Lee Goodwin is not black; however, in a novel re-
plete with psychic displacements, the bootleggers and prostitutes
in *Sanctuary* function as substitutes for a nearly invisible black
community, who cannot play a pivotal role, because white identity
hinges on black marginalization. Quite possibly without conscious
awareness, Faulkner racializes the men and women of Frenchman's
Bend. Popeye, for example, is himself a black figure. In his tight,
black suits, he is repeatedly described as "black" (42, 49, 109;
Sanctuary: The Original Text 9). Miss Reba's white brothel is shad-
owed by the black brothel that Clarence Snopes favors for its rea-
sonable rates. And, in a scene that Faulkner positioned as the first
chapter of the original text, Lee Goodwin, in his jail cell, nightly listens to the doomed black man in the next cell, his black double,
who sings of a certain death that betokens Lee's own. Narcissa even
anticipates a joint hanging: "Maybe they'll wait and hang them both
together. . . . They do that sometimes, dont they?" (134). Most
pointedly, the pressure to alienate this not-so-white underclass—
Ruby cannot stay in Horace's house nor in the town hotel, and Narcissa is outraged that Horace would "mix [him]self up" with such
people (117)—subliminally figures the racial segregation that historically characterizes Faulkner's South.

Given its structure as a primal scene, this racialized lynching—
and by extension, all racial lynchings—is performed to impart a
material form to the Freudian construction of the scene, that is, the

indomitability of the phallic (white) father. Just as the presumed castration of the mother-figure in the primal scene appears to support the Freudian equation that "active was the same as masculine while passive was the same as feminine" (17: 47), so the castration, or its equivalent, of a black man is enacted to symbolize the supremacy of the white patriarch. *Sanctuary*'s representation of this primal scene, however, leaks a forbidden meaning. Beneath the surface level, images of black-white merging suggest that the prohibition against miscegenation merely betokens white difference and supremacy and that this symbolization ineffectively opposes an assimilatory instinct.

The lynching is evoked like a dream, the place where repressed meanings and desires return disguised. Horace is trying to sleep and may be asleep when, as in a dream, "from nowhere," figures "emerge in midstride out of nothingness" (295). Defined by the flames they set, the lynchers appear to be shadows: "Against the flames black figures showed, antic" (296). Like Popeye, the white "black man" in the novel, these white "black figures" are imagoes, symbolizations of the dark, repressed self as well as disguised signifiers for a breakdown of black-white difference. The fire, which is compared to "a voice in a dream," figures a forbidden desire for incorporation. Its engulfing flames consume all distinctions: what was once Goodwin is now "indistinguishable, the flames whirling in long and thunderous plumes from a white-hot mass" (296). In this conflagration, the difference between white lynchers, themselves "black figures," and the racialized lynched man dissolves. Even as a man with a coal oil can sets fire to Goodwin, he himself is consumed in the fire: through "a fleeting gap" in the throng, Horace sees "a man turn and run, a mass of flames, still carrying a five-gallon coal oil can which exploded with a rocket-like glare while he carried it, running" (296). As well, in a scene of dissolving identity, the crime and its punishment elide, as the lynchers imply when they threaten Horace: "Do to the lawyer what we did to him. What he did to her. Only we never used a cob. We made him wish we had used a cob" (296). Goodwin, castrated or sodomized with a weapon, becomes a double for Temple, raped with a corncob, as the castration of the racialized Goodwin, performed to prohibit racial merging, becomes the site of an annihilation of all distinctions. Castration, the defining element of the primal scene, is performed to symbolize the "phallic," that is, omnipotent, father, who enforces culture's definitions; but *Sanctuary*'s versions of the primal scene subliminally reveal that the violence performed to signify paternal interdiction is enacted by players who are themselves bodies in an ever-dissolving material world that eradicates the artificially constructed designations—like white-black difference—enjoined in the name of the mythic phallic father.

While a disguised subtext in *Sanctuary* undermines the notion of a phallic authority that secures the social order, Faulkner himself also spoke out publicly on behalf of that authority. On February 15, 1931, approximately a week after the publication date of *Sanctuary*, a letter written by Faulkner appeared in the Memphis *Commercial Appeal*; he writes in reply to W. H. James, a black man, whose letter, published a week earlier, had commended the ladies of Mississippi for uniting to prevent lynchings. Faulkner protests, "I hold no brief for lynching" (qtd. in McMillen and Polk 6); at the same time, however, he speaks approvingly of an instinct or drive for power:

> the natural human desire which is in any man, black or white, to take advantage of what circumstance, not himself, has done for him. The strong (mentally or physically) black man takes advantage of the weak one; he is not only not censured, he is protected by law, since (and the white man the same) the law has found out that the many elemental material factors which compose a commonwealth are of value only when they are in the charge of some one, regardless of color and size and religion, who can protect them. (4)

While Faulkner's meaning is veiled by evasive language and convoluted constructions, he seems to be saying that the cultural order relies on a ritual of dominance, which puts "the elemental material factors which compose a commonwealth" in the hands of someone who can "protect" them and imbue them with "value." This "some one" seems to allude to a phallic father, a supreme and final authority, who guarantees the cultural (patriarchal) order. In effect, the letter expresses Faulkner's deep psychic investment in the dream of phallic power: it even can be read as itself an attempt to wield that power since, with words as his weapon, Faulkner is virtually unchallengeable—like the mythic phallic father—and the letter effectively defeats and silences his black correspondent. Troubling as this letter is on so many levels, it is not incompatible with *Sanctuary*. The letter rationalizes the same rites of dominance that are ceaselessly reenacted in the novel: as Pettey observes, "the novel works through series after series of symbolic castrations" (76). The defining and saving difference between public statement and fiction is the novel's textual unconscious; that is, fiction, like dreams, is the site of a ceaseless interplay of meanings, the place where refused, unacceptable meanings return disguised. Faulkner himself seems to acknowledge this difference between an author's text and a citizen's public statement by signing his letter "William Falkner," the old family name, which he had not used for more than a decade. While Faulkner's novel, like his letter, stages gestures to claim the role of primal father, keeper of the law that orders material existence, the novel, unlike the letter, lets slip a forbidden meaning, the terrible transformative powers, identified with matter and the mother, that culture seeks to control with a symbol—the phallus.

We look to the father in the primal scene as the author of being, the original, stabilizing point of reference. In *Sanctuary*'s central primal scene, the rape of Temple Drake, Faulkner positions Popeye as father, and, initially, Popeye fools us as he temporarily fooled Temple. With this move, by positioning as "phallic" representative a man who, as we eventually learn, relies on phallic substitutes—the corn cob, Red—to mask impotence, the text suggests that the father in the primal scene only symbolizes difference and that this act of symbolization is not the origin we seek, but another in a series of substitutions that point to an always absent referent. As the reader gradually discerns, Popeye's phallic pose disguises Oedipal desire. The novel's opening scene, which depicts a man (later identified as Horace) drinking from a spring, who sees Popeye in "the broken and myriad reflection of his own drinking" (4), alerts us to Popeye's role as Horace's double.[11] Wearing tight black suits that prompt Temple to call him "that black man" (42), Popeye is an expression, disguised so as to elude censorship, of Horace's buried Oedipal desire, prohibited in the moment of identity-formation, which, variously transformed, has surfaced throughout the novel. Even as Popeye poses as the phallic father, his brutalization of Temple, a daughter-figure, who calls him "Daddy" (236), figures a scarcely veiled violation of the incest taboo. Information revealed only in the coda—each year he makes a trip "home" to his mother—marks him again as the son who has not renounced his identification with the mother. And when finally Popeye is exposed as a disguised exponent of regressive desire, that desire must be driven underground again, and the novel moves inexorably toward Popeye's expulsion, which arrives appropriately in the form of the primal scene.

Popeye's execution, like Goodwin's lynching, is yet another variation on a witnessed scene of symbolic castration performed to enforce prohibition. In this version, the sheriff who hangs Popeye assumes the role of father; the witnesses to the hanging are the child-spectators; and Popeye, as a racialized figure, represents the disallowed other, whose alienation signifies a token for the assertion of difference. Once again Faulkner's primal scene is marked by an outbreak of an unconscious drive toward fusion that the image of the primal scene purports to prohibit. As he is hanged, Popeye, bound and helpless, merges with Goodwin bound to a post in the middle of a roaring blaze and with Horace's nightmare image of a female victim bound on her back to a flat car. As Popeye falls through the trap to his death, his punishment seems to fuse with his crime, and death, sex, and birth appear to coalesce. At one level, the fall though the trap door is a repetition of the rape of Temple Drake: to gain access to Temple in the corn crib, Popeye lowered himself through a trap door. But the fall through the trap is identified with Temple's rape in another sense as well: it symbolically performs sexual intercourse, another entry through a narrow passageway. Popeye's fall through the trap also images birth, the infant's descent through the birth canal. And, as Popeye falls and hangs from a noose around his neck, he fuses with the victim of Horace's rape-fantasy, who "would swing faintly and lazily in nothingness filled with pale myriad points of light" (223). The conflation of this legal execution (for a crime Popeye did not commit) with Goodwin's lynching and with Temple's rape points to, as Matthews observes, "the institutionalized savagery of the law" (264). All three events reprise the primal scene; that is, they perform a figurative castration in an attempt to literalize phallic authority and guarantee the law; but—and herein lies the conundrum—castration, performed to symbolize the law, is an expression of the brutal instincts prohibited by the law, and these instincts open onto a breakdown of the social order, a return to a primal inmixed existence, identified with the phallic mother.

The primal scene is an origin story; and, for both Freud and Lacan, it is a male story: the father authorizes identity and social meanings. For Freud, for whom "anatomy is destiny" (19: 178), the father's phallic authority derives from biological difference: a man is empowered simply by being the bearer of a penis. For Lacan, who rewrites Freud in terms of contemporary language theory, the father's authorizing power is not natural but cultural: culture assigns power to the penis. Despite this important qualification, Lacanian theory and applications are obsessively concerned with the figure of the father as the bedrock of the social order. Even while Lacan acknowledges that the phallus is a symbol, still, given its role "in the structuring and securing (never secure) of human subjectivity," it is the "transcendental signifier" (Rose 86), that is, "the symbol of the authority Lacan assigns to the concept of Law" (Mellard 31). By this kind of verbal equivocation, Lacanian theory seems to extend even as it rescinds the promise of a legitimization of identity and social meanings in the shadowy figure of the Symbolic or dead father.[12]

The primal scene poses an answer to the critical question— what makes a father? In Freud's reading, the father's role is defined by castration: the father appears to be castrating the mother and holds the son thrall by the threat of castration. This interpretation seems to inscribe primitive belief: by removing the sign of power, one is empowered. For Lacan, these functions always operate at the level of signification; nevertheless, an equivalent model of father/phallus obtains; that is, selfhood originates with repression, the psychic equivalent of castration, and the father or phallus represents the law that ordains castration. Castration, the cutting off of a part, makes possible difference and signification, since, as Saussure points out, one term is what it is by excluding another. Paradoxically, then, the father's constitutory power is contingent upon castration.

The problematics of this psychological definition of fatherhood are ceaselessly interrogated in Faulkner's novels. For example, in *Absalom, Absalom!* Thomas Sutpen compulsively reenacts this model of fatherhood: often by proxy, he symbolically castrates son-figures in accordance with an exclusionary model of identity-formation. As Carolyn Porter writes in her astute Lacanian analysis of fatherhood in the novel, the "son, of course, must die, must be sacrificed, so that the father's mastery is sealed once and for all, but at least this will have made a difference" (189). Porter's Lacanian application accepts as axiomatic that the death of the son (the symbolic analogue for castration) is regrettable, but essential: it invents the phallic distinction, the basis for difference and meaning. Faulkner's *Sanctuary*, however, subliminally suggests that the son's death/castration only figures a difference and does not seal "once and for all" the father's mastery. The novel's reenactments of the primal scene, the image of primary repression, which register disguised formations of forbidden desire, point to another axiom of psychoanalytic thought, namely, that it is the nature of repression always to evoke the repressed material. In his essay "Repression" (1915), Freud asserts that "repression itself . . . produces substitute formations and symptoms . . . indications of a return of the repressed" (14: 154); and Lacan, echoing Freud, writes: "repressed, it reappears" (*Écrits: A Selection* 297). In his landmark study *Doubling and Incest/Repetition and Revenge*, Irwin sees repression as an analogue for castration and death because repression "shatters once and for all the sense of bodily integrity, and as such is a partial foreshadowing of the ultimate dissolution of bodily and psychic integrity that is death" (89). Paradoxically, then, repression marks the boundaries of the self by a severance that invokes a sense of unboundedness.

Read for its latent content, *Sanctuary* discloses that a meaning-making system based in alienation, symbolized by the phallic, castrating father, is its own undoing. In later novels, particularly in the novels published in 1942 and after, Faulkner may be trying to revise the Freudian/Lacanian narrative of identity-formation in exclusion. In *Go Down, Moses*, for example, Ike McCaslin rejects the image of a castrating father, modeled by his grandfather, Old Carothers, who impregnated his own enslaved, unacknowledged daughter, and then made a slave of their son. Ike's subsequent dilemma, however, seems to confirm the Freudian paradigm; having refused a repressive model of fatherhood, Ike finds that he is "father to no one" (3) and that in "saving and freeing his son, lost him" (335). Faulkner revisits the Freudian definition of fatherhood in *A Fable* (1954), a *fabula* that he described as "the tragedy of a father who has to decide whether his son shall live or die" (*Faulkner at Nagano* 159). This novel, which he labored over for a decade and regarded as his "magnum o" (Cowley 91), has been largely ignored by readers and discounted by critics, apparently with justification, because its highly experimental form drains the text of any narrative power or excitement; however, the novel's stylized techniques may aim to oppose or attenuate language's exclusionary tactics. For example, the novel's tedious detailing of seemingly countless items in a series or ranks or levels in a hierarchy, as well as its sweeping focus, which favors archetypes and the human aggregate over the individual, may work to level distinctions defined by exclusion. These later novels also subversively recast black men, like Sam Fathers and Lucas Beauchamp, in the role of father. These men, who are both former slaves and father-figures, combine within themselves the polarities of the master-slave dialectic. Lucas Beauchamp, in particular, seems to represent a new model of paternity, patterned after "Uncle" Ned Barnett, an elderly black man, widely respected for his dignity, who was both servant and father-figure to Faulkner.[13] In *Intruder in the Dust* (1948), Lucas refuses to "be a nigger" (22); in Freudian terms, he is proof against the castration threat that defines the son's position in the father/son, white man/"nigger" coordinates, and, for threatening a (white) phallic distinction (and not, as the text discloses, for an alleged murder, which he did not commit), he is to be lynched. Like the lynching, the rape, and the execution in *Sanctuary*, this lynching would reenact a scene of castration to mark a difference, but in *Intruder* the lynching is prevented by a marginalized, alternative community, composed of a white boy, a black boy, and an elderly white woman.

While Faulkner's later novels sometimes appear to be searching for an alternative to an authority generated by repression, these departures from a phallic script seem to be tempered by reassuring reaffirmations of the logic of difference. In *Intruder in the Dust*, for example, Gavin Stevens is Lucas's foil. On the one hand, Lucas seems to personify a new order of fatherhood, which is not contingent upon the castration threat; on the other, "Lawyer" Stevens is the garrulous spokesperson for a cultural order that locates (white) identity by (black) repression. The last third of the novel is dominated by Stevens, who argues the "Go slow" delay tactics of Southern racism. Specifically, he contends that white Southerners must be allowed "the privilege of setting [Lucas] free ourselves. . . . But it wont be next Tuesday" (151–52). While Stevens never overtly advocates racism, his argument to delay integration in the name of Southern "homogeneity," a code word for white difference, thinly veils a dread of egalitarianism as a loss of white identity and dominance.

In a thoughtful discussion of Faulkner's representation of racial difference, Wesley and Barbara Alverson Morris determine that he "could not think beyond difference as exclusive/inclusive, as the struggle of master and slave, but how many modernists can?" (235). The Morrises may be right, but Faulkner, like everyone who speaks, is trapped in language. We construct meanings in culture with language, a closed, artificial signifying system that works by erasure; that is, we assign one meaning to a word and exclude all others. This linguistic strategy for devising meaning is written as law in our origin narratives, which ordain dislocation, and psycholinguists theorize that language's method of displacement reflects psychic processes; hence, Lacan writes, "the unconscious is structured like language" (*Four* 20). As the Morrises observe, an authoritarian guarantee of difference appears to be elemental; it even may be what makes us human: "Difference is, therefore, grounded in the universal origins of human society, giving us an order, a law without which we are subject to savage violence" (235). The case for difference based in exclusion is compelling; within the terms of its own logic, it appears to be incontestable, as psycholinguists teach that a difference created by repression—psychological and social—is our only defense against an omnipresence of meanings tantamount to meaninglessness. We embrace difference so as to invent a separate identity, but, as *Sanctuary*'s successive expositions of the primal scene reveal, difference is itself a form of "savage violence." While Faulkner may not have found a solution to the dilemma of an identity carved out by repression, because his project is to search out first principles (to ask, "Who made me?") he does relentlessly challenge the logic of difference. If we are ever to find, in the words of the Morrises, "a different kind of difference, a difference that did not mythologize itself in exclusive/inclusive oppositions" (235), or if we are to find an alternative to difference, that is, a system of meanings not based in exclusion but perhaps, as feminist theorists suggest, in identification, we must look to our writers—female, male, and of every race and ethnic group—who, like Faulkner, are profoundly aware of the difference words make.

Notes

1. Freud writes that scenes of observing sexual intercourse between parents at a very early age "[p]ossibly . . . are part of the regular store in the–conscious or unconscious–treasury of memories" (17: 59). According to Laplanche and Pontalis, the primal scene is a regularly recurring, unconscious image that functions like a collective myth: through such imaginary scenarios "neurotics and perhaps all human beings seek an answer to the central enigmas of their existence" (332). For Lacan, as James Mellard lucidly explains, "[o]rigins can never be available to us (even if they exist); what is available, Lacan would say, is a capacity for symbolization expressed in language, that covers over the metaphysical or ontological gap where an origin might have been" (7).

2. Arguably, Freud is unable to explain satisfactorily these processes in girls because of the phallocentric bias of his theory. He posits "a corresponding development" for females; however, because, in his view, castration anxiety motivates the boy to turn away from the mother and to identify with the father and because "the girl accepts castration as an accomplished fact," he acknowledges that "a powerful motive drops out for the setting up of a superego and for the breaking-off of the infantile genital organization" (19: 178).

3. To the castration complex, Freud attributes "the profoundest importance in the formation alike of character and of neurosis" (20: 37). Lacan maintains that Freud "designate[s] the very instigation of the subject by the name of castration" (*Feminine Sexuality* 116). In Lacan's revision of Freudian theory, the analogue for the castration complex is alienation, the rupture or division that gives rise to the fictive subject: "Alienation . . . condemns the subject to appearing only in that division which . . . if it appears on one side as meaning, produced by a signifier, it appears on the other as '*aphanasis*' or fading" (*Four* 210).

4. My interpretation owes a debt to important, earlier studies by Polk and Matthews. In his seminal Freudian reading of *Sanctuary*, Polk locates two representations of the primal scene in the novel and observes that "the primal scene is indeed everywhere implied in the overwhelming emphasis throughout the novel on voyeurism" ("Dungeon" 74). Whereas I read these scenes as revising Freud and evoking the merely symbolic nature of the father's authority, Polk applies Freudian formulas to the novel and interprets these scenes as a manifestation of a repressed fear of the mother: *Sanctuary* "is at least in one sense, Horace's nightmare," the return of "*something* connected with sex and aggression and death and disgust and his mother; we may, then, legitimately wonder whether Horace's mother were not in fact much more akin to Caroline Compson than to the frail, helpless wraith of a woman he insists upon remembering" ("Dungeon" 73, 75). Citing Freud, Matthews examines the return in the novel of prohibited Oedipal desire, which, he finds, poses a threat to the social order. Unlike my essay, Matthews's interpretation does not identify the novel's unmasking of phallic authority, but his reading complements my own, particularly in his finding that *Sanctuary* reveals "the radical interpenetration of chaos and order, nature and the law, instinct and custom, innocence and evil" (247).

5. In an early, discerning discussion of the novel, Lawrence S. Kubie observes that rape functions as a substitute for castration, and men who rape or fantasize rape are driven by a sense of their own impotence.

6. Laplanche and Pontalis state that Freud never recognized "the full implications of the primal link to the mother" (285). The pre-Oedipal phase, or Lacan's imaginary stage, is difficult to describe because it is the very disruption of the imaginary that gives rise to language and conceptualization. The key point that emerges from Lacan's discussion of this early register of being is that there is no difference, no self and no other, and the child exists as one continuous totality of being. In the words of Ellie Ragland-Sullivan, the imaginary "is the domain of the imago and relationship interaction" (130–31).

7. This interpretation builds on thoughtful feminist readings of Faulkner by Mortimer, Jones, Gwin, Clarke, Dunleavy, and Eddy. In particular, my approach has been influenced by Jones, who, in an essay that interprets war as a boundary that closes out the feminine, calls for studies that critique the phallocentric biases of Freudian and Lacanian theory so as to "find a way to the mother and the preoedipal" (51); by Dunleavy, who demonstrates that the novel locates sexual difference not in biology but in social configurations of power; and by Eddy, who finds that rape functions as a policing of gender that leaks homoerotic desire. Finally, this study builds on my book, *Faulkner: The Return of the Repressed* (1997), a psychoanalytic reading of five of Faulkner's major novels (not including

Sanctuary). In the course of writing this book, I discovered that just as Lacan rewrites Freudian principles so also writers, like Faulkner, interpret psychic processes in ways different from both Freud and Lacan.

8. In revising *Sanctuary*, Faulkner shifted the focus from Horace Benbow's Oedipal desires for his mother, sister, and stepdaughter to Temple Drake's rape and abduction; in the original text, the Oedipal complex is even directly named (16). See Millgate (121), Polk ("Afterword" 305), Irwin ("Horace Benbow" 546–47), and Clarke (60–62). On the revisions, see Massey (195–208), Meriwether (192–206), Millgate (113–23), Langford (3–33), Polk ("Afterword" 293–306), Bleikasten (*Ink* 213–20), and Cohen (54–66). Polk writes that Faulkner may have rewritten the novel to "get us outside of Horace Benbow's cloyingly introspective, narcissistic personality" ("Afterword" 300); in a subsequent essay, he analyzes the "nightmarish qualities" of the original text in Freudian terms and concludes that Faulkner rewrote the novel to obscure the self-revelation of the early draft ("Space" 18); Bleikasten contends that Faulkner refused to publish the early version for "aesthetic reasons" (*Ink* 216); Cohen agrees, but adds that Faulkner revised the book to make it more commercially saleable as well (56).

9. Some of this identificatory imagery, in particular, Horace's identification with both Temple and Popeye, has been recognized and variously interpreted by critics. For example, Polk reads Horace's dual identification as "fulfilling his own rape fantasy" ("Dungeon" 72–73): Temple is "his female self" ("Dungeon" 73), and Popeye "is much more Horace's double than has generally been allowed" ("Dungeon" 70). For Matthews, this scene is emblematic of the "fragility of the prohibition that protects culture from nature" (257). In an essay that interprets incest in Faulkner's novels in terms of primary narcissism, a self-love that manifests itself as a desire for the mother of the mirror-stage, Irwin argues that Horace's dual identification functions to double Popeye and Temple with Horace and Little Belle: "what the physically impotent Popeye does to Temple with a corncob is an image of what the spiritually impotent Horace would like to do to his stepdaughter" ("Horace Benbow" 558); according to Pettey, the merging of male and female in this scene reflects Horace's ambivalent sexual identity (81); in a Freudian reading that focuses on oral expulsion, Greg Forter argues that the novel stages "a drama of failed differentiation" from "a maternal being-in-the-world" and that "vomit is the ruin of masculinity that collapses the reader it imagines as male into the maternal object-to-be-mastered" (86, 92).

10. In his groundbreaking psychohistorical study of white racism, Kovel states that the lynchings of black men for the alleged rape of a white lady (with "rape" defined to include even imagined gestures or looks of desire) "often included a castration of the black malefactor; and even when it didn't, the idea of castration was

immanent in the entire procedure" (67). Reading these literal or symbolic castrations in terms of Freud's Oedipus complex, Kovel argues persuasively that white racists in the American South projected onto black men the roles of both father and son in the Oedipal triangle so as to satisfy conflicting infantile desires: by lynching the black man, the white racist "is castrating the father, as he once wished to do, and also identifying with the father by castrating the son, as he once feared for himself" (71–72).

11. On this doubling, see Polk ("Space" 23), Matthews (263), Bleikasten (*Ink* 261), Irwin ("Horace Benbow" 558). Adamowski traces Popeye's "pathetic lapse" from a figure "who is transcendent into a dependent creature of weakness" when "others know him" (47).

12. For example, Davis and Bleikasten apply a Lacanian formula to *Absalom, Absalom!* in an attempt to account for Sutpen's failure to represent a legitimate phallic authority, a project that leads them finally to invoke the shadowy figure of the dead father. Bleikasten writes that Sutpen is "dead, but not dead enough" to "act the role of the dead father" ("Fathers" 143), who guarantees the law. This conclusion raises the question: what does a father have to do to be "dead enough" to guarantee the law?

13. Blotner identifies Ned Barnett as a model for Lucas Beauchamp (1246); quite possibly, "Uncle Ned's" death may have moved Faulkner to write *Intruder in the Dust*. He died in December of 1947 and, in January of 1948, Faulkner put aside the manuscript of *A Fable* to write *Intruder*. Blotner's portrait of "Uncle Ned" suggests that he was both father-figure and servant to Faulkner (52, 998, 1006).

Works Cited

Adamowski, T. H. "Faulkner's Popeye: The 'Other' as Self." *Canadian Review of American Studies* 8 (1977): 36–51. Rpt. in *Twentieth Century Interpretations of* Sanctuary. Ed. J. Douglas Canfield. Englewood Cliffs: Prentice, 1982. 32–48.

Bleikasten, André. "Fathers in Faulkner." *The Fictional Father: Lacanian Readings of the Text*. Ed. Robert Con Davis. Amherst: U of Massachusetts P, 1981.

———. *The Ink of Melancholy: Faulkner's Novels from* The Sound and the Fury *to* Light in August. Bloomington: Indiana UP, 1990.

Blotner, Joseph. *Faulkner: A Biography*. 2 vols. New York: Random, 1974.

Clarke, Deborah. *Robbing the Mother: Women in Faulkner*. Jackson: UP of Mississippi, 1994.

Cohen, Philip. "'A Cheap Idea . . . Deliberately Conceived to Make Money': The Biographical Context of William Faulkner's Introduction to *Sanctuary*." *Faulkner Journal* 3.2 (1988): 54–66.

Cowley, Malcolm. *The Faulkner-Cowley File: Letters and Memories, 1944–1962*. New York: Penguin, 1978.

Davis, Robert Con. "The Symbolic Father in Yoknapatawpha County." *Journal of Narrative Technique* 10 (1980): 39–55.

Derrida, Jacques. *Of Grammatology*. Trans. Gayatari Chakravorty Spivak. Baltimore: Johns Hopkins UP, 1974.

Dunleavy, Linda. "*Sanctuary*, Sexual Difference, and the Problem of Rape." *Studies in American Fiction* 24 (1996): 171–91.

Eddy, Charmaine. "The Policing and Proliferation of Desire: Gender and the Homosocial in Faulkner's *Sanctuary*." *Faulkner Journal* 14.2 (1999): 21–39.

Faulkner, William. 1936. *Absalom, Absalom!* New York: Vintage, 1990.

———. *Faulkner at Nagano*. Ed. Robert A. Jelliffe. Tokyo: Kenkyuska, 1956.

———. *Faulkner in the University: Class Conferences at the University of Virginia, 1957–1958*. Ed. Frederick L. Gwynn and Joseph Blotner. Charlottesville: U of Virginia P, 1959.

———. *Go Down, Moses*. 1942. New York: Vintage, 1990.

———. *Intruder in the Dust*. 1948. New York: Vintage, 1991.

———. *Lion in the Garden: Interviews with William Faulkner*. Ed. James B. Meriwether and Michael Millgate. Lincoln: U of Nebraska P, 1980.

———. *Sanctuary*. 1931. New York: Vintage, 1993.

———. *Sanctuary: The Original Text*. Ed. Noel Polk. New York: Random, 1981.

Forter, Greg. *Murdering Masculinities: Fantasies of Gender and Violence in the American Crime Novel*. New York: New York UP, 2000.

Fowler, Doreen. *Faulkner: The Return of the Repressed*. 1997. Charlottesville: U of Virginia P, 2000.

Freud, Sigmund. *The Standard Edition of the Complete Psychological Works of Freud*. Ed. and trans. James Strachey. 24 vols. London: Hogarth, 1953–74.

Gallop, Jane. *The Daughter's Seduction: Feminism and Psychoanalysis*. Ithaca: Cornell UP, 1985.

Gwin, Minrose C. *The Feminine and Faulkner: Reading (Beyond) Sexual Difference*. Knoxville: U of Tennessee P, 1990.

Homer. *The Odyssey*. Trans. Robert Fitzgerland. New York: Anchor, 1963.

Irwin, John T. *Doubling and Incest / Repetition and Revenge*. Baltimore: Johns Hopkins UP, 1975.

———. "Horace Benbow and the Myth of Narcissa." *American Literature* 64 (1992): 543–66.

Jones, Anne Goodwyn. "Male Fantasies? Faulkner's War Stories and the Construction of Gender." *Faulkner and Psychology*. Ed. Donald M. Kartiganer and Ann J. Abadie. Jackson: UP of Mississippi, 1994. 21–55.

Kovel, Joel. *White Racism: A Psychohistory*. New York: Vintage, 1971.

Kubie, Lawrence S. "William Faulkner's *Sanctuary*: An Analysis." *Saturday Review of Literature* 11 (1934): 218–25.

234   Doreen Fowler

Lacan, Jacques. *Écrits*. Paris: Seuil, 1966.

———. *Écrits: A Selection*. Trans. Alan Sheridan. 1966. New York: Norton, 1977.

———. *Feminine Sexuality: Jacques Lacan and the "École Freudienne."* Ed. Juliet Mitchell. Trans. and ed. Jacqueline Rose. New York: Norton, 1982.

———. "Les formations de l'inconscient." *Bulletins de Psychologie* 2 (1957–58): 1–15.

———. *The Four Fundamental Concepts of Psycho-Analysis*. Ed. Jacques-Alain Miller. Trans. Alan Sheridan. New York: Norton, 1981.

Langford, Gerald. *Faulkner's Revision of* Sanctuary. Austin: U of Texas P, 1972.

Laplanche, Jean, and J. B. Pontalis. *The Language of Psycho-analysis*. Trans. Donald Nicholson-Smith. New York: Norton, 1973.

Lukacher, Ned. *Primal Scenes*. Ithaca: Cornell UP, 1986.

Massey, Linton. "Notes on the Unrevised Galleys of Faulkner's *Sanctuary*." *Studies in Bibliography* 8 (1956): 195–208.

Matthews, John T. "The Elliptical Nature of *Sanctuary*." *Novel* 17 (1984): 246–65.

McMillen, Neil R., and Noel Polk. "Faulkner on Lynching." *Faulkner Journal* 8.1 (1992): 3–14.

Mellard, James M. *Using Lacan, Reading Fiction*. Urbana: U of Illinois P, 1991.

Meriwether, James B. "Some Notes on the Text of Faulkner's *Sanctuary*." *Papers of the Bibliographical Society of America* 55 (1961): 192–206.

Millgate, Michael. *The Achievement of William Faulkner*. New York: Vintage, 1963.

Mitchell, Juliet. Introduction. Lacan, *Feminine Sexuality* 1–26.

Morris, Wesley, and Barbara Alverson Morris. *Reading Faulkner*. Madison: U of Wisconsin P, 1989.

Mortimer, Gail L. *Faulkner's Rhetoric of Loss: A Study in Perception and Meaning*. Austin: U of Texas P, 1983.

Obholzer, Karin. *The Wolf-Man: Conversations with Freud's Patient—Sixty Years Later*. Trans. Michael Shaw. New York: Continuum, 1982.

Pettey, Homer B. "Reading and Raping in *Sanctuary*." *Faulkner Journal* 3 (1987): 71–84.

Polk, Noel. "Afterword." Faulkner, *Sanctuary: The Original Text* 293–306.

———. "'The Dungeon Was Mother Herself': William Faulkner: 1927–1931." *New Directions in Faulkner Studies*. Ed. Doreen Fowler and Ann J. Abadie. Jackson: UP of Mississippi, 1984. 61–93.

———. "The Space between *Sanctuary*." *Intertextuality in Faulkner*. Ed. Michel Gresset and Noel Polk. Jackson: UP of Mississippi, 1985. 16–35.

Porter, Carolyn. "*Absalom, Absalom!* (Un)making the Father." *The Cambridge Companion to William Faulkner*. Cambridge: Cambridge UP, 1995. 168–96.

Ragland-Sullivan, Ellie. *Jacques Lacan and the Philosophy of Psychoanalysis*. Urbana: U of Illinois P, 1986.

Ramas, Maria. "Freud's Dora, Dora's Hysteria." *In Dora's Case: Freud—Feminism—Hysteria*. Ed. Charles Bernheimer and Claire Kahane. New York: Columbia UP, 1985. 149–80.

Rose, Jacqueline. Introduction. Lacan, *Feminine Sexuality* 27–57.

CHAPTER 14

THE PICTURE OF CHARLES BON

OSCAR WILDE'S TRIP THROUGH FAULKNER'S YOKNAPATAWPHA

Ellen Crowell

One day I determined to paint a wonderful portrait of you. It was to have been my masterpiece. It is my masterpiece. But as I worked at it, every flake and film of color seemed to me to reveal my secret. I grew afraid that the world would know of my idolatry. I felt, Dorian, that I had told too much. Then it was that I resolved never to allow the picture to be exhibited.
—Oscar Wilde, *The Picture of Dorian Gray*

But I never saw it. I do not even know of my own knowledge that Ellen ever saw it, that Judith ever loved it, that Henry slew it, so who will dispute me when I say, Why did I not invent, create it? . . . It would not even need a skull behind it; almost anonymous, it would only need vague inference of some walking flesh and blood desired by someone else even if only in

Originally published in *Modern Fiction Studies,* Autumn 2004.

some shadow realm of make-believe.—A picture seen
by stealth, by creeping . . . into the deserted midday
room to look at it.
                    —William Faulkner, *Absalom, Absalom!*

In 1882, a near-bankrupt Jefferson Davis was living in semi-exile on Mississippi's Gulf Coast at Beauvoir. Attempts to reinvigorate Briarfield, his family's Mississippi plantation, were failing, and his two-volume *Rise and Fall of the Confederate Government*, published in 1881 as a "monument to his cause," received mostly faint praise; reviewers depicted him as "a man of the past, out of touch with the world of 1881" (Cooper 619, 620). It was this insolvent and out-of-touch Davis who sat on Beauvoir's breezy Gulf-front verandah as a twenty-eight-year-old Oscar Wilde walked up the stately drive for an afternoon visit.

For Wilde, Davis was a relic of the South's heroic past. For Davis, Wilde was a harbinger of a less heroic future. Although Davis's wife Varina and daughter Vinnie were captivated by Wilde's eccentricity, Davis found the artist's effeminacy distasteful. One critic singles out this visit as the "single episode" most "emblematic of the changes the world was experiencing while it left [Davis] behind," arguing that Wilde "was the twentieth century knocking at Davis's door that day, and he simply didn't know what to do with it" (Rev. of *Jefferson Davis*). The defeated leader had another reason to refuse any association with one so flamboyantly effeminate; Davis was rumored to have donned women's clothing while attempting his 1865 escape from the victorious Yankee forces, and this "evidence" of effeminacy became compelling fodder for Northern presses' mockery of Southern manhood. Nancy Silber records that immediately following this incident, images of Jefferson Davis "decked out in crinoline and skirts" appeared in periodicals, advertisements, and even popular music, all of which "offer[ed] a symbolic display of the Northern view of southern gender confusion at the close of the war" (30). Lewis and Smith suggest that because "Jeff Davis . . . had been captured wearing his wife's raincoat," he "had been lampooned savagely enough to merit now the sympathy of a lampooned aesthete" (367). The modern, androgynous figure in "dandyish dress" knocking at the door of Beauvoir repelled Davis because in Wilde he saw embodied the very gender indeterminacy of which he and men of his class stood accused.

Yet the ruined Davis attracted Wilde because in this defeated Mississippi statesman Wilde saw embodied that particular combination of heroism and decay that informed his later aesthetic philosophies. The influence of the "ruined" South reemerges in Wilde's gothic novel *The Picture of Dorian Gray,* a novel that in turn prompted another backward-looking Mississippian to requeer the South. Forty years after Wilde left Davis on his verandah, William Faulkner brought this Irish dandy back to Mississippi. At the center of *Absalom, Absalom!,* buried in chapter 6, readers encounter the novel's sole direct allusion to another writer: Mr. Compson, the most decadent-minded of Faulkner's narrators, imagines a grave-yard melodrama staged on the grounds of Sutpen's plantation:

> It must have resembled a garden scene by the Irish poet, Wilde: the late afternoon, the dark cedars with the level sun in them, even the light exactly right and the graves, the three pieces of marble . . . looking as though they had been cleaned and polished and arranged by scene shifters who with the passing of twilight would return and strike them and carry them, hollow fragile and without weight, back to the ware-house until they should be needed again; the pageant, the scene, the act, entering upon the stage. (157)

This decadent Wildean stage is complemented by the characters who enter: a "magnolia-faced woman . . . created of by and for darkness whom the artist Beardsley might have dressed," and a "little boy whom Beardsley might not only have dressed but drawn—a thin delicate child with a smooth ivory sexless face" (157). The Wildean *fin de siècle* is embodied by these opulently aristocratic, satin-draped, and eroticized mourners—and to their theatrical decadence Faulkner adds a twist at once characteristically Faulknerian and, as I will argue, surprisingly Wildean: this graveyard melodrama is about miscegenation. This magnolia-faced Southern Belle, "walk-ing beneath a lace parasol" and attended by her "bright gigantic" servant, is shrouded in a veneer of "civility," which fails to mask her racial identity. Because "the octoroon" (the only name Faulkner gives her) performs the "bright dramatic pageantry" of a segre-gated aristocracy that denies her, she, as much as her "sexless" son, fits seamlessly into Wilde's decadent iconography. For Wilde's modern gothic tale, like Faulkner's, concerns false aristocracy, mixed blood, and the aesthetics of ruin—a combination Wilde found dramatically embodied in the South's post–Civil War landscape. By placing Wilde squarely within the racial, sexual, and ancestral bat-tleground of the Southern aristocratic family romance, Faulkner suggests that the "Irish poet" is a figure paradoxically at home in the postbellum 1930s South.

Critics have noted Faulkner's early interest in Wilde's *Salome* (1893) and his 1925 visit to the artist's tomb as important glimpses

into his own *fin de siècle* leanings. Lothar Hönnighausen demonstrates that reading Faulkner's *Marionettes* (1920) against *Salome*
illuminates Faulkner and Wilde's shared fascination with "the poetic
quality of biblical prose and the imaginative beauty and unrealistic
nature of its images" (*William Faulkner* 159). Although Hönnighausen briefly examines Wilde's influence on Faulkner's later novels,
he limits his investigation to the echoes of Swinburnian decadence
and Beardsleyesque exoticism that Faulkner's direct and indirect
references to Wilde evoke. Yet Faulkner engages with more than
"implications and lingering connotations" when he imports the
Wildean *fin de siècle* into the American South (158). In this essay,
I hope to show how all facets of the Wilde figure—Irish aesthete,
homosexual dandy, cultural pariah—are in fact central to the decadent landscape of *Absalom, Absalom!*

The Picture of Dorian Gray and *Absalom, Absalom!* are novels
joined by their shared fascination with the erosion of moral values
and the multiple forms amorality can take. This in itself is not revelatory; many modernist texts incorporate and transform *fin de
siècle* discourses of degeneration to explore moral decay. In the
sections that follow, however, I will show that Faulkner's Charles
Bon is a literary figure anticipated by the androgynous pseudoaristocrat Oscar Wilde, who, like Bon, came down from Oxford to find
himself first in Mississippi (visiting with Jefferson Davis on a gracious verandah) and then in New Orleans (where he was escorted
on a tour of the city by Civil War hero General P. T. Beauregard).

Wilde's trip through the "ruined" South crystallized the artist's lasting preoccupation with the relationship between beauty
and decay, a preoccupation that found its fullest expression in the
figure of Dorian Gray, a beautiful gothic monster in whom physical
decline and aestheticism merge. We can therefore read *The Picture
of Dorian Gray* as a novel whose Gothicism was in part born of the
same aesthetics of ruin as *Absalom, Absalom!* Because Wilde wrote
first, and established an entire philosophy of dandyism that could
at once pay homage to and mock the ideologies that produced
him, I argue that in Wildean dandyism (as expressed through both
Wilde's self-aestheticization and his prose) Faulkner recognized a
model through which to augment his critique of the multiple performances of Southern aristocracy. Thomas Sutpen, the planter-
patriarch who wills himself into existence and invents aristocracy on
his own terms, uses the principles of Wildean dandyism to set into
motion his self-described "design."

Wilde's presence in *Absalom, Absalom!* also draws attention
to the way another dandy-aristocrat exposes the equally theatrical
category of Southern whiteness. In the corrupted beauty of Dorian

Gray, we see the seeds of Faulkner's Charles Bon: another dandy-aristocrat whose bodily "corruption" operates as a metaphor for progressive cultural ruin. Wilde's effeminacy, as represented by him and for him in fiction and public life, is always read in ways that reflect a reader's own assumptions about embodied sexuality. Reading Charles Bon against the Wildean dandy—both fictional and biographical—highlights the similar way Bon's relative "whiteness" or "blackness" is "read" by the narrators of *Absalom, Absalom!*: these "readers" similarly expose their own assumptions about the relationship between external appearance and racial categorization. Just as the portrait in *Dorian Gray* is read for moral and sexual perversion, Bon's body is read for mixed blood, which within the landscape of Sutpen's Hundred is a form of moral perversion.

Through allusions to *Dorian Gray* that illuminate the homoerotic nature of Charles Bon's relationship with Sutpen's son Henry, Faulkner rearticulates sexual "otherness" as racial unassimilability. By reading Faulkner through Wilde, we can see that Faulkner does not use miscegenation to symbolize homosexuality, or homosexuality to symbolize miscegenation.[1] Rather, he presents the two transgressions as imbricated in order to highlight the particular fear of "sameness" each breach of Southern morality engenders. Reading Wilde through Faulkner in turn draws attention to the multiple ways Wilde's own sexual "otherness" was likewise racialized; Wilde's race—his Irishness—was cast as yet another in a long list of sexual transgressions.

Wilde about the South

When, toward the end of his 1882 American tour, Oscar Wilde was offered a set of lecture engagements that would take him through the Deep South, he responded immediately: "I have received a good offer for two months light lecturing in the South, which I am anxious to visit" (*Complete Letters* 163). Wilde's "southern enterprise" began at Memphis's Leubrie Theater on June 12, 1882, where he was greeted by "a cultivated audience of six hundred people" eager to hear a lecture entitled "Decorative Art" (Lewis and Smith 358). Wilde spoke next in New Orleans and then traveled to Texas, Alabama, Georgia, South Carolina, and Virginia, finally completing his southern tour on July 14 at the Vicksburg Opera House in Mississippi.[2]

To modern readers, the fact that Oscar Wilde toured America at the age of 28, lecturing on topics as diverse as interior decorating, the Aesthetic movement, and Irish nationalism, in locations as far-ranging as San Antonio, Montgomery, and Sioux City, fascinates by virtue of unexpected juxtaposition: the Irish aesthete shaking hands with the Colorado cowboy; blue velvet knee-breeches showing up against somber late-Victorian black; and lectures on "The House Beautiful" ceremonially intoned for the farmers of Griggsville, Illinois. But fascinating as each leg of Wilde's American tour remains, his trip through the postbellum South emerges as its most surprising and illuminating segment.

On July 4, an *Atlanta Constitution* reporter conducted an extended interview with "the Great Esthete." In the interest of advance publicity for the lecture at De Give's Opera House scheduled for that evening, Wilde peppered his ruminations on art with praise for the South:

> It should be—the south [*sic*]—the home of art in America, because it possesses the most perfect surroundings, and now that it is recovering from the hideous ruin of the war I have no doubt that all these beautiful arts, in whose cause I will spend my youth in pleading, will spring up among you. The south produced the best poet in America—Edgar Allan Poe: and with all its splendid traditions it would be impossible not to believe that she would continue to perfect what she has begun so nobly. The very physique of the people in the south is far finer than that in the north, and a temperament infinitely more susceptible to the influences of beauty. ("Oscar Wilde: Arrival" 8)

Wilde flatters Southerners by suggesting that their "splendid traditions," played out against the backdrop of "perfect surroundings," create the ideal conditions for American art. Wilde is arguing for a Southern renaissance, which he graciously implies is already under way. This renaissance is only slightly delayed by the "hideous ruin of the war," a ruin from which the South is, in Wilde's on-the-record estimation, quickly recovering. However, in a private letter composed the next day from Augusta, Georgia, Wilde praises instead the great aesthetic possibilities offered by the ruined South. Although the aesthete falls into predetermined Southern stereotypes, readers familiar with Wilde's later preoccupation with the relationship between art and ruin will detect hints of *Dorian Gray* in his observations:

> I write to you from the beautiful, passionate, ruined South, the land of magnolias and music, of roses and romance: picturesque too in her failure to keep pace with your keen northern pushing intellect; living chiefly on credit, and on the memory of some crushing defeats. And I have been to Texas, right to the heart of it, and stayed with Jeff Davis at his plantation

(how fascinating all failures are!) and seen Savannah, and the Georgia forests, and bathed in the Gulf of Mexico, and engaged in Voodoo rites with the Negroes, and am dreadfully tired. (*Complete Letters* 175–76)

Passion and ruin, beauty and failure are twinned forces that comprise the weight of the South's impact on Wilde. Wilde's mention of Poe as the South's greatest poet underscores the kind of Southern aesthetics he values, and one senses that economic recovery is the last thing Wilde would have found essential to a renaissance in Southern art.

Wilde was aware of what Southerners wanted to hear from a "great esthete," namely, that their war-torn cities were more cultivated and refined than those in the North. As the son of Speranza, the Irish nationalist poet, Wilde was well versed in the rhetoric of underdog nationalism and the poetics of romantic defeat, and he used this knowledge to ingratiate himself with audiences across the South. But what also becomes clear through these interviews is that even in 1882 Wilde was preoccupied with the relationship between art and ruin. Upon returning from his visit to Beauvoir, Wilde was asked to describe his visit:

[Davis] lives in a very beautiful house by the sea, amid lovely trees. He impressed me very much as a man of the keenest intellect, and a man fairly to be a leader of men on account of a personality that is as simple as it is strong, and an enthusiasm that is as fervent as it is faultless. . . . Because although there may be a failure in fact, in an idea, there is no failure possible. The principles for which Mr. Davis and the South went to war cannot suffer defeat. ("Oscar Wilde: Arrival" 8)

Although readers of the *Atlanta Constitution* might have been touched by Wilde's unrestrained admiration for "the principles for which . . . the South went to war," most modern readers are shocked to find Wilde espousing such blindly conservative and racist politics. Yet two principles that guided Wilde's political and aesthetic beliefs are at work here. The first, learned from his Irish nationalist mother, was that individuals bound together by tradition and common interests have a right to self-governance and a mandate to rebel against an oppressive imperial power. The second was to become Wilde's central aesthetic principle: that the twinned aesthetics of classical beauty and decadent ruin form the crux of modern art. Wilde's conflation of Davis's personal failures with the South's military and ideological failures is therefore significant to the artist's later work; for Wilde, every ruin, and perhaps especially the national ruin of frustrated rebellion, is a human condition to be analyzed and aestheticized. In the world of ideas, as in Wilde's world of art, complete ruin is an aesthetic impossibility.

Richard Ellmann records that, after Wilde returned from America, he would explain that "in the South, whenever one would mention anything, people would reply, 'you should have seen it before the War'" (196). Wilde claimed to have underestimated the ruining power of war "until one night in Charleston he turned to someone and said, 'How beautiful the moon is!' and had for a reply, 'You should have seen it, sir, before the War'" (Ellmann 196). Within this lighthearted vignette lies a central Wildean principle, put most succinctly in his combative preface to the 1891 version of *The Picture of Dorian Gray*: "It is the spectator, and not life, that art really mirrors" (3).

Aesthetic Wills-to-Power

And the mentor, for whose sake [Henry] had repudiated not only blood and kin but food and shelter too, whose clothing and walk and speech he had tried to ape, along with his attitude towards women and his ideas of honor and pride too, watching him with that cold and catlike inscrutable calculation, watching the picture resolve and become fixed, and then telling Henry, "But that's not it. That's just the base, the foundation. It can belong to anyone."

—William Faulkner, *Absalom, Absalom!*

The aesthetical costume Wilde donned for his American tour varied little from venue to venue. Occasionally he would write to his agent requesting replacements, all in the romantic style that advertisements promised and audiences expected:

Dear Colonel Morse, Will you kindly go to a good costumier (theatrical) for me and get them to make me (you will not mention my name) two coats, to wear at matinees and perhaps in the evening. They should be beautiful; tight velvet doublet, with large flowered sleeves and little ruffs of cambric coming up from under the collar. . . . Any good costumier would know what I want—sort of Francis I dress: only knee-breeches instead of long hose. Also get me two pair of grey silk stockings to suit grey mouse-coloured velvet. The sleeves are to be flowered—if not velvet then plush—stamped with a large pattern. They will excite a great sensation. . . . They were dreadfully disappointed at Cincinnati at my not wearing knee-breeches.[3] (*Collected Letters* 141)

In the South, Wilde's wardrobe was "shocking," "peculiar" ("Oscar Wilde: A Visit" 4), and a "spectacle . . . long to be remembered" ("Oscar Wilde: Arrival" 8). Word of Wilde's self-presentation had preceded him, and one New Orleans *Daily Picayune* reporter set out to uncover the "real man" behind this advance hype. The gentleman he found at the hotel, however, was still attired in a version of his "peculiar" costume: "His hair is long and straight, not curling, and hangs upon his shoulders in heavy masses. He was dressed in a black velvet jacket, gray tight fitting pantaloons, not knee breeches, red silk stockings and slippers. His shirt collar was loosely tied with a dark scarf" ("Oscar Wilde: A Visit" 4).

In her recent treatment of dandyism and decadence, Rhonda Garelick places Wildean dandyism within a transatlantic tradition of self-aestheticization for a public audience:

> Both the early social dandyism of England and the later, more philosophical French incarnations of the movement announced and glorified a self-created, carefully controlled man whose goal was to create an effect, bring about an event, or provoke reaction in others through the suppression of the "natural." Artful manipulation of posture, social skill, manners, conversation, and dress were all accoutrements in the aestheticizaton of self central to dandyism. (3)

These newspaper responses show that Wilde embodied, as early as his American tour, the subversive potential of the late-Victorian dandy: an "artfully manipulated" figure that highlights both the theatricality of the self and the theatricality of colonial culture. The identity Wilde donned for Southern audiences was that of the aesthetic aristocrat; his eccentric attire, combined with frivolous lecture topics, signified the ease of affluence as much as they did the principles of aestheticism. It is through this over-the-top parody of aristocratic privilege that we first see Wilde embodying his distinctive dandyism: using mimicry to expose as fluid those national, racial, and sexual identities upon whose fixity colonial power structures depended.

Wildean dandyism distinguishes itself through its reliance on the sublime tension that structures the dandy's consciousness: a gothic version of Immanuel Kant's psychological sublime, in which the desire to transcend "natural" limitations creates its own unique monstrosities.[4] In *Critique of Judgment* (1790), Kant maintains that the sublime resides not within natural objects themselves, but in the mind of whoever contemplates the sublime object. Because it divorces the sublime experience from the realm of Christianity (or morality) and places it squarely in the mind of the spectator, Kant's sublime is clearly linked to the dandy's aesthetic will-to-power: the human mind is first paralyzed by a feeling of helplessness before an overwhelming force and then experiences the exultation of human possibility that comes with the capacity for resistance, which "gives us courage to be able to measure ourselves against the seeming omnipotence of nature." The ability to experience the sublime exemplifies, on the one hand, the limitations and weakness of finite humanity and, on the other, humanity's "preeminence over nature," even when confronted by the "immeasurability" of nature's magnitude and the "irresistibility" of its might (309–10).

Wilde felt the sublime force of English class and race distinctions when he left Ireland at twenty to "pit himself against the most ancient university in England" (Ellmann 36). The volatile colonial relationship between Ireland and England at the end of the nineteenth century demanded a rhetoric of racial difference, which segregated the categories of "Irish" and "English"; to upper-class English Victorians, subtle distinctions between Anglo-Irish aristocrats and the "common" Irish remained invisible. Born in Dublin into the increasingly bankrupt Anglo-Irish upper-middle class in 1854, Wilde in late-Victorian London was just another suspicious Irishman. The English "high polish" of Wilde's prose did not come naturally, and as an Oxford undergraduate Wilde was "naïve, embarrassed," with a "convulsive laugh, a lisp, and an Irish accent" (38). Despite talking well and amusing his peers, Wilde committed several social blunders, which were attributed to his Irish birth. Thus rebuffed, "Wilde determined to be beyond rather than behind the English. His lisp and native intonation disappeared" (38), along with all other markers of his Irish upbringing:

> His father had been laughed at by society, so he would mock society first. His father had been unkempt, so he would be fastidious. From his mother he had inherited a gigantic and ungainly body, which Lady Colin Campbell compared to a "great white caterpillar," and which recalled all too poignantly the gorilla-like frame of the stage Irishman in [English] cartoons. To disarm such critics, Wilde concealed his massive form with costly clothes and studied the art of elegant deportment. (35)

By carefully ridding himself of the markers of Irishness, Wilde sought to become the perfect "English" gentleman, and in so doing suggested that aristocratic "Englishness" was less dependent on bloodline than on a set of entirely reproducible cultural stances.

Dorian Gray's sublime experience follows Wilde's own. When Lord Henry Wotton's seductive treatise on amorality "touches some secret chord that had never been touched before" in Dorian Gray (20–21), who until that moment had been a passive sitter for painter Basil Hallward, his calculated words transform the young man:

> I believe that if one man were to live out his life fully and completely, were to give form to every feeling, expression to every thought, reality to every dream—I believe that the world would gain such a fresh impulse of joy that we would forget all the maladies of medievalism. . . . The only way to get rid of a temptation is to yield to it. Resist it, and your soul grows sick with longing for the things it has forbidden itself, with desire for what its monstrous laws have made monstrous and unlawful. (20)

In the brief time it takes Lord Henry to "corrupt" Dorian's soul, Basil completes his masterpiece—spurred on by the subtle tinge of corruption that spreads across Dorian's rapt face, a tinge that somehow produces "the effect I wanted—the half-parted lips, and the bright look in the eyes." For his part, Lord Henry "knew the precise psychological moment in which to say nothing" and felt "intensely interested" in the effect his art of words has had on his subject. "He had merely shot an arrow into the air. Had it hit its mark?" (21). Together, Basil and Henry, in a fantastic act of male-male reproduction, give birth to a new, fragmented Dorian: a beautiful, static portrait and a wild, morally unhinged dandy. And upon experiencing the results of this birth—his nascent hedonism twinned with the force of the ideal beauty standing before him—Dorian makes his corrupting wish: "If only it were the other way! If it were I who was always to be young, and the picture that was to grow old! . . . I would give my soul for that!" (26). Dorian immediately wishes for and begins living out the immortality (and amorality) he believes only his portrait can enjoy. Once he realizes that his wish has come true, Dorian uses his status as ageless aristocrat to plumb the depths of his own psyche, believing he will emerge unscathed.

William Faulkner's own careful and contrived staging of his public image rivals Wilde's in its scope and intention, and several critics have identified this obsession with public "masks" as further evidence of what was clearly an ongoing investment in *fin de siècle* dandyism. Hönnighausen maintains that "a study of Faulkner's masking practice will show [that] the elusive master employed not one but a multitude of masks to transform himself" (*Faulkner* 4), and James Watson, in *William Faulkner: Self-Presentation and Performance*, argues that Faulkner's self-presentations as gentleman, dandy, soldier, and farmer become mirrored in his prose, where they become separate but interlocking elements of his fictional representation (5). Hönnighausen obliquely links this role-playing to the artist's interest in dandyism, arguing that "while it is tempting to dismiss Faulkner's dandyism as a means for him to compensate for his diminutive size, there is little doubt that such a simplistic approach would prove unsatisfactory" (*Faulkner* 4). Delineating the specifics of why this approach remains unsatisfactory is my goal in this section. Faulkner's various self-aestheticizations, including his Oxford dandy, bohemian artist, country farmer, and Anglophilic aristocrat poses, are *all* manifestations of a particularly Faulknerian type of dandyism, a type that, on examination, looks distinctly Wildean.[5] This dandyism is evident in Thomas Sutpen, whose late-blooming class consciousness prompts an elaborate and painstaking attention to aristocratic performance. Faulkner's readers cannot read about the artist's infatuation with masks without also remembering this pseudoaristocrat, whose own decadent "design" sets *Absalom, Absalom!* into motion. Like Wilde's Dorian Gray, Faulkner's own dandy-aristocrat is haunted by the desire to transcend, and through sublime transcendence deem "unnatural," the limitations of class that maintain aristocracy's cultural, political, and economic hegemony.

Thomas Sutpen's design erupts into existence through a moment of psychological crisis, in which he at once recognizes what one might desire (the physical wealth of the plantation) and the class structures in place that prohibit the realization of that desire. Sutpen's "trouble," as General Compson recalls, "was innocence" (178): an obliviousness, in Sutpen's case, to the subtle distinctions of class. Sutpen is descended from Scots-Irish "cracker" stock, and although his sheltered boyhood taught him "the difference between white men and black ones," he remained unaware of any class system that could place one white man over another (183). Sutpen had assumed that any man "would be as pleased to show him the balance of his things as the mountain man would have been to show the powder horn and bullet mold that went with the rifle" (186). But when he is turned back from the front door of a grand plantation house by an opulently dressed black servant, who tells him to take his business around back, "it was like that . . . like an explosion—a bright glare that vanished and left nothing, no ashes nor refuse: just a limitless flat plain" (192). The face of the slave at once becomes the "balloon-faced" symbol of plantocracy (187), and Sutpen instantly apprehends the futility in either hating or killing a symbol: one must instead infiltrate what stands behind the symbol.

Therefore, out of a sublime combination of horror and desire, Thomas Sutpen creates a "design" that demands the adoption of a carefully aestheticized identity. He wants to beat the Southern aristocrat at his own privileged game, and to do so he methodically refashions himself in the aristocrat's physical and moral image. The horror Sutpen feels when he realizes that class divisions put some white people below black servants becomes the catalyst for his systematic ascension to the planter class:

> If you were fixing to combat them that had the fine rifles, the first thing you would do would be to get yourself the nearest thing to a fine rifle you could borrow or steal or make, wouldn't it? . . . But this ain't a question of rifles. So to combat them you got to have what they have. . . . You got to have land and niggers and a fine house to combat them with. You see? (192)

"He left right then," Mr. Compson tells Quentin (193). The instant Sutpen realizes first his desire, then his potential to achieve that desire, and finally the meticulous design his desire requires, is also the instant at which he realizes that the clock is ticking. Like Dorian Gray, Thomas Sutpen is obsessed with the threat posed to his desires by the fact of his mortality—so, like Gray, he makes a devil's bargain to stop time: his design, the all-encompassing motive for his every action, robs him of humanity as it assures immortality.

Later, after learning that his rejected son has returned to pervert his "design," Sutpen asks himself, and General Compson too, what he did wrong. In his recitation of this story to his son Jason Compson, the General again identifies a profound "innocence" as the cause of Sutpen's undoing. This innocence is itself a willed performance. Sutpen's willed innocence allows him to see his "design" as wholly of his own making rather than as complicit in the colonial project. Daniel Singal argues that the willed innocence of the Victorians is dictated by their "struggle to build an unassailable wall between themselves and the uglier aspects of life, and in their pre-Freudian conviction that human evil—that the twentieth century would call the unconscious and the preconscious mind—could be held at bay by a firm act of will. Here was the basis for that incorrigible naiveté, that willful innocence" (12). In order to fully "ape" Pettibone, the planter whose servant turns the young Sutpen from an opulent front door, Sutpen keeps himself from acknowledging the cultural, moral, and sexual implications of slavery. Yet Sutpen's white privilege, the same privilege that allows his "design" to take root, derives from a racial system that oppresses others to keep itself "innocent." Sutpen loses his innocence at the exact moment when he strikes his devil's bargain and begins formulating his design. The system he desires to enter is already corrupted, and by acquiring the planter's wealth and status, Sutpen himself is corrupted, even if he cannot clearly see the decay surrounding him.

The visual trappings and modulated language of decadent dandyism and the combative logics of the Wildean dandy's pose are always present in descriptions of Sutpen's transformation from country boy to aristocrat, even when narrators are not immediately identifiable as decadent enthusiasts. Sutpen, like Wilde, uses "decorum . . . if not even elegance of appearance" as "the only weapon (or ladder, rather) with which he would conduct the last assault on what Miss Coldfield and perhaps others believed to be respectability" (28). "Respectability" here is not general; Faulkner means to suggest that Sutpen's revolutionary "design" is meant as an assault on the codes of gentility, white manhood, and morality that bind the Victorian South. In chapter 2, Mr. Compson describes as "alertness" the sheer force of will Sutpen's aristocrat's pose required:

> That . . . alertness which he had to wear day and night without changing or laying aside, like the clothing which without doubt and for a time at least he had to sleep in as well as live in, and in a country and among a people whose very language he had to learn and where because of this he was to make that mistake which if he had acquiesced to it would not even have been an error and which, since he refused to accept it or be stopped by it, became his doom; that unsleeping care which must have known that it could permit itself but one mistake; that alertness for measuring and weighing event against eventuality, circumstance against human nature, his own fallible judgment and mortal clay against not only human but natural forces, choosing and discarding, compromising with his dream and his ambition like you must with the horse which you take across country, over timber, which you control only through your ability to keep the animal from realizing that you actually cannot, that actually it is the stronger. (41)

Compson here paradoxically characterizes Sutpen as a powerless man using the power of dandyism to convince the Southern aristocracy of his rightful place there. As Jershua McCormack succinctly observes, "the Dandy represents the transactions by which the powerless, the nobodies, assume power and importance" (88),[6] and here, the dandy-jockey takes the Southern plantocracy for a ride. Declan Kiberd finds an apt definition of dandyism in Wilde's confession to having "strained every muscle in his body to achieve mastery of a London dinner-table" (374), and here we see Sutpen's similar dandyism in the South, one in which an alert, ambitious, "unsleeping care" in regard to clothes, language, and human nature is the means by which the powerless can control an "animal" that "actually is the stronger."

By affecting the architectural trappings of the planter class, Sutpen exposes the fallacy of class division. Sutpen's design is dictated by the dandyism of the self-made aristocrat. But Sutpen, again like Wilde and his character Dorian Gray, fails from the first to pull off this pose: his performance of aristocracy is always a bit too florid, always in danger of exposing itself *as* performance, as camp. Mr. Compson describes Sutpen's shortcomings as an aristocrat:

> [He] saluted them with that florid, swaggering gesture to the hat (yes, he was underbred. It showed like this always, your grandfather said, in all his formal contacts with people. He was like John L. Sullivan having taught himself painfully and tediously to do the schottische, having drilled himself and drilled himself in secret until he now believed it no longer necessary to count the music's beat, say . . .).[7] (34–35)

Sutpen is unaware of these shortcomings. Although he might concede that other men "might have done it a little more effortlessly than he," he would never admit that any man "could have beat him in knowing when to do it and how" (35). The dandy, of course, makes it his sole purpose to know the whens and hows of "formal contacts," and in this knowledge Sutpen is right in thinking himself unbeatable. But his lack of aristocratic breeding shows through despite careful study, and in this Sutpen is a failed dandy. If the other gentlemen in Jefferson understand his pose to be a "raree show" (20), then his entire "design" is flawed from the start.

Nevertheless, Sutpen's self-mastery, Mr. Compson tells Quentin, cements his place in Jefferson's community: "anyone could look at him and say, *Given the occasion and the need, this man can and will do anything*" (35). "Sutpen's power," as Sean Latham argues, "derives not from any claim to the natural superiority of his skin-color but from the spectacular and violent display of his own primitive will-to-power" (457). Once he secures his entrance into polite Jefferson society through his marriage to Ellen Coldfield, the respectable daughter of a local merchant, "some of the faience appearance which the flesh of his face had when he [first] came to town" disappears (36). The word "faience" is instructive here; the glaze of flashy newly acquired wealth that remained, despite Sutpen's alertness, a marker of his difference has lost some of its gaudy luster. But the glaze still barely hides the simple earthenware beneath. Sutpen's will-to-power cannot completely obscure his origins, nor perhaps does he mean to do so. For Sutpen's design is twofold: to first *become* the aristocrat, and to then *outrage* the aristocracy by the ease with which he is able to mimic them. Sutpen's failure to flawlessly mimic the planter patriarch is therefore an essential part of his dandyism: the cracks in Sutpen's aristocratic mask constitute his greatest weapon—the ability to provoke the indignation of the class he mocks.

When Miss Rosa tells Quentin Compson that Sutpen "wasn't a gentleman . . . wasn't even a gentleman" (9), readers see the emotional effects of Sutpen's provocation. Rosa, obsessed with Southern manhood, cannot condone Sutpen's mockery of her cherished institution. In her denial of Sutpen's ambitions, Rosa exposes her own romanticized notion of a strict cultural boundary between "demon" and "gentleman":

> No: not even a gentleman. Marrying Ellen or ten thousand Ellens could not have made him one. Not that he wanted to be one, or even be taken for one. No. That was not necessary since all he would need would be Ellen's and our father's name on a wedding license (or any other patent of respectability) that people could look at and read . . . just as anyone could have looked at him once and known that he would be lying about who and where and why he came from by the very fact that apparently he had to refuse to say at all. (11)

For Rosa, a gentleman is someone who "knew who his father was in Tennessee and who his grandfather had been in Virginia" (11): a Southerner with a consanguineous relationship to (white) Southern history. Sutpen's transparent attempt to will these blood ties to the "respectability" of Yoknapatawpha aristocracy "was proof enough" for Rosa "that what he fled from must have been some opposite of respectability too dark to talk about" (11).[8]

Rosa's observation that Sutpen "came here and set up a raree show which lasted five years and Jefferson paid him for the entertainment" is both literal and metaphorical (12): Sutpen supplies Jefferson with a "raree show," or a "peep show," by inviting gentlemen to watch him wrestle his own slaves. Sutpen, out behind his gentlemanly plantation home, creates a theater of domination that paradoxically literalizes both the assertion of white racial supremacy and its underside, the interdependence of master and slave:

> [O]n certain occasions, perhaps at the end of the evening, the spectacle, as a grand finale or perhaps as a matter of deadly forethought towards retention of supremacy, domination, he

> would enter the ring with one of the negroes himself. Yes.
> That is what Ellen saw: her husband and the father of her chil-
> dren standing there naked and panting and bloody to the
> waist and the negro just fallen evidently, lying at his feet and
> bloody. (21)

Through this spectacle, Faulkner's Sutpen redefines Wildean dandyism: the dandy's subtle, humorous, and highly aestheticized
mockery of aristocratic performance here becomes literal and brutal. By taking on his own slaves to entertain the aristocracy and the
"riff-raff" who serve them, Sutpen (perhaps unwittingly) exposes
the brutality of the crucible in which master and slave are inexorably joined. Sutpen's spectacle of Southern paternalism relies on the
"gentlefolk": Sutpen presents his audience with a mirror of their
own relationship to their slaves, a mirror that denies plantocracy
its pastoral myth. As Godden points out, the hidden irony of the
planter's power—that the position of "master" is created by and
maintained through slave labor—is an irony the planter must deny
through claims of cultural supremacy (6–7). Instead, Sutpen's
sideshow-aristocrat performance mocks the viability of these
claims. The "raree show" that so outrages Rosa and her kind becomes a metaphor for Sutpen's extended performance of Southern
aristocracy; he is always the main attraction in a show meant to
put this institution on graphic and public display.

What makes the sublime moments and transcendent wishes of
these two dandies gothic is the fact of their failures. If Dorian's
movement outside time and decay had gone off without a hitch, if
Sutpen's "design" had been built and maintained as planned, *Dorian
Gray* and *Absalom, Absalom!* would be utopian rather than gothic
novels. Instead, the mask Dorian Gray dons to maintain an ever-
youthful exterior eventually exposes those parts of himself he is
both obsessed with and seeks to deny, and this denial forces
Dorian's eventual demise. By stepping out of the system of time
and aging, and thus rebelling against Victorian class and sexual mores, Dorian invites his own downfall. Sutpen, too, is undone by
those parts of himself and his culture that he seeks to deny. Charles
Bon, his infinitely more refined son-in-dandyism and in blood, returns as Sutpen's "double," his own portrait. Bon's stylized and ambiguous aristocratic presence on the grounds of Sutpen's Hundred
pulls Sutpen back into the hidden culture of miscegenation he
sought to escape. Sutpen fails because in adopting the trappings of
the planter class he unwittingly adopts also their code of racial ethics. When standing face to face with Charles Bon, Sutpen refuses to
acknowledge their blood relationship. He cannot accept as son a

man raised for privilege who has surpassed his father in gentility, intelligence, and fashion—a perfect dandy who, in all respects, has succeeded in passing as an aristocrat.

Volitionless Seductions

He is the curious one to me. He came into that isolated Puritan country household almost like Sutpen himself came into Jefferson: apparently complete, without background or past or childhood—a man a little older than his actual years and enclosed and sur-rounded by a kind of Scythian glitter, who seems to have se-duced . . . without any effort or particular desire to do so, who caused all the pother and uproar.

—Mr. Compson on Charles Bon in William Faulkner,
Absalom, Absalom!

In *Oscar Wilde's America: Counterculture in the Gilded Age*, Mary Blanchard contextualizes American responses to Wilde's strangeness in terms of his impact on a nation still recovering from the Civil War. The new mode of feminine masculinity Wilde sug-gested to American audiences stood "in dialectical relation to a more persistent and visible [masculine] ideal—the man as soldier" (4). In 1882, wary Victorians read Wilde's effeminacy not merely as a marker of his cultural or aesthetic difference, but as homosexual. Like their European counterparts, late-Victorian Americans were becoming aware of "inversion" theories espoused by sexologists like Karl Ulrichs and Edward Carpenter: during the 1880s and 1890s American medical journals began analyzing sexual "uranism," a term Ulrichs coined to describe the sexual "perversion" of a woman's soul trapped within a male body.

American journalists in 1882 linked Wilde's effeminate physi-ology to his "inverted" sexuality. Reporters repeatedly described his face as "womanish" and "fleshy," descriptors demonstrating that Wilde's effeminacy was read as homosexuality. In San Fran-cisco, members of the Bohemian Club "referred to Wilde as a 'Miss Nancy,'" and in New York the upper-class members of the Century Club, to which Wilde had been invited, asked, "Where is she? Well, why not say 'she'? I understand she's a 'Charlotte Ann'" (Blanchard 12). Southern reporters remarked on the bizarre and effeminate nature of Wilde's wardrobe and physique: "His personal appear-ance is perhaps the most striking thing about him. He is very tall, over six feet, with a large frame. His head is large, features all large, and fat rather than strong in expression, but his face has an air of youthful, almost infantile sweetness, which perhaps is the real secret of Mr. Wilde's power over the people who admire him" ("Oscar Wilde: A Visit" 4). Characterizing Wilde as "fat rather than strong" feminizes him, and he is infantilized by what this reporter deems his sweet, cherubic face. Together, these qualities explain the "secret power" Wilde can exert if one admires him, and the homoerotic overtones here are subtle but clear. Although Wilde, a twenty-eight-year-old college graduate at the time of his tour, could claim the status of adulthood without objection, reporters insisted on his youth. "He looks to be quite young," the reporter continued, "not much beyond twenty, is beardless, with a florid complexion . . . and his face wears a somewhat over-fat or bloated look, but it does not at any time lose its attractiveness" ("Oscar Wilde: A Visit" 4). Despite the fact that the words "giant" and "effeminate" do not go hand in hand, reporters cast Wilde's largeness as evidence of sexual inversion. The artist's physical bulk and verbal dominance made his sexuality confrontational. The *Daily Picayune* characterized Wilde as outsized and pathological, despite the fact that the reporter cited as evidence the fact that at "over six feet in height" Wilde "would weigh evidently about 180 pounds" ("Oscar Wilde: Arrival" 8). By today's standards, a man over six feet tall, weighing 180 pounds, is certainly not "bloated."[9] Reporters allowed their impressions of Wilde's "strangeness" to distort their sense of his physical presence, and Wilde's "gorilla-like frame" became evidence of racial, as well as sexual, difference. John Tenniel's "Irish Frankenstein," famously depicted in the May 1882 issue of *Punch* after the Phoenix Park murders, accentuated a perceived connection between the African "savage" and the dangerously revolutionary Irish "paddy," and the *Atlanta Constitution* drew on this connection:

> The spectacle that met the astonished gaze of the reporter was one long to be remembered. In the farther end of the room, seated in a large rocking chair, was the great esthete. His appearance was striking in the extreme, so odd he appeared. His hair was long and fell about his shoulders. It was parted near the middle and was rather stiff and in great abundance. His face was large, his lips exceedingly so, and his nose prominent. ("Oscar Wilde: Arrival" 8)

This reporter's language uses physical traits to imply a racial ambiguity he sees in Wilde's physiognomy. Wilde's large lips and prominent nose, in addition to his long, abundant hair, together imply both sexual and racial "difference." In the end, as much or more attention was paid to Wilde's physiology as to his carefully arranged aesthetic dress. Wherever Wilde aligned himself in terms of culture, national-ity, and breeding, observers insisted on aligning him both with the "native" Irish (and by extension the African "savage") and the effeminate "queer."

In *Queering the Color Line: Race and the Invention of Homosexuality in American Culture*, Siobhan Somerville maintains that the increasingly binary-driven definitions of sexuality emerging in the United States at the end of the nineteenth century "had to do with concurrent conflicts over racial definition and the presumed boundary between 'black' and 'white'" (3). The 1892 *Plessy v. Ferguson* case "formally and explicitly hardened racialized boundaries in new ways" and "ushered in a nationwide and brutal era of 'Jim Crow' segregation, an institutionalized apartheid that lasted well into the twentieth century" (Somerville 1). Against this 1892 case Somerville juxtaposes Wilde's 1895 trial for gross indecency under the 1885 Labouchere Amendment, an act that criminalized "gross acts" between men in Great Britain. Although prominent sexologists Havelock Ellis and Richard von Krafft-Ebing had already published influential tracts on "sexual inversion," the Wilde case, due to its sensational nature and its (in)famous defendant, galvanized the field of sexology on both sides of the Atlantic. Wilde, who was already a suspiciously effeminate transatlantic icon of Aestheticism, became, through the sensationalism surrounding his trials, "a transatlantic icon of [explicit] homosexuality and decadence" (Somerville 2).

During an evening lecture in Rochester, New York, Wilde was interrupted by "the brutal behavior of Rochester students":

> At Oscar Wilde's lecture here to-night considerable disturbance was caused by the students of Rochester University. They occupied seats in the gallery and busied themselves by groaning, hissing, and sighing at opportune moments. They also dressed up an old Negro in a swallow tailed coat and knee-breeches, with a huge bunch of sunflowers in his buttonhole, and had him walk down the center aisle after the lecture had commenced. This caused a great laugh. The gallery students became so much of a nuisance that the opera house policeman commanded them to leave. They answered him insolently and he struck two of them across the face with a cane. A row then occurred, during which the gas in the gallery was turned off by accomplices of the students. . . . During the noise and the disturbance Mr. Wilde folded his arms on his breast and looked savagely at the students, but said nothing. He finished his lecture before a very small house. ("Insulting Oscar Wilde" 2)

As we see in this dramatic instance, students mocked Wilde's aestheticism through race. This public mockery extended also to the realm of Victorian advertising; merchants across the United States began placing Wilde's image on trade cards to sell anything from cigars (see figure 1) to décolleté cream (see figure 2). Although many of these merchants used Wilde's image with verisimilitude, many others chose to link a perceived sexual queerness with a perceived racial difference; Wilde's Irishness, in the tradition of Victorian caricature, was imagined as black (see figures 3–4). Wildean dandyism, then, outrages first because it seeks to perform an aristocratic identity, which the dandy cannot claim by birth. This dandyism doubly and triply outrages because the Wildean dandy's outward show of aristocratic gentility, a show that has gained him entrance into the inner circles of high society, masks the gothic fact that his blood may be infected with unnamed pollutants.

In *De Profundis*, Wilde's prose explication of his fall from grace, the artist labeled himself a "born Antinomian" (*Collected Letters* 732). This does not mean that Wilde rejected all moral codes; instead he argued that ideally the individual should pursue a perfect identity, not a perfect morality. The theological definition of an antinomian is one who believes Christians to be free from moral law by virtue of grace: the freely given and unmerited favor of God, which regenerates and strengthens humans against evil. Wilde's personalized definition of antinomianism reflected his training as a decadent aesthete of the Pater school: if a thing is beautiful or brings one pleasure, it can contain no evil. If Wilde was a "born" antinomian, he was so only in a parody of the Christian sense; an innate distrust of strict moral codes informed Wilde's infatuation with "grace," an ideal he defined as "elegance or beauty in form, manner, motion or act" (*Collected Letters* 642). However, when Michael Foldy, following a trend in Wilde criticism, argues that by substituting "a complete and utter faith in oneself for faith in God," Wilde "replaced the redemptive goal of eternal salvation with the more immediate and worldly goals of pleasure and success" (99), he fails to recognize the extent to which Wilde's art hinges on and is shaped by conventional Victorian morality. Although in Ellmann's estimation Wilde's art conducted, at its best, "an anatomy of his society, and a radical reconsideration of its ethics" (24), Wilde never broke free of Victorian ethics altogether. His attachment to beauty as the benchmark of moral purity was, in fact, quite Victorian. Nineteenth-century conventions of physiognomy demanded that the human body display either virtue or corruption in its limbs and features, and, as L. Perry Curtis reminds us, "not only were these conventions invested with the authority of art and science," they were also "reinforced by nov-

OSCAR WILDE.

Straiton and Storms cigars of New York. Trade card advertisement, ca. 1882. Author's collection.

elists, who drew on physiognomical codes to delineate the moral or emotional character of their protagonists" (xvii). Wilde's insistence on the inherent goodness of the beautiful, then, was not itself revolutionary. It is instead Wilde's manipulation of Victorian ethics to produce a shocking and sensational effect—his juxtaposition of evil acts and beautiful actors—that "belongs more to our world than Victoria's" (Ellmann 589). Critic Daniel Mendelsohn maintains that *Dorian Gray*, "for all its haphazard construction, still suggests—with its almost prurient and (whatever post-facto demurs) never quite unadmiring portrait of beauty wholly divorced from morals—why [André] Gide could have thought of Wilde as 'the most dangerous

Marie Fontaine's Moth and
Freckle Cure. Trade Card
advertisement, ca. 1882.
Author's collection.

product of human civilization'" (31). Wilde's Victorian readership
was indeed up in arms after the novel's publication. Because the
ambiguously corrupted and corrupting Gray remained separate
from the moral markers of his sins for most of the novel, readers,
like Gray's own victims, cannot rely on physiognomy to decode morality. Even though Dorian Gray's final attempt to destroy the evidence of his sin ends in gruesome failure and plays out the physical-
moral connection in spades, Wilde implies that if Dorian had not
initiated his own destruction, he could have lived on forever—
beautiful and young—completely impervious to physical markers of
immorality.

THE ÆSTHETIC CRAZE.

What's de matter wid de Nigga ?   Why Oscar you's gone wild !

"The Aesthetic Craze" caricature of Wilde by Currier and Ives, 1882. Courtesy of the William Andrew Clark Memorial Library, University of California, Los Angeles.

In his own juxtaposition of evil acts and beautiful actors, Faulkner manipulates Victorian physiognomy in Wildean fashion. Despite the crucial question of his racial ancestry, Charles Bon remains the most refined, handsome, educated, and genteel example of white, Southern manhood in *Absalom, Absalom!* Bon is "a man with an ease of manner and a swaggering gallant air in comparison with which Sutpen's pompous arrogance was clumsy bluff and Henry

"Ise gwine for to wuship dat lily" caricature of Wilde by Duval,
1882. Courtesy of the William Andrew Clark Memorial Library,
University of California, Los Angeles.

actually a hobble-de-hoy" (58). Young Southern aristocrat Henry
Sutpen and his clumsily dandyesque father are "troglodytes" whom
Bon, with the careful attention of a "scientist watching the muscles
of an anesthetized frog," contemplates "from behind [a] barrier of
sophistication" (74). Although, as Kevin Railey argues, Bon is "very
much like Sutpen in the way that both men choose to will themselves into existence, choose to define and invent themselves on
their own terms" (139), Bon is quite unlike Sutpen in the level of his

dandyism's success. "In short," Railey continues, "Bon is the real thing" (138). But what "thing" is he?

"The coalescence of blood, race, and sexuality in Charles Bon," Michael Davidson argues,

> raises important questions about the integrity of blood as a marker of national identity. . . . Bon's threat to the postbellum South—and ultimately to Reconstruction America—is the fiction of racial and sexual pollution that will corrupt patrilineal descent. His identity is articulated through a cultural imaginary that includes figures at the heart of American romance from Poe and Hawthorne to Anne Rice and Jewell Gomez: feminized invalids, aristocratic recluses, and vampiric predators. (51)

And, I would add, fallen aesthetes. Bon certainly reminds readers of these gothic, aristocratic icons from American literature, but Wilde in the South stands as his clearest cultural antecedent. Faulknerian dandyism, embodied first in the clumsy, outsized figure of Thomas Sutpen, finds its perfect (and already "ruined") expression in the foppish, genteel, Wildean Charles Bon, who represents "the return of a tragic history to the American South—in the guises first of white Creole decadence, then of blackness and in the form of retributive justice" (Ladd 357).

The "aesthetic" Bon reclines his way through Faulkner's novel, dressed in an opulent fashion of which Wilde would have approved:

> This man whom Henry first saw perhaps riding through the grove at the University on one of the two horses he kept there or perhaps crossing the campus on foot in the slightly Frenchified cloak and hat which he wore, or perhaps . . . reclining in a flowered, almost feminized gown, in a sunny window in his chambers—this man handsome, elegant, even catlike, and too old to be where he was, too old not in years but in experience, with some tangible effluvium of knowledge, surfeit: of actions done and satiations plumbed and pleasures exhausted and even forgotten. (76)

Bon's secret obscures his age. His "elegant, catlike" presence gives no clue as to his years yet does suggest his sexual corruption; he has "plumbed" and "satiated" all of his (unnamed) desires to the extent that, in true decadent form, he has grown bored. His matriculation to the University of Mississippi at Oxford and to the Oxford university life for which he is "too old" in experience sparks excitement in overawed undergraduates who "admire him" in all of his "Scythian glitter" (74). Mr. Compson's imagined Oxford, Mississippi, a decadent intellectual climate in which Charles Bon effortlessly seduces local youths, reinforces connections between the University of Mississippi and that other "Oxford" across the Atlantic where Wilde's antihero Dorian Gray also inspires intense emotions in his younger and less-worldly peers.[10]

Consider these two descriptions, the first from Wilde: "Indeed, there were many, especially among the very young men, who saw, or fancied that they saw, in Dorian Gray the true realization of a type of which they had often dreamed in Eton or Oxford days, a type that was to combine something of the real culture of the scholar with all the grace and distinction and perfect manner of a citizen of the world" (*Picture of Dorian Gray* 129). And the second from Faulkner,

> Yes [Henry] loved Bon, who seduced him as surely as he seduced Judith—the country boy born and bred who, with the five or six others of that small undergraduate body composed of other planters' sons whom Bon permitted to become intimate with him, who aped his clothing and manner and (to the extent which they were able) his very manner of living, looked upon Bon as though he were a hero out of some adolescent Arabian Nights. (*Absalom* 76)

Gray's self-presentation belies the corruption underneath; he is a "true realization of a type," but not the "type" his admirers expect. Similarly, Faulkner's "Arabian Nights" metaphor here functions as euphemism; by thus orientalizing Bon, Mr. Compson perhaps unknowingly alludes to the fact that Bon is racially "other"—these young, rich planters' sons are "aping" the refinements of one whose ancestry is in question.

As Somerville demonstrates, the figure of the sheik in American culture had by 1920 become a powerful, anti-Victorian symbol for an effeminate, "colored," sexually ambiguous man:

> Within popular culture in the United States during the 1920's, the term "sheik" itself was racialized and seems to have been used to characterize a specific type of sexualized masculinity, an eroticized and ironically somewhat feminized object of desire, but one who also enacted unbridled sexuality. The "sheik" figure . . . troubled the larger cultural insistence on the bifurcation of "black" and "white" identities. The "sheik" did not fit neatly into either category, and that was, in part, the source of his fascination. (153)

Like Dorian Gray, another dandy associated with orientalism, Bon is an "elegant, esoteric hot-house bloom" capable of laissez-faire seduction through a nonchalant performance of aristocratic satiation (77). Bon is as much part-effeminate as he is part-black—his "unbridled sexuality," masked as it is in "feminized" decorum, is what gains the admiration of the young men at "Oxford." This admiration is distinctly homoerotic, yet Faulkner chooses not to cast it in stereotypically feminine/masculine terms. Bon is effeminate, as Mr. Compson's sumptuous descriptions of him show, but he is the dominant partner in his relationship with Henry Sutpen, the most sensitive and effeminate of all Sutpen's progeny. As John Duvall observes, "At the time Faulkner was writing, the model of inversion was the standard way of naming deviance; in this model, the homosexual male can only be effeminate. Yet part of the way that Faulkner's texts refuse to disavow homosexuality is by unhinging the presumed conjunction of heterosexuality and masculinity. In other words, one can be a male and a heterosexual and still not be a 'man'" ("Faulkner's Crying Game" 52). And following this logic, in *Absalom, Absalom!* one can be both male and homosexual and still not be effeminate. In Charles Bon, as in Wilde himself, we witness a linking of racial and sexual deviance, which makes the sexual "deviant" masculine and monstrous rather than effeminate and pitiable—a redefinition that casts the dandy as a powerful gothic antihero.

Neither author is candid about the real "secret" of the power these dandies hold over those who admire them, and this curious attractiveness is the central narrative mystery in each novel. Faulkner's novel, read once, cannot be reread without linking Bon's difference, his peculiar and calculated attractiveness, to his ambiguous racial status. Similarly, Wilde's *Dorian Gray* cannot be read as a mere morality tale once one understands the novel's homoerotic subtext, which was used as evidence against the artist in his trials. The influences Dorian Gray and Charles Bon exert on members of their respective enemy-aristocracies are, within the logic of late Victorian culture, capable of corrupting in two distinct but related ways; through infectious, dandified talk and pose—the twinned viruses of homosexuality and miscegenation—these dandies "pass" the "bad blood" infecting aristocracy on both sides of the Atlantic. In *Skin Shows: Gothic Horror and the Technology of Monsters*, Judith Halberstam maintains that the dandy, as embodied by such figures as Bram Stoker's Count Dracula and Wilde's Dorian Gray, is a "gothic monster" whose horror is multipurpose: "He represents too much and too little, excess and paucity; the dandy represents the parasitical aristocrat and the upwardly mobile bourgeois" (62). A beautiful object, to be "read" only at the peril of the spectator, the gothic dandy performs a part loving, part hateful send-up of the aristocratic identity he embodies. The dandy is terrifying and, therefore, gothic because he both foretells ruin and is himself ruined by the culture he both adores and mocks.

In the case of Bon, Halberstam's "too much and too little" takes on a distinctly racial tone; he has "too little" black ancestry to be detected by the Southern aristocracy that almost universally falls in love with him, and therefore his mixed blood is rendered all the more dangerous because of its indecipherability. Especially in Mr. Compson's account, Henry and Judith Sutpen, their mother Ellen Sutpen, and her sister Rosa Coldfield, as well as various starstruck Oxford undergraduates, all fall hopelessly in love with Bon or with their own imagined "pictures" of him. Among the novel's central characters, only Thomas Sutpen, Bon's own father, escapes this dandy's genteel seduction. Although, according to Quentin and Shreve, Bon actively and repeatedly seeks his father's recognition—his definition of which becomes increasingly liberal as time passes—his attempt to entice his own father into acknowledging paternity stands as the novel's only failed seduction.[11] Bon performs, and through performing anatomizes, the society that denies him. Because he is capable not only of passing as an aristocrat but of surpassing the best Southern aristocratic gentility has to offer, Bon, as the black dandy, utilizes his insider understanding of aristocratic boundaries and prohibitions to both seduce and outrage. And yet, true to the principles of dandyism, he remains embroiled in the very cultural ethics he willfully subverts. Even though Bon recognizes as arbitrary those moral codes eroded by his presence within the plantation landscape, he still respects the conventions—so like those of his own upper-class New Orleans upbringing—of the aristocracy that denies him.[12] His prodigal son's return, by invitation, to Sutpen's Hundred is an act Faulkner therefore characterizes as neither mere adoration nor mere revenge. By both admiring and toying with the white Southern aristocracy's staid conventions and prohibitions, Bon cements his status as dandy: one who, in the words of Jershua McCormack, admits to the power of cultural conventions while at the same time "suffering from and revenging [himself] upon them, and pleading them as excuses against themselves, dominating and being dominated by them in turn" (89).

In Mr. Compson's homoerotic version of the Sutpen story, Charles Bon loved his half-sister Judith "after his fashion," but he loved his half-brother Henry "in a deeper sense than merely after his fashion" (86). Bon acts as Sutpen's "double," to use John Irwin's influential characterization of the novel's mirroring aesthetics, but he is more than a mere double to Henry. Formally, as Sutpen's sons—one abandoned by his father because of blood, the other who "repudiated [his] blood birthright" (71)—the two men act as perfect opposites, and therein lies their narcissistic attraction. That Bon loved Henry and Henry loved Bon makes doubly significant Faulkner's reference to Wilde's "Ballad of Reading Gaol" in chapter 4: Faulkner alters Wilde's original "each man kills the thing he loves" when Mr. Compson imagines Bon "reversing the order" and learning to "love the thing he has injured" (86). Bon "injures" Henry by corrupting his Southern gentlemanly sense of right and wrong; Bon's threat to defy the incest taboo by marrying Henry's sister is a moral battle that Henry eventually loses. Bon corrupts Henry into accepting incest as unavoidable if he wants to keep the man he loves in the family.

But Mr. Compson, not privy to this version of the Bon-Henry story, creates another "reason" for Bon's murder. In chapter 4 Compson imagines a homoerotic temptation scene much like the one between Dorian Gray and Lord Henry Wotton in Wilde's novel to explain how Bon "injures" Henry. Although Compson's temptation scene is almost wholly imagined and certainly gets the core of the later-developed story wrong, his interpretation of Bon and Henry's relationship as seducer and seduced is one reaffirmed by each narrator in the novel. When Duvall characterizes Bon as "volitionless seducer" in the Wildean mode (*Faulkner's Marginal Couple* 110), one is reminded of Mr. Compson's imagined *Dorian Gray*–esque temptation scene:

> Yes, I can imagine how Bon led up to it, to the shock: the skill, the calculation, preparing Henry's puritan mind as he would have prepared a cramped and rocky field and planted it and raised the crop which he wanted. . . . I can imagine him, the way he did it: the way he took the innocent and negative plate of Henry's provincial soul and intellect and exposed it by slow degrees to this esoteric milieu, building gradually toward the picture which he desired it to retain, accept. (86–87)

Here, Bon is Lord Henry Wotton, calculating the precise moment to let his "arrow fly" into Dorian's innocent mind. "The terror of society, which is the basis of morals, the terror of God, which is the secret of religion," Lord Henry begins, "these are the two things that govern us. And yet," and here Lord Henry pauses, making certain his "field" is, in Compson's words, prepared for sowing. And indeed, "at that moment a look had come into the young lad's face that [Basil] had never seen there before."

"And yet," continued Lord Henry . . . "I believe that if one man were to live out his life fully and completely, were to give form to every feeling, expression to every thought, reality to every dream, I believe that the world would gain such a fresh impulse of joy that we would forget all the maladies of medievalism. . . . But the bravest man among us is afraid of himself. *The mutilation of the savage has its tragic survival in the self-denial that mars our lives. We are punished for our refusals.*" (20; emphasis added)

Lord Henry, like Charles Bon, is by degrees pulling back the curtain on a new model of morality, one that takes Wilde's antinomianism as its creed.

Mr. Compson, who has read enough of Wilde to refer to him directly in his graveyard soliloquy, imagines this process in words that recall Wilde's novel. The temptation, first initiated through language, continues, as in *Dorian Gray*, in silence: "A dialogue without words, speech, which would fix and then remove without obliterating one line the picture, this background, leaving the background, the plate prepared and innocent again: the plate docile, with that puritan's humility toward anything which is a matter of sense rather than logic, fact" (88). Here Henry *becomes* the "plate" on which Bon composes his "picture" of amorality, using sense (or sensuality) to override Henry's provincial Puritanism. Bon, "watching him with that cold and catlike inscrutable calculation, watching the picture resolve and become fixed," tells Henry that the corruption he has so far been allowed to peer at behind the curtain is "not it. That's just the base, the foundation. It can belong to anyone." "You mean it is still higher than this, still above this?" Henry, the "plate," asks in reply. Faulkner's almost overemphasis here on the language of painting, portraiture, and photography reiterates the connection between his own and Wilde's temptation scenes. As Henry waits "for the next picture which the mentor, the corruptor, intended," Bon continues, "Talking . . . lazily, almost cryptically, stroking onto the plate himself now the picture which he wanted there. I can imagine how he did it—the calculation, the surgeon's alertness and cold detachment, the exposures brief, so brief as to be cryptic, almost staccato, the plate unaware of what the complete picture would show" (88). And at the temptation's end, after returning exhausted to his rooms, Bon, "the mentor," is "watching again . . . thinking *have I won or lost?*" (91).

Bon, like Lord Henry after tempting Dorian Gray, must pull back and watch for markers of his temptation's success or failure. Readers by now attuned to Faulkner's extended dialogue with Wilde's novel will note the similarities in each seducer's calculated retreat. When Dorian Gray tells Lord Henry to "Stop! You bewilder me! I don't know what to say. There is some answer to you, but I cannot find it. Don't speak. Let me think. Or rather, let me try not to think" (20), Lord Henry obliges: "With his subtle smile, Lord Henry watched him. He knew the precise psychological moment when to say nothing. He felt intensely interested. . . . He had merely shot an arrow into the air. Had it hit its mark?" (21). *Absalom*'s Henry Sutpen, described by Mr. Compson as a "façade shuttered and blank," and who is like Dorian innocent before his "fall" into amorality, is likewise infiltrated and corrupted by a "bland and cryptic voice" whispering "secret and curious and unimaginable delights" (89). Bon, stepping back from Henry to let the youth come to his realization alone, is now "impotent even with talk, shrewdness, no longer counting upon that puritan character which must show neither surprise nor despair, having to count now (if on anything) on the corruption itself, the love" (91). In an instant, Henry apprehends Bon's complete picture, the force of which dissolves some "blank and scaling barrier" in his mind, "striking straight and true to some primary blind and mindless foundation of all young male living dream and hope" (89).

Mr. Compson imagines that the arrow with which Bon strikes true into Henry's most animal, "young male" desires has a woman's name on it. For here readers are first ushered into the boudoir of Faulkner's Wildean octoroon widow: a place made "by and for darkness" where beautiful courtesans are raised for the pleasure of white men. Compson assumes that Henry—who accepts miscegenation when it is regulated by the power dynamics of the plantation, and whose own sister Clytie is a product of these dynamics—suffers a psychic and moral breakdown when he encounters the notion of "marriage" between a nonwhite, aristocratic-looking woman and a man in whom he finds embodied the ideals of Southern aristocracy. But the success of Bon's temptation, according to Compson, depends on "the corruption itself, the love." Since Henry is not being asked to choose a courtesan for himself, readers are left wondering what love Bon is counting on. His subtle and progressive seduction, calculated to lead Henry by degrees into accepting sexual love between members of different races, may have as its first goal Henry's acceptance of the octoroon. But as Lord Henry prepares Dorian for his progressive and cumulative descent into amorality, so Bon acts as a proactive seducer—preparing the ground of Henry's mind for the more explosive revelations about mixed-race desire to come.

Although Faulkner's novels, like Wilde's writings, consistently anatomize the codes of Victorian morality, Singal reminds us that "by contrast to the Victorians, his gaze was not outward and broad-ranging, but inward and intense. Moral significance was to be found in consciousness, not in some abstract code based on natural or supernatural law" (195). Augmented by its complex dialogue with Wilde's own exploration of moral consciousness, *Absalom, Absalom!* goes furthest in exploding those "natural laws" that gave moral significance to sexual acts. The core of Lord Henry's temptation of Dorian rests in this phrase: "The mutilation of the savage has its tragic survival in the self-denial that mars our lives. We are punished for our refusals." This is the rationale Lord Henry gives Dorian for shaking off the twinned terrors of society and religion, "the basis" of the moral codes "that govern us" (20). Dorian is compelled by this reasoning, and although he begins his foray into the New Hedonism fairly innocently—venturing into new parts of town, enjoying low-brow theater—his experimentations with amorality increasingly provoke scandalous gossip in his aristocratic circles. Mr. Compson asks us to believe that what Bon attempted to seduce Henry into accepting was his own mulatto wife—and, by extension, marriage between a white man and his mulatto courtesan. If one reads Faulkner's New Orleans temptation scene through its corollary in *Dorian Gray*, it becomes clear that Lord Henry's warning about the denied savage who returns and "punishes us for our refusals" also informs Bon's decidedly more transgressive seduction of Henry himself. When Mr. Compson himself admits that Bon's marriage to a mulatto courtesan "does not explain" why Henry later murdered Bon, Faulkner invites readers to look for another explanation—one implied by Compson's imagined seduction. For by subtly seducing Henry into shedding part of his aristocratic moral code, Bon, like Wilde's Lord Henry, prepares Henry Sutpen to accept even greater transgressions of the codes he was raised to uphold.

Readers are led to conclude that Bon is Henry's half-brother, and are thus placed in the same position as Henry: should Bon still marry Judith, his half-sister, and thus keep the Sutpen "design" alive? Henry's eventual, tortured answer is "yes." In response to his father's strict *"He must not marry her,"* Henry cries, *"Yes. I said Yes at first, but I was not decided then. I didn't let him. But now I have had four years to decide in. I will. I am going to"* (283). Here it is Henry who, speaking as bride, accepts Bon's proposal of marriage (I said yes, I will, I am going to). His desire for Bon, his desire "to give form to every feeling, expression to every thought, reality to every dream" (Wilde, *Picture of Dorian Gray* 14) has outweighed the religious taboo against incest. Bon's temptation has been successful on one count. But when Henry finds out, as it seems Bon imagined he would, that his half-brother is part black—"*He must not marry her, Henry. His mother's father told me that her mother had been a Spanish woman. I believed him; it was not until after he was born that I found out that his mother was part Negro*" (283)—Bon's temptation fails. "*So it's the miscegenation*," Bon hisses to a despondent Henry, "*not the incest, that you can't bear*" (285). Most readers attribute Henry's murder of Bon at the gates of Sutpen's Hundred to Bon's resolve to marry Judith. But Henry is also violently rejecting a lover he now sees as black. Although the force of his own sexual desire overrides the incest taboo—he accepts Bon, his brother, as a mate for (himself and) his sister—that same desire cannot supplant his culture's taboo against miscegenation. Although Bon, in Lord Henry fashion, has warned his acolyte against those punishments that arise from our refusals, Henry Sutpen must refuse this desire. And indeed he is punished for this denial; when Henry kills Bon, he kills a narcissistic love. Because Henry sees Bon as a stand-in for himself, fratricide becomes suicide. Henry disappears after this murder, only returning to die at the novel's end. Henry's murder of Bon at the gates of Sutpen's Hundred therefore formally matches Dorian Gray's killing of his own portrait.[13] In both cases the killing hides an aberrant sexuality—miscegenation, homosexuality, or incest. In both cases, "each man kills the thing he loves" and kills himself in the process.

Through his picture of Charles Bon, Faulkner asks his contemporary readers, many of whom were reckoning with new definitions of morality, to themselves create a hierarchy of taboo. Is incest worse than miscegenation? Will we condone one before the other? If a man, a perfect cavalier in all other respects, wants acceptance as son, brother, and husband, can one ignore his race and ambiguous sexuality? Sutpen, of course, could not. The man who began as a self-made dandy, acquiring the planter's trappings and poses, ends by also adopting the planter's morality and is thus undone. Sutpen gets caught up in the "raree show" of aristocratic culture and forgets the first principle of his "design": that the Southern aristocracy is no more than a show. Because he allows this show to define his life to the degree that it does, Sutpen cannot step back from it when confronted with his forsaken son. He has allowed the performance of aristocracy to become his sole reality, and he must keep performing for his life to have meaning. Faulkner's readers, in the end, *do* find a moral tale in *Absalom, Absalom!*: in the words of Wilde, "alas! they will find that it is a story with a moral. And the moral is this: All excess, as well as all renunciation, brings its own punishment" (Wilde, *Artist as Critic* 240).

Faulkner's Wildean forms code his Southern aristocrats as dandies, and those Southern dandies perform aristocracy by merging the Victorian discourses of race and homosexuality. When one reads *Absalom, Absalom!* through Wilde, Faulkner's examination of Southern culture through dandyism emerges as one of the most central preoccupations in the novel. At the same time, reading Wilde through Faulkner allows readers to recognize late-Victorian responses to Wilde in London and the U.S. as reactions piqued by Wilde's embodiment of both sexual and racial otherness. Wilde and Bon symbolize the deepest desires and the deepest fears of their respective cultures. When, in *De Profundis*, Wilde claims that he was a symbol of the age that produced him, readers are returned to his preface to *Dorian Gray*, which could stand in as a preface to *Absalom, Absalom!*: "All art is at once surface and symbol. Those who go beneath the surface do so at their peril. Those who read the symbol do so at their peril. It is the spectator, and not life, that art really mirrors" (3).

Notes

1. Altman draws a similar conclusion about Faulkner's earlier use of lesbianism in *Mosquitoes* (1927). She argues that unlike many writers of the 1920s, Faulkner resists using the figure of the homosexual in a purely metaphorical way:

   > I resist the impulse . . . to tie up *Mosquitoes* neatly, and see the [l]esbians at the heart of it as somehow a "key" to understanding it. . . . But there is a political point here, and it may have been one that Faulkner, with his heterogeneous friendships, could appreciate: lesbianism is not a "key" to anything, not a metaphor, nor a theme, not a stand-in for something else. In fact, it's a part of life. Even in Yoknapatawpha. (66)

2. Although Lewis and Smith record Wilde's last southern lecture as occurring in Richmond, Virginia on July 11 (376), Ellmann records Vicksburg, Mississippi as Wilde's last stop, after which he returned to the East Coast (189–90). Ellmann does not record his source for the Vicksburg lecture, but for the purposes of this argument I prefer to imagine a Mississippi setting for Wilde's final performance.

3. Saurony's photographs of the artist in this "theatrical" costume, taken in New York in 1882, are undoubtedly the most famous portraits of Wilde, and audiences assumed that the dramatic wardrobe Wilde donned in these images reflected his own aesthetic philosophy. Although he might have enjoyed wearing velvet knee-

breeches, Wilde was in fact required to affect this singular style: his tour was contracted as publicity for Gilbert and Sullivan's *Patience*, and the play's "aesthetic" character Bunthorne (who many believed was a parody of Wilde himself) was outfitted in a similar manner.

4. Kant's idea of the sublime draws on Edmund Burke's, which juxtaposes the "beautiful" (based on passionate love) and the "sublime" (that which provokes pain, peril, or terror). Although Burke ultimately argued that all sublime forms of power derive from the "infinite power of a stern and just God" (Abrams 102), I would further argue that this concept of sublimity contains an underlying class element. Both Faulkner and Wilde locate the sublime in the "vast, limitless, infinite" powers of aristocracy, wealth, and youth.

5. After purchasing an old plantation house and taking up his position as resident artist of Oxford, Mississippi, Faulkner occasionally staged "English" foxhunts for which all members of the household, black and white, dressed in costume. See Blotner 991–93.

6. McCormack's reading of dandyism is indebted to Charles Baudelaire's *The Painter of Modern Life,* which rejects the idea that the dandy is, to quote from Carlyle's *Sartor Resartus* (1833), merely "a clothes wearing man" (38), and instead links dandyism to those times in history when shifting politics demand ambiguous political stances—particularly when democracy is flowering but aristocracy still retains some cultural power. This Baudelarian dandyism is also the brand most applicable to Faulkner's sense of Southern culture in *Absalom, Absalom!* Sutpen, a self-made man who nonetheless embraces and performs Southern aristocracy, well embodies the schism between encroaching capitalism and Southern aristocratic paternalism—a schism Faulkner seeks to illuminate in this novel.

7. Here Faulkner again links the performance of Southern aristocracy to a flamboyant, brute Irishman who tries to "pass" as a civilized, cultivated gentleman.

8. Rosa's reference to Sutpen's "dark" past operates as part of Faulkner's elaborate system of hints and allusions to racial secrets in the novel.

9. This reporter's emphasis on the "hugeness" of Wilde's presence is significant: sexologists linked large hands and frame to female inversion, citing a connection between an overactive pituitary gland and an excess of sexual desire. In an appendix to *Trials of Oscar Wilde* entitled "The Problem of Wilde's Inversion," Hyde cites Wilde's mother's oversized physiognomy as biological evidence of Wilde's own homosexuality:

    Lady Wilde, the poetess "Speranza" . . . exhibited certain peculiar physical characteristics, due to the excessive development of the pituitary gland, which were reproduced in her son. This excess manifests itself in a general physical overgrowth. Mr. Bernard Shaw, for instance, recalls that her hands were enormous, "and the gigantic splaying of her palm was reproduced in her lumbar region." To Shaw, Wilde thus appeared as an overgrown man with something not quite normal about his bigness. . . . "I have always maintained that Oscar was a giant in a pathological sense," Shaw has written, "and that this explains a good deal of his weakness." (367)

10. For a discussion of "Dorianism" and the cult of boy love in late-Victorian (English) Oxford, see Dowling.

11. One could argue that Sutpen fails to seduce Rosa Coldfield, since she refuses to become his mate. However, Sutpen's seduction of Rosa worked perfectly. Rosa herself admits that she was mesmerized by Sutpen's "florid boast" of a marriage proposal (132), and because she is perpetually seduced by the romantic figure of the Confederate soldier, her acceptance of this proposal is not a surprise. It is only when Sutpen, thinking practically and not romantically, asks Rosa to "breed together for test and sample" before marrying, to ensure that their progeny is male, that Rosa refuses (144).

12. This delicate balance of subversion and adoration shared by both Sutpen and Bon is eventually upset by a third generation: Bon's own son, Charles St. Etienne de Valery Bon, purposefully rejects the (white) aristocratic trappings he was raised to embrace in favor of an African-American culture that rejects him.

13. One could also extend this idea to Quentin Compson's suicide at the end of *The Sound and the Fury*; like Dorian Gray, Quentin is likewise attempting to kill those parts of himself that remain culturally taboo: his sexual desire for his sister and (possibly) his Harvard roommate Shreve, and his ambivalent half-hatred of his inherited Southern lineage.

Works Cited

Abrams, M. H. *Natural Supernaturalism: Tradition and Revolution in Romantic Literature*. New York: Norton, 1971.

Altman, Meryl. "The Bug That Dare Not Speak Its Name: Sex, Art, Faulkner's Worst Novel, and the Critics." *Faulkner Journal* 9.1 (1993–94): 43–68.

Blanchard, Mary. *Oscar Wilde's America: Counterculture in the Gilded Age*. New Haven: Yale UP, 1998.

Blotner, Joseph. *Faulkner: A Biography*. New York: Random, 1974.

Carlyle, Thomas. *Sartor Resartus: The Life and Opinions of Herr Teufelsdrockh*. Ed. Rodger L. Tarr. Berkeley: U of California P, 2000.

Cooper, William J. *Jefferson Davis, American*. New York: Knopf, 2000.

Curtis, L. Perry. *Apes and Angels: The Irishman in Victorian Carica-ture*. Washington: Smithsonian, 1997.

Davidson, Michael. "Strange Blood: Hemophobia and the Unexplored Boundaries of Queer Nation." *Beyond the Binary: Reconstructing Cultural Identity in a Multicultural Context*. Ed. Timothy Powell. New Brunswick: Rutgers UP, 1999.

Dowling, Linda. *Hellenism and Homosexuality in Victorian Oxford*. Ithaca: Cornell UP, 1994.

Duvall, John. "Faulkner's Crying Game: Male Homosexual Panic." *Faulkner and Gender*. Ed. Donald M. Kartiganer and Ann J. Aba-die. Jackson: UP of Mississippi, 1996. 48–72.

——. *Faulkner's Marginal Couple: Invisible, Outlaw, and Unspeakable Communities*. Austin: U of Texas P, 1990.

Ellmann, Richard. *Oscar Wilde*. New York: Knopf, 1988.

Faulkner, William. *Absalom, Absalom!* 1936. Ed. Noel Polk. New York: Vintage, 1990.

Foldy. Michael. *The Trials of Oscar Wilde: Deviance, Morality, and Late-Victorian Society*. New Haven: Yale UP, 1997.

Garelick, Rhonda. *Rising Star: Dandyism, Gender, and Performance in the Fin de Siécle*. Princeton: Princeton UP, 1998.

Godden, Richard. *Fictions of Labor: William Faulkner and the South's Long Revolution*. Cambridge: Cambridge UP, 1997.

Halberstam, Judith. *Skin Shows: Gothic Horror and the Technology of Monsters*. Durham: Duke UP, 1998.

Hönnighausen, Lothar. *Faulkner: Masks and Metaphors*. Jackson: U of Mississippi P, 1997.

——. *William Faulkner: The Art of Stylization in his Early Graphic and Literary Work*. Cambridge: Cambridge UP, 1987.

Hyde, H. Montgomery. *The Trials of Oscar Wilde*. Baltimore: Penguin, 1962.

"Insulting Oscar Wilde. The Brutal Behavior of Rochester Students: Rowdyism Last Night." *Easton Express* 8 Feb. 1882: 2.

Irwin, John. *Doubling and Incest/Repetition and Revenge: A Specula-tive Reading of Faulkner*. Baltimore: Johns Hopkins UP, 1975.

Kant, Immanuel. *Critique of Judgment*. Ed. James C. Meredith. Oxford: Clarendon, 1961.

Kiberd, Declan. *Inventing Ireland*. Cambridge: Harvard UP, 1995.

Ladd, Barbara. "'The Direction of the Howling': Nationalism and the Color Line in *Absalom, Absalom!*" *Subjects and Citizens: Nation, Race and Gender from Oroonoko to Anita Hill*. Ed. Michael Moon and Cathy Davidson. Chapel Hill: Duke UP, 1995. 345–60.

Latham, Sean. "Jim Bond's America: Denaturalizing the Logic of Slav-ery in *Absalom, Absalom!*" *Mississippi Quarterly* 51 (1998): 453–62.

Lewis, Lloyd, and Henry Smith. *Oscar Wilde Discovers America*. 1882. New York: Harcourt, 1936.

McCormack, Jershua. "The Wilde Irishman: Oscar as Aesthete and An-archist." *Wilde the Irishman*. Ed. Jershua McCormack. New Ha-ven: Yale UP, 1998.

Mendelsohn, Daniel. "The Two Oscar Wildes." Rev. of *The Importance of Being Earnest*, dir. Oliver Parker. *New York Review of Books* 10 Oct. 2002: 23–24.

"Oscar Wilde: Arrival of the Great Esthete and His Lecture." *Atlanta Constitution* 5 July 1882: 8.

"Oscar Wilde: A Visit to the Apostle of Modern Art." *Daily Picayune* 15 June 1882: 4.

Railey, Kevin. *Natural Aristocracy: History, Ideology, and the Production of William Faulkner*. Tuscaloosa: U of Alabama P, 1999.

Rev. of *Jefferson Davis, American*, by William J. Cooper. *History House*. 14 Jan. 2003. 12 May 2004 [[www.historyhouse.com/book0394569164]].

Silber, Nancy. *The Romance of Reunion: Northerners and the South, 1865–1900*. Chapel Hill: U of North Carolina P, 1993.

Singal, Daniel. *The War Within: From Victorian to Modernist Thought in the South*, 1919–1945. Chapel Hill: U of North Carolina P, 1982.

Somerville, Siobhan. *Queering the Color Line: Race and the Invention of Homosexuality in American Culture*. Durham: Duke UP, 2000.

Watson, James. *William Faulkner: Self-Presentation and Performance*. Austin: U of Texas P, 2002.

Wilde, Oscar. *The Artist as Critic: Critical Writings of Oscar Wilde*. Ed. Richard Ellmann. Chicago: U of Chicago P, 1982.

——. *The Complete Letters of Oscar Wilde*. Ed. Rupert Hart-Davis and Merlin Holland. New York: Holt, 2000.

——. *The Picture of Dorian Gray*. 1890. Ed. Donald Lawler. New York: Norton, 1988.

CHAPTER 15

EXTREMITIES OF THE BODY
THE ANOPTIC CORPO-REALITY OF *AS I LAY DYING*

Erin E. Edwards

From the point of view of death, disease has a land, a mappable territory, a subterranean, but secure place where its kinships and its consequences are formed; local values define its forms. Paradoxically, the presence of the corpse enables us to perceive it living—living with a life that is no longer that of either old sympathies or the combinative laws of complications, but one that has its own roles and its own laws.
—Michel Foucault, *The Birth of the Clinic*

Martin Jay claims that the materializing body, that physical otherness recalcitrant to mental self-conception, threatens to reduce bodily experience to "the sameness of the cadaver" (175). The cadaver at the center of *As I Lay Dying*, however, markedly refuses to function according to "sameness." While Addie Bundren's corpse does suggest the inert material "stuff" immune to psychic and discursive definitions of the body, it also attains a macabre animation

Originally published in *Modern Fiction Studies,* Winter 2009.

as it decomposes during the protracted trip toward burial. Extending beyond the borders of the singular body, the corpse, I argue, also becomes a more abstract and ubiquitous presence through a figurative corporealizing and cadaverizing of both the natural world and characters' perceptual, subjective experiences. *As I Lay Dying*'s "necropoetics," an experimental and vertiginously uncertain tropology through which the body is composed and decomposed, becomes the defining mode of corporeal experience in the novel.

Turning between a cadaverous materiality and more abstract figurations, the novel's tropology anticipates recent theoretical debates about the status of the body, which tend to take polar forms: the Foucauldian body produced or "inscribed" by social power and the body whose materiality precedes the influence of culture. The Foucauldian body perhaps never attains the certainty of form; he writes, famously, "The body is the inscribed surface of events (traced by language and dissolved by ideas), the locus of a dissociated self (adopting the illusion of a substantial unity), and a volume in perpetual disintegration" ("Nietzsche" 83). The Foucauldian body is not only material other, an occasionally betraying strangeness failing us in moments of duress, illness, or death; it exists as a state of perpetual inscription, perpetual destruction, perhaps as that which is thus always elusive. Foucault's commentators have discussed the ontological difficulty of his conception of the body; Judith Butler in particular notes that his most pointed descriptions of bodily ontology—the body as a "surface," for example—necessarily revert to metaphorical terms ("Foucault" 603). Theorists of embodiment, in contrast, claim the primacy of the body as a certain base from which culture and discourse emanate, such that a notion like "progress" would follow from the basic sensorimotor experience of navigating space.[1] Thus, for Foucault, discourse creates a body that can only be understood as metaphor; for theorists of embodiment, discourse, culture, and knowledge are metaphorical extensions of an ontologically prior body.

This article claims metaphor as the salient hinge between these two conceptions, arguing that relations among body, subject, and power are most significantly questioned and negotiated in *As I Lay Dying* through its unstable figurative bodies, rather than through the necessarily allegorical fate of characterological bodies. Deviating from criticism that upholds the mimetic value of the corpse as a signifier of sheer materiality from which consciousness is necessarily disembodied, I argue that the novel uses the corpse to stage a range of interrogative representational strategies. "What is a body?" is a question the novel continually poses through the corpse whose ontology is outside traditional conceptions of the body. Butler points out that models of inscription tend to imagine the prediscursive body as cadaverously passive, its prior or "underlying" materiality the "blank and lifeless page" that is "always already dead" (*Bodies* 4). *As I Lay Dying* would seem to reverse this formulation, the corpse inaugurating the strange life of a previously unaccountable corporeality, while cultural definitions of bodily form in the novel tend to ossify and render the body dead. Where culture would define the body through, for instance, the medical diagnosis, the anatomical model, the illustrative cadaver, or the discrete image, the novel erodes such certainty, showing that which escapes inscription—the body's dimensionality, its densities and volumes, the "terrific hiatus[es]," to use Darl's phrase, that comprise bodily existence (12). *As I Lay Dying*'s experimental bodily tropes trouble the poles of the discursive-materialist debate, exploring the extremities of bodily form that neither yield, nor yield to, the symmetries of discourse.

The form of the novel itself poses the question of how readers should relate the belated, interiorized monologic sections to the characters undergoing the physical ordeal of burying Addie. While much criticism of the novel has regarded this seeming disembodiment as paradoxically gesturing toward and reinforcing authorial presence, I suggest that such a reading privileges a "notional body," a containing boundary that separates reflection from action, and the interior of the text from the exterior. Caught in the volatility of trope, the novel's mutable corporeality discourages conceiving subjectivity or authorship in relation to such predictable bodily form. The novel instead describes absences from and returns to matter, decompositions that dissolve the boundaries of the body and the text, and local, partial processes that never arrive at the completion of form. As I will discuss through comparison of the corpse with Gilles Deleuze and Felix Guattari's notion of "becoming-animal," the corporeality authorized by Addie's corpse becomes a site of transformation and escape in the novel. What Foucault describes as "the locus of a dissociated self" thus becomes a generative dissociation: the anoptic, ambient bodily tropology unhinges representation from the visual forms of power that have traditionally structured the normative body, allowing for new definitions of both corporeality and subjectivity.

A Decomposing Scene

Addie's death is the inaugural event of *As I Lay Dying*, but of what does she die? Anse somewhat incomprehensibly curses the road as the cause of death, and Peabody, the doctor he belatedly summons to attend her, offers no diagnosis, but declares her already "dead these ten days" on his arrival (43). Peabody, however, not only refrains from diagnosing; he determines her dead, and thus in some sense already a corpse, without a visual examination of her body. His visit suggests an inversion of the Foucauldian model of medical power and the subject, in that the scene depicts Peabody as the subject of Addie's gaze rather than the reverse:

> She looks at us. Only her eyes seem to move. It's like they touch us, not with sight or sense, but like the stream from a hose touches you, the stream at the instant of impact as dissociated from the nozzle as though it had never been there. She does not look at Anse at all. She looks at me, then at the boy. Beneath the quilt she is no more than a bundle of rotten sticks. (44)

Peabody's metaphorical reconfiguration of Addie substitutes for a body that he does not directly perceive, transforming her outward appearance into reflection that is more revelatory of his subjectivity than Addie's physical condition. More to the point, it seems that there is no body present to examine or diagnose. Peabody displaces Addie's body onto a haptic gaze, which, like the stream escaping from the nozzle, is as disconnected from a corporeal origin "as though it had never been there." It is only after dying, in the uncertain passage between death and burial, that Addie acquires corporeal presence, becoming a substantial material burden and an invasive effluvium, defining a new mode of corporeality that also involves the bodies of those who mourn her.[2]

Foucault argues that the corpse comes to occupy a privileged role in Enlightenment epistemology, no longer shrouded by religious and moral strictures, but a source of medical and anatomical knowledge: "A fine transmutation of the corpse had taken place: gloomy respect had condemned it to putrefaction, to the dark work of destruction; in the boldness of the gesture that violated only to reveal, to bring to the light of day, the corpse became the brightest moment in the figures of truth. Knowledge spins where once larva was formed" (*Birth* 125).[3] Examination of the corpse in a sense completes the process by which the entirety of the body, and consequently the subject, are made available to view, surpassing with a penetrating gaze the limits of the bodily surface and making both the internal and external operations of the body subject to analysis and categorization. But Foucault's claim also paradoxically implies an elision of the body—a transformation of the bodily viscera into knowledge, a mode of examination through which the body is, to use his metaphor, only a chrysalic pause on the way to understanding. Foucault implies an epistemology through excorporation—knowledge as that which comes out of, but also thus simultaneously erases, the body. In contrast to the cadaver whose interiority can be translated into a discourse of pathological causality, the emaciated "bundle of rotten sticks" lying under the quilt at the beginning of *As I Lay Dying* disallows exploratory penetration: one can imagine that an autopsy of Addie's body would discover not a landscape of organs ravaged by disease, but only a kind of aridity. Addie's absent body functions as an epistemological aporia, a blind spot that undoes the certainty of medical diagnosis and knowledge about the body. Through Addie's corpse, *As I Lay Dying* reasserts the bodily materiality that Enlightenment thought has elided, but as that which escapes the control, understanding, and visual structures of power.

Corpses often figure prominently in early twentieth-century novels, signaling an anxiety about the status of the body in the modern period; we might consider, for example, Myrtle Wilson and Jay Gatsby in *The Great Gatsby*, Catherine Barkley in *A Farewell to Arms*, and Mary Dalton in *Native Son*. But while these corpses typically maintain their ontological certainty within the plot, the corpse in *As I Lay Dying* is radically uncertain; it is known not through visual inspection but through anoptic penetration—a blind, often grotesque familiarity with an ambient corporeality, which reformulates all corporeal and subjective possibilities in the novel. Although Foucault describes the centrality of the corpse to medical knowledge, he considers death itself as "power's limit, the moment that escapes it" (*History* 138). The eerie animation of Addie's corpse—which "resists, as though volitional" (97), which "go[es] faster than a man" in water (151), and which speaks to Darl and Vardaman through the coffin—seems to protract or equivocate this moment of death. Death in *As I Lay Dying* is not so much a discernible moment as a liminal and unpredictable domain, and Addie's cadaver lives, in Foucauldian terms, with "its own roles and its own laws," marking places of escape within the gaze of power (*Birth* 149). Mourning Addie, the characters are physically, often agonistically involved with her corpse; as I will show, they undergo uncertain tropological decompositions of bodily form through which they negotiate escapes from power as well. The novel's corporeal decompositions demand new ways of thinking about novelistic character: the novel insists on the discreteness of character in assigning each section to a different speaker, even as the unity of characterological body as a reliable "container" of subjectivity is continually undone.

Cora Tull, the Bundrens' officious neighbor, implies that the soul and the cadaver might be analogously explored and transformed into knowledge when she urges on Addie a kind of autopsy model of Christian salvation. She claims, "He alone can see into the heart, and just because a woman's life is right in the sight of man, she cant know if there is no sin in her heart without she opens her heart to the Lord" (167). Self-knowledge, according to Cora, depends on "opening" the heart to the gaze of an authority outside the self, thus illuminating the otherwise obscured recesses of the soul. But just as Addie's corpse defines a mode of bodily existence outside the visual structures of power, subjective life in *As I Lay Dying* can neither be translated into visual terms nor mapped according to the predictable contours of the normative body. There are often radical hiatuses in mental life and its relation to the body, and consciousness often follows from the experience of localized body parts, which are inertly reified or grotesquely animated, and thus not easily assimilable to ideas of character or personhood. The novel continually defamiliarizes the normative body and the panoptic perspective on which realist representations of the subject have traditionally depended.

Departing from this panoptic perspective necessitates reconceptions of the ways we know and map the body and redefinitions of the body's relation to space. Medical and discursive definitions of the body have often presented us with isolated two-dimensional representations, which deny that the body exists "in the round" and cannot be perceived in a single instant or image. Catherine Waldby identifies this representative problem in the history of anatomical study as "the incommensurability between the opaque volume of the body and the flat, clean surface of the page," and she claims that a spatial conception of the body was necessary to overcome this incommensurability: "This problem was resolved to some extent through the creation of analogies between anatomical and cartographic space, analogies evident in the fact that the book of anatomy is known as an atlas. If the interior of the body could be thought of and treated as *space,* rather than as a self-enclosed and continuous solid volume, then it could be laid out in ways which are amenable to mapping" (qtd. in Lippit 47). When Anse repeatedly claims that the *road* kills Addie, he similarly spatializes her body, conceiving it as structured by the vertical and horizontal axes through which he understands the landscape.[4] He speculates, "When He aims for something to be always a-moving, He makes it long ways, like a road or a horse or a wagon, but when He aims for something to stay put, He makes it up-and-down ways, like a tree or a man" (36). Deviating from this vertical/horizontal perspective, which posits a disembodied viewer assessing the scene from a removed position, bodies in the novel are related to the landscape through haptic contingencies of localized parts, through variable speeds and specific densities. Bodies resist being mapped in their entirety and are not clearly demarcated from their environment, as bodily experience is tropologically displaced onto a corporealized landscape. Interrupting the spatialized hierarchy through which, in Jay's terms, "the spiritualizing, formalizing head" predominates over the "materializing, grotesque body," the unruly bodily tropes unseat the suzerainty of the mind, marking hiatuses in the mind's possession of the body (175). Deleuze and Guattari claim that every "great American author creates a cartography, even in his or her style," and the novel's stylistic experiments have a similarly cartographic dimension (520). Even as the burial trip can be tracked on the Yoknapatawpha map of which Faulkner named himself "sole owner and proprietor," the novel's tropes bring us to the limits of two-dimensional cartography in accounting for the body, encouraging us to ask what a cartography of the body would be if it allowed for modes of perception in addition to the visual, if it used the auditory, the olfactory, and the haptic to disrupt the reliable externality of the visible world.

Before Addie's death, the novel insists on the boundary between external, visible form and subjective inwardness only to demonstrate continually its breachability; after her death, this boundary is eroded altogether. The novel opens with a series of choreographed passes between Darl and Jewel, who are simultaneously passing between interior and exterior spaces. Darl is initially in front of Jewel as they make their way along the path from field to house; Jewel then assumes the lead after passing through the windows of the cottonhouse, which Darl circumvents; Darl gains the lead on the path again when Jewel stops to take a drink. The novel's careful tracking of these spatial navigations, which are repeated but reversed once they reach the main house, suggests the tenuous reversibility of interiors and exteriors. Unlike before, Darl passes directly through the house to the back porch via the hallway, while Jewel this time avoids the interior passage, coming and going around the outside of the house. Their thoughts during these different passages, however, reverse the perspective of their physical orientations to the house. Darl ignores for the moment the pressing event of Addie dying inside the house, attending to the external scene of Cash's construction of the coffin, an outward container that functions as an anticipatory synecdoche for Addie's metamorphosis into just matter. Jewel, on the other hand, projects his thoughts inside the house, inhabiting Addie's perspective and lamenting that her dying must be a spectacle, "with every bastard in the county coming in to stare at her" (15). Throughout the novel,

Darl is able to see "into the inside of" others, but here he attends to exteriors (125); Jewel, frequently compared to wooden objects and described as having "eyes like wood"—a spectacle to behold rather than an agent of vision—attends to the interior (4).

The opening sections of the novel thus dislocate thought from bodily location and describe a disparity between characters as they can be visually interpreted by others and the "contents" of their subjective life. This disparity between body and thought is apparent in a fatal ignorance about bodily operations, which runs through the novel and motivates its central events—Anse's belatedly futile summoning of Peabody, his belief that he will die if he sweats, Dewey Dell's pregnancy and her misguided attempt at abortion, and Cash's loss of inches and inches of skin after the family, incredibly, uses concrete to set his broken leg. The problematic relation between body and thought dramatically culminates in Addie's narrative, whose origins are not easily reconcilable with the dead body being carried to Jefferson. These disparities, however, are not simply a reiteration of the familiar Cartesian divide between body and mind; though separate, the two are not cleanly cast apart, but inextricably tethered, oscillating in uneasy temporal and spatial lags. Despite an apparent ignorance about bodily existence, self-definition in the novel depends on the body, returning to and taking its shape through phenomenological experience. Unlike the base materialism of the Cartesian body, however, the body to which the mind is tethered in *As I Lay Dying* is not consistently substantial; it falters, is marked with phenomenological hiatuses, and, as I will discuss, requires the work of language in order to be "fleshed out." *As I Lay Dying* is thus not a narrative of bodies experienced and existing a priori; the novel requires acts of language—specifically the displacements of figurative language—in order to create bodily form.

The novel also significantly dislocates thought and knowledge from vision. In the opening paragraph, Darl remarks, "Although I am fifteen feet ahead of him, anyone watching us from the cotton-house can see Jewel's frayed and broken straw hat a full head above my own" (3). He continues to describe Jewel crossing the cottonhouse "with the rigid gravity of a cigar store Indian" even though he is ahead of Jewel and has already turned the corner of the cottonhouse (4). Darl's remote descriptions, as well as his allusion to a disembodied "anyone" watching their progress along the path, conjure the specter of an absent omniscient narrator and would seem to suggest that he has taken on this ability in the narrator's stead. But his awareness of "anyone watching" elides the most significant act of vision at this point in the novel—Addie watching Cash build her coffin from the bedroom window. Darl's vertical perspective on the scene, which aligns him with divine or authorial panopticism and omniscience, is thus adopted because of an invisible motive that is very much "inside" the fictive world. This elision suggests, not authorial surrogacy, but that both Darl's vision and his willful blindness are psychologically motivated.

The novel departs from a common trope of the realist novel—the window as a figure for authorial observation in which the body remains stationary while the mind imaginatively enters into visual engagement with the world.[5] Here, Jewel passes bodily through the windows, typically an aperture for vision, but he does not see his setting at all. The novel describes the death of a stationary mode of viewing—either a stationary viewer who watches the world passing or a disembodied viewer who moves with cinematic fluidity through a stationary world.[6] Darl's narration of the unseen culminates in his remote, disembodied viewing and narrating of Addie's death, but the motive for Darl's trip with Jewel discourages linking his narration with a panoptic perspective. Darl is not just an omniscient narrator but a motivated one who has arguably arranged their absence from Addie's deathbed as revenge against Jewel. Thus while thought and interior monologues might be separated from bodily location, the disembodied nature of thought does not necessarily encourage an analogical reading between character and a disembodied author—bodily location is continually reasserted to reground the textual dynamic "within" the fictive world of the novel.

Peter Brooks points out that the separation of thought from our bodies and from what we can physically see is, of course, something of a norm of mental life—and perhaps never more so than during reading and writing. Their various separations in *As I Lay Dying* nevertheless mark an important departure from the conventions and epistemological methods of realist fiction. Brooks explains:

> The dominant nineteenth-century tradition, that of realism, insistently makes the visual the master relation to the world, for the very premise of realism is that one cannot understand human beings outside the context of the things that surround them, and knowing those things is a matter of viewing them, detailing them, and describing the concrete milieux in which men and women enact their destinies. To know, in realism, is to see, and to represent is to describe. (88)

The characters in *As I Lay Dying* do enact their destinies within circumscribed locations. Their milieu, however, is not concrete, but involves a significant amount of "bleed" between character and context. No external narrator or perspective fixes them in their fictive world; surroundings are instead introjected, made strange, and subsequently reconstructed. Rather than the visual study and description of a stable context in which bodies take their place with ontological certainty alongside other fictive objects, knowledge in the novel occurs through inconsistently embodied perspectives in interface with the outside world.

The opening section begins by mapping a predictable Cartesian space, tracking bodies that move through space mapped along horizontal and vertical axes, but Darl's concluding onomatopoeia marks a representative mode that operates not just through visual description, but through sound. He is no longer followed by Jewel, whose body can be located in space, but by the ambient "Chuck. Chuck. Chuck." of Cash's adze (5). His consciousness thus involves from watching a scene perceived as external to the more internal, embodied experience of audition. The onomatopoeia achieves its mimetic effect by emphasizing the visual spacing of the words on the page, transgressing the "invisibility" of the printed word through which fictive worlds are created.[7] Yet, the dichotomy of the exterior of the metatextual and the interior of the fictive world does not hold. Even as the onomatopoeia and the spacing of the words draw attention to the visual and representative aspects of the text, they also, paradoxically, return us to the fictive, internal world of *As I Lay Dying*—the rhythmic spacing of the "Chuck. Chuck. Chuck." links the time of our reading to the experiential time of character. This linkage between reader and character depends on certain "bodily" aspects of the text—the auditory aspects of rhythm and onomatopoeia—but bypasses the visual externality of bodily description.

This positing of, and subsequent withdrawal from, the visible world structures many of the early sections of the novel; before Addie's death, most of the sections begin with visual description or references to seeing but end with speech, sounds, or echoing quotations of what someone "says." The certainty of the external scene gradually erodes, becoming subjectivized and incorporated. Characters are often perceived by others through the echo of their voices—acousmatic separations of voice from body, which are received by an auditor outside visual context. Despite the fact that Addie is just "a bundle of rotten sticks," her voice remains "harsh and strong" the moment before her death. Like the mythological Echo, Addie is also just a voice without a body, as her self-echoing call of "Cash . . . you, Cash!" follows Peabody outside her bedroom (46). Departing from the visual mappability of the body, the novel relies on auditory perceptions of bodies unmoored in space, perceptions that, in Darl's terms, "sound as though they were speaking out of the air about your head" (20). Addie's death radically changes dynamics of seeing, hearing, and bodily existence in the novel. The section immediately following her death is Vardaman's first in the novel, offering a childish or new perspective that describes not a passage from the visual to the auditory, as the previous sections do, but a reconfiguration of bodily form altogether, as his body is uncertainly involved with that of Peabody's horse. Rather than knowing through the visual description of bodies, Vardaman's consciousness, and those represented in the sections following Addie's death, develop from bodily experience.

When characters describe other bodies in visual terms, their descriptions emphasize the corporeal and visual limits of both gazer and other, rather than reinforcing the epistemological power of the observer. Descriptions often focus on parts of the body that are not easily visible to the self, those aspects of bodily life that resist self-perception. The novel contains numerous, idiosyncratically specific descriptions of Anse's hump and the backs of bodies and necks; Darl, for instance, fixates on Jewel's neck, which is "trimmed close, with a white line between hair and sunburn like a joint of white bone" (39). Unlike the fictive bodies of the realist novel, freely available to the untrammeled vision of a panoptic narrator, images of blind backsides in *As I Lay Dying* emphasize not only the impenetrable corporeality of the one gazed on, but also the limited, embodied, and necessarily subjective perspectives of observers, the fact that each of the viewers in the novel also operates from a position of partial blindness. The novel, then, describes more than the dislocation of body from thought: even the experience of "embodiment" implies a kind of dislocation in that parts of the body always escape self-conception. Characters are often depicted looking over one shoulder, turning to look backward, emphasizing the positional limits of the visual field and the body's orientation in space. Characters are insistently present as material bodies with specific locations; Anse, for instance, is frequently depicted as rubbing his knees, an emblematic, gestural tic that does not admit penetration to character interiority. The body of the other becomes an obdurate surface, such that Anse's eyes, "like pieces of burnt-out cinder", and his brogans, "hacked with a blunt axe out of pig-iron," are equal in their reified enervation, both unyielding, material objects that bar discovery (32, 11).

The reification of these blind backsides and of Anse's body suggests that a cadaverous materiality overtakes many of the bodies of the novel, not just Addie's; the corpse that is hidden from view is everywhere reproduced. But while the corpse defines an inert corporeality that fails to yield knowledge through visual examination, it also gives rise to a vivified, anoptic corporeality. Addie dies somewhat anticlimactically early in the novel, but she has a strange afterlife, reappearing in bodily tropes and acts of perception. The dual nature of the corpse, both reified and animated, signifies the liminal ontology of the body in modernity, having departed from the Cartesian dualism that characterized nineteenth-century thought and the realist novel, but unable to become fully "embodied." Jani Scandura and Michael Thurston argue that the corpse is symbolically significant in modern thought, because it encrypts the past through a kind of willed forgetfulness:

> The modern does not so much imply an erasure of the past . . . as an encryptment of certain uncomfortable narratives. Indeed, the suggestion that progressive modernity throws itself to the future is itself a denial of the obsessive attention that modern cultures paid to "looking back" to Darwinian origins, nostalgic folk histories, and the childhood wounds of oedipal dramas. Still, modernist nostalgia was not marked so much by a longing for a past, as by a desire for not having had one. (5)[8]

Different acts of retrospection and retrogradation similarly constitute Addie's corpse, suggesting that modernity's departure from past perspectives on the body is not always an easy, or even a desired, passage. Her inverted placement in a "clock-shape[d]" coffin to accommodate her wedding dress is a spatial inversion that also implies a temporal return to her wedding day, and her burial entails the retrograde motion toward Jefferson, which signifies both personal and national origins (88). But this journey, which Darl describes as "so dreamlike as to be uninferant of progress," becomes an alienating odyssey rather than a return home (108). And, from a narrative perspective, the novel never reaches this origin, as Addie's burial in Jefferson is never directly narrated, and Cash's proleptic description of their life with the new Mrs. Bundren seems to erase Addie's death. Her death, then, involves both a retrograde return and a proleptic forgetting. Anse seems to recognize both the relevance and the impossibility of retrogression, claiming, with his characteristic homespun philosophy, "It aint no luck in turning back" (140). Wandering for most of the novel between the modernity promised by New Hope and the past suggested by Addie's origins in Jefferson, the characters are caught between troubling memories and forgetfulness, which each town—and the various desires it inspires—promises to deliver.

Dewey Dell's corporeality is similarly positioned between the old and the new, a juncture depicted as a function of death. She fixedly anticipates the future during the approach to New Hope ("New Hope. 3 mi. it will say. New Hope. 3 mi. New Hope. 3 mi."), but she turns back in this section toward the past, conflating child-hood experience and phantasmic memories with their present er-rand: "That was when I died that time. *Suppose I do. We'll go to New Hope. We wont have to go to town.* I rose and took the knife from the streaming fish still hissing and I killed Darl" (120–21). Dewey Dell immediately "encrypts" this violent fantasy of having killed Darl within her own bodily experience. Beginning as a night-marish absence but ending with a waking awareness of her body located again in space, her liminal corporeality suggests that the interruption of the mind's attachment to the body is not solely the domain of death, but that there are death-like breaches within bodily life and the skein of awareness.

> *I had a nightmare once I thought I was awake but I couldn't see and couldn't feel I couldn't feel the bed under me and I couldn't think what I was I couldn't think of my name I couldn't even think I am a girl I couldn't even think I nor even think I want to wake up nor remember what was opposite to awake so I could do that I knew that something was passing but I couldn't even think of time then all of a sudden I knew that something was it was wind blowing over me it was like the wind came and blew me back from where it was I was not blowing the room and Vardaman asleep and all of them back under me again and going on like a piece of cool silk dragging across my naked legs.* (121–22)

Dewey Dell's recollection destabilizes the notion of a somatic base from which subjectivity extends. It is not merely that conscious-ness bleeds outward from bodily form; there is no prior body whose bounds could be transgressed. Bodily form requires the work of trope to delineate its borders, becoming tenuously articulated only with the simile of the wind passing over her "like a piece of cool silk." The simile points to a phenomenological aporia, in that her body is not naturally possessed but brought into understanding through a claim of what it is "like." Her comparison of the wind to silk sounds "natural," even clichéd, but it is drawn from outside her quotidian experience, as nothing in the Bundren household would suggest that familiarity with silk is "natural" to Dewey Dell. The bodily "naturalness" with which the passage concludes thus con-tains the alien as a constituent element. The novel does not just claim moments of sensory mortification; it makes the more radical suggestion that the body must be continually constructed from prior absences. Her uncertain negativity undercuts more than the primacy of the cogito in favor of the phenomenological: even the phenomenological must be created.

Figurative language is central to this creation: perception, self-consciousness, and bodily experience in the novel continually occur through tropological negotiations that enact corporeality as a stage of flux or becoming, in contrast to visual descriptions that operate through the assignation of distinct attributes.[9] Darl's complex description of Dewey Dell's face, for instance, develops into an anxious self-awareness: "Her face is calm and sullen, her eyes brooding and alert; within them I can see Peabody's back like two round peas in two thimbles: perhaps in Peabody's back two of those worms which work surreptitious and steady through you and out the other side and you waking suddenly from sleep or from waking, with on your face an expression sudden, intent, and concerned" (103). Darl's description of worms boring through Peabody's back suggests visual penetration of the body to understand character, but it occurs here within the distortion of the convex mirrors of Dewey Dell's eyes, emphasizing corporeal, binocular vision, rather than the transcendent vision of an ideally positioned, omniscient viewer. The ocular reflection of "two round peas" makes of the doctor a kind of literal "peabody," implying the inextricability of body and language, imagining a body that fulfills the meaning of its name, or a name become flesh. The passage between the body and language, however, is not easy or mutually reinforcing, but produces the experience of shock or astonishment—the image of a subject momentarily come awake through awareness of being seen, although not, in this case, by an outsider. From what position *could* Darl see Peabody reflected in Dewey Dell's eyes? Such a reflection could only be seen in intimate proximity and would thus reflect himself, rather than Peabody. Moreover, we might have trouble envisioning Peabody—who takes his ministrations over the ailing, dying Bundrens in stride, as so many figures already entered into the "dead accounts" of his books—experiencing such a disturbing awakening (43). Darl's trope functions more as a self-description; or, to be more precise, Darl describes an uncanny awakening that occurs through trope. The troubled exchange between the body and language problematizes the notion of an intact narrator who operates outside the opacity of linguistic representation and can narrate for certain what a body is. Darl's description vacillates between the convex distortions of the physical eye and the equally distorting realm of his imagination; his trope of penetrative vision seems to be a displaced enactment and indictment of Peabody's failure to examine Addie, and the scene decomposes as the image of a body riddled with worms intrudes into his field of vision. Addie's illness and the particular materiality of her corpse are tropologically displaced onto characters who become sites of decomposition—but this is decomposition with a difference, producing a shocked, excess awareness through the erosion of body, vision, and the fictive frame that would contain them.

The material world in *As I Lay Dying* is thus not brought into the mind to be articulated according to the form of the human figure; the novel deviates from the notion of a Cartesian "homunculus" inside the mind—a mental model of an intact, complete bodily figure according to which perception of the outside world is structured. Nor is the body easily demarcated from the stuff of the world. The novel describes a perpetual, labored dislocation of the body onto its surrounds and a distorting reconstruction of the outer world through perception. Several critics have remarked on the relation between reified bodies and personified objects in the novel, such that Jewel, for example, is frequently "wooden-backed" (94), while the thwarting river log "surged up out of the water and stood for an instant upright" (148).[10] André Bleikasten comments:

> The animate and the inanimate, the human and the nonhuman are brought into a relationship of reciprocal metaphor, and so are Faulkner's language and Faulkner's "world," one mimicking the other without allowing us to determine which is "one" and which the "other." In the never-ending process of slippage and change, everything is thus eventually reabsorbed in the pervasive metaphoricity of a single language and gathered within the frame of a single vision. (168)

Bleikasten's characterization of the "frame of a single vision" is itself a kind of "looking back" toward the literary past. He argues that "this shifting, swirling world of movement and metamorphoses, of death and madness, of water and fire, has a striking resemblance to the art and literature of the baroque era" (168). I would argue, however, that Faulkner's metamorphoses, the strange transformations of physical forms and the passages from fictive object to self-conscious metaphor and back, yield not a baroque fullness but rather a poetics of negativity. If, through the novel's linguistic play, the body and the inanimate world seem to metamorphose into one another, these transformations, rather than reinforcing a single vision, work to erode both body and world. Like the dual worms that bore through Peabody's back, "like two round peas," metaphors tend not just toward exchange or "reabsorption," but to project characters into uncertain spaces that jarringly extrude from the frame of the fictive world. The eventual return to the fictive world leaves that world all the more tenuous, rather than reinforcing the fullness of authorial vision. While many of the novel's metaphors draw on the same set of images and can be considered, as Stephen Ross notes, to have a distinctively "'Faulknerian' ring," the tropes are nevertheless anoptic, decomposing viewership through a play of shifting surfaces and linguistic figures, rather than self-reflexively reinforcing an equation between authorial vision and text (304).[11] Like Darl's description of "waking . . . from sleep or from waking," the novel continually erodes the distinction between the imaginative enchantment of the fictive and awareness of the absence outside the world of the novel.

There is an excess in the displacements between animate and inanimate, an ambient corporeal remainder that resists definite form. Darl's description of the river, for instance, conjures the diseased corporeality that Addie herself never inhabits. He remarks on its "yellow surface dimpled monstrously" (141) as though with fatty excess, and he describes it as "yellow, skummed with flotsam and with thick soiled gouts of foam as though it had sweat, lathering, like a driven horse" (141–42). Darl's allusions to "gouts," sweating struggle, and a kind of sluggish circulation displace onto the landscape all the fleshy corporeality and diseased travail that Addie, in her emaciated, quiet extinction, escapes. The thickly "skummed" surface of the river cannot be visually penetrated but "talks up to us in a murmur" like a person (141); Addie's corpse, conversely, with its "little trickling bursts of secret and murmurous bubbling," sounds like a river 212). Neither speech is decipherable; both emit textured sounds, grained and tautological. Foucault claims that death provides a point at which disease can be translated into diagnostic discourse, but here no such interpretive discourse exists.

These displacements between animate and inanimate therefore become sites of power negotiations in the novel. Characters experience the natural or inanimate world as already invested with power so that fighting the river or the elements is a struggle against a providential force but also proof that this power is granting one salvation through struggle. As I Lay Dying is rather claustrophobic; its tropes, with a few notable exceptions, are drawn from the immediacy of the natural world and thus have a metonymic quality as well. But here that immediacy has an uncanny quality; what's immediately tangible is also immediately strange, and the natural world and one's sense of place are already Other, already an opaquely monitoring force that awakens self-reflection. Power, like corporeality, thus functions as an ambient force, rather

than being housed in characterological or institutional agents: Whitfield and Peabody are inept figures of power, and the Bundrens are
largely immune to the force of law in Jefferson. Faulkner claims
that he introduced Peabody to provide an external point of view on
the Bundrens, and there is a way in which the neighbors and townspeople function, in Bleikasten's terms, as a kind of "Greek chorus"
providing moral context and judgment (153).[12] Yet, despite the fact
that these observers' sections often sound as though they are in-
dicting the "outrage" of events or defending their own involvement
with the Bundrens to some outside auditor, their perceptions are
too idiosyncratic to function as external gauges, becoming instead
points of involvement.[13] Tull's dilatory metaphorizing, for instance,
quickly traverses the boundary of the objective and the visible, as
his "spy-glass" is invaded by figurative negotiations of gendered
bodily form:

> When I looked back at my mule it was like he was one of these
> here spy-glasses and I could look at him standing there and
> see all the broad land and my house sweated outen it like it
> was the more the sweat, the broader the land; the more the
> sweat, the tighter the house because it would take a tight
> house for Cora, to hold Cora like a jar of milk in the spring:
> you've got to have a tight jar or you'll need a powerful spring,
> so if you have a big spring, why then you have the incentive to
> have tight, wellmade jars, because it is your milk, sour or not,
> because you would rather have milk that will sour than to
> have milk that wont, because you are a man. (139)

Tull proves to be an intentional metaphorist, reflecting elsewhere
that Anse looks "like a uncurried horse dressed up: I don't know"
(123). His reflections are thus not just quotations of idiomatic regional speech, but self-conscious usages of tropological language.
Tull's tropes turn midway from the expansiveness of sweat and the
land pouring out of the mule to the constrictive containment of Cora
and the milk. Tull's metaphors, like Darl's, produce a kind of self-
reflection: the comparison of Cora to a jar of milk becomes lost in
a Barthesian "metonymic skid" (92), which no longer refers to
Cora but to the possibility of losing her, and simultaneously losing control over himself and language. Tull's identity and masculinity are called into question through this metonymic skid and
must be reconstituted, however unconvincingly, at the end of the
passage.[14]

Jonathan Crary explains that the optical devices central to the
nineteenth-century culture of visual realism are "inextricably dependent on a new arrangement of knowledge about the body and

the constitutive relation of that knowledge to social power." He argues further, "These apparatuses are the outcome of a complex remaking of the individual as observer into something calculable and regularizable and of human vision into something measurable and thus exchangeable" (17). Tull's description of "looking back" at the mule offers a model of vision that is clearly neither calculable and regularizable, nor measurable and exchangeable. If we take Faulkner's tropological description as illustrative of new conceptions of vision in modernism, however, it is not the case that Faulkner's viewer, though his vision is no longer normative, is more in "possession" of what he views. In Tull's puzzling comparison of his mule to a "spy-glass," and in Darl's later reference to a "spy-glass" that "had a woman and a pig with two backs and no face," the gross corporeality of the animal, like that of the corpse, obtrudes into the field of vision (254). The body is the perpetual mote in the eye of the viewer, and these optical devices, metonyms for the function of the eye itself, fail as boundaries between viewer and vision so that the viewer's body itself becomes subject to circulation, displaced onto a scene no longer securely external to the self.[15]

Becoming a Corpse

Anse, whose mourning of Addie is not particularly profound, is an exception to bodily experience in the novel. Unlike the other Bundrens, who suffer physical trauma and attrition, Anse experiences a bodily increase, his new teeth making him "look a foot taller" by the novel's conclusion (260). Although power functions most significantly in the novel as a ubiquitous presence, rather than being wielded by particular characters or social institutions, Anse does exert control over his family's fate so that their conditions are worsened because of his actions. Despite this control, however, the tropological reformations of the body that define mental life continually elude his grasp and indeed the very notion of characterhood that his control suggests. Anse's repeated references to the vertical/horizontal axes that structure the body are undone by the novel's bodily tropology; the novel thus poses this patriarchal model of control and locationality as a foil against which corporeality is figured.

When Anse uses upright images to depict the body, he claims its absolute orientation in space as dictated by some outside divinity. He imagines Addie suffering a kind of dying fall: she is upright and "well and hale" until she takes to her bed, her prone form then making her as good as dead (37). Deleuze similarly uses a vertical bodily image to describe a dominant and limited mode of cognition:

"the image of a naturally upright thought, which knows what it means to think" (*Difference* 134). Deleuze describes the tyranny of this form of cognition, the way in which iteration of this a priori bodily image substitutes for the more violent "encounter" that defines the actual process and event of thought (139). Anse's static, upright body functions in the same way as a foregone substitute for actual thought, leading him to such inept conclusions as, "Because if He'd a aimed for man to be always a-moving and going somewheres else, wouldn't He a put him longways on his belly, like a snake?" He further casts thought into upright bodily form, noting, "It *stands* to reason He would" (36; emphasis added).

Despite the many images of inversion and retrogradation that constitute Addie's body, the corpse enacts its resistance not just through a simple inversion of the "naturally upright" human figure in relation to the world, or the world turned upside down, but also by giving rise to a radical reconfiguration of human form. We can see such a reconfiguration in the Deleuzian violent encounter between Jewel and his horse, which offers a protracted, uncertain response to Anse's deceptively simple question, "Where's Jewel?"

> When Jewel can almost touch him, the horse stands on his hind legs and slashes down at Jewel. Then Jewel is enclosed by a glittering maze of hooves as by an illusion of wings; among them, beneath the upreared chest, he moves with the flashing limberness of a snake. For an instant before the jerk comes onto his arms he sees his whole body earth-free, horizontal, whipping snake-limber, until he finds the horse's nostrils and touches earth again. (11–12)[16]

In characterizing the image of upright thought as "know[ing] what it means to think," Deleuze claims the complacency of an easy analogy between thought and predetermined bodily form; Darl's description, in contrast, uproots both the body and consciousness from the certainty of the image. The rapid violence of the encounter would seem to disallow physical sight, but sight occurs here within the uncertain bodily geography of singular moments, rather than participating in a socially constructed, regularized tradition of vision. That Jewel "sees his whole body"—a perspectival impossibility—suggests the coincidence of becoming and awareness of becoming, a radical positionality through which control and the certainty of bodily location are suspended. And Darl, although ostensibly an outside observer, is also reformed, momentarily "earth-free" through the precarious regress of "seeing" Jewel "see his whole body." Bodily location and visual perception are mobile and depend on the figural: in the fleet serpent and "glittering maze" of hooves and wings, Darl conjures the figures of a caduceus or a Pegasus, but they never coalesce into final form. His description "turns back" toward Classicism even as this meeting of the perceptual and the figural evokes something unrecognizably new.

Posing a question that could aptly refer to Jewel's encounter with the horse, Deleuze and Guattari ask, "Who has not known the violence of these animal sequences, which uproot one from humanity, if only for an instant . . . ?" They describe the process of "becoming-animal" by which a subject not only mimics or exists in analogical relation with an animal, but experiences a "block" of animality "in the interstices of [the] disrupted self" (240). For Deleuze and Guattari, these moments of animality do not represent atavism or some way to locate the human on a scale of evolution or devolution; becoming-animal, they claim, is a real, and not necessarily uncommon, experience that escapes traditional articulations of the human. Citing a 1976 study conducted by Rene Schérer and Guy Hocquenghem of so-called "wolf-children," Deleuze and Guattari write that these children

> appeal to an objective zone of indetermination or uncertainty, "something shared or indiscernible," a proximity "that makes it impossible to say where the boundary between the human and animal lies," not only in the case of autistic children, but for all children; it is as though, independent of the evolution carrying them toward adulthood, there were room in the child for other becomings, "other contemporaneous possibilities," that are not regressions but creative involutions bearing witness to "*an inhumanity immediately experienced in the body as such*," unnatural nuptials "outside the programmed body." There is a reality of becoming-animal, even though one does not in reality become animal. (273)

Darl's metaphors not only describe Jewel as *like* a serpent, or the horse as *like* a winged creature; they provide a language for the invisible reality of the inhuman within the body, a reality that occurs outside "programmed" conceptions of the body.[17] Simultaneously ophidian, equine, avian, and human, the becoming-animal of Jewel and horse challenges normative taxonomies, performing the "unnatural nuptials" that exist outside or alongside traditional classificatory models. These becomings problematize diachronic conceptions of evolution. The novel's tropological reformation of corporeality escapes modernism's fixation on primitivism and progress, allowing for "other contemporaneous possibilities" beyond such linear exigencies. Jewel's relation with the horse is thus not merely a substitute for Addie; the intercorporeality through which Jewel, horse, and, arguably, Darl are momentarily inseparable exceeds the logic of substitution. Even as Darl's repeated claims that "Jewel's mother is a horse" homonymously and insultingly recall Addie's infidelity and Jewel's "bastardy," the tropological confusion of Jewel, horse, and viewer defines a competing notion of generation that challenges the paradigm of the family and its rules of legitimacy and illegitimacy (95).

Although I have argued against the logic of reciprocal exchange or analogy in the novel, I would nevertheless suggest a kind of relationship between character and authorial subjectivity—a relationship not of analogy, but of becoming, something that is more difficult to locate because its becoming erases what it identifiably was. Deleuze and Guattari include authorship in the processes of becoming-animal, noting, "If the writer is a sorcerer, it is because writing is a becoming, writing is traversed by strange becomings that are not becomings-writer, but becomings-rat, becomings-insect, becomings-wolf, etc." (240). Granting and withholding life where we least expect, *As I Lay Dying* may well be animated by a kind of sorcery, and we can consider a textual awareness not as merely contained within identifiable characterological bodies, but as traversing a range of family resemblances among the Bundren "pack," coming to be through some of the more fantastic tropes of the novel. Agreeing with Bleikasten that Faulkner is possessed by "the demon of analogy" (39), Eric Sundquist argues that the novel's individual sections, which, like Addie, fail to cohere as a unified body, paradoxically point us toward the author: "the authorial 'I' . . . is dead as a single identity but still alive in the episodes that continue to refer themselves to that identity and continue to constitute it even more emphatically in our desire to locate Faulkner's own 'language,' his own 'story,' in the voices of his characters" (40). I think it is not drawing too fine a distinction, however, to suggest that the absent author "outside" the text is not just analogically "like" the corpse, but rather that the writing is possessed by something of a "becoming-corpse," which can be understood neither as an absence nor as a predictable decomposition. A textual awareness obtains that does not just refer to the absent author, but, "like" Addie, has a particular kind of animation that resists discursive definition. The corpse thus provides for Faulkner what the animal provides for Deleuze and Guattari: both serve as sites of transformation and becoming, redefining the human outside traditional notions of "personology" (*Plateaus* 264).

Foucault usefully describes death not in terms of disembodiment or absence, but as a "teeming presence," noting, "long after the death of the individual, minuscule, partial deaths continue to dissociate the islets of life that still subsist" (*Birth* 142). The "becoming-corpse" of the novel similarly outlives the moment of death, acting not just through the discernible figures of Addie's corpse or characterological bodies, but through "teeming presences," miniscule and partial bodily phenomena that escape the individual. Deleuze and Guattari, using similar terms, argue that becoming occurs through localized microprocesses that reform the body and its perceptual apparatuses, noting, "the affects of a becoming-dog . . . are succeeded by those of a becoming-molecular, microperceptions of water, air, etc." (249). Rippling outward from Addie's death, such microperceptions reformulate the body in relation to a natural world that is sporadically vivified into "islets of life." Darl's description of drinking from a water bucket, for instance, mingles the properties of water and air, uncertainly casting them into the form of a spectral body: "It would be black, the shelf black, the still surface of the water a round orifice in nothingness, where before I stirred it awake with the dipper I could see maybe a star or two in the bucket, and maybe in the dipper a star or two before I drank" (11). He relocates the sky in miniature within the dipper, his "dipper" a punning reference to the constellation such that it is both an instrument of reflection and reflected image, and Darl the viewer is uncertainly located between sky and water. His comparison of the water's surface to an "orifice in nothingness" conjures a body, but it is a negative body, vertiginously dependent on the pivots of language, tracing in spectral form the irredeemable body whose loss has imparted a corporeal resonance to the natural world.

Faulkner juxtaposes this spectral, tropological corporeality, which temporarily escapes the restraint of any force that would shape it, with the bluntly material body that so emphatically bears the imprint of economic necessity. Darl's reverie immediately precedes a flatly prosaic description of Anse's feet as "badly splayed, his toes cramped and bent and warped, with no toenail at all on his little toes, from working so hard in the wet in homemade shoes when he was a boy" (11). Anse's body in this passage is more corpse-like than anything we can associate with Addie herself; the novel's experimental, tropological bodies thus offer fleeting curatives for the formative social pressures of regionalism, describing bodily, subjective possibilities not available to characters within the plot. The novel shuttles between two distinct bodily modes: the characterological body rooted within its social context, and the tropological corporeality unleashed from such constraints. Citing

Nathalie Sarraute, Deleuze and Guattari claim that the modern novel is characterized by two distinct "planes of writing": "a transcendent plane that organizes and develops forms (genres, themes, motifs) and assigns and develops subjects (personages, characters, feelings); and an altogether different plane that liberates the particles of an anonymous matter, allowing them to communicate through the 'envelope' of forms and subjects, retaining between them only relations of movement and rest, speed and slowness, floating affects" (267).

As I Lay Dying similarly passes between two different planes. The novel, on the one hand, is ostensibly about social deprivation—Addie's death is only the most pronounced symptom of a disease from which all the Bundrens suffer—but this death simultaneously gives rise to a liberating reorganization of matter and subjectivities. This is not to diminish the novel's investment in representing a specific social milieu; character and setting are "envelopes" to which the novel repeatedly returns, but the experimental tropes reorganize the "anonymous matter" of a corporeality that escapes this milieu, marking the death of the completed form of the body in favor of an ambient corporeality and subjectivity, or, in Deleuze and Guattari's terms, the death of molarity in favor of molecularity. Against the entropy of the plot—the sense that all possibilities of redemption for the Bundrens have been foreclosed by the novel's end—the novel poses the liberations of tropology. If the cadaver typically suggests bodily form at its most objective, finite, and available to view, *As I Lay Dying*'s necropoetics, those tropes emanating from or haunted by the figure of the corpse, paradoxically announce the death of such bodily finality. Far from being merely morbid or undesirable processes, then, the corpse and the tropological reformations it compels erode the body traditionally constituted as and controlled through the certainty of the image, claiming instead an emergent ontology of the body, continually reiterated and reformed.

Notes

I would like to thank the readers at *Modern Fiction Studies* and Gabriel Wolfenstein, whose insights greatly improved this article, and I am particularly grateful to Dorothy Hale for her valuable contributions at every stage of composition.

1. See Mark Johnson, who argues that metaphor is not merely a rhetorical device, but "one of the chief cognitive structures by which

we are able to have coherent, ordered experiences" (xv). The metaphors through which we commonly structure experience, he claims, are founded on primal bodily experience. He argues, for instance, that "balance" is an *activity we learn with our bodies* and not by grasping a set of rules or concepts" (74).

2.   John K. Simon notes that Addie is "treated as a corpse before her unobtrusive demise and as a sort of strangely living entity afterwards" (20); Eric Sundquist claims that "dying maintains a figurative power far succeeding the literal event of Addie's death" (30).

3.   Foucault argues that this perception of the status of the cadaver in the eighteenth century is actually historically inaccurate and exaggeratedly benighted. This reconstruction of the past nevertheless functions as kind of truth in the nineteenth century, demonstrating the extent to which medical and other forms of power are dependent upon rhetoric (*Birth* 125).

4.   Donald Kartiganer's discussion of verticality and horizontality in *As I Lay Dying* associates the figurative language used at the Bundren farm with verticality, metaphor, and Being, and that during the journey with horizontality, metonymy, and Becoming. Kartiganer aligns these oppositions with Saussure's diachronic and synchronic, Jakobson's metaphor and metonymy, New Criticism's the miraculous and the mundane, de Man's symbolic and allegorical, and Lacan's Imaginary and Symbolic. Rather than invoking these axes of signification, my discussion is interested in the novel's use of vertical and horizontal images to situate the body in a predictably mappable visual field; the novel's figurative language, shifting between metonymy and metaphor, continually disrupts this field and reconfigures the body. See also Hortense J. Spillers's provocative discussion of Faulknerian "geography as a living agent" (548), in which "the subjective component of space turns it into an infinite series of authorships" (535).

5.   Peter Brooks notes, "The window, like the mirror, is a traditional metaphor of realist vision directed at the world" (89). The window provides a model of authorship for Henry James, who writes, famously, "The house of fiction has . . . not one window but a million." These windows, he claims, are "nothing without the posted presence of the watcher—without, in short, the consciousness of the author" (46). See also Homer B. Pettey, who includes the window within the "metaphorical frames" that "serve as sites of death" in the novel (29).

6.   For Simon, in contrast, cinematic vision is a useful analogy; he compares the novel's disjunctive points of view to "a movie scenario where we watch a character's back as he walks into a house and then see him coming towards us as he enters from outside" (3). Simon argues that, despite the disruption of vision, the external world of the novel remains autonomous and "fundamental" (5).

7. See Michael Kaufmann's discussion of the interplay between narrative events and "paginal space," the printed surface of the page, in *As I Lay Dying*.

8. Jessica Baldanzi and Kyle Schlabach argue that the "outrage" prompted by Addie's corpse represents a failure of such encryptment; the corpse "thwarts all attempts to close off our personal and national narratives" (52).

9. See John T. Matthews, whose discussion of the "play of Faulkner's language" opposes the notion that the experience of external reality precedes language. Calvin Bedient, on the other hand, writes that the novel's metaphorical prose "gets in the way of the reality it describes, or better, the language . . . secretly flouts and overcomes reality, achieving a proud independency" (151). My discussion follows Matthews, suggesting that the experience and representation of the body, whose materiality is bound with discourse, particularly necessitate, and even accelerate, such tropological play.

10. See, for instance, both Sundquist and Simon.

11. Pettey argues that vision fails as the dominant mode of perception in the novel, replaced by a "network of symbols" that "negate" reality (29). I would suggest that the novel stages this failure of vision in order to offer, in its wake, new perceptual and representative modes.

12. Sundquist writes, "Bringing in Peabody from what Faulkner called 'comparatively the metropolitan outland' allows the reader to admit of the Bundrens that 'maybe they do exist. Up to that time they were functioning in this bizarre fashion almost inside a vacuum, and pretty soon you wouldn't have believed it until some stranger came in as a witness'" (32).

13. Ross comments, "None of the sections is framed by a storytelling situation, yet many 'sound' publicly told" (304).

14. Kaja Silverman notes that at an earlier point in history "the phallus . . . seemed to fit as smoothly over the penis as a condom," but that "over the past two centuries, the male subject has increasingly dissociated himself from the visible, attempting thereby to align himself with a symbolic order within which power has become more and more dispersed and demateral" (26). Tull's language similarly dissociates the physical from the visible, but the derangement of bodily form suggests a contestatory relationship with power, rather than an alignment.

15. I am indebted here to Karen Jacobs's discussion in *The Eye's Mind* of the relation between corporeality and vision.

16. Bleikasten refers to this passage not in narrative terms at all but as a "pure kinetic poem" (165).

17. Arguing that the "becoming-animal" should be understood as a kind of transformative encounter rather than as an analogic relation

between discrete entities, Deleuze and Guattari write: "The word 'like' is one of those words that change drastically in meaning and function . . . when they are made into expressions of becomings instead of signified states or signifying relations. . . . The actor Robert De Niro walks 'like' a crab in a certain film sequence; but, he says, it is not a question of his imitating a crab; it is a question of making something that has to do with the crab enter into composition with the image, with the speed of the image" (274).

Works Cited

Baldanzi, Jessica, and Kyle Schlabach. "What Remains? (De)composing and (Re)covering American Identity in *As I Lay Dying* and the Georgia Crematory Scandal." *Journal of the Midwest Modern Language Association* 36.1 (2003): 38–55.

Barthes, Roland. *S/Z.* Trans. Richard Miller. New York: Hill, 1974.

Bedient, Calvin. "Pride and Nakedness: *As I Lay Dying.*" *Faulkner, New Perspectives.* Ed. Richard Brodhead. Englewood Cliffs: Prentice, 1983. 136–52.

Bleikasten, André. *The Ink of Melancholy: Faulkner's Novels from* The Sound and the Fury *to* Light in August. Bloomington: Indiana UP, 1990.

Brooks, Peter. *Body Work: Objects of Desire in Modern Narrative.* Cambridge: Harvard UP, 1993.

Butler, Judith. *Bodies That Matter: On the Discursive Limits of Sex.* New York: Routledge, 1993.

——. "Foucault and the Paradox of Bodily Inscriptions." *Journal of Philosophy* 86. (1989): 601–7.

Crary, Jonathan. *Techniques of the Observer: On Vision and Modernity in the Nineteenth Century.* Cambridge: MIT P, 1990.

Deleuze, Gilles. *Difference and Repetition.* Trans. Paul Patton. New York: Columbia UP, 1994.

Deleuze, Gilles, and Felix Guattari. *A Thousand Plateaus: Capitalism and Schizophrenia*. Trans. Brian Massumi. Minneapolis: U of Minnesota P, 1987.

Faulkner, William. *As I Lay Dying.* New York: Vintage, 1990.

Foucault, Michel. *The Birth of the Clinic: An Archaeology of Medical Perception.* Trans. A. M. Sheridan Smith. New York: Pantheon, 1973.

——. *The History of Sexuality, Volume 1: An Introduction.* Trans. Robert Hurley. New York: Random, 1978.

——. "Nietzsche, Genealogy, History." *The Foucault Reader.* Ed. Paul Rabinow. New York: Pantheon, 1984. 76–100.

Jacobs, Karen. *The Eye's Mind: Literary Modernism and Visual Culture.* Ithaca: Cornell UP, 2001.

James, Henry. *The Art of the Novel.* Ed. R. P. Blackmur. New York: Scribner's, 1934.

Jay, Martin. "Returning the Gaze: The American Response to the French Critique of Ocularcentrism." *Perspectives on Embodiment: The Intersections of Nature and Culture*. Ed. Gail Weiss and Honi Fern Haber. New York: Routledge, 1999. 165–83.

Johnson, Mark. *The Body in the Mind: The Bodily Basis of Meaning, Imagination, and Reason*. Chicago: U of Chicago P, 1990.

Kartiganer, Donald M. "The Farm and the Journey: Ways of Mourning and Meaning in *As I Lay Dying*." *Mississippi Quarterly* 43 (1990): 281–303.

Kaufmann, Michael. "The Textual Coffin and the Narrative Corpse of *As I Lay Dying*." *Arizona Quarterly* 49.1 (1992): 99–116.

Lippit, Akira Mizuta. *Atomic Light (Shadow Optics)*. Minneapolis: U of Minnesota P, 2005.

Matthews, John T. *The Play of Faulkner's Language*. Ithaca: Cornell UP, 1982.

Pettey, Homer B. "Perception and the Destruction of Being in *As I Lay Dying*." *Faulkner Journal* 19.1 (2003): 27–46.

Ross, Stephen M. "'Voice' in Narrative Texts: The Example of *As I Lay Dying*." *PMLA* 57 (1979): 300–310.

Scandura, Jani, and Michael Thurston. *Modernism, Inc.: Body, Memory, Capital*. New York: New York UP, 2001.

Silverman, Kaja. *The Acoustic Mirror: The Female Voice in Psychoanalysis and Cinema*. Bloomington: Indiana UP, 1988.

Simon, John K. "The Scene and Imagery of Metamorphosis in *As I Lay Dying*." *Criticism* 7 (1965): 1–22.

Spillers, Hortense J. "Topographical Topics: Faulknerian Space." *Mississippi Quarterly* 57 (2004): 535–68.

Sundquist, Eric J. *Faulkner: The House Divided*. Baltimore: Johns Hopkins UP, 1983.

MODERNITY AND MODERNIST TECHNIQUE

CHAPTER 16

FAULKNER'S *PYLON* AND THE STRUCTURE OF MODERNITY

Donald T. Torchiana

In a letter to the *New York Times*, December 26, 1954, William Faulkner examined an idea and its consequences which, it seemed to him, lay behind the crash of an Italian airliner at Idlewild airport. In the letter Faulkner assumed, for the moment, that the pilot's instruments had failed, that his instinct after so much experience in the air told him what was wrong, and, yet, that "he dared not accept that knowledge and . . . act on it." Faulkner then concluded:

> He dared not so flout and affront, even with his own life too at stake, our cultural postulate of the infallibility of machines, instruments, gadgets—a Power more ruthless even than the old Hebrew concept of its God, since ours is not even jealous and vengeful, caring nothing about individuals.
>
> He dared not commit that sacrilege. . . . I grieve for him, for that moment's victims. We all had better grieve for all people beneath a culture which holds any mechanical [sic] superior to any man simply because the one, being mechanical, is infallible, while the other, being nothing but man, is not just subject to failure but doomed to it.

Originally published in *Modern Fiction Studies,* Winter 1957.

Faulkner's letter was printed under the caption "The Cult of the Machine." The next Sunday a reader wrote an answer to Faulkner in the same paper. Terming Faulkner's letter "an interesting display of literary skill," the reader proceeded to his main attack. Faulkner's mistake was to suggest that a pilot disregard his instruments and rely on intuition and judgment. Yet had the pilot done so, and then crashed, "there would be no story for Mr. Faulkner to write." And finally:

> When the Aeronautics Board presents the results of their investigation perhaps then we may arrive at sound judgments. For if accuracy is our aim it would be well for pilots as well as literary creators to resort to evidence. When this is done "gadgets," in the form of precision instruments, will continue to serve the function of increasing the accuracy of our judgments.
>
> OTTO KRASH
> Assistant Professor of Education
> Hofstra College

It would seem that Mr. Krash misunderstood Faulkner's letter, for the intuition and experience Faulkner speaks of are professional and result from a year-to-year acquaintance with "precision instruments" on which a pilot must rely. Nevertheless, he must also check and correct them. Instruments cannot correct themselves. The pilot is master of his instruments, and mastery calls for intuition and judgment based on experience. In the second place, Faulkner's conjecture was no more than that. The crash was a possible case in point demonstrating our veneration of the machine and neglect of the human. This view does not stand or fall by the findings of the Aeronautics Board; for were we even certain that the pilot had wilfully disregarded his instruments, there would still remain "the almost religious awe and veneration" with which moderns regard machines. And Mr. Krash's letter, in holding the mechanical superior to the human, thus actually tended to substantiate Faulkner's point.

More important still is the fact that Faulkner *has* written about a pilot who died ignoring "his instruments and . . . basing his judgment on intuition and experience" of the highest sort. It is a story of a man who did "flout and affront" that "Power" which cares "nothing about individuals." It is the story of a people and a culture for which we should all grieve. I refer to Faulkner's novel *Pylon.* Roger Shumann is the pilot; the "Power" is the cash nexus of value; and the culture is our own urban one.

Pylon is perhaps Faulkner's most neglected work.[1] Superficially, to be sure, the neglect seems partially deserved: the confused point of view is especially troublesome with the result that one is never entirely sure of how a character's actions are meant to be taken. The obvious case in point is the Reporter. On the one hand, the Reporter, his perceptions, and surroundings and, consequently, the very point of view of the book reflect Faulkner's heavy borrowing from Eliot. Beyond the name J. Alfred Prufrock and the Reporter's attendant Prufrockian idiosyncrasies, one thinks of the airfield reclaimed from a "waste land," the sterile and desiccated urban scene partially reclaimed in a death by water as in Eliot's own poem, and then all the actual echoes and repetitions of phrases from other poems like "Gerontion," Burbank with a Baedeker," "Preludes," and "The Hollow Men." Yet all these tend to clash, on the other hand, with the humorous, rough-and-ready, maverick side of the book, again also seen in the Reporter, who risks his life riding in an experimental plane, curses with the best of reporters and airmen, looks like a jackstraw, and spends a disconcerting amount of his time drunk. Absinth, not tea, is his beverage. Thus the Reporter, the sensitive go-between in the novel, is alternately the tough, alert reporter of American newspaper tradition or his more detached, urbane, Eliotic contemporary. As a consequence, the meaning of the book is often split or blurred. Like the Reporter's last scribbled note and two accounts of Shumann's death, *Pylon* becomes variously farcical, sardonic, and heroic from the standpoint of plotting and point of view. However, as I hope to show, the iron structure of modern life that rises from the mechanical, determined, and inhuman content of the book serves only to test Faulkner's major formal assertion: heroism is still possible in our age. In this last regard few of his novels are any more pertinent to our age of the mid-fifties, an age which seems to revere only deadly efficiency, whether in a jet bomber, a suburban parent, or a coaxial cable. For in *Pylon,* as in his future letter to the *Times,* Faulkner only affirms earlier that our efficient culture continues to harass the pilot, man (Italian or otherwise), as much as ever.

At first glance, the predominant theme in *Pylon* appears to be the modern inversion of life and eros into death and destruction by means of the Cult of the Machine, which, in turn, is impelled by the Power of money. Yet there is an opposite theme of equal force. Herein lies the main action: the triumph of life in the self-sacrifice of Shumann, and the affirmation of life by his fellow flyers—Holmes, Laverne, and Jiggs—while they all strenuously pursue death. Perhaps most memorable is the controlling symbol of both these themes, the pylon. It is the symbolic reminder of man's aspirations and his limits: the hate and the love, the dying and the begetting, the creative phallus and the fatally extended death wish for those who fly. From the very first we witness its ambivalent attraction when Shumann takes second place in an air race by flying the pylons closer than the other racers; thus in risking death he maintains the sexual *menáge à trois* he has fostered, and he assumes responsibility for the baby (not his) to come. Perhaps the Reporter has best suggested this last creative, life-giving meaning of the pylon. Mulling over the daily montage of newspaper print, the chaotic headlines of our world, he thinks of Shumann, Holmes, and Laverne:

> Farmer's boy, two farmers' boys, at least one from Ohio anyway she told me. And the ground they plough from Iowa; yair, two farmers' boys downbanked; yair, two buried pylons in the one Iowadrowsing womandrowsing pylondrowsing. . . . [2] (110)

The most violent and dramatic definition of these two themes, symbolized by the pylon, is rendered in the account of Laverne's exhibition parachute jump in a small Kansas town. Here the action also suggests the day-to-day relationship of the flyers to society. For at the height of risk, waiting to jump from the wing of the airplane, Laverne turns to Shumann "with an expression that he was later to realize was not at all fear of death but on the contrary a wild and now mindless repudiation of bereavement as if it were he who was the one about to die and not her" (195–96). This act pits wild, teeming life against problematical death and asserts the force and integrity of the couple's own personal existence. In the next moment, however, Laverne become and center of the public inversion of her own inner being. Landing naked and muddy, in the bondage of the chute, she is a figure to titillate the crowd with the lurid attraction of death delivered nubile and obscene from the air. A sadistic policeman, frenzied at the sight of her on the ground, epitomizes the unnatural curiosity of the crowd. Later, escaping from the final crazed pursuit of the policeman, Shumann sees in him the inversion of the natural love that Laverne had offered in the air. The ideal representative of society, defender of the insane modern order, and sexual psychopath, the policeman screaming

> I'll pay you! I'll pay her! I'll pay either of you! Name it. Let me . . . her once and you can cut me if you want! (200)

reveals to Shumann "almost a counterpart of that terror and wild protest against bereavement and division which he had seen in Laverne's face while she had clung to the strut and looked back at him" (200). It is this fantastic episode which stands like the pylon at the center of the two ways of the novel.

Echoes of this traumatic scene resound through the book. They are projected by the dynamism of the airplane, the beautiful and deadly machine, as it swings in a metaphorical orbit around the double meaning of the mastering symbol, the pylon.

Always the airplane possesses a fatal beauty and attraction for the flyers. The Reporter, the central observer of the novel, can liken flying to an orgasm (97), and at the same time compare a racing plane to a device of self-destruction "where you burn the engine up or fly out from between the wings and the undercarriage" (47). Like Bayard Sartoris and Quentin Compson, Roger Shumann and the other flyers are possessed; they have a compulsion to fly. They are aware of the danger, the searing, vibrating, brutal risk of the air; but fly they must. Even in the midnight wake of the Press after Shumann's death, one of the reporters comes close to uttering this truth. Flyers like Shumann fly "because they have got to do it, like some women have to be whores. They can't help themselves." And in the same breath: "Ord knew the ship was dangerous, and Shumann must have known it as well as Ord did . . ." (292). This personal ambivalence attached to flying becomes, in the face of the means society has provided for making money, a calculated risk. Shumann's attitude is professional. It is best seen before his last race when he answers Colonel Feinman's query on the plane bought from Ord:

> Now Feinman turned to Shumann.
> "Is it dangerous to fly?" he said
> "They all are," Shumann said.
> "Well, are you afraid to fly it?" Shumann looked at him.
> "Do you expect it to fall with you this afternoon?"
> "If I did I wouldn't take it up," Shumann said. (226)

Here, all at once, Shumann has denied openly courting death, and at the same time, Feinman, ironically, has uttered Shumann's daily anxiety—is the airplane all right? This conversation, then, hints his compulsion and his fate. With this exception: Shumann's last pylon, the turn before his death, finds him beyond considerations of risk; there his attitude is confessional rather than professional.

Even the Reporter has some inkling of this antinomy in the lives of the flyers, but he never sees his own fate as common to theirs. Nevertheless, his devotion to the printing press, his forced compliance with the demands of news readers, and his dedication to alcohol rather than speed permit him a partial understanding of the flyers. He knows that neither money nor glory serves them as a final end. He can even fathom the peculiar twist of sex and death that contorts their life and work. To him, Shumann's racing plane "trembles like a bride" when rounding the home pylon on a wingtip (47). And despite the fact that the flyers appear subhuman when piloting such a bride, the Reporter admits to their life and creativity when a woman like Laverne will give herself, "opened for the profound, unsleeping, the inescapable, and compelling flesh," as the bride of Shumann (63). Yet the Reporter can never see that both he and they are driven, denied creativity by the very instruments they have chosen, for the airplane and the printing press in the service of finance capitalism are at the beck of the forces of evil.

The extent of this evil can best be seen in the life of Laverne, the most strained and wretched character in the story. She fiercely exults in the life of the air, but she hates with equal intensity its mercantile denial of her femininity, her motherhood, and her humanity. She dresses like a man; she can repair an engine; and after Shumann's death she gives up her son rather than quit the air. Yet always she is torn by pain and anxiety and denial. The first time we see her we learn that it was she who started the cruel airport joke on her son Jack. The Reporter explains:

> And they told me how it wasn't them that started saying "Who's your old man?" to the kid; it was her, and the kid flailing away at her and her stooping that hard boy's face . . . down to where he can reach it and saying "Hit me. Hit me hard. Harder. Harder." (49)

She is determined to exact all the torment possible from her freely chosen role as mate to two flying men. Even after Shumann's first mishap she can offer herself to him only when she has cursed and struck him for the chance he took in the afternoon race. Nor will she relax her rigid stoicism as she watches Roger's plummeting racer disintegrate. While all around her are screaming, she can only desperately curse him: "Oh damn you Roger! Oh damn you! damn you!" (234).

In the same way, the other flyers and those who help them become victims of frustration and pent-up violence that portend great discipline and devotion at war with a natural human rage for life. Because, for example, Shumann's prize money is withheld, Holmes punches Jiggs, who in turn gets drunk and lands in jail. Ord and the Reporter both try to help Shumann; they provide him with his last airplane. Afterwards, in burning the promissory note, they brim with the fear and hate which each harbors for his part in promoting Shumann's death: Ord ambiguously curses the Reporter, while at the same time the Reporter all but burns himself in burning the note. Thus hatred and rage are distilled from their marvelous sympathy and mutual excitement at the prospect of Roger's winning. Neck and neck with Shumann at the end of the race, Ord had given him more than enough room to pull up and cut the pylon close. In doing so Shumann met his end.

And even in themselves, not as instruments of economic competition but as extensions of man's will, the airplanes embody the conflicts of the flyers. On the one hand the machines answer a psychic need for control and skill. One recalls the fascination of jet planes today with their thrust, maneuverability, and roar. Their speed, like the speed of the 1935 racer, dimly approaches the myth of absolute speed: the desire of man to reduce time and space to one event, one instant, the trilling diastole of the human moment protracted for all time. At least something like this balances, on the other hand, the promise of death or *nada* which draws the crowds and braces the flyers. The fierce symmetry of the planes,

> Waspwaisted, wasplight, still, trim, vicious, small, and immobile. . . . (18)

the harsh sounds of the airport,

> . . . vicious highpitched ejaculations . . . the announcer's voice harsh masculine and disembodied . . . the snarl and snore of the engines . . . the scuffle and murmur of feet on tile . . . and the band . . . faint and almost trivial. . . . (25–26)

and the cut-jewel effulgence, the diffusion of human and nonhuman effort when six racing planes rise

> raggedly and dissolved, converging, conveying toward the scattering pylon out in the lake. . . . (30)

all betray a vacuous, deadly splendor which even Faulkner may not write down.

But he never allows us to forget the vulgar reductions of the poised delicacy and power of the airplane dynamism. Two especially come to mind. One is the roadster that Hagood the editor owns, "a machine expensive, complex, delicate and intrinsically useless . . ." (87). The other is the present Jiggs and the Reporter give to the boy Jack. It is a blue and yellow toy airplane which they find "hanging by a piece of cord . . . in similitude of flight" (272). Yet this toy strongly suggests the reduction of real airplanes to amusing toys hanging in the similitude of death above the spectators in a "promoted" airshow. And perhaps no other event better marks the comparable reduction of man's powers and aspirations to mere animal cunning in the press for survival than does the image of the Frenchman in inverted flight twenty feet above the runway. He passes, "his head and face beneath the cockpitrim motionless and alert like that of a roach or a rat immobile behind a crack in a wainscot, his neat short beard unstirred by any wind as though cast in one piece of bronze" (230). Each in its way, then, the roadster and the toy, is a reminder of the superb machine which can attract the gallantry and courage of a man, yet give him nothing in return but a marginal living, an occasional prize, and eventually the wage of death itself. Or as Faulkner goes on to describe the image of the Frenchman in inverted flight, "the bilious aspect of an inverted world" (230).

II

The force that works this inversion is finance capitalism. As we have seen, its mode is the machine, and its death-dealing, iron laws are emblematic of the rigid, arbitrary, course-marking pylon. This force can be equated with the profit motive, especially where it is based on the sale of money rather than the consumption of production goods. It may also be likened to the "business as usual" slogan which battens on the excitement of Mardi Gras and air race alike. The radiance of this cash nexus illuminates, ironically, the multifarious economic activities of the book: in this light Colonel Feinman, manipulator, promoter, and self-styled apologist for "business," and Uncle Isaac, the pawn broker, pursue the same ends by the same means. Between them are the merchants and hucksters catering to the Comus rout of the Mardi Gras season; they are more respectable and less despised than their Jewish brothers, yet are certainly no less avaricious. As we may come to see, Faulkner's stereotyped use of the Jew in this role is characteristic of Eliot, his partial model.

Thus it is in a "kike" (72) clothing store, described in the opening pages of the novel, that this theme is struck. Briefly, Jiggs makes a purchase on terms which become the efficient cause for Shumann's death. For had the store manager agreed to stay open until seven, Jiggs would have learned of the withheld prize money and might not have disastrously "borrowed" twenty dollars from Holmes. Painfully obvious in this scene is the mutual suspicion of the airman and the merchant. The sartorial elegance of the salesmen, their impersonal glitter, and their condescending haggling over the final disposition of Jiggs' beloved boots contrast sharply with Jiggs' halting assertions and strange motley. Even his subsequent easy ticket settlement with a bus driver mocks the final "agreement" Jiggs has made with the merchants. Nor is it misleading to dwell at such length on this opening episode; for if nothing else all this chaffering is an ironic reminder, strange and wonderful, that the real business relationship is being reversed. It is, after all, Jiggs and the other flyers who are attracting buyers and business to the city during Mardi Gras. This curious irony underlying the be-grudged sale of the boots and Jiggs' catastrophic payment is as transparent as the store window separating Jiggs from his desired boots. Through the plate glass we see the actual relationship: the flyers ostensibly subsidized by the merchants are actually the fly-ers whose potential deaths help throng New Valois with spectators. There it is: boots on a pedestal beside the placard bearing a photo-graph of the "trim vicious fragile aeroplanes and the pilots leaning upon them in gargantuan irrelation . . ." (1).

Since the airmen are to be paid in prizes, the investment of the businessmen in the airmeet is purely financial speculation with no product resulting but the risked lives of the performers. Colonel Feinman, the chairman of the sewage board, represents the cloacal association Faulkner discovers in the monetary values of the city. And to epitomize Feinman's transactions there is Shumann's final entry that helps balance accounts; his death dive into the accumu-lated sewage and refuse of the city at the bottom of Lake Rambaud is "profitable" and, at the same time, is a shattering identification of profit value.

However, on two other occasions, especially, we see Feinman or his emissary exploiting this strange accounting system which automatically deprives the flyers of money or safety when a profit is in the offing.

At one juncture the assembled flyers are told there will be a $2^1/_2\%$ cut in their prize money; one of their number has been killed; thus the program is misleading and must be reprinted at their ex-pense. Yet here the bland voice of the representative of business and Colonel Feinman can assure them that this fantastic piece of equity finds the flyers as "benefactors" and the businessmen acting in "good faith" (153–54). The Reporter compares the flyers here to miners being sent into a condemned mine with a dock in pay; and to underscore the exploitation of the airmen and the fact that they are legally depressed, Jiggs is arrested immediately after the meeting, beaten, and thrown in jail for brawling over the payment of a drink. Since the meeting and Jiggs' absence leave the valves unchecked, Roger's dead-stick landing in the next race follows naturally, then, from the normal course of business. Feinman's ma-jor personal appearance, however, is in the role of pleader for Shu-mann's death. In getting Ord's condemned airplane approved for flight, Feinman also improves on one of the many myths of high fi-nance. It is part of the greater myth that Thurman Arnold has described in *The Folklore of Capitalism,* a myth which allows a corporation to identify itself as an individual before the law. The corollary of this view is belief in the wickedness of a government that interferes in the economic affairs of such an individual. The realities behind this myth make Feinman's plausible defense of business a fantastic plea for death by racing plane: the government inspector is interfering with the harvest of the air; a condemned plane should be flown because customers have paid to see it fly. And at last the economic myth of laissez faire easily yields to the anonymity of modern guilt when Feinman himself waives the qualifying requirements for Shumann's plane in the name of the citizens of New Valois and Franciana.

Caught in the machinery of the profit motive, the flyers with their disdain for money as such and their quixotic devotion to flying appear to be absurd. At the beginning, Shumann flies his plane on commission since he doesn't own one; there are but two trench coats between Shumann, Laverne, and Holmes; at the end Jiggs receives but $5.00 for boots which cost $22.50. This amount, which Jiggs receives from Uncle Isaac, is the ultimate expression of the smooth fact of usury, "a charge for the use of purchasing power levied without regard to production, often without regard even to the possibilities of production," as Ezra Pound once put it.[3] It is also probably the clearest evidence of the basic financial operations in *Pylon*.

Two concluding scenes best point up this absurdity of good will, charity, and compassion as motives in competition with the allure of profit.

With the $5.00 Jiggs buys presents for Laverne, Holmes, and young Jack in order to ease their journey after Shumann's death. Yet these presents are actually a further reduction of Uncle Isaac's pittance by the merchants of New Valois, and may only be termed ironic:

> . . . a box or chest of candy about the size of a suitcase and resembling a miniature bale of cotton lettered heavily by some pyrographic process: *Souvenir of New Valois. Come back again* and three magazines—Boys' Life, The Ladies' Home Journal, and one of the pulp magazines of war stories in the air. (273)

Thus a lady, a boy, and an airman may regale each other with memories of a dead pilot and busy, bustling, profitable New Valois. The humane motive always fails. Like Holmes at the end of his crippling jump, humane values land smack against a refreshment booth—or a cash register. Yet like the heroic actions of Holmes and Shumann, humane values demand a conscious choice from those absurd enough to uphold them, absurd enough to be human. The theme is struck early. It occurs in the early picture of the airport at dusk: against the lights like "bloodless grapes" and despite the voice of the amplifier, "apocryphal, sourceless, inhuman, ubiquitous, and beyond weariness or fatigue," there is a puny smear made on the horizon by the parachutist Holmes. He trails from the "soundless and breathless void" into the "accomplished and ineradicable" evening. Nonetheless, we are told that his parachute blooms in the face of it, blooms above the emblazoned and electrified name, Feinman, on each hangar roof (39–40).

III

There remains to be described the connection between the master symbol, the pylon, and the economic motivation which the novel catches in the open. The connection is eminently metaphorical, recalling many of the reviews of *Pylon* which describe it as one of Faulkner's most poetic efforts. As one might suppose, the metaphorical texture is rendered largely in terms of locale and characters. It is here that economic theories operate; it is here that symbols derive their meaning; here, then, is the center of the structure of modernity.

The locale is urban. Logos has become "garblement" (209) and ethos a presence odorous, tropical, and massive; the very innards of the city exude the uncanny blend of modern commerce and ancient decay:

> . . . brick walls which seem to sweat a rich slow overfecund smell of fish and coffee and sugar, and another odor profound faint and distinctive as a musty priest's robe. . . . (15)

Nor may one escape it. The smell of the city, its brown horizon, and sweating metal geometry are beyond time and distance, even beyond death. Shumann's grave is the repository of the final alchemy of the city. Even in death he must repose on "shards of condemned paving and masses of fallen walls and even discarded automobile bodies—any and all of the refuse of man's twentieth century" (236–37). Land, water, and sky are outraged. The city is the landscape of nightmare. A like vehicle, the airport is simply a more fearsome extension of the city's massive oppressiveness. A "terrific and purposeless reclamation," its buildings are "low," "dead," and "unnatural" (17). Likewise the newspaper office, the conscience of the city, is no less furiously meaningless. Although "the insoluble enigma of human folly and blundering" is the constant subject of the newspaper, the completed daily is a dead thing: "the dead instant's fruit of forty tons of machinery and an entire nation's antic delusion" (111). Caught in this quotidian round of unreality, the Reporter, the sensitive observer of the novel, articulates the constricted sensibility of modern man. In the dark loneliness of his room he is fully conscious of a passing moment; it is the moment between darkness and light in which the "illimitable unforgetting" and the "immobility of fleeing" pause, "unbreathing and without impatience and incurious, for him to make the move" (263). The city permits this much felt life, this much synthesis and no more in a still moment.

The tenor of this locale is an impersonal, determined clock time. Here at least two images come to mind as pressing reminders that man's days are irrevocably numbered. The first is the airport beacon light with the initial F for Feinman on one side and, on the other, the flat swordlike beam which flicks by, literally and metaphorically:

> Steadily, with clocklike and deliberate precision, the long sicklebar of the beacon swept inward from the lake, to vanish at the instant when the yellow eye came broadside on and apparently halted there with only a slow and terrific centrifugal movement within the eye itself until with that gigantic and soundless *flick!* the beam shot incredibly outward across the dark sky. (252)

The other figure appears at the same juncture of the novel; in the hands of a screaming newsboy, the headline announcing Shumann's death is also described as flicking away (240). Frozen and short of breath, witness to the unsuccessful salvage operations, the Reporter only dimly perceives the blending of these two vanishing eidolons in the bright dawn.

Both images are also one in echoing the grim click of actual clock time as it measures out the brief encounter of the Reporter and the flyers. Previous to their meeting, the Reporter's lack of attachments coincided with his disregard for watches and time pieces; time to him was simply evanescent, "vanishing slowly like the damp print of a lifted glass on a bar" (201). But the more he commits himself to the welfare of the flyers, the more the Reporter becomes aware of time as "the mechanical regimentation of hours" (210). The chapter title "And Tomorrow" suggests the tenor of the rushing ticks of clock time, the interminable yet finite tension of stressed life that is hurried and enjambed in the grinding passage of determined events. After Shumann's death the sound reaches a crescendo in the new tone of holiness which breaks from the cathedral clock as it tolls the hours remaining before Laverne, Holmes, and Jack leave. Yet the Reporter may only audit the incantation of that moment; he does not see them leave. Sitting in the station, he can only mark "the thin spidery splash" (281) of the second hand which signals the departure of their train. Needless to say, the opening explosions of the airmeet, characteristically monotonous and shattering, actually prepared us for the mechanical tenor of the rigid steel, glass, and masonry of the city. For who can forget the reverberations of the starting bomb as it counters the human beat and throb of the novel, as it mechanically jars the fluid, pulsing elan of the master symbol and lends that symbol a terrible silence?

A second vehicle of the metaphorical structure is the gross population of New Valois or any other city. Its leaders, Feinman and the wild-eyed sadist smitten with Laverne, both exploit the mob in the name of order and solicitude. Hagood, too, panders to the mass appetite for blood, fornication, and murder, while at the airport the announcer insinuates the great sensorium of the mass mind into the very cockpit of a doomed pilot. Thus, whether by turnstile, pistol butt, printing press, or amplifier, each of these leaders practices on the myth perpetrated by the murals in the rotunda, the myth of man's conquest of the "infinite and impervious air" (37–38). Feinman and his fellow priests offer urban man a blood ritual; having scented blood, seeing Shumann's plane disintegrate, the crowd hastens to the only heroic dish it knows, the feast of the eyes. All become scavengers. A mile line of cars, headlights staring, patiently monitor the futile salvage operations through the night; small boats and skiffs do a brisk business as sightseers strain for a glimpse of the disinterment of their myth and their lust. Nevertheless, it is a professional scavenger, a photographer, one of the gentlemen of the press gathered to pick over the facts of Shumann's demise, who epitomizes the denial in mass man of any compassion for his brothers. For an awkward moment he speculates with the Reporter:

> Jesus, I tell you I feel bad too. Here, smoke a cigarette. Yair. I could vomit too. But what the hell? He aint our brother. Come on, now! (238)

The tenor of this abandoned activity is identical with the jangling, coruscating hilarity of the Mardi Gras celebration. The sacrificial death of Shumann comes just before Ash Wednesday and turns the pageant of restless, senseless living into a *danse macabre,* with the snarling death-flirtation of the air race at its center. Shumann's screaming death dive is its final orgiastic release, and the dance of machines and men in blood frenzy has as its orbit all America. Even the Reporter is reminded of the blind necessity propelling the revelers once a year to and from New Valois. They celebrate the fact that they must celebrate (281). They gather round their death tree, the pylon, in a masquing rite that reveals the horror, the truth of the average men in an average city.

Shumann's death also belongs to the victims. Those who are also compelled, those who disregard the profit motive, who are harried by its agents, they, the victims, force the double meaning of the pylon symbol. So far the metaphoric structure of the novel has only suggested death as the dominant value of Faulkner's novel. But Shumann's death denies death and affirms life, his own life and the lives of his fellow victims, Laverne, Holmes, Jiggs, and young Jack.

The essential difference between the flyers and the audience they amuse is that the flyers are aware of their degradation as men. They realize that a passion for the air gets them only supreme hazard and a miserable return. Thus each has a studied behavior which furtively reveals an acute reaction to the outrages against his life. In Jiggs it takes the form of muscular tension, tight clothing, and a propensity for brawling and drink. Laverne is quick to anger, tightlipped, and strong in her ruthless rejection of domesticity. Holmes is pugnacious, quick to pretend to the economic values of the society which mocks him, yet obdurate in refusing to steal from the Reporter. Shumann with his air of rigid calm cannot belie his own absolute dedication to the others: he flies the pylons close, he steals, and he dies for the others all in full consciousness of his deeds. Even the boy Jack fights automatically, breathlessly and furiously against any who question his parentage. And each has some reminder, some talisman to preserve his awareness. Jiggs wears expensive boots; Shumann affects an impeccable Homburg; despite her mannish dress, Laverne keeps her abundant yellow hair long. Holmes has a handsome, brutal, disreputable, yet feminine look about him. The boy daubs his face with grease. All are from nowhere; in one way or another each is adrift from the normal bonds of family and place. They are a band of grotesques. But theirs is the only real community of the book.

For, contrary to the earlier statement of the Reporter, and contrary to the populace and locale surrounding them, the flyers are the real human beings, the eminently sane men. Their "crime," with Shumann kneeling before them all to complete the robbery of the drunk Reporter, has no joy in it. Denied their prize money, they must eat and sleep, and further their own degradation to do so. Yet all attempt to make restitution to the Reporter. Their "crime" stands in delicate contrast to the approved sharp practices of the businessmen who profit by Shumann's death. Unlike those men, the indifferents, the flyers are aware of their act and atone for it. But ironic testimony to their sanity and decency is best seen in the early exchange between the Reporter and the elevator man in the newspaper office. The topic is air racing.

"I think they are all crazy," the elevator man said. . . . "Them
that do it and them that pay money to see it." (52)

Superficially he is right, but he has failed to realize that the insan-
ity of those who pay to see a race is different from the apparent
irrationality of the flyers who maintain themselves as only they
can. The elevator man's mode of life explains his mistake. He is the
prudential man; he is enclosed, as we are told, in his cage. The instruments of his work and pleasure define him: the shallow stack
of newspapers he sells, the dollar watch which holds them in place,
the stinking, "dead stained cob pipe," and his caged, mechanical,
and regular occupation. By contrast the flyers are the *saltim-
banques* of the modern age, without tickets to their own air circus,
part of the cosmic rule of poverty without which the world seemingly could not exist. Yet they are alive and he is dead. By virtue of
their individual awareness they exercise conscious choice, deny
cosmic necessity, and elicit sympathy from those who would understand them: Ord, the Reporter, and the madame of a whorehouse. Though the flyers may only choose between the means
of defeat offered them, their mode of living continues to be charitable and sacrificial, not acquisitive and egotistical. Their apparent
schizophrenic existence is actually consciousness of choice and its
frightful vistas.

Shumann, specifically, is the exemplar of the freely chosen
sacrifice that counters the virulence of finance capitalism and lends
such provoking ambiguity to the otherwise death-dealing pylon. So
far as I know, the only critic who has given any serious attention to
Pylon finds the book a "definition of sacrifice," and Shumann "reenacting . . . the ceremony of Christ on the Cross."[4] There is much
to back up this contention. Shumann does literally shepherd the
little group, even to the extent of forcing food on Jiggs to keep him
relatively sober and useful. Under Shumann's guidance they all
work as a perfect team in maintaining their racing plane. His death,
coming at the beginning of the Lenten season, betokens that period of austerity, fasting, and penitence preceding the sacrifice of
Christ. In fact, the Sunday morning after Shumann's death is the
first to usher in a day of clear sunlight; the streets are quiet "with
a certain slow tranquility as though the very brick and stone had
just recovered from fever" (267). Again the most significant statement in this regard is made by the photographer: "For Christ's
sake, we never made him go up in it [the condemned airplane]"
(240). Of course, "we," they did. For Shumann's sacrifice did not
stop at the bounds of his "family." By virtue of his concern for Laverne's unborn child and by virtue of his zooming "out of the path

of the two aeroplanes behind while he looked down at the close-peopled land and the empty lake, and made a choice before the tailgroup came completely free" (234), Shumann's act partially redeems the guilt of all men. One feels that the ferro-concrete world of city and airport has trembled and is momentarily calmed and emptied of its terror.

Sacrifice and its freedom, however, come hard for ordinary men. Only full knowledge of his predicament establishes Shumann's freedom to die on his own terms. The pain of that knowledge is also met by Laverne and Holmes when they give up the boy. Jiggs, too, in choosing to relinquish his beloved boots that he may perform a charitable act, takes a heavy loss on them; but for the ordinary man the attitude taken toward Shumann's death is a variation on further remarks of the photographer: *I might be a bum and a bastard but I'm not out there in that lake"* (252). And Dr. Shumann, Roger's father, a man who sacrificed his family home in order to pay for Roger's flying, even he at the end cannot go on sacrificing himself interminably. His jerry-built town house, in contrast to his former country seat, symbolizes the disintegration of his will. Even he finally surrenders to the values of the city. Earlier he had accepted Roger's flying, Laverne, and the fact that her child Jack might or might not be Roger's. But then he was younger. Or at least he sees his apostasy in that light when at the end of the novel he warns Laverne that, while he and his wife live, she must not see her son again:

> We are old; you cannot understand that, that you will or can ever reach a time when you can bear so much and no more; that nothing else is worth the bearing; that you not only cannot, you will not; that nothing is worth anything but peace, peace, peace, even with bereavement and grief—nothing! nothing! (306)

Finally, the tenor of Roger's act, and the tenor of the lives of the flyers, is dramatically strengthened following Dr. Shumann's reversal in at least three tableaux of unbelief. First the old man Pharisaically asks Laverne for a sign, some sign that Jack is Roger's son. Then, more ironically, as the representative of an adulterous and unbelieving generation, Dr. Shumann condemns to the fire the money in the airplane, money given in charity which he assumes Laverne had acquired by adultery. Lastly, there is the spectacle of the old man sobbing in his wife's lap; before him stands the boy, the doctor of toy machines, resolute in a man's shirt and ready to leave; then while he clutches to his chest the toy destroyed by Dr.

Shumann, that grief-ridden man hysterically claims the boy as his own. The only other sound is the faint roar of the flames in the stove as the money passes into nothing and its values triumph. Thus Faulkner has ultimately rendered the structure of modernity in the Christian concepts of sacrifice and unbelief. In the modern wasteland, under the enormous pressure to conform, most men will eventually accept the passive, the dead, or the inert rather than endure the pain of man's middle state between God and beast, as Pope has said. The pylon, sexual symbol of Godhead or inert reminder of man's bestiality, is a superstructure of these limits at once mysterious and exacting. In this world all men must measure their course by that pylon if they are even to endure.

IV

In concluding his chapter on *Pylon*, William Van O'Connor has made a provocative statement which is initially hard to resist here:

> *Pylon* . . . invites one to question the wholehearted anti-modernity which is usually attributed to Faulkner. Laverne and Shumann and Jack are as heroic as creatures half-human and half-metallic can be. They live within their own morbid and masochistic idealism. . . . One is asked, not to like such characters, but to give them a little margin of admiration for having come to terms with a mechanized order, finding a part of their being in it. If this is so, one would like to be able to see a little more deeply into the forces motivating them, to understand . . . the dialectical leap from machine to human spirit.[5]

In questioning Faulkner's anti-modernity in *Pylon*, O'Connor has certainly put his finger on a serious problem in the novel, yet his drift seems essentially wrong. For Faulkner is so decidedly anti-modern in *Pylon* that he seems to have accepted Eliot's prescriptive, now classical image of the modern city, a waste land, at almost secondhand. In this case, his anti-modernity is *a priori*, when it ought to have been a discovery. Indeed, his real discovery seems to have been the essential humanity of the flyers, despite their "half-metallic" appearance, and the essential inhumanity of the ordinary human being in New Valois. O'Connor's use of the word "idealism" strikes the right note, but the idealism is not morbid, and if it is masochistic, as in the case of Laverne, the perversion is caused by other hands, other forces than personal weakness. The rapacious force of finance capitalism works through the machinery of the modern city. The city becomes the condition of modernity or evil just as the Snopeses, lynch law, and a decayed aristocracy serve the irrational evil of Yoknapatawpha County. The leap, then, is not from machine to human spirit, but from inhumanity to humanity, from death to life. Machines, the printing press and the airplane, help extend man's inhumanity impersonally and efficiently. Yet both may also establish the authority of normal human failure. The Reporter is still capable of writing his first account of Shumann's death, though he tears it up; and Roger Shumann, even more positively, wrests his own destiny, his own integration from a condemned airplane at its moment of disintegration, his moment of choice.

When asked recently why he wrote, Faulkner gave an answer which may bear out this analysis of *Pylon:*

> Writers have private illusions at the origin of their books. I intend my writing as the phrase which appeared all over on the walls during the last war (in America) "Kilroy was here!" Kilroy has been here. I write to say No to death.[6]

But modern life does not say No to death, and therefore Faulkner must. Critics often go to Faulkner's review of Jimmy Collins' *Test Pilot* in the *American Mercury* of November, 1935; there they discover Faulkner voicing his disappointment in not finding Collins' book a "folklore of the speed itself," and, in turn, accuse Faulkner of the same failure in *Pylon.* But *Pylon* is not *Test Pilot* nor was meant to be. No. *Pylon* is a book which says No to our death-in-life by showing how the compassionate may conquer it through love, sacrifice, and personal discipline. Consequently, despite the blurred view in *Pylon,* Faulkner has remained true to his vision, the conditions of death and their denial.[7] In depicting this "bilious inversion" of values, this dance of death where few prevail, some endure, and all fail, Faulkner has presented not the folklore of speed but the folklore of modernity. Treacherous, mysterious, and life-giving, the lonely pylon is its totem symbol.

Notes

1. After writing this essay, I discovered that even a popular reviewer like Harvey Breit could dreamily term *Pylon* "the most undeservedly neglected book" in the past quarter century. He describes himself as never being "the same about planes after *Pylon . . .*" (*American Scholar,* XXV [Autumn, 1956], 474).

2. Unless otherwise noted, all quotations are taken from the first edition of *Pylon* (New York: Harrison Smith and Robert Haas, Inc.,

1935). I have capitalized the "reporter" in order to distinguish him from his fellow newsmen.

3. Cited by Guy Davenport, "The Nuclear Venus: Williams' Attack on Usura," *Perspective,* VI (Autumn–Winter, 1953), 183.

4. John R. Marvin, "*Pylon:* The Definition of Sacrifice," *Faulkner Studies,* I (Summer, 1952), 20–23. Although I cannot agree with some of Mr. Marvin's conclusions, for instance, that "Shumann obviously is not tragic," still his essay appears to be the only one to point out the undeniable elements of individual consciousness, sacrifice, and Christian value in the book.

5. William Van O'Connor, *The Tangled Fire of William Faulkner* (Minneapolis, 1953), pp. 92–93. The same point is made even more adamantly by George Marion O'Donnell: "*Pylon* is his most conspicuous failure; and his imperfect sympathy with, and his inability to control the protagonists, who should be antagonists, seems to account for the failure" ("Faulkner's Mythology," *William Faulkner: Two Decades of Criticism,* ed. Frederick J. Hoffman and Olga Vickery [East Lansing, Michigan, 1951], p. 59).

6. A. M. Dominicis, "An Interview with Faulkner (translated from the Rome Weekly *La Fiera Letteraria*, February 14, 1954, pp. 33–37 by Elizabeth Nissen)," *Faulkner Studies,* III (Summer–Autumn, 1954), 35. See also Faulkner's address in *The New York Times Book Review,* February 6, 1955, pp. 2, 4, on the occasion of his receiving the National Book Award.

7. Worth quoting here are some of Faulkner's remarks on the general theme of his works as Cynthia Grenier has recorded them in "The Art of Fiction: An Interview with William Faulkner," *Accent,* XVI (Summer, 1956): "There isn't any theme in my work, or maybe if there is you can call it a certain faith in man and his ability to always prevail and endure over circumstances and his own destiny" (171). And in answer to the questions why his characters are usually trapped by faith, why so many go down, and what is the right way of going down: ". . . there is always some one person who survives, who triumphs over his fate. . . . That they go down doesn't matter. It's *how* they go under. . . . It's to go under when trying to do more than you know how to do. It's trying to defy defeat even if it's inevitable" (172).

CHAPTER 17

GOTHICISM IN
SANCTUARY
THE BLACK PALL AND
THE CRAP TABLE

David L. Frazier

There are, I suggest, two large categories of elements in *Sanctuary,* the conventional gothic and the unconventional modern; and the theme of society-directed indignation which characterizes the book is expressed, when it is not explicit, through satire effected by contrasting them. It is the juxtaposition of the conventional gothic stimulus element, the *black pall,* and that characteristically modern, the *crap table,* or more generally the modernistic finishing treatment given that which began taking conventional shape, that gives *Sanctuary* much of its shocking power and ultimately its force of moral censure; and it is this function which needs most to be understood if the book is to be justly evaluated. Accordingly, I shall not attempt here to catalogue *Sanctuary's* gothic elements, but shall only note such, with their horror and allusive values, as seem necessary to indicate their instrumentality.

In this connection the account of Red's wake, in chapter 25, is a significant scene. In its relatively small wholeness may be more easily seen the general contrast treatment, the transition from the

Originally published in *Modern Fiction Studies,* Autumn 1956.

predominantly traditional condition with nontraditional touches to the predominantly nontraditional ending in which the contrasting traditionalism becomes vestigial, which forms the structure of the book as a whole. In it the gothic and modern elements are mixed with compression, and from it are taken the terms used for convenience to denote these classes of elements:

> The archway to the dice room was draped in black. A black pall lay upon the crap table, upon which the overflow of floral shapes was beginning to accumulate. People entered steadily, the men in dark suits of decorous restraint, others in light, bright shades of spring, increasing the atmosphere of macabre paradox. (Modern Library edition, p. 292)

The scene sets a situation in which traditional behavior is demanded and in which there is at the start a predominantly suitable gothic atmosphere, although incongruity exists in the crap table features and in the cast, whose attempts at fitting manners resemble apish mimicry. From the black pall and the crap table the action rushes along a catenation of contrasts with a bier and a bouncer, hymns and jazz, crosses and wreaths and bootleg booze, until their bestiality masters the actors and the wake becomes a funereal orgy in which even the semblance of traditional comportment vanishes and death and its trappings are stripped of their gothic awfulness and dignity. In the beginning the crap table, at the end the black pall is incongruous; the passage is from a black pall to a crap table atmosphere, and the final effect is one of horrified disgust at the grotesque hoodlumism, at the backstage view of the gothic scene, the wires, grease paint, mummery disclosed. The satirical quality of the book becomes salient in the sharp juxtaposition of incongruous details, in the "macabre paradox," in the fusion of Poe and Capone. Conventional Gothicism is instrumental to the effect of disgust which attaches to modern gangsterism. The appropriateness of the scene, which is not a tightly integrated part of plot, is thematic; its theme is the breakdown of traditionalism implicit in the major action. It is the key to the largest function of Gothicism in the book.

This scene is also one of several which serve to establish the comic-terrible atmosphere that enables the moods of horror and indignation in the use of the conventions. Faulkner's solution to the problem of maintaining suspense and pace—dramatic presentational form—is that with which early Gothicists met the problem; but his creation of the comic-terrible atmosphere is a significant departure from gothic dramatic formula, significant because it parallels the transition in the story from the largely black pall to the largely crap table conditions. The action at the Old Frenchman place is close to gothic conventionality; and, consistently, the mood is one of terror and the presentation formulistic. With the transition to Miss Reba's brothel, the modernistic locale, the element of comedy enters: the departure from formula coincides with the shift and corresponds with the breakdown of traditionalism in the plot movement. Comic interlude occurred in the gothic romance on nothing like the scale in *Sanctuary;* a little comedy gave needed relief and by contrast intensified the horror, but it was strictly limited, from the danger of its marring the effect of high seriousness for which the early Gothicists strove. Comedy in *Sanctuary* begins small, with Miss Reba and her dogs, and has the intensifying effect, but soon grows large. Faulkner, approaching the close of the story, with the Clarence Snopes train scene, the Virgil Snopes bawdy house scene, the wake scene, the Uncle Bud tea party scene brings horror and comedy to balance. The marring effect occurs but is no defect, for the result is a tone over the events of horrible humor and humorous horror, paradox, grotesquery, that makes harmonious background for the caustic parody and ironic contrast by which the feeling of outrage is communicated.

Sanctuary begins, to repeat, in traditional form. The circumstances of the Old Frenchman place are largely conventional and establish the book's Gothicism. Perhaps the most conspicuous and highly conventionalized feature of gothic formula was the setting; the locale of the action was almost invariably a massive dark building remote from civilization in the midst of wild nature, surrounded by a dark wood which deepened its gloom and air of foreboding. Setting is also a conspicuous feature of the first part of *Sanctuary* and conspicuously gothic. From the first pages, with the reflecting pool, mysterious silence, descending darkness, deepening gloom, black jungle, and swooping owl Faulkner creates the atmosphere for a gothic setting. Such elements make the proper frame for the gothic building, and the Old Frenchman place looms from the blackness a proper gothic ruin: "A moment later, above a black, jagged mass of trees, the house lifted its stark square bulk against the failing sky" (p. 6).

Like Clara Reeve, Faulkner finds a manor house, a ruined plantation manor house, an equivalent for a medieval pile and makes it a fit place for gothic horror and crime. It is hulking and grim and compares favorably with the traditional ruined abbeys and castles: "It was set in a ruined lawn, surrounded by abandoned grounds and fallen outbuildings . . . a gaunt weather-stained ruin in a sombre grove through which the breeze drew with a sad murmurous sound" (p. 47). The Old Frenchman place corresponds closely in architecture and landscaping to the setting of gothic tradition; and, traditionally, it functions mainly as a horror device. It is a suitable container for murder and rape and imparts to them the flavor of its own horror taint. But if it is largely a black pall ingredient and a large one, its presentation is not completely traditional, for it is inhabited by no person of any sort whose presence is traditional. It is infested by a pack of vermin of a modern strain, bootleggers; and they, like the actors in the wake scene, are incongruous. The august ruined mansion calls for occupants of commensurate stature and of a nature consistent with its tone: if evil, grandly evil. But the bootleggers are at most animalistically vicious; in the mansion they seem creeping, crawling things; and this impression is enforced by the presence of the rats, with which in their movements, sounds, glowing eyes, and other traits the bootleggers are identifiable. The gothic locale, too, has its crap table element; and the contrast feelingly implements the implicit moral judgment on bootlegging, bootleggers, and the society that produces them which it later made explicit, as truth in *Sanctuary* frequently is, through Ruby: "God, if I had my way, I'd hang every man that makes it or buys it or drinks it, every one of them" (p. 193).

The action at the Old Frenchman place is enough like gothic plot to prompt comparison, but in it the crap table strain becomes increasingly articulated. The plot of the old romance for which the gothic structure was fabricated revolved about a crime, frequently one of illicit or incestuous love. This crime was the source of much of the horror in the tale, and the movement of the plot was toward prevention or retribution of it. So, too, the plot of *Sanctuary* revolves about a crime. The gothic plot situation most like that of *Sanctuary*—the plot of Walpole's *The Castle of Otranto* exemplifies it—found a sterling maiden, separated from family and in a strange place (the gothic locale), running about frenetically trying to escape being but ever on the verge of being deflowered by the monomaniacal villain; she was aided in her escape by the young hero and eventually saved by the appearance of her father. And this might serve as a sketch of the plot of *Sanctuary,* the skeleton of it, but it says nothing of the noteworthy variations which Faulkner makes upon tradition.

The centric sexual crime in *Sanctuary* is no conventional matter of illicit or incestuous love, though the story contains sufficiency of one and suggestion of the other; a crime involving either would have been too traditional, too human for Faulkner's purposes. Paradoxically, the conventional gothic villain of the pursuing amorous sort is represented by Goodwin, who is not the villain; and the paradox emphasizes the perversion of the corncob rape, which is identified through Popeye with modernism. Goodwin's pursuit of

Temple is similar to the basic horror-stimulating situation in *Otranto,* Manfred's pursuit of Isabella, but it stimulates little if any horror in *Sanctuary.* Goodwin's pursuit creates the expectancy of conventional treatment, prepares the reader for a black pall crime; the crap table crime which actually occurs is therefore shocking. The contrast reveals in relief the pathology of Popeye's crime and effects augmented reprehension of modernism.

Similarly, the flight involved with the sexual crime is close to gothic conventionality in broad outline but has crap table qualifications which make it expressive of moral censure. Temple's situation bears obvious resemblance to that of the gothic heroine; and she runs through the halls, rooms, stalls, trap doors, and lofts of the Old Frenchman place as the gothic heroine ran through corridors, passageways innumerable in her flight from the villain. But thereafter the contrast enters: the gothic heroine wanted only to escape, while Temple wants in part to be caught; and the flight of the heroine was wholly a flight of escape, while Temple's running is like an animalistic, feintingly evasive mating dance. Paradoxically, it is such that she lets herself be caught and such that it is actually a provocation. Implicit in the contrast is condemnation of the immorality of "modern" young womanhood, the flapperhood Temple personifies. It is an expression of the general attitude underlying the treatment of Little Belle, the girls on the train, the girls at Temple's university.

The object of the heroine's flight through the romance was a place of sanctuary. The corncrib in connection with Temple's flight is an important ironic element. Since it is so closely connected with the crimes that lie at the gravitational center of the book, and since it is the pivotal point in the plot's black pall to crap table turn and a symbolic focal point of the moral condemnation, the crib, with the word's connotation of the prostitute's workroom, is the most important of the several quasi-sanctuaries in the book. Temple, like the gothic heroine, runs for sanctuary but, unlike her, does not seek and find it in a holy place. Her refuge is the crib, and it suits her motivation; she both fled and sought her fate, and accordingly the crib figures as a place where she may escape her potential ravishment and a place where she may submit to it. And more, it becomes a symbol of the holding of the harvest of what Faulkner seems to consider part of man's original sin in the land, his plowing-exploiting-ravaging of the earth and prostitution of his moral dignity. In the crib Temple prostitutes herself and is violated. The crib as temple is violated; the body as the temple is violated; Temple is violated. She is ravaged in turn, plowed with furrows of fire by a symbol of fecundity horribly used, through the possession of one who represents evil in modern society, its tin gods mechanism, materialism, and perverted sexuality. The corncrib becomes a religious shrine appropriate to the unholy worship, and the prostitution-rape action a rite of the worship. With Temple, the movement of the plot with its increasing modernism comes to a climax in the corncrib, and there traditionalism dies. It is the pivotal point in the transition from the traditional with nontraditional touches to the nontraditional with gothic overtones; after it Temple substitutes one kind of crib for another, and the movement which began with the gothic ruin and its elements of modernism proceeds to the modernistic locale of the brothel with its gothic sights and sounds as a few remaining stimuli of traditional attitudes and values.

The parallel in *Sanctuary* to the key role of the father in the gothic plot, a parallel, it may be, in which there are variations on the conventional gothic element of prophecy about the crime and on the stock horror touch of the living statue and an expression of the recurrent idea of the blind inadequacy of legal justice as the agency of right, also comes to a crystallization in the crib. The prophecy may be indicated by Temple's cry, "I told you it was! . . . I told you! I told you all the time!" (p. 122), the confirmation, perhaps, of a presentment she had tried to communicate to her father that because of the risks she ran in her escapades and her own vulnerability something like the rape would happen to her. The variation on the horror touch is the presentation of the blind man at the ruin as a living statue. When Temple first sees him she is terrified by his eyes, the blank eyes of a statue. He moves about the ruin with sculptured insentience and seems to follow Temple—even in her trip to the toilet, grotesque parody on gothic convention. His terror effect on Temple is constant, and the possibility that she prophesied to her father that something was going to happen to her may elucidate this effect. It may be that the statue represents her father, that his following her about corresponds to her father's constant presence in her thoughts at the Old Frenchman place, and that the statue's frightfulness is increased by fear she felt for her father, fear evoked because she is sexually tempted.

Judge Drake policed Temple's behavior and caused fear-based inhibitions in her, but gave her no sounder basis for ethical behavior; as a father he personified law. The relationship was inadequate for her needs; and she responded to the injunctions and the threats with resentment and took advantage of her opportunities to express by her actions her resentment and, indirectly, her need for understanding discipline and control. But her father was blind to what she was thereby trying to show him, and there is heavy irony in his being the judge, as Temple repeats over and over. It is to him, symbolized by the blind man, that she screams the I-told-you-so as the disaster approaches her with Popeye:

> She could hear silence in a thick rustling as he moved toward her through it, thrusting it aside, and she began to say Something is going to happen to me. She was saying it to the old man with the yellow clots for eyes. "Something is happening to me!" she screamed at him, sitting in his chair in the sunlight, his hands crossed on the top of the stick. "I told you it was!" she screamed . . . until he turned his head and the two phlegm clots above her where she lay tossing and thrashing on the rough, sunny boards. "I told you! I told you all the time!" (p. 122).

The interpretation may seem fanciful, but it explains a few otherwise obscure points in the book. Moreover, the image of Judge Drake presented at the end of the book calls up irresistibly the image of the blind man: "Beside her, her father sat, his hands crossed on the head of his stick . . ." (p. 379). If it is correct, it represents an interesting adaptation of the conventional gothic usage of the father.

The heroine of the romance found herself in her plight because her father was not present to protect her. That Temple's father is absent during her nightmare in the ruin, then, is conventional. But there is a more important sense in which his absence results in her predicament, and that is in his absence as a proper father from the first. Not physical presence, but guidance to assure safety in parental absence is necessary for the emancipated heroine which Temple is. But Judge Drake is inadequate, and he shares with society the blame for Temple's catastrophe. His failure to save the heroine as the gothic father saved her is the consequence that illuminates his general moral failure. The gothic father's arrival is parodied, because Temple's father arrives too late; the catastrophe has befallen her, and she is totally corrupted. He remains blind and inadequate to the last: her predicament is moral, but he removes her only from its physical setting, the whorehouse, and attempts to set things right by giving her a trip to Europe. The presentation is a modern twist given conventionality, and he emerges a part of reprehensible modernism.

Religion, not only the sort of which Popeye is the priest or icon, but also traditionalistic religion enters largely into *Sanctuary* as it did in the romance, where it was usually a force working for the right and occasionally a horror device employed for its mystery value. But in *Sanctuary* religion is neither good nor black in an occult sense; it is devoid of any supernaturalistic connection. It is no source of consolation or of sanctuary; it is blind, dogmatic unreason, prejudice with fanatic zeal; the right for which it works is morally wrong, and its working hampers justice and fosters inequities. The minister's sermon which Benbow recounts to Miss Jenny may well have been the germ of the idea that, given impetus by the district attorney, led the mob to drag Goodwin from jail and burn him alive. It was a committee of religious ladies that hounded Ruby and her sick child from the hotel where Benbow placed them. When the time of judgment came in the gothic plot, poetic justice of divine rightness, often tempered with mercy, was meted out. Justice in *Sanctuary* is vicious and blind and fits neither the crimes nor the virtues of the characters. It is not divine, but legal justice; and the blindness and inadequacy of law is the last ironic twist of the knife. Religion fails to promote justice, and without religion law cannot succeed.

Horace Benbow represents the union of morality and law and is the foil of Judge Drake. He tries to save Little Belle as Judge Drake did not try to save Temple; he works for the right judgment upon Goodwin which the law confounds and Judge Drake thwarts. Benbow exerts the only motive force toward the right which is operative in *Sanctuary*; but it is, of course, direction frustrated: the opposed collective maleficent force of modernism is finally overwhelming. Much could be said of Benbow and of Ruby Lamar, the other major approvable character in the book, but their gothic qualities need no great elaboration. It is perhaps sufficient to say of Benbow in this connection that he personifies the traditional values of the gothic romance in the modern conditions of *Sanctuary* and that his failure is the failure of traditionalism. Ruby bears strong resemblance to the suffering matron figure in the romance, to Hippolyta, the wife of the villain in *Otranto*. Loyalty and fidelity, too, are the keynotes of Ruby's character; but they are of a kind that transcends narrow moral definition. She is a whore of necessity, but she is uncorrupted; she is the foil, then, of Temple, who is not a whore but is spiritually rotten. Ruby is not, either, religious in the conventional way of the gothic matron but has her own naturalistic ethic in which love, hard work, and honesty are the main principles. Ruby is the virtuous gothic matron as she can only exist in modern society; and the differences between Ruby and the matron are the effects of, and point up, the evils of modern society. She embodies the basic virtues which neither perverted sexuality, parental failure, vicious law, nor corrupted religion can destroy.

Ruby, as teller of truth, describes exactly what Temple is with the one word *honest,* employing all the traditional ironic values of the word: "Oh, I know your sort. . . . Honest women" (p. 66). The irony of Temple Drake is that while she is placed in the role of the gothic heroine and resembles her superficially in several respects—enough to establish the identification so that her unlike qualities are the more striking—she is, beneath all, worse than whore because a selfish hypocrite who gives nothing for all she receives. The sentimental heroine was customarily chaste, knew no evil. Temple was a virgin before the crib, but only technically; she had no virginal attitudes and therefore no purity of mind as armor against evil as had the gothic damsel. The evil which overcame Temple came in part from within her. She was not raped, but seduced—perhaps merely given opportunity. Removed from her father and brothers, her inhibitors, her concupiscence, a result of the corrupting influence of modern society, begins to control her; and she submits to her latent nature as frenziedly as she ran from and toward it before. In the middle portion of the action, after the pivotal rape scene, she undergoes the typical black pall to crap table change. She changes from the gothic heroine with unconventional qualities to a creature of modernism, a nymphomaniac, with gothic overtones:

> When he [Red] touched her she sprang like a bow, hurling herself upon him, her mouth gaped and ugly . . . as she writhed her loins against him.
>   . . . With her hips grinding against him, her mouth gaping in straining protrusion, bloodless, she began to speak. "Let's hurry. Anywhere." (p. 287)

The image of Temple in the entire scene is striking in its ugliness, and the effect owes much to the blending of black pall and crap table motifs, the blending of the vampire and the vamp.

In the closing action Temple again becomes identifiable with the gothic heroine; and the change from the first of the book to the last parallels Benbow's vision in the episode involving the photograph of Little Belle (p. 200). The photograph, one of the most effective variations on the magical glass imagery which includes the pool at the beginning, the mirror in which Benbow detects Little Belle's dissimulation, the clock in the brothel, and the compact used by Temple in the end, discloses the eternal expression in pure form of the propensity to evil which characterizes Little Belle, Temple, and all women back to Eve. The image, with the precarious balancing, the shifting, the distorted but clear vision of evil, the flattening, and the vacant musing, suggests a schematization of the changes Temple undergoes in the course of the novel.

What Temple is to the heroine, Gowan Stevens is to the gothic hero; and he is an even more obvious parody on gothic convention. Among the peasants of Mississippi he by virtue of his Virginia education and alcohol is a noble youth, a gentleman. So Benbow describes him: "The Virginia gentleman one, who told us . . . about how they taught him to drink like a gentleman. Put a beetle in alcohol, and you have a scarab; put a Mississippian in alcohol, and you have a gentleman" (p. 29). Faulkner draws him with heavy sarcasm. The gothic hero too, like Theodore in *Otranto,* was often a noble youth among peasants in some disguise. Further, the hero had flawless virtue, a heart of gold, and absolute courage; and after his accidental involvement with the heroine he did all in his power, faced death bravely, to save her. Stevens' courage is drunken bellicosity, his honor a parody on the medieval conception. Instead of finding the heroine in her plight, Stevens puts her into it. He realizes that he is obligated to protect her—"'Got proteck . . .' Gowan muttered '. . . girl' 'Ginia gem . . . gemman got proteck . . .'" (p. 86). And he picks a fight with Van, gets beaten up, and passes the night in a drunken stupor. When Temple needs him most he fails her, leaves her in her plight because of his shame at not having held his liquor like a gentleman. In his farewell letter to Narcissa he discloses that he, like Theodore, is afflicted with a great soul-sadness; it is a burlesque upon even Sentimental self-pity. Stevens is the jellybean in Faulkner's general moral condemnation of modern youth.

As might be expected, Popeye is a prime exemplification of the black pall and crap table relationship in the book. He begins as the monster and ends as the criminal; he is the personification of evil, the equivalent of the gothic villain, and the gangster, a case for sociological study. In his final effect he is the personification of evil still, but of social evil, and a monster, but a Frankenstinian monster whose creator was society. He is a human, but in his mechanism and amorality hardly recognizable as human. He is a demon, but neither his origins nor powers are supernatural; and accordingly his demonical attributes are all normally modern: his glowing eye is a cigarette, the smoke that accompanies him tobacco smoke, his demoniacal aura the smell of brilliantine, his deathly power a deadly pistol.

Perhaps Popeye becomes at the last too much a case for sociological study; but Faulkner's last minute attempt to humanize, or at least explain, him—an attempt that resembles Mrs. Radcliffe's far-fetched final explanations and like them seems a greater improbability than the improbability it is meant to remove—is not a fault simply because it is a naturalistic explanation. *Sanctuary* is constructed by a naturalization process, a going from tale of terror conventionality to naturalism of a lowest depths sort; and the naturalistic explanation of Popeye could be defended on this ground. Yet the explanation is an aesthetic blemish. Through most of the book Popeye is an abstraction, an embodiment of the ultimate extensions of the modern values which Faulkner condemns; the explanation at the end particularizes him in a way that robs him of his symbolic value. Until the end the theme is objectified, embodied; in the explanation it is no longer implicit, but explicit, and the effect is that of a pointing of the moral. Seen in perspective, however, the fault is a minor one; and in spite of it Popeye, the black pall and crap table villain, is one of the striking evil characters in literature. He is the source of the evil operative in most of the plot and the antithesis of Benbow. Since his source is society, evil and society become equated in him.

It is unimportant that Popeye, like the usual gothic villain, is an Italian; it does, however, matter that he has a physical defect, as the gothic villain often had. Popeye is impotent, and since he represents death forces alone this is a symbolic defect. The pistol, the machine consistent with his mechanism, is a more appropriate phallic symbol in *Sanctuary* than it usually is in literature where it functions as such. It ejaculates death; and the irony of Popeye's circumstance is that since he wishes to possess Temple he cannot use upon her even his phallic substitute, but must bring in Red and the danger of losing her. Popeye's dilemma arises from the fact that he is not totally inhuman; for so long as he is mastered by no desire—and Popeye is an ironically ascetic figure—he is invincible. His desire for Temple, then, is an ironic twist upon the tragic flaw of the conventional amorous gothic villain, who was good except for the evil sexual obsession that brought about his downfall. Pardoxically, sexual desire, in Popeye's case, brings about the downfall of evil; it is a life force that defeats death. Popeye's is an internal collapse; he does not wish to escape death. And perhaps it is his dilemma, his awareness of his own black futility, that keeps him deathly impassive until he is mechanically flipped off, dropped by society to dangle like its puppet.

To a large degree the horror and mystery, and therefore the very Gothicism, of the gothic romance was a cumulative effect of the battery of stock props and devices included in it. Certain uses of these elements in *Sanctuary,* the dark woods, the ruin, the owl, the statue, the objects of the magical glass sort, and others, have been mentioned. To them could be added the corpses, the blood, the mysterious sounds, the tomb imagery in Temple's hallucination, the incubus-quality of her night in the room at the ruin, the suggestion of the Cannibal Bridegroom motif in her wild rides with

Popeye. These, along with conventionalities of presentational mode, plot, character types, give *Sanctuary* a markedly gothicesque quality. Yet, however gothicesque it may be, *Sanctuary* is more than the old romance and different. It is not simply a tale of terror, not simply, as Faulkner called it, the "most horrific tale" (p. vi) that he could contrive. The gothic elements contribute to the horror effect of the book, but their horror effectiveness has become lessened, staled, in time; and therefore their main effect is to highlight the greater horribleness of the modern elements with which they are linked.

In addition, and more importantly, the gothic elements are evocative of traditional values which serve as implicit standards by which the modern conditions may be judged. In a sense, then, the elements serve as stimuli of stock responses; they create pendent expectancy of conventional treatments and suggest the traditional values the conventional treatments embody. When the presentation of a character, an action, a setting suggests identification with gothic convention, that convention becomes a standard with which the presentation is implicitly compared. Should the presentation deviate from conventional expectation, the deviation is therefore distinctly noticeable. If the deviation conflicts with the moral values inherent in, associated with, the convention, it is seen as moral deviation. And insofar as this deviation is identifiable with modern conditions, modern behavior, modernism is implicitly condemned. With modification suitable to particular instances of its application, then, this is the mode of expression of outrage employed throughout the book. If the gothic qualities or the deviations are sensational, still *Sanctuary* is not spectacular in the way of the old romance, in which the spectacle was its own end. The sensationalism *Sanctuary* contains is necessary for the force of its criticism; because of the contrast process no element, black pall or crap table, however shocking, is merely sensational in its final effect.

CHAPTER 18

FAULKNER'S STORIED NOVEL

GO DOWN, MOSES AND THE TRANSLATION OF TIME

Ronald Schleifer

Go Down, Moses is a book of initiations, the depiction of Lucas' and Isaac's confrontations, with the world and with the past. Ultimately, it is an exploration of initiation in terms of possession, and to this end it creates multiple versions of initiation in the apparently discrete stories which it contains. Initiation is not usually regarded in terms of possession, yet in this book Faulkner is trying to create images of initiation within the context of a host of things—the land, the heritage, other people, and most of all the past—which are all treated as either possessing or possessed. Of course, one can possess things in the world: Molly's reed-stem pipe which she always has around the house is a good example, or Lucas' fifty-year-old hat. Yet more than with the possession of *things*, Faulkner is concerned in *Go Down, Moses* with time and events in time as objects of possession. How can an "object" of the past—old Carothers for instance, or merely his blood, his name—be an object of possession for Lucas? How can Ike's remembrance of something which happened to him forty years ago be his own?

Originally published in *Modern Fiction Studies,* Spring 1982.

Faulkner's characters' preoccupation with the past is an expression of insufficiency of strength and vision in a world where they, like all of us, are latecomers;[1] his particular problem, from *The Sound and the Fury* on, is to find an appropriate "novelistic" form which allows for the depiction, without despair, of the failure of vision overwhelmed by the past. Initiations, after all, take the *form* of short stories: they are particular, unique events that take on ongoing significance; they provide a single event with lifelong meaning. That is why, as Jerome Beaty has argued, so many stories represent initiations—which are themselves representative events.[2] Stories in Faulkner represent their own representative power; and strangely brought together in *Go Down, Moses,* they depict the limitations—the fictionality—of that power. One way the short story differs from longer fictional forms is just the sense of its momentary representational power, what Faulkner calls in a different context its "condensation" of time. It is no accident that Joyce developed his term "epiphany" in relation to the fragments of experience he depicts in *Dubliners.* And many of his stories, insofar as the epiphanies are those of his characters, take the form of successful or unsuccessful initiations. That is, the short story attempts somehow to recast its participants' relation to time, to make them, as initiations at least illusorily do, time's subject instead of its object. Thus, the characters of *Go Down, Moses* are dispossessed and in need of finding some authentic relation to their land and their past: what Isaac and Lucas seek is a sense of home in the world—a sense of possession—and this is what Faulkner's novel seeks to create. "Our pleasure in ourselves," Nietzsche has written, "tries to maintain itself by again and again changing something new *into ourselves*; that is what possession means."[3]

Possession, then, refashions the world, and to possess the past—to recreate antecedents—is the difficult task of Faulkner's characters and his novel. This can be seen in the form of the novel itself: the most striking and problematic aspect of *Go Down, Moses*—one which I have already articulated in my contradictory references to the book as a collection of stories and as a novel—is its narrative attempt to refashion fictional forms by offering what I am calling his "storied novel." By means of this "recreated" form, Faulkner refashions his world and creates the possibility of depicting the success and failure of vision facing its own origins; in one way or another, he makes room for the past amid a living present.

What the form of *Go Down, Moses* offers, that is, is a modern sense of the short story: the story that both is and is not itself in a book that attempts to *possess* storytelling. Recently, André Bleikasten has written of Faulkner's work that "one may choose to consider Faulkner's novels as discrete, autonomous units; it is no less legitimate to read them as so many fragments of a single text, each novel functioning as a supplement to the previous ones and requiring in turn the supplementarity of its followers—not to be made whole, but to allow the process of completion to continue."[4] Bleikasten's last phrase suggests the kinds of changes Faulkner's texts imply in the relation between literary form and the presentation and representation of time: by placing the "completion" implied in both initiation and the short story in the context—the "process"—of time, Faulkner reenvisions—"revises"—the story itself. The whole of this description of Faulkner's work and of its problematic vision of the relation between form and time is enacted in his late work, *Go Down, Moses.*

I

The means of initiation and possession in *Go Down, Moses*—of changing something into oneself, fashioning versions of the self—is ritual violence and ritual love, hunting, and courtship. Within the forms of ritual, the characters of Faulkner's book try to find a place for themselves in the world, sometimes adhering strictly to conventional forms and sometimes transforming them. The opening story, "Was," depicts two courtships, one that is successful within the limits of the story and one which we learn elsewhere will ultimately succeed. Both are highly conventional: Turl participates in a formalized contest, a race, to win his lady, while Buck adheres strictly to a mode of chivalry learned from Walter Scott in his contact with Sophonsiba. The contrast between these courtships is important. Turl utilizes the conventions in which he participates as a vehicle for his ends so that the race becomes an expression of his love, and the ritual seems his *own.* Buck, on the other hand, is trapped in the conventions so that the code obliges him to propose to Sophonsiba after entering her room. Buddy wins that obligation back in a card game, but eventually, Faulkner tells us outside the context of his "story," Buck is captured. Buck is trapped by the conventional forms of courtship, and rather than expressing and creating himself within and through these forms, he becomes a version of them, exhibiting and manifesting the forms as he is controlled and determined by them.

Both of these courtships are forms of initiation. Initiation—whether it be courtship, communion, or a hunt—is a formalized behavior to test the self which, if found worthy, enters into possession of some special community, the estate of adulthood. That such behavior is formalized makes the initiation as a whole an encounter with the past—the very conventions of initiation, like the fathers the initiate joins, are antecedent to him. Yet when successful, initiation refashions origins (or creates the illusion of refashioned origins) just as Turl refashions the conventions of courtship: it repeats the past in ways that make the repeated act seem original and prior to the past, that is, "Was." Initiation is a "rebirth," a repetition which, unlike our first birth, is chosen and possessed. Through it a man can own his past, his circumstances: as Isaac says in "Delta Autumn," "most men are a little better than their circumstances give them a chance to be. And I've known some that even their circumstances couldn't stop."[5] There is an irony in this because Isaac is a man bound by his circumstances and hardly better than they are, yet there is also some truth to what he says. Initiation is the act of possessing one's own past and is thus the recreation of the self; it allows a man to enter the world a little better than his circumstances, his antecedents.

In *Go Down, Moses* the rituals of courtship and the hunt are the means through which the participants confront the world in an attempt to create a place for themselves, their own estate. In a way they are complementary—they are forms of love and violence—yet, as Faulkner uses them, courtship often leads to violence and the hunt to deep reverence and love. For Isaac and Lucas, the objects of these rituals are different. The hunt for Isaac is a means of escaping time, leaving the world to enter a primeval "essential" realm of truth and freedom. It is no accident that the dream of Isaac in "Delta Autumn" is that of the hunt: as he himself says to Cass, he seeks to escape from the world to the "freedom" which is his inheritance from Sam Fathers. In the dream of "Delta Autumn,"

> suddenly he knew why he had never wanted to own any of it, arrest at least that much of what people call progress, measure his longevity at least against that much of its ultimate fate. It was because there was just exactly enough of it. He seemed to see the two of them—himself and the wilderness—as coevals, his own span as a hunter, a woodsman, not contemporary with his first breath but transmitted to him, assumed by him . . . from that old Major de Spain and that old Sam Fathers who had taught him to hunt, the two spans running out together, not toward oblivion, nothingness, but into a dimension free of both time and space . . . where the wild strong immortal game ran forever. . . .
> He had been asleep. (p. 354)

The hunt for Isaac is an initiation into a realm without time. From the very moment he shot his first deer—the timeless, forgotten moment (p. 103)—and saw the vision of its avatar walking proudly before him, Ike was attempting to live a Keatsian moment when truth and beauty coalesce.[6]

The alternative is Lucas' way, through courtship to marriage and the world. Lucas is not content merely to watch "the beginning of the end of something" as Isaac says he is (p. 226), and his dream is not that of the past but of future wealth. Even though Isaac dreams of the past, he seeks to avoid it as he does time itself; he seeks to avoid the name and the crimes he associates with his patrimony. Lucas, on the other hand, is a "fatherless" black man who must create a family to produce a past and a name for himself.

There is an emphasis on pairs that runs through the "stories" of *Go Down, Moses* and, as we shall see, structures them into something that is more than merely a collection of stories. This emphasis is based on the dichotomy between ritual hunt and ritual courtship, and it forces us to examine the actions of Lucas and Isaac in terms of one another. Lucas and Isaac are faced with the same challenge. They are the two male heirs to the McCaslin name (even though Lucas bears his mother's name), and both attempt to create themselves before the awful burden of their common past— invisible in the case of the black man—and the land on which they live. Each must change, as Nietzsche says, their common though divergent heritage into a version of himself and by so doing create a place for himself in the world.

The crisis in the life of Lucas is the moment of his encounter with Zack Edmonds after Zack had taken Lucas' black wife to his home—an encounter with someone whose name recalls "Isaac." This is the first courtship portrayed in "The Fire and the Hearth"; Lucas' original courtship of Molly occurred well before any of the times depicted in the story. At this moment, however, when Lucas faces Zack in Zack's room at dawn one morning, the preservation of his marriage becomes a test for Lucas, a challenge to his place in the world. Over the bed after Zack has goaded Lucas by saying that maybe he "aint even a woman-made McCaslin" but just a "nigger"—a "boy"—and Lucas has gained the gun, he says to Zack,

> "You thought I wouldn't didn't you?" Lucas said. "You knowed I could beat you, so you thought to beat me with old Carothers, like Cass Edmonds done Isaac: used old Carothers to make Isaac give up the land that was his because Cass Edmonds was the woman-made McCaslin, the woman-branch, the sister, and old Carothers would have told Isaac to give in to the woman-kin that couldn't fend for herself. And you

thought I'd do that too, didn't you? You thought I'd do it quick, quicker than Isaac since it aint any land I would give up. All I have to give up is McCaslin blood that aint even mine or at least aint even worth much. . . . And if this is what McCaslin blood has brought me, I don't want it neither. And if the running of it into my black blood never hurt him any more than the running of it out is going to hurt me, it wont even be old Carothers that had the most pleasure.—Or no. . . . No!" Lucas cried; "say I dont even use this first bullet at all, say I just uses the last one [to commit suicide] and beat you and old Carothers both. . . ." (pp. 56–57)

In one breath Lucas is contrasting himself with Ike, who has acted as if he weren't a McCaslin, trying to justify Ike's action in terms of blood, and finally repudiating old Carothers absolutely by offering to shed the blood which runs in his, Lucas', veins. Lucas is wrong when he says that Cass made Ike give up the land, yet when he says Ike was forced to give up the land because of the past—in the forms of ritual obligations and the felt presence of old Carothers—he approaches the truth.

Lucas repudiates the past by offering to destroy its embodiment in himself. This repudiation is the ground for initiation because the denial of the past—even one's own past—creates the space within which one can build oneself. As Lucas says, if his loss of Carothers' blood in dying hurts more than the loss of the same blood by old Carothers in engendering the black line—if Lucas' is the greater repudiation—then *his* will be the greater pleasure, because the blood will be his own. Thus, in this encounter Lucas makes himself the equal, and more than the equal, of his grandfather: it allows him to seem to possess time. In his contempt for the blood of his sire and for his own past expressed in words he thinks will be his last, he translates those things into versions of himself. Later Roth thinks in horror:

> *He's more like old Carothers than all the rest of us put together, including old Carothers. He's both heir and prototype simultaneously of all the geography and climate and biology which sired old Carothers and all the rest of us and our kind, myriad, countless, faceless, even nameless now except himself who fathered himself, intact and complete, contemptuous, as old Carothers must have been, of all blood black white yellow or red, including his own.* (p. 118)

The bullet that Lucas carries is an apt symbol of this initiation, containing, as he says, both his and Zack's lives. That content is more than the fact that they were saved from death by its misfire; it is the fact that they both stood before death and defined one another and their past in speech. Lucas' fight with Zack, their "embrace" over the bed, was an attempt by Lucas to enter—or reenter—the community of marriage. "'How to God,' he said, 'can a black man ask a white man to please not lay down with his black wife?'" (p. 59).

The emblem of the community of marriage, not only in "The Fire and the Hearth" but in "Pantaloon in Black" (in which Rider consciously imitates Lucas) and in "Go Down, Moses," is the burning hearth, first lit by Lucas on his wedding night and burning for forty-five years; lit by Rider, too; and still smoldering at the Worsham estate as the novel closes. Lucas comes furiously close to putting out his fire with a bucket of water a day before he goes to Zack to demand his wife; and after Molly's return when he waits, with thoughts of murder, for Zack to come and claim his child on the night before their encounter, he finds the flames out but the hearth still warm.

> It was hot, not scorching, searing, but possessing a slow, deep solidity of heat, a condensation of the two years during which the fire had burned constantly above it, a condensation not of fire but of time, as though not the fire's dying and not even water would cool it but only time would. (p. 51)

This heated brick of the hearth is the best image of the notion of possession which Faulkner develops in the book. Possession here means to contain, yet so inextricably that the heat seems a part or an aspect of the brick. The brick "contains" the heat, and is itself transformed by it. Yet this passage translates the content of the brick, the heat, into an image of Lucas' married state by translating it into temporal terms. And here a remarkable thing occurs: the time which "contains" the brick in its own dimension has become the brick's own possession, of which the heat, its content, is merely the outward sign. Here is "translation" with a vengeance, an act of appropriation by means of a word, a name. In a sense the brick— Lucas' brick—possessing heat, possessing time, has "fathered" itself. Heat becomes a version of time for the brick, and thus translated the brick becomes a means of possessing time, in just the way, as the novel shows, that the marriage and its namings come to possess rather than repeat time.

These are the terms in which Cass describes the acquisition and possession of the land by old Carothers,

> who saw the opportunity and took it, bought the land, took the land, got the land no matter how, held it to bequeath, no

matter how, out of the old grant, the first patent, when it was a wilderness of wild beasts and wilder men, and cleared it, translated it into something to bequeath to his children, worthy of bequeathment for his descendants' ease and security and pride and to perpetuate his name and accomplishments. (p. 256)

Fatherhood, Joyce has suggested, is a mystical estate: it is founded, as he says, on the void, on fiction. Here Faulkner uses the linguistic metaphor of "translation" to render the fiction of fatherhood. Such fatherhood is the constant preoccupation of Faulkner: when it takes place without a sense of its fiction, characters like Quentin Compson, his father, and grandfather "duplicate," as Bleikasten says, "one another; they form a timeless, frozen series of identical units, not an unfolding sequence of differential terms."[7] That is, the failure of the father/son relationship—the "freezing" of roles without the "differential" sense of their fictionality—leads to units rather than sequence, "stories" rather than a "novel." Here, then, as John Irwin notes, are two conceptions of time:

> the struggle between the father and the son inevitably turns into a dispute about the nature of time, not just because the authority of the father is based on priority in time, but because the essence of time is that in the discontinuous, passing moment it is experienced as a problem of the endless displacement of the generator by the generated, while in the continuity of the memory trace it is experienced as a problem of the endless destruction of the generated by the generator.[8]

The "continuity" of memory "generates" the story, the frozen unit, a "cold pastoral"; it never allows us to forget an unpossessed—a *dispossessing*—antecedent that leads to the destruction of the present, in which, as Henry James says, "relations stop nowhere" and one is always and only a "son," already *complete*.[9] And the "discontinuous" experience of time "generates" the endless displacements of the novel, the overwhelming of the past by the present in which the son becomes the father.[10] The *translation* of this opposition into a dialectic—into a "sequence of differential terms" (son/father, past/present) which enacts both conceptions of time—is the aim of Faulkner's fiction.

That is, Faulkner's fiction attempts to see "father" and "son" not as absolute designators, but as roles—that is, "positions"—which, like the signifiers of language, are susceptible to translations because, like language, they themselves are prior to their particular manifestations: Lucius McCaslin, Isaac McCaslin. "Really, universally," James writes,

> relations stop nowhere, and the exquisite problem of the art-
> ist is eternally but to draw, by a geometry of his own, the
> circle within which they shall happily *appear* to do so. He is in
> the perpetual predicament that the continuity of things is the
> whole matter, for him, of comedy and tragedy, that the conti-
> nuity is never, by the space of an instant or an inch, broken,
> and that to do anything at all, he has at once intensely to con-
> sult and intensely to ignore it.[11]

To consult continuity is to define oneself, as Isaac does, as simply and absolutely a son, a "unit" that is "complete"; to ignore it is to translate oneself, as Lucas does, into a father and to embed oneself in the "process" of completion.

Thus, the fiction of fatherhood, like Cass's and Faulkner's prose—like the brick's "possession" of time—seems simply a rhe-torical figure, simply a metaphorical activity, the "translation" of the land into a name. Yet the action of metaphor resists ("ignores") a prior world by giving it a human name: it changes something into ourselves. Jacques Lacan has noted that in psychoanalysis the op-erative "cure" of hysterics is not memory but verbalization: the patient "has made [memory] passage into the *verbe* or more pre-cisely into the *epos* by which he brings back into present time the origins of his own person."[12] As we shall see, listening to Sam Fa-thers, Ike fails to make such a narrated retrieval, fails to pos-sess—to author—his origins. Lucas, though, resists old McCaslin; he resists the McCaslin blood, "simply by possessing it. Instead of being at once the battleground and victim of the two strains, he was a vessel, durable, ancestryless, unconductive, in which the toxin and its anti stalemated one another, seethless, unrumored in the outside air" (p. 104). He resists his grandfather as the brick, symbol and element of the hearth, resists time, by the action of metaphors—"toxin and its anti"; "condensation of the two years the fire had burned"—the action of "translation." Translation creates versions, it marries language and language, heat and time, and, in Carothers' case, land and self. It consults and ignores continuity by measuring language not only against reality, but against another language. It creates "fiction": the fiction of fatherhood, the fiction of possession. Language joins the man to his world and creates the possibility of vision; it makes that world his own.

I've used the metaphor of marriage because marriage trans-forms antecedents and self and exhibits, at least in *Go Down, Mo-ses*, the (at least "illusory"; at least "fictional") possession of time.

Moreover, marriage enacts the kinds of naming I have been discussing. In its outward form, marriage literally changes the woman's name, and for the characters of *Go Down, Moses* its children also become versions of the parents. It is no accident that every man who is a scion of old Carothers (with the exception of Zack, who bears his own grandfather's name) bears some part of old Carothers' name. Lucas, "most like old Carothers," bore his full name, Lucius Quintus Carothers McCaslin [Beauchamp], yet being most like him he changed it:

> . . . not *Lucius Quintus* @c @c @c, but *Lucas Quintus*, not refusing to be called Lucius, because he simply eliminated that word from the name; not denying, declining the name itself, because he used three quarters of it; but simply taking the name and changing, altering it, making it no longer the white man's but his own, by himself composed, himself selfprogenitive and nominate, by himself ancestored, as, for all the ledgers recorded to the contrary, old Carothers himself was. (p. 281)

Such translation of origins, of self, is the literal and metaphoric prerequisite to marriage: as Rider says of his old life on the eve of his marriage, "Ah'm thu wid all dat" (p. 138). Like the brick from Lucas' hearth, marriage contains time by refashioning (translating) its antecedents; in *Go Down, Moses* it is a means to conquer time, as Cass says, by perpetuating a name. The courtships that create marriages in "The Fire and the Hearth," whether in violence with Zack or with the simple bag of candy for Molly at the end, initiate and effect an accommodation with the past.

This accommodation, and especially the *repeated* courtship with Molly, is central to the "accommodation" Faulkner is attempting to render between the "two conceptions of time" Irwin describes. It is central because the position of the husband joins the pride of the father with the humility of the son and in so doing brings together the past and the present, the moment and ongoing time, violence and love. At the end of "The Fire and the Hearth," Lucas gives up his hunt: "Man has got three score and ten years on this earth, the Books says. He can want a heap in that time and a heap of what he can want is due to come to him, if he just starts in soon enough. I done waited too late to start . . ." (p. 131). Lucas, husband and father, recognizes despite those roles—along with those roles—the belatedness of the son: even his name-changing cannot quite change that. Faulkner too changed his name. As Bleikasten says,

> No sooner did he begin to publish than he changed his patronym from "Falkner" to "Faulkner," thus inscribing the

difference, prophetically, in his very name. His was indeed the romantic dream of autogenesis, the fantasy of giving birth to an *oeuvre* and being reborn in it—son and father to his work. And in a sense his dream came true. Yet one might argue as well that the experience of writing dispelled the dream, for its agonies and ecstasies taught him humility rather than pride. The experience led him to the sobering realization that writing is a process of dispossession and dismemberment rather than self-creation. . . . The experience made him discover that the artist is not the father or god of his creation but only one of its conditions, and that the name with which he signs his work is a kind of imposter. . . . :"It is my ambition to be, as a private individual," Faulkner wrote, "abolished and voided from history, leaving it markless, no refuse save the printed books. . . . It is my aim . . . that the sum and history of my life, which in the same sentence is my obit and epitaph too, shall be them both: He made the books and died."[13]

Thus writing, like the naming I've been speaking of—and especially like the naming that is the aim and result of courtship—combines the self and time in just the dialectic I have suggested: writing joins the pride of the father with the humility of the son by conceiving the father impersonally as the *ritual* of language that, in its system and manifestations joins the past and the present, and *manifests* time. At the end of "The Fire and the Hearth," Lucas recognizes time and reclaims his place in the middle term as husband, which, like son and father joined—as they are joined in that other middle role of storyteller—also brings together *desire* and *due*: "He can want a heap in that time and a heap of what he can want is due to come to him, if he just starts in soon enough."

II

A second ritual form explored in *Go Down, Moses* is that of the hunt. Isaac's hunts signal his entrance into manhood, and they form his attempts to find his true estate within the world. In his sixteenth year, four years after his first kill, which in some way prepared him for this moment, Isaac witnesses the deaths of Old Ben, Lion, and Sam Fathers; five years later he "witnesses" the origin and crimes of his race in the history-ledger books. The hunt is the ritual through which Isaac approaches and attempts to appropriate the past, and hunting is performed by him on two planes— before the wilderness and before the tamed land.

Issac himself is faced with multiple versions of initiation-hunts in the wilderness. First, as a child, after learning through patience the humility and pride necessary to be a man, he kills his first buck. At eleven, he faces and gives himself up to the wilderness and to Old Ben by relinquishing his gun, compass, and watch to the wilderness ("he relinquished completely to it"—p. 208). When he is thirteen, he learns bravery from the fyce and sees Old Ben face to face (although he refuses to shoot). And at eighteen, he is brought back from a vision of deathlessness in the garden-wilderness by his "grandfather" the snake. Entering the wilderness is a method of engaging the past for Ike, yet this confrontation with the past is not as violent for him as it was for Lucas, because Ike doesn't resist as Lucas does. Ike avoids the conflict through relinquishment—so much so that Faulkner's sentence, quoted above, makes relinquish an intransitive verb—and in so doing, I believe, his initiations fail.

The first time the word *relinquish* appears in "The Bear" is significantly related to the sense of possession Faulkner develops in the novel.

> On the third day he had even found the gutted long where he had first seen the print [of Old Ben]. It was almost completely crumbled now, healing with almost unbelievable speed, a passionate and almost visible relinquishment, back into the earth from which the tree had grown. (p. 205)

It is in terms such as these that Lucas regards Ike's actions. He believes that Ike sold his birthright not for "*peace but obliteration*" (p. 109). The log and Ike relinquish themselves and become aspects of their own past: both are possessed by the past. Isaac's relinquishment consists in giving himself up to the wilderness and to the past in the person of old Sam Fathers. Sam would talk to Isaac

> about those old times and those dead and vanished men of another race . . . gradually to the boy those old times would cease to be old times and would become part of the boy's present, not only as if they had happened yesterday but as if they were still happening. . . . And more: as if some of them had not happened yet but would occur tomorrow, until at last it would seem to the boy that he himself had not come into existence yet. . . . (p. 171)

The past becomes more than the boy's present; like the earth to which the log returns, Ike's past so overwhelms him that it becomes his future, too.

Ike's constant attempt to possess the past is far different from Lucas': his returning to the wilderness is his attempt to create a world for himself that is nonexistent, to find a place for himself within a past that is gone. Every year presents a renewal of initiation for Ike because his initiation is never complete. Not only does Ike find for fifty years his constant yet annually new "home" in the big woods peopled by men long dead, each year he must face again the brooding past which the woods represents. Lucas, Roth says, is "impervious to time" (p. 116) because he was able to contain and possess time as well as space in the hearth-fire of his marriage. The hunt for Isaac, on the other hand, is his attempt to create a community with his fathers that ends with Isaac's relinquishment of himself to his fathers. Isaac is completely dominated by the past: his initiations fail because he translates himself into something other than himself and becomes a version of the past. The image of the receding woods "contains" time just as Lucas' brick "contains" time, yet Ike does not possess the woods literally or symbolically as Lucas possesses the brick. Rather, it and the past it represents are the space for his action: he is "contained"—possessed—by the woods.[14]

Isaac's second hunt is a more literal engagement with the past. Like Lucas, Isaac faces the domination of Carothers in his hunt through the "wilderness" past of the history of the family. Under his eyes those books—like the stories of Sam Fathers—take "substance and even a sort of shadowy life with their passions and complexities too as page followed page" (p. 265). These two encounters with the past, in the wilderness and in the books, contrapuntally come together to make Isaac what he is. In his dialogue with Cass on his twenty-first birthday, both contribute to his decision to relinquish his patrimony, and together they reveal the extent of his initiations.

Section Four of "The Bear" is probably the climax of the book as a whole. All the stories which preceded and follow it—with the possible exception of "Go Down, Moses"—are suggested and "contained" within its moment. Both "Was" and the self-named Lucas are in the ledger. Ike's marriage and his wife's demands are there, threatening and precipitating divorce and separation just as Molly and Rider's wife Mannie did. "Delta Autumn" is foreshadowed there in the person of the fatherless old Ike, uncle to half a county. More terribly, the crime of Carothers McCaslin, which is discovered in Section Four, is repeated by Isaac McCaslin in "Delta Autumn" when he lovelessly sends Roth's mistress away as old Carothers had sent his mistress and daughter away, with money that was easier and cheaper than saying *My son to a nigger*" (p. 269). Section Four is very difficult. Its single quotation marks and the breadth of its time indicate that somehow its discourse is related: as Faulkner said, it is remembered by Ike,[15] a memory he constantly returns to, just as he annually returns to the woods.

The discourse with Cass is the crisis in Isaac's life, and in that dialogue Ike attempts to explain himself just as Lucas explained himself to his cousin, Zack.

> Let me talk now. I'm trying to explain to the head of my family something which I have got to do which I don't quite understand myself, not in justification of it but to explain it if I can. I could say I don't know why I must do it but that I do know I have got to because I have got myself to have to live with for the rest of my life and all I want is peace to do it in. . . . (p. 288)

Further on in the conversation, a few pages later, Ike says the Negroes will endure, outlast them. Again, Ike is trying to understand and explain himself as far as he can.

> 'They will outlast us because they are—' it was not a pause, barely a falter even, possibly appreciable only to himself, as if he couldn't speak even to McCaslin, even to explain his repudiation, that which to him too, even in the act of escaping (and maybe this was the reality and the truth of his need to escape) was heresy: so that even in escaping he was taking with him more of that evil and unregenerate old man who could summon, because she was his property, a human being because she was old enough and female, to his widower's house and get a child on her and then dismiss her because she was of an inferior race, and then bequeath a thousand dollars to the infant because he would be dead then and wouldn't have to pay it, than even he had feared. (p. 294)

Ike falters when he is about to say that Negroes will endure because they are better, because they are free. Ike's faltering is the refusal of language, the refusal of translation: unlike Lucas, at the moment of crisis he cannot speak.

Most of all Isaac seeks freedom. He seeks to be free from the possession of the evil past, of that old man. Implicit in his decision to relinquish the land is the fact that the land did belong to old Carothers. The land was his, "translated" by him and thereby cursed, "not only the blood, but the name too; not only its color but its designation" (pp. 298–99). Yet Isaac is completely possessed by old Carothers, and even in escaping he is destined to repeat his crime just as he repeats the "cursed" name: he is another version of Carothers. Rather than resisting ("repudiating") the past, he relinquishes the land and not only allows the same crime to be repeated by Roth, he concurs in that act. Lucas is more like Carothers than Carothers himself because he has appropriated his past—old Carothers—to make himself. This is the freedom that Ike seeks, the freedom that he lacks.

"Sam Fathers set me free," Isaac explains (p. 300), yet his freedom is the same as that of Sophonsiba and her black husband, ineffectually reading through lensless glasses, who also went to the head of the family, Cass, not to ask but to inform, to explain himself. "'Fonsiba. Are you all right?'" asked Isaac. "'I'm free,' she said" (p. 280). Fonsiba is terribly tied to the past, to her color, and to the crimes of our nation, and her pathetic response is an apt comment on Ike's assertion. Ike's assertion that he is free is simply sophistry which he doesn't recognize. Instead of making his name his own as Lucas did, of repudiating the past, and of leaving old Carothers' house—his unfinished "monument"—to his black children and building his own home as Buck and Buddy did, Isaac tries to escape. In so doing his inheritance becomes the debts of and to the past, a burlap sack whose tin contains its own history in discrete "units" of I.O.U.s. Late in life Isaac thinks, "No wonder the ruined woods I used to know dont cry for retribution! he thought: The people who have destroyed it will accomplish its revenge" (p. 364). His grandfather destroyed it, and he does, too, by not acting as he could have, by not translating the land into something to bequeath as his grandfather had done. To escape his grandfather he relinquished the land and yet enacted again his crime. That was the revenge.

Ike's attempt to explain himself is another form of initiation. It is his attempt to translate the past—the land—into himself through confession. He falters and fails because he tries to possess the past by living in it, and ironically his repudiation is, in fact, a relinquishment: he tries to repudiate his blood by imagining "that he himself had not come into existence yet, that none of his race . . . had come here yet" (p. 171). The memory of the dialogue with Cass related in Section Four thus becomes a symbol and momento of an "initiation" that he carries with him as Lucas carries the bullet. Yet because that memory contains something that Isaac still strives for, something that isn't acknowledged and repudiated as past, it possesses and directs his life rather than being his own.

That thing that dominates the whole dialogue with Cass, significantly never spoken in their conversation, is the ultimate and timeless moment of the hunt when Ben and Lion and Boon appeared to be "almost" statuary and Sam Fathers began to die. This moment controls Ike's life just as his blood controls his life. At that moment, just as at the moment three years earlier when he and Sam refused to shoot Old Ben when the fyce bayed him, Ike refuses to shoot and fails as a hunter. His engagement with the past results in the victory of the past: by not shooting he repeats his father's, Sam Fathers', action in an attempt to join a community which is already dead. His "faltering" at the hunt is the same as his faltering in his dialogue with Cass: he is acting out a version of the past.

This is why the ritual of hunting for Ike is ultimately a dream, and his initiation unsubstantial. After Ike fails to shoot Ben when the fyce attacked him, Cass asks why and then reads "Ode to a Grecian Urn" to him. Then Ike thinks,

> *Somehow it had seemed simpler than that, simpler than somebody talking in a book about a young man and a girl he would never need to grieve over because he could never approach any nearer and would never have to get any further away. He had heard about an old bear and finally got big enough to hunt it and he hunted it four years and at last met it with a gun in his hands and didn't shoot . . . and Sam Fathers could have shot at any time during the interminable minute while Old Ben stood on his hind legs over them. . . .* (p. 297)

Isaac didn't want to grieve, he didn't want to accept the past, yet could not "ignore" it, and, therefore, strove throughout his life to make it present, not through possession and transformation, but through relinquishment and dream. Even when he has a chance to possess and to redeem the past—in another version of initiation—he says to Roth's mistress, "*Maybe in a thousand or two thousand years in America*, he thought. *But not now! Not now!* He cried, . . . 'You're a nigger!'" (p. 361). Faced with the present, again he escapes into— and is possessed by—the past.

III

Violence and love define, in large part, the function of time in Faulkner's novel. Love, as we have seen, is a function of ongoing time—of tradition, of names, of bequeathment—the hearth that continuously burns. Violence, on the other hand, is momentary: time seems to stop or at least seems momentarily captured, in Lucas' bullet as much as in Ike's memory. Successful initiation combines love and violence in such a way that they seem versions or translations of one another in which present and past are joined: initiation joins what Irwin calls "the discontinuous, passing moment" and "the continuity of the memory trace." As with Carothers' taking the land "no matter how" to bequeath it or Lucas' "pleasure" in spilling his blood to make it his own, possession requires and combines both reverence and violation.

The structure of *Go Down, Moses* reflects the novel's preoccupation with such translations by offering somewhat discrete stories that repeat versions of initiation in terms of ritual violence and love. The novel then seemingly "translates" these stories into one another, complementing violence and love within each and within the novel as a whole. The book divides itself into two thematically coherent sections. The first three stories are primarily concerned with the love ritual of courtship performed against a background of race relations, the violence of black and white brothers. Here, however, even the violence is bound up with courtship: Turl becomes human "game" in the hunt to get his wife; Lucas struggles with Zack to maintain his marriage, and later struggles with Molly and courts her once again with a bag of candy; and Rider kills Birdsong to express his grief at the loss of his marriage. The next three stories, on the other hand, are primarily concerned with the violence ritual of the hunt performed before the background of kin relations, the love between fathers and sons. Here, however, the love is bound up with the hunt: Ike and Fathers are juxtaposed before the wilderness; Ike and Cass are juxtaposed before the tame land (and the hunt through the ledgers); and finally, Roth and Ike are juxtaposed before the two earlier relationships, both wilderness and inheritance.

The hunts in the courtship stories—Buck and Buddy's hunt for Turl, Lucas' hunt for gold, Rider's attempt to kill his grief—are readily apparent, and they demonstrate the necessity of the dialectic integration of love and violence—of present and past—to create a place for oneself. More important, however, is the element of courtship in Ike's stories of hunting, because the recurrent metaphoric failure of marriage in these stories helps to emphasize Ike's failure to attain adulthood. In "The Old People" Ike's "courtship" with the wilderness is his courtship by Sam Fathers and his forgotten tongue, and "Delta Autumn" hinges on the hunt for the "doe," Roth's divorce from his cousin-mistress. Most importantly, however, the failure of Ike's initiation is explored in "The Bear" in terms of marriage itself. Not only do the past and the hunt come between Ike and his wife (Lucas gives up his hunt for buried treasure for the sake of his wife), but Ike's attempt to avoid the grief and responsibility of his inheritance also destroys the possible son who would have fulfilled their marriage. Thus Ike sees "himself and his wife juxtaposed in their turn against that same land, that same wrong and shame from whose regret and grief he would at least save and free his son

and, saving and freeing his son, lost him" (p. 351). Ike refuses responsibility for the sake of a dead past and fails to perpetuate his
name. He remains throughout his life fatherless, seeking to find
that father he never had; and throughout his life he remains uncle
to half a county but father to no one.

The last and title story of the book, "Go Down, Moses," in
some way stands outside the framework I have been constructing
in terms of love and violence, the initiations of courtship and the
hunt. Nevertheless, "Go Down, Moses" does present a version of
initiation and links it in a vital way to ritual commemoration. Samuel Beauchamp returns home to Jefferson and is finally admitted
into society—finally finds a place for himself—but only through
death. Here is the ritual of funeral, yet it is merely a form without
widespread grief. Even the grief Molly feels is not so much directed
at Sam's death as at his exclusion, something which the funeral
remedies.

More important, however, is Molly's participation in the ritual,
for it points out Lucas' success and Ike's failure. In Molly's reaction
to the death of her grandson is another manner of relation to the
past and discovery of the self that I have been discussing under the
term initiation. In response to Sam's death, Molly chants an elegy—
"Go Down, Moses." Elegy is another form of ritual which allows for
the possession of the past; it is the translation of a past life into a
version of one's own. It is literally a translation, another naming
that articulates past and present together. When Molly chants of
Benjamin and Pharaoh she is really speaking of her lost grandson
Samuel. Yet her sorrow and her elegy find expression because they
are aspects and responses to her own life; in a way Molly's grief is
for herself, for her years of bondage and sorrow. Molly translates
her grandson's life into a version of her own, and her grief is real.
Molly's chant is her recognition and her possession in speech of the
past.

Yet, in another way, her grief is also for those seemingly more
perfect days with which the book opened. This too is a suitable form
of elegy, and because commemoration, like initiation, is a manner
of appropriating the past and translating it into the present, this
chant, this story, is an appropriate way of ending this book. Moreover, this multileveled title—song, story, novel—brings to attention
a last version of initiation found in the language of *Go Down, Moses*
itself. The book constitutes an initiation for the reader using these
same elements of violence and love so that at once he possesses
and is possessed by the volume he reads. To this end Faulkner manipulates time, point of view, and even semantics throughout his
work to arrest the reader and call attention to the language itself.

For my purposes, however, it is most significant to examine how Faulkner strives to possess the reader and at the same time to relinquish his language to the reader. In *Go Down, Moses* Faulkner is dealing with the past—that of his characters and his readers—and the book creates two versions of the past, timeless moments and elegy, corresponding to its self-contradictory form as a collection of stories and a novel; in this way it creates its own ambiguous version of novelistic form. Both versions engage the reader, indeed, depend on him, and it is this dual engagement which constitutes a last form of initiation.

The characteristic unit of speech in Faulkner is the sentence, and throughout *Go Down, Moses*, within the sentence, Faulkner brings the past and the present together to play off one another, to be translated into one another. After Ike's first kill he sees, with Sam, a vision of a buck who watches them and then continues its course before them.

> It did not even alter its course, not fleeing, not even running, just moving with that winged and effortless ease with which deer move, passing within twenty feet of them, its head high and the eye not proud and not haughty but just full and wide and unafraid, and Sam standing beside the boy now, his right arm raised at full length, palm-outward, speaking in that tongue which the boy had learned from listening to him and Joe Baker in the blacksmith shop, while up the ridge Walter Ewell's horn was still blowing them in to a dead buck.
> "Oleh, Chief," Sam said, "Grandfather." (p. 184)

In this passage Faulkner creates a sense of the timeless past which so seduced Ike, yet he does so with himself in full possession of time. This sentence lists present participles incessantly and hypnotically until the image that it creates seems to move along. Alliteration contributes to this movement, and together these carry the reader to the end of the sentence which, because it is built merely upon participles, actually doesn't take the reader anywhere. In fact, this is hardly a conventional sentence at all. Rather, Faulkner creates his own version of a sentence, accumulating phrases on the narrow base of the verb *does not alter* and linking them on the principle of contiguity in space and time. The image this sentence creates seems to move, yet the whole is a static image of the past, composed into a picture, a remembered moment, and based on a negated verb. In this way Faulkner violently translates a traditional form into his own: like Turl, he makes the form an expression of himself.

Faulkner creates the buck largely out of what it is not. Negative attributes clear a space for the buck and create an image

which is suggestive and tautological rather than definite: "not fleeing, not even running, just moving with that winged and effortless
ease with which deer move." In the terms that I have been devel-
oping, the negatives constitute the repudiation, the violence which
precedes initiation. They deny past conceptions of deer—fleeing,
running—and then translate those conceptions into a new image
of a deer—Faulkner's buck.

From the buck the sentence expands to an image of Sam
(standing next to the boy who has entered the dying community)
and, to explain this, to the past: to the primeval past of the strange
and dying tongue, and then to the "past" of the story, Joe Baker
(whose name this sentence translates, however, from the "Jo-
baker" of the story). The sentence, again explaining itself, also expands to the future: both the "future" of the story in Walter Ewell's
slain buck and, more importantly, the future six years later when
Issac would say to the snake, "speaking the old tongue which Sam
had spoken that day without premeditation either: 'Chief,' he said:
'Grandfather'" (p. 330). These expansions are explanations, making meaningful rather than changing the referents, filling with all
time, as it were, this moment of Sam Fathers' invocation. Like Lucas' brick, this sentence contains time. Its movement within its own
static form and its condensation of time within that form overwhelm
and engulf the reader, draw him in, in an almost esthetic wonder,
until he is caught by the past which seems so timeless: it is as if its
silent form teases us out of thought.

Yet, despite these extraordinary moments, Go Down, Moses
creates and gives us the past, as elegy does, to make our own. The
picture Faulkner draws here of deer and Indian is not timeless even
if it is an image and a vision. It is part of Isaac's past, his twelfth
year, which is repeated in his eighteenth year—and his sixteenth
year, too—and its "content" of time creates a sense of the past that
is only lost when it is taken to be autonomous and timeless, as
Isaac takes it to be: it is lost to the short story. The past is made
present in grief. It is made present—and transformed into commemoration and elegy—when it is put into the context of time and
change, the context of a tongue that will die (or has already died)
and evil that Isaac must encounter (or has already encountered).
This sentence's movement renders a moment, yet that moment is
also within time itself: it exists within a novel. Here, then, is the
dialectic of the discrete "units" of short stories and the continuity
of a novel upon which Go Down, Moses is based. The two versions
of time in this sentence—and the two versions of this incident itself, both a story and a chapter—create an image of a past that is
irrevocably past, yet the confrontation and engagement with which

in the continuing present allow Lucas or Molly or Isaac to name—to speak, to narrate—himself or herself. Isaac didn't want to grieve, so he tried to escape from time into the timeless past; he faltered, relinquished himself, and was possessed by the past. Yet Lucas—and Faulkner, too, in his "novel"—can face the past, grieve over and repudiate it, and in so doing re-form it into a storied novel, a translation of himself.

Notes

1. For a fine articulation of this theme in Faulkner, see John Irwin, *Doubling and Incest/Repetition and Revenge* (Baltimore, MD: Johns Hopkins University Press, 1975) and the essays in *The Fictional Father: Lancanian Readings of the Text*, ed. Robert Con Davis (Amherst: University of Massachusetts Press, 1981).

2. See *The Norton Introduction to Literature: Fiction* (New York: Norton, 1973), p. xxiii, and also the arrangement of stories in the book.

3. *The Gay Science*, trans. Walter Kaufman (New York: Vintage, 1974), p. 88.

4. "Fathers in Faulkner," in *The Fictional Father*, p. 137.

5. *Go Down, Moses* (New York: Random House, 1942), p. 345. All subsequent citations are from this edition and will be identified parenthetically within the text.

6. Jacques Derrida calls a dream such as this a dream of the impossible time of pure presence "before" the "linguistic catastrophe," "before" speech: a time out of time. The fact that Isaac dreams but cannot effectively speak—to tell stories and to define himself against the family, traditions, and language that he is born into—marks, as we shall see, the limit of his "initiation." See *Of Grammatology*, trans. G. C. Spivak (Baltimore, MD: The Johns Hopkins University Press, 1976), pp. 279–80 & passim.

7. "Fathers in Faulkner," p. 128. Such "duplication" denies relationship: as Bleikasten says a few pages later, "To Sutpen fatherhood and sonship are in fact only complementary modes of his ideal self. . . . So just as he denied his father, he must deny his sons, for if he acknowledged them as sons he would have to abide by the law of patrilineal succession and envision the transmission of his power to his descendants" (p. 140). Thus, ultimately, it denies the *process* of time.

8. *Doubling and Incest,* pp. 108–9.

9. See R. C. Davis, "The Discourse of Jacques Lacan," in *The Fictional Father*, p. 189.

10. For Wordsworth's struggle with these conceptions of time and the "imaginative" dialectic between them, see my "Wordsworth's Yarrow and the Poetics of Repetition," *Modern Language Quarterly*, 33 (1977), 348–66.

11. *The Art of the Novel*, ed. R. P. Blackmur (New York: Scribner's, 1934), p. 5.

12. *The Language of the Self*, trans. Anthony Wilden (Baltimore, MD: The Johns Hopkins University Press, 1968), p. 17.

13. "Fathers in Faulkner," pp. 145–46.

14. The difference is that between *repudiation* and *relinquishment.* The first, Lucas' way, is a form of *repression*: as Regis Durand says, "the essential process behind the so-called paternal metaphor . . . is a repressive gesture, the constitutive repression: a passage from a world of pure difference and meaningless oscillation to an *anchoring*, a stabilization through some key symbols. The paternal metaphor, when it is successful, casts a kind of 'signifying mesh' or network and acts as a ballast. When it is *not* completely successful, as in the case of psychotic subjects, what has not been properly repressed and made symbolic becomes forecluded (*Verwerfen*) and threatens to return in the real as hallucination. The whole symbolic process is affected by the failure of the paternal metaphor (one of the consequences being that it becomes impossible to distinguish between the symbol and the thing symbolized, word and thing presentation, for instance)" ("'The Captive King': The Absent Father in Melville's Text," in *The Fictional Father*, pp. 50–51). *Repudiation* "ignores" continuity and is a "proper" repression that allows the subject to possess the estate of adulthood; *relinquishment* leaves the subject in "a world of pure difference and meaningless oscillation" and results, as we shall see, in the repetition of what Bleikasten calls "a timeless frozen series of identical units" ("Fathers in Faulkner," p. 139).

15. *Faulkner in the University*, ed. Frederick L. Gwynn and Joseph Blotner (New York: Vintage, 1965), pp. 3–4.

CHAPTER 19

FROM PLACE TO PLACE IN *THE SOUND AND THE FURY*
THE SYNTAX OF INTERROGATION

Cheryl Lester

I

Because the individual sections of *The Sound and the Fury* are not intelligible in themselves, readings of this novel depend on the complex interplay between the sections. For this reason, the analytical approach generally brought to bear on this novel can analyze, in its most successful application, only the critical or fictional synthesis into which its individual sections have been read. Yet studies of *The Sound and the Fury* that proceed from section to section, like those of Olga Vickery or Wolfgang Iser, or that concentrate on one section alone, like that of George Stewart and Joseph Backus, give the mistaken impression that the significance of the novel is the sum of four independently meaningful parts, individually calculated and added up.

Analyses of *The Sound and the Fury* generally refer to the relationship among the sections only in order to characterize the

Originally published in *Modern Fiction Studies,* Summer 1988.

development of the novel as a whole. The novel is most often said to shift, particularly with the fourth section, from obscurity to clarity, from privacy to universality, or from subjectivity to objectivity. Describing this development, André Bleikasten writes, "No longer constrained to adopt the narrowly limited viewpoint of an idiot or the distorted vision of a neurotic, we can at last stand back and take in the whole scene" (176); Wolfgang Iser holds that "the identical world of the Compson brothers [is released] from the first-person point of view" (151); Olga Vickery argues that the novel "emerge[s] from the closed world of the Compson Mile into the public world as represented by Jefferson" (46); and Cleanth Brooks, in a more florid vein, claims that we "break into the sunlight of the world—an objective world. . . . Here the solipsism of the private world is expanded into something communal" (25). Yet these assumptions about liberation and enlightenment, about the novel's progress from obscurity to clarity, from privacy to publicity, or from subjectivity to objectivity are assumptions less about the novel than about the nature of signification in general.

Signification itself is at stake in the development of *The Sound and the Fury*, as Michael Millgate has recognized. He notes that the final section "forces us to view some aspects of the earlier sections in a radically different way" and that "meaning proves on closer inspection to dissolve into uncertainty and paradox" (Millgate 167–71). The development of the novel, or, in other words, the interplay among its parts, is crucial, then, because it represents the level of the text on which meaning at once emerges and dissolves. To address this level of the novel is to confront the uncertainty and paradox of one's own claims about its meaning.

The sort of analysis that has dominated the criticism of this novel confines itself to the semantic level of the text. The syntax of the novel is either condemned as fragmentary and hence flawed or salvaged in a proposition concerning the novel's "development." Yet the syntactic level of the text is not easily extricated from the meaningful, semantic level. In predominantly semantic readings, the peculiar disposition or arrangement of the novel returns, like the repressed, as evidence of an evasion.

By articulating a reading according to the novel's most apparent itinerary or architecture, one may appear to have left the stubbornly divided form of the work pure and intact. Yet the manifest allegiance of section-by-section analyses to the objective form of the work becomes a meaningless and empty gesture, which merely uses form as a ready-made, pigeonholed container for self-presentation. Such presentations fail to acknowledge the fact that the significance they attribute to each ostensibly independent section comes belatedly and from without, that the sections in themselves are largely unintelligible, and that what appears to ameliorate this discomfiting absence of meaning is the play of relations among the individual sections. To represent the dynamics of this novel as a genetic development is not only to reduce a structure productive of countless possible meanings to one decisive meaning and form; it is also to deny the divagations, the *sine qua non*, of reading *The Sound and the Fury*.

How have the sections of the novel been traditionally marked off from and related to one another? Readers mark the four original sections of the novel off from one another chronologically, according to the date that entitles each part, and perspectivally, according to each narrator. The first section of the original text is thus taken to represent the point of view of Benjy and to take place on April 7, 1928; the next section, the point of view of Quentin on June 2, 1910; and the next, that of Jason on April 6, 1928. The last section is understood to take place on April 8, 1928, but the character of its narrator is not explicit. This narrator has generally been characterized as omniscient, neutral, objective, or, at the very least, less subjective, as Margaret Blanchard points out, before arguing that the narrator of the fourth section is a figure for an ideal or, in other words, acutely perceptive reader (555, 557). This figure must be compared, at any rate, with the narrator of the appendix, "a sort of bloodless bibliophile . . . [who] knew only what the town could have told him," as Faulkner suggested (Cowley 44). What kind of reader is this bibliophile, who is able to cover, as well as cover up, more than two centuries' time?[1]

Let us first examine the identification of the sections with the perspectives or points of view of their narrators, by means of which readers evade numerous crises of uncertainty. Many readers presume that although on the one hand the multiplication of points of view makes it impossible to see the novel as a whole from any single point of view, the singular perspective of each section, on the other hand, offers the view of a single unified whole. Because each section represents a different point of view, it is hastily reasoned that each of these sections must constitute a unity of perspective. That the first three sections are cast as soliloquies encourages readers to identify these sections with the subject, particularly with consciousness and with all that has been traditionally thought under its name, that is to say, identity, presence, unity, autonomy, and so on. Because the identification of the first three sections with the characters that narrate them is endemic to the criticism of this novel, I cannot exhaustively describe but rather can illustrate the extent of its consequences.

In a study noted for its attention to the formal structures of this novel, Irena Kaluza states that her aim is to "describe the linguistic structures of *The Sound and the Fury* in formal categories, that is, . . . objectively, and then to find out whether they form a meaningful artistic system in the novel" (8). Kaluza, however, restricts her study of linguistic structures to those that represent "stream-of-consciousness" or, in other words, "mental processes" (8), because, as she notes, her reading has been "moulded" by Vickery, "who treats the four-part structure of the novel as representative of four ways of perceiving experience, dramatizing the progression from a private to a public world" (41). Having decided that the linguistic structures under study correspond to private "ways of perceiving experience," Kaluza must first of all entirely exclude the fourth section and the appendix from consideration. But then, too, she must exclude from the first three sections whatever material cannot be construed as a way of "perceiving experience." Thus, based on the argument that they are "traditional narrative devices" or "directly quoted utterances" (44), as opposed to representations of Benjy's stream of consciousness, Kaluza omits from her study, according to her own calculation, seventy-seven percent of the sentences in the first section. Following the same logic, she excludes from her study of the second and third sections, respectively, "all sentences between two quotation marks . . . as well as the accompanying narrative routine units of the 'he-said' type" and "all direct utterances contained between two quotation marks" (61, 92).

Kaluza's criterion for separating each narrator's "own" language from "mere" citation or from what she considers a narrative "routine" or "device" underlines the problem raised by the application of such broad and unthought formalistic categories to these sections. As her systematic exclusions point out, the first three sections do not simply or even primarily represent single voices, perceptions of experience, or perspectives.

If such readings reduce the differences of which the first three sections are composed to representations of each narrator as a consciousness, they quickly reach their limits. Whereas systematic omissions make it possible to characterize these sections as "interior monologues," as unities in the form of human subjects, the critic cannot turn to the subject, to character, or to consciousness as a way of accounting for the manners in which the monologues interrelate. Because the monologues are not communicated but uttered in the silence of mental soliloquy, even a model of intersubjectivity is unable to explain what motivates the interaction of the first three sections of the novel. Criticism that refashions the text in the mold of the subject is unable to *account* for these relations; nevertheless, it employs them in the form of an ideal-ized network of intersubjective relations upon which, in lieu of the literary work, it passes judgment.

Interpretations that identify the first three sections with their narrators are embarrassed by the fourth section of the novel. Un-like the narrators of the "monologues," who are also characters in the novel, the shadowy, anonymous narrator of the fourth section, rather like the narrator of the appendix, hovers in a space and time, that is, in a "world" that the novel does not represent. This embarrassment is turned to advantage when critics argue that the lofty perspective of this otherworldly narrator sees beyond the lim-ited perspectives represented in the monologues and in this man-ner bridges or relates the monologues to one another. As such a medium of totalization and dissolution, the narrative of the fourth section is typically described as broader in scope, explanatory, and clarifying.[2] In other words, although the fourth section frustrates the totalization of the sections on the grounds of narrative per-spective, it is recuperated as the perspective that unites all singu-lar perspectives, dissolving their differences in a higher totality.

Although the novel puts in play the conservative intentions of point of view (self-presence, continuity, unity, autonomy, exclusion of difference, purity, and so on), as well as those of genealogy (lin-eage, breeding, continuity, transmission of value, purity, exclusion of difference, and such), it challenges rather than confirms their status. Rather than affirming that such constructs can unite what is disparate, the fourth section separates itself off from the other sec-tions of the novel and lends them character through its difference. The appendix, as a genealogical narrative written from a "biblio-philic" point of view, draws out the character of the other sections of the novel by pointing out their difference from and incommensura-bility with simple genealogy.[3]

Chronology, as I have mentioned, is also invoked to identify and order the sections. The sections are identified with the dates that serve as their titles and are thus understood to take place not in the order they are given but in the sequence their titles can be said to signify: accordingly, the second section ("JUNE SECOND 1910") would come "first," the third section ("APRIL SIXTH 1928") would come "second," the first section ("APRIL SEVENTH, 1928") would come "third," and the fourth section ("APRIL EIGHTH 1928") would remain "fourth" and last. What disturbs the simple reshuffling of the sections is that their given order *signifies*, if only to signify their difference from chronological order.

The four original sections seem to offer little resistance to such reordering, but the appendix, which is titled "Appendix. Compson 1699–1945," poses a peculiar problem. The dates that appear in the title of the appendix, "1699–1945," which Faulkner wanted typeset like the birth and death dates on a tombstone, include and exceed the time identified with the original sections of the novel. By giving this fifth section a three-part title—at once appendix, patronym, and time span—and by wishing to place the appendix not at the end of the novel but at its beginning, Faulkner draws out many of the contradictions involved in the relationship between a title and the text it entitles. With the appendix, it is difficult to assert that the title establishes the topic and time of the section it entitles. Although the title of the appendix is related to the titles of the other four sections, it does not function according to the same logic. If the punctual dates of the original sections can be scrambled and restored to chronological order, where is one to locate a time span that engulfs that order? On the basis of the dates in its title, the question of whether to place the appendix first or last is a false question, because neither possibility can reconcile a span of time with a series of points in time. Because it has no place in the order the first four sections can be understood to signify, the appendix is rarely treated as a section in itself but is discussed here and there, with reservations about its status, to bolster particular interpretations of character or chronological order. But the appendix simply draws out what the original sections of the novel already suggest: that is, that this novel opposes itself to the conventional manners in which temporal difference is signified. To examine the novel from the perspective of a temporal order is to relinquish the radical form in which it questions the temporality no less than the spatiality of signification.

A sequential rearrangement of the sections is unable to recognize the specific differences between the sections, even in terms of temporality alone. A simple enumeration of the sections in their "proper"—chronological—order obscures the basic question of why Faulkner eschewed such an order, as well as a variety of questions raised by the sections' chronological determinations. Why, for example, is the "time" between the sections that are chronologically first and second (June 2, 1910 and April 6, 1928) so much greater than that which separates the others (April 6, 7, and 8)? A chronological reading of the sections has difficulty maintaining the specific differences between such temporal leaps, and it blurs the fact that the temporal differences between the chronologically consecutive sections cannot be expressed as a uniform and formalistic interval. In the order Faulkner gives them, the first section (April 7) is one day after the third (April 6), and the third section (April 6) is two days before the fourth (April 8). But relations of anteriority and posteriority in fact fail to do justice to these interrelations, for each section, taken on its own terms, stakes an equal claim on the present and rearranges the others accordingly. From the perspective of the first section, the third section is the day before; but from the perspective of the third section, the first section is the day after. The fact that the sections' titles may refer to more than one chronological time and to more than one kind of time—to a span of time, to a time before or after, to a first or last time, to a consecrated or a forgotten time—may explain why the sections are most commonly referred to in terms of proper names: as the Benjy section, the Quentin section, the Jason section, and (alas) the fourth section.

Only when the various perspectives raised by the section titles are eliminated in favor of their referral, above all, to the sections "themselves" and when all the sections are therefore understood to partake in the single, common element of chronological time do the section titles offer the promise of a medium in which all the individual sections might be united. Time answers to the hope for a form, not quite discovered in consciousness or point of view, that would bring all the sections together in a single, homogeneous medium. Yet such a hope can be fulfilled only by subordinating the novel's complex textualization of time to some unthought notion of Time. In *The Sound and the Fury*, the essence of time, if that is to be the name for the medium of provisional totality, is nothing simply temporal.

Let us examine the section titles one last time, with reference to the order in which they are given. The only section titles that can be stretched in place to represent a forward-moving, linear sequence or continuum are the first (April 7) and fourth (April 8). Yet, this sequence is interrupted by what stands in the space of its unthinkable middle, a middle or medium without which it could not be a sequence. What comes to light in this space is curiously incompatible with its apparently formal logic, precisely because in this middle semantics and syntax collide. What appears in the middle of this sequence is not the syntactic middle of what its semantic order suggests; indeed, what could or should there be between the 7th and the 8th? Conversely, since April 6th appears between the 7th and the 8th, what appears in the middle of these two dates no longer functions as a satisfactory semantic middle either, as it would if it appeared, say, between the 5th and the 7th. In sum, the construction of a semantic unity invariably opens a middle that exceeds that unity. Semantic unities are thus inhabited and divided by a space that they can neither regulate nor do without. This is the sort of "medium" in whose unruly space and time *The Sound and the Fury* lets loose its significations.

Because they do not simply add up, line up, or cancel each other out but articulate their differences, the section titles cannot serve to rearrange the novel in the temporal order they at once suggest and disrupt. Like Luster and Benjy, who at the end of the novel double back in disruption around the statue of a Confederate soldier, a monument to a lost cause, the section titles circle around time, which Jason *père* refers to as "the mausoleum of all hope and desire" (93). Like "point of view," which hovers like a succubus over the voices through which this novel speaks, chronology is in no position to account for the fury of referrals or relays in which it participates and which gives the novel over to the apocryphal stories they lead us to construct. Measurements such as point of view and chronology, failing to account for the relays of which they too are made, can only situate the novel with respect to the very banalities from which it escapes.

II

One instance of the sort of illegibility for which *The Sound and the Fury* is famous occurs toward the end of the first section, when Benjy turns his gaze upon himself. What Benjy gazes upon when he looks at himself is unclear: "*I got undressed,*" we read, "*and I looked at myself, and I began to cry.*" The coincidence of this troubled reaction with Benjy's sight of himself is immediately remarked by Luster: "*Hush, Luster said. Looking for them aint going to do no good. They're gone*" (90). The significance of Luster's remark is obscure. What, the curious reader must ask, or who, is it useless to look for? Who or what is gone? For the moment, at any rate, it does the reader as little good to ask who or what "they" are as it does Benjy to look for "them."

We can better understand if not explain the puzzles of this passage by pointing out that the antecedent of the objective and subjective pronouns "them" and "they" has been withheld. Certainly, withheld antecedents are familiar to readers of Faulkner, especially to those of us who continue to mull over the dazzling epigraph that introduces Faulkner's second novel, *Mosquitoes*, in which the author *seems* to be writing about mosquitoes yet never calls them by their name. Aside from arousing our curiosity and perhaps our irritation, a pronoun that precedes its antecedent has something to say about the topography and chronology of signification.

In the absence of an antecedent, a pronoun is not altogether insignificant. On the contrary, it signifies that it does not in itself indicate *what* it signifies (in opposition to the manner in which a substantive is held to signify) and, from anyone who cares to know what is intended, it solicits a question. Instead of referring to something, the pronoun invites the reader to ask: "To whom or to what are you referring?" The lack of an antecedent, like a surplus of antecedents, *troubles* the referring function of the pronoun, but it does not abolish it. Even in the absence of a decidable referent, the pronoun refers. "You *are* referring," we say to the troublesome pronoun, "but to *whom* or to *what* are you referring?" As any hand-book makes clear, and as any writing instructor knows only too well, it is the proper *placement* of the antecedent that allows the pronoun to signify as it *should*. But in defiance of the grammatical imperative, the pronouns in Luster's reply signify as they do. Be-cause they refer to no neighboring word, because their antecedent or referent is not in the area that precedes them, the reader can only hope to recover their referent in time.

The question we are left with is whether this pronoun will ever recover its "antecedent," but the question we have already forgot-ten is what Benjy was looking at when he looked at "himself." If I outline a course or itinerary of referrals leading back to this pas-sage and to the antecedents of this passage, I must confess from the outset that the latter question will never be answered. It is not simply Benjy's gaze at himself that will lead us back to this passage but the fact that it coincides with Benjy's ambiguous cries and Lus-ter's ambiguous words. It will never be certain that what Benjy was looking at when he looked at himself corresponds to what Benjy began to cry about or to what Luster declared he was looking *for*. Indeed, what will lead us back to this passage with its long-since forgotten ambiguity will be the very question we have declared ourselves unable to answer: what *would* Benjy think about when "he'd happen to take a look at himself"?

Because this "backwards" referral comes in the third section, whose title "APRIL SIXTH" might be said to indicate the day before the first section, we might have to concede that Faulkner's grammar is correct, after all. The narrator is Jason.

Well at least I could come home one time without finding Ben and that nigger hanging on the gate like a bear and a monkey in the same cage. Just let it come toward sundown and he'd head for the gate like a cow for the barn, hanging onto it and bobbing his head and sort of moaning to himself. That's a hog for punishment for you. If what had happened to him for fool-ing with open gates had happened to me, I never would want to see another one. I often wondered what he'd be thinking about, down there at the gate, watching the girls going home from school, trying to want something he couldn't even re-

member he didn't and couldn't want any longer. And what he'd
think when they'd be undressing him and he'd happen to take
a look at himself and begin to cry like he'd do. But like I say
they never did enough of that. I says I know what you need,
you need what they did to Ben then you'd behave. And if you
don't know what that was I says, ask Dilsey to tell you. (315)

Although this passage may begin to "clarify" the passage we discussed above, it also generates ambiguities in its own right. Which
uncertainty is the reader of this passage to focus upon—what
strange composite beast (caged bear/cow/hog) serves to describe
Benjy, what happened to Benjy for fooling with open gates, what
they never did enough of, why Jason, of all characters, would wonder what Benjy would think, "down there at the gate" or when
"they'd be undressing him and he'd happen to take a look" at his
naked body, or who Jason addresses when he suggests that "you
need what they did to Ben"? Few readers pursue the first and last
questions because, unlike the others, they do not promise to efface
themselves by clarifying other passages memorable for their obscurity. Few readers choose to puzzle over the odd plurality of animals to which Benjy is compared—not only in this passage from
the third section but also in passages from the first section, where
Benjy is compared to a hound because he can smell death (41), and
from the fourth, where Benjy is compared to a "trained bear"
(342)—because such a menagerie interferes with the reader's desire to give Benjy's "voice" a "visible form." Nor do readers question the fact that it is Jason who expresses concern or at least curiosity about what had happened to Ben. It is by way of Jason that
we are referred back to two previously unconnected passages: one
in which Benjy looks at himself undressed and the other in which
Benjy "fooled" with the open gate. Jason's remarks newly characterize the passage in which Benjy fooled with the open gate, bap-
tizing it as the antecedent of the passage in which Benjy looked at
himself and began to cry. If Jason's remarks "clarify" the relation
between these two passages, they also suggest that Jason may
have been the architect of their relation. Rather than explaining
obscurity away, Jason's remarks introduce new, more sinister ob-
scurities. Still, the reader has become more or less aware, by way
of this overcharged chain of referrals, of what critics refer to, in
sum, as Benjy's castration. He or she finds out even more when, at
the conclusion of the third section, Jason resumes his meditation
on what happened to Benjy.

I could hear the Great American Gelding snoring away like a
planing mill. I read somewhere they'd fix men that way to give

them women's voices. But maybe he didn't know what they'd
done to him. I dont reckon he even knew what he had been
trying to do, or why Mr Burgess knocked him out with the
fence picket. And if they'd just sent him on to Jackson while
he was under the ether, he'd never have known the difference. But that would have been too simple for a Compson to
think of. Not half complex enough. Having to wait to do it at all
until he broke out and tried to run a little girl down on the
street with her own father looking at him. Well, like I say they
never started soon enough with their cutting, and they quit too
quick. I know at least two more that needed something like
that, and one of them not over a mile away, either. But then I
dont reckon even that would do any good. Like I say once a
bitch always a bitch. (328–29)

In order to trace this passage back to the passages with which we
are concerned, we must overlook the questions it evokes, questions we will never be in a position to answer: whether Benjy knew
"what" they had done to him, who "they" are, and which two people, according to Jason, also needed "something like that." With
this passage, the first section's passages about the open gate are
clarified both with respect to events that "took place" (Benjy "tried
to run a little girl down on the street" and her father, Mr. Burgess,
"knocked him out with the fence picket") and with respect to the
castration that results from those events ("Gelding," "they'd fix
men that way to give them women's voices," "what they'd done to
him," "while he was under the ether," "Having to wait to do it,"
"they never started soon enough with their cutting"). Nevertheless, this passage does not simply clarify select passages from the
first section of the novel; rather, it allows certain readers the opportunity to decide upon the significance of passages untranslat-
able in themselves. The extent to which these previously unintelligible passages are affected by Jason's remarks can be illustrated
by a summary Edmond Volpe offers of the passage in which Benjy,
as this critic puts it, "assaults the Burgess girl and is castrated."

> Mr. Compson asks Jason if he had left the gate open. Jason
> denies it, saying the family is bad enough without this kind of
> thing happening. He tells his father that now he will have to
> send Benjy to Jackson, that is, if Mr. Burgess does not shoot
> the idiot first.
>   The next scene, beginning "It was open when I touched
> it" presents Benjy's recollection of the incident. The school
> girls know that the gate is always locked, and they stop to

watch Benjy. When the idiot touches the gate, it opens. They run, but he catches one of them.

This memory merges into the castration operation: "and she screamed and I was trying to say and trying and the bright shapes began to stop and I tried to get out. I tried to get it off my face." *He is fighting the anesthesia mask, but he breathes in and goes off to sleep.* (359; emphasis added)

According to Volpe, Benjy's recollection of the "incident" merges into "the castration operation," but it is more accurate to say that Volpe's description of this passage merges with what certain passages from the third section of the novel allow him to imagine. Yet in order to focus on the *significance* of these passages one must of course refer to some other passage or passages. In order to give significance to a passage whose referents are either plural or absent, one must locate some "antecedents," if you will. One must turn to other passages in which it is identified or "marked," as Southern farmers say of castrated livestock. Yet the critic who would in this way mark a passage already marked by its unreadability ought to acknowledge his or her hand in the operation of castration. Volpe, for example, fails to acknowledge that he has identified this passage in a particular manner, excluding not only its own peculiar markings but also any other manner in which it may be marked. Jason's remarks, however dramatic their effect, do not exhaust the referrals into which this passage enters.

Oddly enough, Benjy's "fumbling abortive attempt . . . on a passing female child," as this passage is characterized in the appendix (422), is situated at a critical juncture of the first section. At this point in the section, Benjy's movements have come full circle; as at the beginning of the section, he is at the fence, looking at the golf course "through the curling flower spaces" (1, 62). What motivates this return to the beginning of the novel? Just before this critical, violent, and confusing "scene," Benjy comes upon Caddy's daughter, Quentin, "in the swing" with a man, and he is reminded of the time he saw Caddy in the swing with Charlie. Benjy's way of describing this sight, as "two now, and then one in the swing" (56), suggests a way of describing the operation of referral, in which otherness leaves its mark. Referral, the swing between two different but related elements, is the most recurrent structure in the novel and is frequently thematized, as it is in this passage, as a crisis. In such crises, the characters of *The Sound and the Fury* do not recognize but rather suffer the difference between the times and places brought together in the swing of similarity. Benjy has at this point in the section brought together two scenes from whose similarity the narrative seems to flee. As if to end itself here once and for all, the narrative returns to its beginning. Yet instead of exploiting the closure of such repetition, as the narrative does in both the second and third sections, the first section suffers its own differences from itself. What "happens" at the open gate marks the unforeseeable difference of the "same."

The passage at the open gate, in which Benjy sees the girls who "passed with their booksatchels," refers the reader to the passage in which Benjy meets Caddy at the gate when she returns from school. In its return to the "same" place, the narrative emphasizes the violence of difference or rather of the failure to recognize difference. Let us examine the passage Jason's remarks in the third section identify as the cause of what "they" did to Benjy:

> I went down to the gate, where the girls passed with their booksatchels. They looked at me, walking fast, with their heads turned. *I tried to say*, but they went on, and I went along the fence, *trying to say*, and they went faster. Then they were running and I came to the corner of the fence and I couldn't go any further, and I held to the fence, looking after them and *trying to say*. (63; emphasis added)

The relation of this passage to the passage it attempts to repeat, in which Benjy meets Caddy at the gate, will enable us to hear this passage's emphasis on "trying to say." This phrase draws our attention to the obvious yet nonetheless perplexing paradox of Benjy's voice or point of view, which is incompatible with his incapacity or incompetency. Benjy *expresses* himself only through inarticulate cries, or in their cessation, yet he employs articulate language in soliloquy. Perhaps the manner in which we *understand* his soliloquy can be related to the manner in which other characters in the novel "understand" his inarticulate cries. Through his cries, Luster understands that Benjy wants to see the golfers, the flowers, or the fire; Dilsey understands that Benjy smells death; Quentin understands that Benjy doesn't want Caddy to leave; Caddy understands that Benjy thinks it is Christmas, that he wants to hold a letter, that he doesn't like the smell of perfume, and so on. Whether what is understood corresponds to what Benjy means or whether Benjy knows what he means cannot be determined with reference to his soliloquy. What is peculiar to the passage cited above is that Benjy remarks emphatically that he is *not* crying. Instead, Benjy claims, he is "trying to say." Benjy's distinction continues:

> It was open when I touched it, and I held to it in the twilight. *I wasn't crying*, and I tried to stop, watching the girls coming

along in the twilight. *I wasn't crying. . . . I wasn't crying. . . .* They came on in the twilight. *I wasn't crying*, and I held to the gate. They came slow. . . . They came on. I opened the gate and they stopped, turning. *I was trying to say*, and I caught her, *trying to say*, and she screamed and *I was trying to say and trying* and the bright shapes began to stop and I tried to get out. I tried to get it off of my face, but the bright shapes were going again. They were going up the hill to where it fell away and *I tried to cry*. But when I breathed in, *I couldn't breathe out again to cry*, and I tried to keep from falling off the hill and I fell off the hill into the bright, whirling shapes. (64; emphasis added)

To try to understand the difference between crying and trying to say, we cannot turn to "crying," whose significance is decided in particular contexts, by particular characters, and in view of particular interests. Because the significance of Benjy's cries is at once plural and unverifiable, we cannot determine what Benjy means when he says that he is "not crying" but "trying to say." Yet the way Caddy greets Benjy at the gate suggests a way of greeting the ambiguity of this distinction. When Caddy finds Benjy at the gate, she lets loose a battery of questions:

> Did you come to meet me. . . . Did you come to meet Caddy. . . . Did you come to meet Caddy. . . . What is it. What are you trying to tell Caddy. . . . What is it. . . . What are you trying to tell Caddy. What is it. (5–6)

Caddy's questions are remarkable for their tenacity but also because they lack the punctuation proper to interrogation. In fact, none of the questions posed in the first section bear the mark of interrogation. Still, because the distinction between a declarative and interrogative statement in English is also marked by syntax, we can recognize a question even in the absence of a question mark. Such recognition is simple on the level of the sentence but is considerably more difficult on the level of narration. The narrative is obvious when it forecloses questioning, for example, when Luster points his interlocuter to Benjy, a mute witness, for verification of this or that claim (for instance, 82) or when Caddy interjects answers into her unanswerable interrogation of Benjy, which culminates in a last, unanswerable question:

> What is it. . . . Did you think it would be Christmas when I came home from school. Is that what you thought. (6)

But the narrative's interrogative thrust, which characterizes, for example, the indeterminable distinction between crying and "trying to say" or between Quentin *fille* and Caddy in the swing with a man, is more difficult to acknowledge.

It has been argued that Benjy's repetition of "trying to say" is an expression of an urgent desire to communicate. Bleikasten writes that "to speak and be heard [is] the very wish Benjy's monologue is at pains to fulfill. For is not the entire first section a 'trying to say'?" Is not, Bleikasten adds, the entire novel a "trying to say" (83)? Bleikasten interprets "trying to say" in terms of both speaking and being heard because, on the one hand, he cannot be sure which of these very different wishes it refers to and, on the other hand, he projects onto the passage, the section, and indeed the entire novel the wish that speaking and being heard would be the same. But nowhere in *The Sound and the Fury* is it suggested that the relation between speaking and being heard, between utterance or discourse and comprehension or interpretation, tends toward identity, or even toward a modest felicity. With its congregation of intruding voices and sounds, Faulkner's novel affirms nothing so much as the folly and misery of this desire for an illusory identity in communication.

But why should the fundamental separation of the self from itself—whether one chooses to think of this as castration or as trying to say—surface at this juncture as a crisis? Why should the question of self-identity arise here, at a point the first section could have used to fold back over itself, ending itself in the echo of its beginning, as do the second and third sections? It is here, in its first self-encompassing circle back upon itself, returning to "the curling flower spaces," that the first section discovers that its echoes are not answers but questions. Instead of folding back over itself as though in answer to itself, the novel at this point gives itself over to the recombinatory fury of questions multiplied in the echo of referral. By sustaining referral at the expense of simple reference, as does a pronoun in the absence, excess, or deferral of its antecedent(s), by dwelling on the breaking point of designation, language recasts itself as literature.

When merged with their echoes in the third section, the first section's passages at the open gate are translated into the pseudohistorical cause of Benjy's castration. Yet this "clarification" leads only to other questions, for it obscurely suggests that this cause, too, has a cause.[4] Reluctant to entertain the interrogatives of this narrative, which are directed, for one thing, at our haste to rectify and dispel its obscurity, placid translations of *The Sound and the Fury* obscure this novel's furious repetition of its own castration and pacify the violence of its particularly literary affirmation.

Notes

1. Faulkner often dated the "present" in his novels to coincide with the time of writing: thus, "1928" in the section titles coincides with the year in which he wrote *The Sound and the Fury*, and "1945," as the outside date in the title of the appendix, is the year in which he wrote the appendix.

2. Even Walter Slatoff, who argues that the fourth section "seems designed not to interpret or to integrate but to leave the various elements of the story in much the same suspension in which they were offered," evaluates the final section in terms of its explicatory relation to the previous sections of the novel (158).

3. For a "genealogy" of the appendix and its critique of genealogy, see Lester.

4. For Jason's possible agency in this history, see 63, 315, 328–29, 422.

Works Cited

Blanchard, Margaret. "The Rhetoric of Communion: Voice in *The Sound and the Fury*." *American Literature* 41 (1970): 555–65.

Bleikasten, André. *The Most Splendid Failure: Faulkner's "The Sound and the Fury."* Bloomington: Indiana UP, 1976.

Brooks, Cleanth. "Primitivism in *The Sound and the Fury*." *English Institute Essays, 1952*. 1954. Ed. Alan S. Downer. New York: AMS, 1965.

Cowley, Malcolm. *The Faulkner-Cowley File: Letters and Memories, 1944–1962*. New York: Viking, 1966.

Faulkner, William. *The Sound and the Fury*. 1929. New York: Random, 1956.

Iser, Wolfgang. *The Implied Reader: Patterns of Communication in Prose Fiction from Bunyan to Beckett*. Baltimore: Johns Hopkins UP, 1974.

Kaluza, Irena. *The Functioning of Sentence Structure in the Stream-of-Consciousness Technique of William Faulkner's "The Sound and the Fury": A Study in Linguistic Stylistics*. Norwood: Norwood, 1979.

Lester, Cheryl. "To Market, To Market: *The Portable Faulkner*." *Criticism* 19 (1987): 371–89.

Millgate, Michael. "The Composition of *The Sound and the Fury*." *Critical Essays on William Faulkner: The Compson Family*. Ed. Arthur F. Kinney. Boston: Hall, 1982. 155–72.

Slatoff, Walter. *Quest for Failure: A Study of William Faulkner.* Ithaca: Cornell UP, 1960.

Stewart, George R., and Joseph M. Backus. "'Each in Its Ordered Place': Structure and Narrative in 'Benjy's Section' of *The Sound and the Fury.*" *American Literature* 29 (1958): 440–56.

Vickery, Olga. *The Novels of William Faulkner: A Critical Interpretation.* Baton Rouge: Louisiana State UP, 1959.

Volpe, Edmond L. *A Reader's Guide to William Faulkner.* New York: Farrar, 1964.

Appendix A
Alternative Grouping of Essays

The following provides an alternative to the table of contents. Under "General Studies" are essays that trace an issue through several of Faulkner's novels. Those essays focusing on a single work are grouped under the title of the particular Faulkner novel addressed.

General Studies
Chapter 5. "If *Was* Existed": Faulkner's Prophets and the Patterns of History, James G. Watson (1975)
Chapter 7. "So I, who had never had a war...": William Faulkner, War, and the Modern Imagination, Donald M. Kartiganer (1998)
Chapter 9. Faulkner's Garden: Woman and the Immemorial Earth, Karl E. Zink (1956)

Individual Works
The Sound and the Fury (1929)
Chapter 10. "The Beautiful One": Caddy Compson as Heroine of *The Sound and the Fury,* Catherine B. Baum (1967)
Chapter 19. From Place to Place in *The Sound and the Fury:* The Syntax of Interrogation, Cheryl Lester (1988)

As I Lay Dying (1930)
Chapter 4. Enigmas of Being in *As I Lay Dying,* Robert Hemenway (1970)
Chapter 15. Extremities of the Body: The Anoptic Corporeality of *As I Lay Dying,* Erin E. Edwards (2009)

Sanctuary (1931)
Chapter 13. Faulkner's Return to the Freudian Father: *Sanctuary* Reconsidered, Doreen Fowler (2004)
Chapter 17. Gothicism in *Sanctuary:* The Black Pall and the Crap Table, David L. Frazier (1956)

Light in August (1932)
Chapter 1. Christian Symbols in *Light in August,* Beekman W. Cottrell (1956)
Chapter 2. *Light in August:* The Calvinism of William Faulkner, Alwyn Berland (1962)

Pylon (1935)
Chapter 16. Faulkner's *Pylon* and the Structure of Modernity, Donald T. Torchiana (1957–58)

Absalom, Absalom! (1936)

Chapter 3. The Role of Myth in *Absalom, Absalom!*, Donald M. Kartiganer (1963)

Chapter 6. On Lamentation and the Redistribution of Possessions: Faulkner's
    Absalom, Absalom! and the New South, Rebecca Saunders (1996)

Chapter 11. Devious Channels of Decorous Ordering: A Lover's Discourse in
    Absalom, Absalom!, Linda Kauffman (1983)

Chapter 14. The Picture of Charles Bon: Oscar Wilde's Trip through Faulkner's
    Yoknapatawpha, Ellen Crowell (2004)

Go Down, Moses (1942)

Chapter 8. Accounting for Slavery: Economic Narratives in Morrison and
    Faulkner, Erik Dussere (2001)

Chapter 18. Faulkner's Storied Novel: *Go Down, Moses* and the Translation of
    Time, Ronald Schleifer (1982)

The Snopes Trilogy: The Hamlet (1940), The Town (1957), and The Mansion (1959)

Chapter 12. Linda Snopes Kohl: Faulkner's Radical Woman, Keith Louise Fulton
    (1988)

Appendix B
Chronological Listing of All Essays on Faulkner Published in *MFS*

Essays appearing in this volume are followed by an asterisk.

Swiggart, Peter. "Time in Faulkner's Novels." 1.2 (1955): 25–29.

Backman, Melvin. "Faulkner's Sick Heroes: Bayard Sartoris and Quentin Compson." 2.3 (1956): 95–108.

Flynn, Robert. "The Dialectic of *Sanctuary*." 2.3 (1956): 109–13.

Frazier, David L. "Gothicism in *Sanctuary*: The Black Pall and the Crap Table." 2.3 (1956): 114–24.*

Moses, W. R. "The Unity of *The Wild Palms*." 2.3 (1956): 125–31.

King, Roma A., Jr. "Everyman's Warfare: A Study of Faulkner's *Fable*." 2.3 (1956): 132–38.

Zink, Karl E. "Faulkner's Garden: Woman and the Immemorial Earth." 2.3 (1956): 139–49.*

Beebe, Maurice. "Criticism of William Faulkner: A Selected Checklist with an Index to Studies of Separate Works." 2.3 (1956): 150–64.

Cottrell, Beekman W. "Christian Symbols in *Light in August*." 2.4 (1956): 207–13.*

Torchiana, Donald T. "Faulkner's *Pylon* and the Structure of Modernity." 3.4 (1957): 291–308.*

Lamont, William H. F. "The Chronology of *Light in August*." 3.4 (1957): 360–61.

Gwynn, Frederick L. "Faulkner's Raskolnikov." 4.2 (1958): 169–72.

Richardson, H. Edward. "The 'Hemingwaves' in Faulkner's *Wild Palms*." 4.4 (1958): 357–60.

Moses, W. R. "Water, Water Everywhere: 'Old Man' and *A Farewell to Arms*." 5.2 (1959): 172–74.

Watkins, Floyd C., and Thomas Daniel Young. "Revisions of Style in Faulkner's *The Hamlet*." 5.4 (1959): 327–36.

Tritschler, Donald. "The Unity of Faulkner's Shaping Vision." 5.4 (1959): 337–43.

Bouvard, Loic. "Conversation with William Faulkner." 5.4 (1959): 361–64. Translated by Henry Dan Piper.

Gold, Joseph. "Delusion and Redemption in Faulkner's *A Fable*." 7.2 (1961): 145–56.

Berland, Alwyn. "*Light in August*: The Calvinism of William Faulkner." 8.2 (1962): 159–70.*

Meriwether, James B. "The Text of Faulkner's Books: An Introduction and Some Notes." 9.2 (1963): 159–70.

Kartiganer, Donald M. "The Role of Myth in *Absalom, Absalom!*" 9.4 (1963): 357–69.*

Muste, John M. "The Failure of Love in *Go Down, Moses*." 10.4 (1964): 366–78.

Bowling, Lawrence. "Faulkner: The Theme of Pride in *The Sound and the Fury*." 11.2 (1965): 129–39.

Mitchell, Charles. "The Wounded Will of Faulkner's Barn Burner." 11.2 (1965): 185–89.

Hogan, Patrick G., Jr., Dale A. Myers, and John E. Turner. "Muste's 'Failure of Love' in Faulkner's *Go Down, Moses*." 12.2 (1966): 267–70.

Underwood, Henry J., Jr. "Sartre on *The Sound and the Fury*: Some Errors." 12.4 (1966): 477–79.

Miller, David M. "Faulkner's Women." 13:1 (1967): 3–17.

Larsen, Eric. "The Barrier of Language: The Irony of Language in Faulkner." 13:1 (1967): 19–31.

Baum, Catherine B. "'The Beautiful One': Caddy Compson as Heroine of *The Sound and the Fury*." 13:1 (1967): 33–44.*

Hagopian, John V. "Nihilism in Faulkner's *The Sound and the Fury*." 13:1 (1967): 45–55.

Franklin, R. W. "Narrative Management in *As I Lay Dying*." 13:1 (1967): 57–65.

Baldanza, Frank. "The Structure of *Light in August*." 13:1 (1967): 67–78.

Watkins, Floyd C. "What Happens in *Absalom, Absalom!*?" 13:1 (1967): 79–87.

Feaster, John. "Faulkner's *Old Man*: A Psychoanalytic Approach." 13:1 (1967): 89–93.

Kerr, Elizabeth M. "*The Reivers*: The Golden Book of Yoknapatawpha County." 13:1 (1967): 95–113.

Beebe, Maurice. "Criticism of William Faulkner: A Selected Checklist." 13:1 (1967): 115–61.

Stafford, T. J. "Tobe's Significance in 'A Rose for Emily.'" 14.4 (1968): 451–53.

Atkins, Anselm. "The Matched Halves of *Absalom, Absalom!*" 15.2 (1969): 264–65.

Rossky, William. "The Pattern of Nightmare in *Sanctuary*: Or, Miss Reba's Dogs." 15.4 (1969): 503–15.

Hemenway, Robert. "Enigmas of Being in *As I Lay Dying*." 16.2 (1970): 133–46.*

Nash, Harry C. "Faulkner's 'Furniture Repairer and Dealer': Knitting Up *Light in August*." 16.4 (1970): 529–31.

Monaghan, David M. "The Single Narrator of *As I Lay Dying*." 18.2 (1972): 213–20.

Brogunier, Joseph. "A Housman Source in *The Sound and the Fury*." 18.2 (1972): 220–25.

Esslinger, Pat M., et al. "No Spinach in *Sanctuary*." 18.4 (1972): 555–58.

Perry, J. Douglas, Jr. "Gothic as Vortex: The Form of Horror in Capote, Faulkner, and Styron." 19.2 (1973): 153–67.

Hagopian, John V. "*Absalom, Absalom!* and the Negro Question." 19.2 (1973): 207–11.

Spivey, Herman E. "Faulkner and the Adamic Myth: Faulkner's Moral Vision." 19.4 (1973): 497–505.

Naples, Diane C. "Eliot's 'Tradition' and *The Sound and the Fury*." 20.2 (1974): 214–17.

Trimmer, Joseph F. "V.K. Ratliff: A Portrait of the Artist in Motion." 20.4 (1974): 451–67.

Stoneback, H. R. "Faulkner's Blues: 'Pantaloon in Black.'" 21.2 (1975): 241–45.

Strandberg, Victor H. "Between Truth and Fact: Faulkner's Symbols of Identity." 21.4 (1975): 445–57.

Watson, James G. "'If Was Existed': Faulkner's Prophets and the Patterns of History." 21.4 (1975): 499–507.*

Volpe, Edmond L. "Faulkner's 'Knight's Gambit': Sentimentality and the Creative Imagination." 24.2 (1978): 232–39.

Pearce, Richard. "Reeling through Faulkner: Pictures of Motion, Pictures in Motion." 24.4 (1978): 483–95.

Seltzer, Leon F., and Jan Viscomi. "Natural Rhythms and Rebellion: Anse's Role in *As I Lay Dying*." 24.4 (1978): 556–64.

Connolly, Thomas E. "Point of View in Faulkner's *Absalom, Absalom!*" 27.2 (1981): 255–72.

Schleifer, Ronald. "Faulkner's Storied Novel: *Go Down, Moses* and the Translation of Time." 28.1 (1982): 109–27.*

Oriard, Michael. "The Ludic Vision of William Faulkner." 28.2 (1982): 169–87.

Kauffman, Linda. "Devious Channels of Decorous Ordering: A Lover's Discourse in *Absalom, Absalom!*" 29.2 (1983): 183–200.*

Olsen, Lance. "Faulkner's Echo in Robbe-Grillet: Narrative Constructions and Destructions." 29.4 (1983): 609–22.

Allen, Dennis W. "Horror and Perverse Delight: Faulkner's 'A Rose for Emily.'" 30.4 (1984): 685–96.

Hedeen, Paul M. "A Symbolic Center in a Conception Country: A Gassian Rubric for *The Sound and the Fury*." 31.4 (1985): 623–43.

Hoag, Ronald Wesley. "Ends and Loose Ends: The Triptych Conclusion of *Light in August*." 31.4 (1985): 675–90.

McPherson, Karen. "*Absalom, Absalom!* Telling Scratches." 33.3 (1987): 431–50.

Lester, Cheryl. "From Place to Place in *The Sound and the Fury*: The Syntax of Interrogation." 34.2 (1988): 141–55.*

Fulton, Keith Louise. "Linda Snopes Kohl: Faulkner's Radical Woman." 34.3 (1988): 425–36.*

Saunders, Rebecca. On Lamentation and the Redistribution of Possessions: Faulkner's *Absalom, Absalom!* and the New South." 42.4 (1996): 730–62.*

Kartiganer, Donald M. "'So I, who had never had a war…': William Faulkner, War, and the Modern Imagination." 44.3 (1998): 619–45.*

Dussere, Erik. "Accounting for Slavery: Economic Narratives in Morrison and Faulkner." 47.2 (2001): 329–55.*

Fowler, Doreen. "Faulkner's Return to the Freudian Father: *Sanctuary* Reconsidered." 50.2 (2004): 411–34.*

Crowell, Ellen. "The Picture of Charles Bon: Oscar Wilde's Trip through Faulkner's Yoknapatawpha." 50.3 (2004): 595–631.*

Fowler, Doreen. "Beyond Oedipus: Lucas Beauchamp, Ned Barnett, and Faulkner's *Intruder in the Dust*." 53.4 (2007): 788–820.

Edwards, Erin E. "Extremities of the Body: The Anoptic Corporeality of *As I Lay Dying*." 55.4 (2009): 639–64.*

Contributors

CATHERINE B. BAUM was an instructor at Emory University before becoming an independent scholar in Atlanta, Georgia.

ALWYN BERLAND is a professor emeritus of English at McMaster University where he served for a number of years as Dean of the Humanities. He is the author of *Culture and Conduct in the Novels of Henry James* (1982) and *Light in August: A Study in Black and White* (1992).

BEEKMAN W. COTTRELL (1922–2004) completed his dissertation at Columbia and taught at Carnegie Institute of Technology (now Carnegie Mellon University) in Pittsburgh.

ELLEN CROWELL is an assistant professor of English at Saint Louis University and author of *Aristocratic Drag: The Dandy in Irish and American Southern Fiction* (2007). Her current book project, *Oscar Wilde's Body*, illuminates the contested and occasionally macabre processes through which artists, bibliographers, collectors, and critics sought to establish the place Wilde's "body" would occupy in the aesthetic and political landscape of early modernism.

ERIK DUSSERE teaches literature and film at American University. He is the author of *Balancing the Books: Faulkner, Morrison, and the Economies of Slavery* (2003), and he has also published articles on film noir and comic books.

JOHN N. DUVALL is Professor of English and the Editor of *MFS* at Purdue University. Among his books are *Race and White Identity in Southern Fiction* (2008), *The Identifying Fictions of Toni Morrison* (2000), and *Faulkner's Marginal Couple: Invisible, Outlaw, and Unspeakable Communities* (1990). He also has edited several collections, including *The Cambridge Companion to Don DeLillo* (2008) and *Productive Postmodernism: Consuming Histories and Cultural Studies* (2002).

ERIN E. EDWARDS teaches in the English Department at the University of California, Berkeley. She is currently working on a book manuscript that examines the figure of the corpse in modern American literature and film.

DOREEN FOWLER, Professor of English at the University of Kansas, is the author of *Faulkner: The Return of the Repressed* (1997), a psychoanalytic interpretation of William Faulkner's major novels, and the coeditor of eleven collections of essays on Faulkner. Her current project is a study of liminal models of identity-formation in the fiction of Southern writers.

DAVID L. FRAZIER was a professor emeritus of English at Miami University in Oxford, Ohio. His work was primarily in American realism, and he published several essays on William Dean Howells. He died of cancer at age 67 in 1998.

KEITH LOUISE FULTON, former holder of the Prairie Joint Regional Chair in Women's Studies (University of Manitoba/University of Winnipeg), is a professor emerita of English at the University of Winnipeg. In 1999 she received the Clifford J. Robson Memorial Award for Excellence in Teaching and in 2005 was awarded the Robin H. Farquhar Award for Excellence in Contributing to Self-Governance.

ROBERT HEMENWAY retired from the Chancellor's position of the University of Kansas in 2009 after fourteen years at the helm. He remains a faculty member and hopes that he can contribute once again to Faulkner scholarship. In addition to his many articles on African-American and American literature, he wrote the award-winning *Zora Neale Hurston: A Literary Biography* (1977).

DONALD M. KARTIGANER is Howry Professor Emeritus of Faulkner Studies at the University of Mississippi and Director of the Faulkner and Yoknapatawpha Conference. He is the author of the monograph "Process and Product: A Study of Modern Literary Form" and *The Fragile Thread: The Meaning of Form in Faulkner's Novels* (1979). He also coedited *Theories of American Literature* (1972) and seven volumes of the papers from the Faulkner and Yoknapatawpha Conference.

LINDA S. KAUFFMAN's three most recent essays are on Don DeLillo (including one in *MFS* in 2008). She is the author of *Bad Girls and Sick Boys: Fantasies in Contemporary Art and Culture* (1998); *Discourses of Desire: Gender, Genre, and Epistolary Fictions* (1986); and *Special Delivery: Epistolary Modes in Modern Fiction* (1992). She is editor of three volumes, including *American Feminist Thought at Century's End* (1993). She is Professor of English and Distinguished Scholar-Teacher at the University of Maryland, College Park.

CHERYL LESTER is the Director of the American Studies Program and Associate Professor of American Studies and English at the University of Kansas. In addition to her contribution to *MFS*, her essays have appeared in such journals as *Criticism*, *American Studies*, and the *Faulkner Journal*, as well as in such books as *The Cambridge Companion to William Faulkner* (1994), *The Aesthetics of Toni Morrison: Speaking the Unspeakable* (2000), and *A Companion to William Faulkner* (2007). She is completing a book on Faulkner and the Great Migration.

REBECCA SAUNDERS teaches global literatures, theory, and African studies at Illinois State University. Her publications include *Lamentation and Modernity in Literature, Philosophy and Culture* (2007); *The Concept of the Foreign: An Interdisciplinary Dialogue* (2002); and articles on late nineteenth- and twentieth-century European and African literatures and cultural theory. She also served as coeditor of *Comparative Studies of South Asia, Africa and the Middle East* from 2002 to 2007. Her current work focuses on transitional justice, human rights, and philosophical and literary conceptualizations of justice.

RONALD SCHLEIFER is George Lynn Cross Research Professor of English at the University of Oklahoma. He is also Adjunct Professor in Medicine. He has worked widely in twentieth-century literary and cultural studies. His recent books include *Modernism and Time: The Logic of Abundance in Literature, Science, and Culture 1880–1930* (2009); *Medicine and Humanistic Understanding: The Role of Narrative in Medical Practices* (2005, cowritten with Jerry Vannatta and Sheila Crow); and *Intangible Materialism: The Body, Scientific Knowledge, and the Power of Language* (2009). He is currently completing *Modernism and Popular Music: Language and Music in Gershwin, Porter, Waller, Holiday.*

DONALD T. TORCHIANA was a professor emeritus at Northwestern University at the time of his death at age 77 in 2001. A scholar of Irish literature, he authored *W. B. Yeats and Georgian Ireland* (1966) and *Backgrounds for Joyce's Dubliners* (1986), as well as numerous journal articles on modernist literature.

JAMES G. WATSON is Frances W. O'Hornett Professor of Literature at the University of Tulsa. He has authored three books on Faulkner, including *William Faulkner, Self-Presentation and Performance* (2000). He is also editor of the previously unpublished letters in *Thinking of Home: William Faulkner's Letters to His Mother and Father, 1918–1925* (1992) and of the 2007 special Faulkner issue of *Mississippi Quarterly.*

KARL E. ZINK is a professor emeritus of English at the University of Central Washington. In addition to his contribution to *MFS*, his articles on Faulkner appeared in *PMLA* and *South Atlantic Quarterly.*

Index